Cooking Light®
'87

Cooking Light® '87

Oxmoor House®

Copyright 1987 by Oxmoor House, Inc.
Book Division of Southern Progress Corporation
P. O. Box 2463, Birmingham, Alabama 35201

ISBN: 0-8487-0699-4
ISSN: 0884-2922

Manufactured in the United States of America
First Printing 1987

Cooking Light ® '87

Senior Foods Editor: Katherine M. Eakin
Senior Editor: Joan E. Denman
Assistant Foods Editor: Janice L. Krahn
Copy Editor: Melinda E. West
Editorial Assistants: Donna A. Rumbarger, Karen Parris Smith
Director, Test Kitchen: Laura N. Massey
Test Kitchen Home Economists: Bonnie Echols, Rebecca J. Riddle,
 Elise Wright Walker
Photographer: Jim Bathie
Photo Stylist: Kay E. Clarke
Production Manager: Jerry Higdon
Art Director: Bob Nance
Designer: Faith Nance

Project Consultants:
Text Writer: Robert A. Barnett
Recipe Coordinator and Menu Developer:
 Susan M. McIntosh, M.S., R.D.
Recipe Developers: Carroll Sessions Flowers, R.D.;
 Marilyn Wyrick Ingram
Recipe Consultant: Susan L. Curtin, M.S., R.D.
Exercise Physiologist: Dr. Gary Hunter

Cover: *Rum Bavarian Cream with Raspberry Sauce (page 69).*
Back cover: *Easy Dinner For Two (menu begins on page 82).*
Page ii: *Strawberry-Cider Cooler (page 95), Banana-Mango
 Smoothie (page 96), and Cappuccino (page 28).*

Contents

Living Well Is The Best Reward

Welcome to *Cooking Light '87*, an all-new cookbook that celebrates the pleasures of good health. Our low-fat, low-calorie recipes are easy to make, a delight to behold, a feast for the senses.

Guided by the premise that good health and good food are synonymous, our editors developed an approach to eating and cooking that is both healthy and appealing.

In addition, unlike most cookbooks, *Cooking Light '87* contains the very latest in research from the world of nutrition science, exercise physiology, and psychology.

All of the 480-plus recipes are new, including the thirty delicious and attractive menus that offer fresh ideas for family meals, company dinners, and cocktail parties. With *Cooking Light '87* as a guide, you'll learn to minimize the fat, sugar, and sodium in your meals and, at the same time, maximize the vitamins, minerals, and fiber that contribute to a well-balanced diet. The emphasis is on the good taste and texture of fresh wholesome food cooked the light way.

Use this book to begin a lifetime of living well. By making gradual changes in eating habits, increasing physical activity, and providing a little time for relaxation, you'll begin to have more energy and a greater sense of well-being. You'll also improve your chances of living longer and avoiding some of the major chronic diseases of our time. Most importantly, you'll improve your quality of life now.

In short, we're showing you how to take charge of your diet, your physical activity, your health habits, your attitudes, your body, and your mind.

Ensure a healthy blend of nutrients and appetizing meals by choosing a variety of foods from the basic food groups — fruits and vegetables; milk and cheese; meat, fish, poultry, and legumes; and breads and cereals.

Update '87

The more we take responsibility for our own health and well-being, the more we need accurate scientific information upon which to base our decisions. Fortunately, there's growing scientific literature documenting the relationships between health and nutrition, exercise, mental attitude, relaxation, and other lifestyle habits.

Emotions and Health

A good mental attitude isn't important just to our business and personal lives. It may be important to our health as well.

Scientists at the National Institutes of Health in Washington, D.C., and the University of Rochester in New York have recently discovered that the brain and the immune system produce very similar hormones and that hormones from one system can affect the other.

This discovery helps explain how the way we deal with our thoughts and feelings (brain) can affect our resistance to disease (immune system). In one study of diary writers, reported at the annual meeting of the American Psychological Association in August 1986, those who, in their diaries, dealt with their emotions and expressed their feelings about disturbing life experiences, had a higher level of disease fighting immune substances and fewer illnesses compared to those who in their diaries didn't, or couldn't, deal with their emotions and express their feelings.

Clearly, being in touch with our emotions and being able to express them is a healthy skill. Thus, it is not surprising that mental and physical well-being are intertwined.

A New View of Fats

The consensus remains the same this year as last: Most Americans eat too much fat. More specifically, we eat too much saturated animal fat which can raise the level of cholesterol in the blood and increase the risk of cardiovascular diseases. This fact doesn't mean that we should eliminate all fats from our diets. A certain amount of fat is needed in the diet to help the body absorb vitamins A, D, E, and K.

However, new studies indicate that some fats are better for us than others. Recently, there's been good news about two types in particular: polyunsaturated fat found in the oil of fatty northern ocean fish such as salmon, and monounsaturated fats found in products such as olive oil.

Fish oil, a unique form of polyunsaturated fat, protects our cardiovascular system in at least two ways. One, it lowers the levels of cholesterol in the blood. Two, by affecting hormone-like substances called prostaglandins, it reduces the tendency of blood to form clots that can lead to clogged arteries.

Monounsaturated fats also lower blood cholesterol. In particular, they lower the part of cholesterol ("low density lipoprotein") implicated in heart disease. Levels of "good" cholesterol ("high density lipoprotein"), which may protect against heart disease, remain largely unaffected.

Irradiated Foods

Scientists world-wide have known for years that treating certain foods with gamma rays emitted from a radioactive source, usually cobalt, is an effective way of preserving food. However, the United States has been cautious in this regard. In 1983, the Food and Drug Administration approved this method of preserving (irradiation) certain spices and seasonings. In 1986, the FDA approved the irradiation of pork and some fruit and vegetables.

According to the Food and Drug Administration, the international symbol indicating food has been irradiated must appear on foods sold at the retail level. The phrase "treated by irradiation" or "treated with radiation" must also appear on the product or be displayed above the product in the store.

Currently, commercial use of these products is very limited. The first irradiated produce — mangos carrying the international symbol and the phrasing — was test-marketed in Florida in 1986.

In the next couple of years, consumers are likely to see more imported produce that carries the irradiation symbol.

New Dietary Recommendations

The American Heart Association released revisions of its dietary guidelines in September 1986. The recommendations were much more specific and more conservatively limiting in four areas: cholesterol, fats, sodium, and alcohol.

Cholesterol. Consume no more than 100 milligrams of cholesterol per 1000 calories eaten per day. The daily maximum should not exceed 300 milligrams, which is equivalent to the cholesterol in one egg.

Fats. Total fat intake should not exceed 30% of the daily caloric intake. Of this 30%, less than 10% should come from saturated fats.

Sodium. Limit sodium consumption to one gram per 1000 calories consumed per day. This is equivalent to one level teaspoon of table salt. The maximum amount of sodium should not exceed 3 grams per day.

Alcohol. Limit alcohol consumption to no more than one and a half ounces of pure alcohol a day, which is equivalent to two 12-ounce beers, two 4-ounce glasses of wine, or two drinks of distilled liquor. No more than 15% of total daily calories should come from alcohol.

Calcium Reduces High Blood Pressure

Calcium is making news in dropping blood pressure. Scientists at the University of Oregon have found that adding calcium to the diets of people with high blood pressure can actually *lower* it. In one study, about half of the hypertensive patients who took 1,000 milligrams of calcium every day for two months dropped their blood pressure by about 10 points, a significant amount.

Diet and Cancer

The National Cancer Institute (NCI) has in process a number of studies which link diet and cancer. Even though these studies are incomplete, the NCI feels there is enough evidence to give some advice: Reduce your fat intake, eat dark green and deep yellow fruits and vegetables (containing beta-carotene), eat cabbage-family (cruciferous) vegetables, reduce your intake of cured meats, and drink alcohol in moderation.

A number of studies are currently investigating the power of A, C, and E vitamins and the mineral selenium to prevent certain cancers caused by free oxygen radicals (FORs).

Our bodies live on oxygen, but one form of oxygen known as free oxygen radicals (FORs) damages cells, and may eventually lead to cancer if they damage genetic material such as DNA in cells.

FORs are created naturally in the human body, even in healthy people. But smoking, eating cured meats, being exposed to pollutants, and even aging can increase the rate at which FORs are formed.

Fortunately, our bodies have natural enzyme systems which "mop up" these undesirable forms of oxygen. Vitamins A (formed from beta-carotene), C, and E and the mineral selenium, found in whole grains, garlic, and seafood, help our bodies to produce the enzymes needed to mop up the FORs.

To explore the value of beta-carotene, the NCI is conducting a study involving 20,000 physicians. Some are taking pills containing beta-carotene; some are taking a placebo. We won't have conclusive results for years, but meanwhile it's a good idea to eat more of the fruits and vegetables that are high in beta-carotene, says the NCI.

Food and Mood

Past studies have revealed that there is a psychological link between food and mood. In fact, eating a favorite food can often relieve depression and lessen anxiety.

New studies are revealing that certain types of foods may have a physiological effect as well. Scientists at the Massachusetts Institute of Technology (MIT) have discovered that eating a meal high in pure carbohydrate such as fruit or pasta can cause sleepiness within 30 minutes. Carbohydrates affect a brain chemical called serotonin, which has a calming affect and helps us to fall asleep. Eating a high protein meal such as meat has the opposite effect; it increases alertness.

Other substances in foods affect other brain chemicals. Recently, M.I.T. researcher Richard Wurtman teamed up with a major soup company to add a purified form of lecithin to chicken soup. The special pure lecithin raises the level of acetylcholine in the brain — a chemical that's associated with memory. Preliminary studies have found that the souped-up chicken soup helps Alzheimer's patients remember better.

Meditation and Medicine

Training in relaxation, whether by yoga, biofeedback, or other techniques, is used increasingly in modern medicine to reduce stress hormones.

Recent studies, for example, find that such techniques can help asthmatics to widen respiratory passages, diabetics to require less insulin, hypertensives to lower blood pressure, the elderly to strengthen their immune systems, and patients with chronic pain to need fewer pain-killing drugs.

An article in the May 1986 issue of the *Journal of Psychosomatic Research*, for instance, finds that relaxation helps chronic asthmatics reduce the number of emotional upsets that can trigger episodes. It opens up air passages that would normally become constricted in an attack.

To help patients learn relaxation, many physicians now use biofeedback machines, which graphically display physiological changes that signal relaxation. In one study at Duke University, diabetics who practiced relaxation with biofeedback for five days had much lower blood sugar levels than a similar group of diabetics who didn't learn relaxation techniques.

The Food and Fitness Connection

Health, the ancient Greeks believed, comes from a harmony of food and exercise. Indeed, the two are inseparable in a healthy life. By eating a balanced diet and exercising regularly, you can achieve an exhilarating sense of well-being, as well as control your weight.

An added bonus provided by regular exercise is a decrease in stress. Exercise regularly and you'll probably feel calmer. Feeling calmer, you may find it easier to resist eating or drinking too much.

Gradual changes add up. In fact, taking charge in one aspect of your life, psychologists say, often helps you take charge in other areas. Lose a few pounds by adopting *Cooking Light '87* recipes as your own, and you may find it's easier to start that exercise program you've been promising yourself. Conversely, start a brisk walking program, and you may find you have a renewed desire to lighten your cooking and eating habits to achieve a livelier life-style.

Nutrition Basics for *Cooking Light*

In America, new diet programs or plans appear on the scene almost daily. Some promise health, some weight loss, others promise both. But how many diets do you need?

Just one. For generally healthy people, one basic diet, scientists now believe, can help you control your weight and give you energy, while at the same time make you feel better and less susceptible to debilitating diseases.

What is this magic diet? Just what you see reflected in the 480 or so mouth-watering recipes in this book. These recipes are formulated to be high in complex carbohydrates and fiber; low in fat (particularly saturated fat), cholesterol, and sodium; moderate in protein and calories; and full of a variety of fresh foods that provide the balance of vitamins and minerals, including iron and calcium, that our bodies need to function efficiently.

The core of this diet is a healthy balance of the three major nutrients: carbohydrates, protein, and fat. Most of us get a little too much protein, much too much fat, and much less carbohydrates than we need. In *Cooking Light '87*, we've created recipes and menus to help you achieve the daily balance that is recommended by today's leading nutritionists — 50% carbohydrates, 30% fat, 20% protein.

REDUCING FAT IN THE DIET

Reducing the amount of fat in your diet is perhaps the most important step you can take toward a healthy diet.

Fat has more than twice the calories per gram than either carbohydrates or protein.

The kind of fat is important, too. Saturated fat, which is found in animal products like hamburgers and whole milk, as well as in some vegetable cooking oils (including hydrogenated solid shortening), is thought to elevate cholesterol. A little is acceptable, but most of the fat we take in should be monounsaturated, such as olive oil, and polyunsaturated, such as corn or safflower oil. The kind of polyunsaturated fat in fresh fish, in particular, is believed to lower cholesterol.

To help reach the goal of getting no more than 30% of total calories from fat, it's helpful to learn a little math. A gram of fat has 9 calories, a gram of protein or carbohydrate, 4 calories.

Let's say you're looking at a food in the supermarket. How do you find out the percentage of calories from fat in that food? Find the grams of fat in a serving. Multiply by nine. That gives you the number of calories in fat. Then divide that number by the total calories, and you'll get the percentage of calories from fat.

For example, if you're looking at a low-fat yogurt label, work the percentage out this way. The yogurt has 200 calories and 4 grams of fat. Four times 9 is 36. So 36 calories of the 200 calories come from fat. That works out to 18%, an acceptable percentage for fat.

Reducing fat doesn't have to be difficult. By learning where fat hides in recipes, you can serve low-fat variations of foods you love. That's why we created *Cooking Light '87* — to show you how to create delicious low-fat dishes more easily.

And don't worry if you eat high-fat foods once in a while. A few treats rarely wreck a good diet. The important point is to aim for getting only 30% of your calories from fat over the long term.

HIGH CARBOHYDRATE ENERGY

Reducing fat is easier when you increase something else. That something is preferably complex carbohydrates: whole grains such as rice, breads, pasta, beans, and potatoes, as well as other vegetables and fruit. If the calories from fat are reduced to 30% or less, then carbohydrates, preferably complex carbohydrates, need to account for 50% or 55% of the total calories.

Complex carbohydrates are generally the whole foods, not the refined ones. Bread made from whole wheat flour has more fiber, more B vitamins, and certain minerals than most white breads, so it's more nutritious.

Complex carbohydrates are a natural energy

source. Runners may have been the first to discover this fact when they found how much their performance improved after eating a high-carbohydrate diet. Complex carbohydrates fuel the muscles in our bodies.

A diet high in complex carbohydrates is also rich in fiber, the less digestible part of grains, vegetables, and fruit. Once thought useless, fiber is increasingly recognized as an essential element in a healthy diet.

There are two main types: insoluble and soluble. Each serves a purpose.

Insoluble fiber, found in wheat bran, helps foods pass through the intestine, possibly reducing the risk of colon and rectal cancer.

Soluble fiber, found in beans, oats, and certain fruit such as apples and pears, helps lower the levels of cholesterol in the blood. Also, it causes only a slow rise in blood sugar levels, which is beneficial for diabetics because their need for insulin is reduced. Soluble fiber may also reduce the risk of adult-onset diabetes.

Cooking Light '87, with its emphasis on whole foods, includes recipes with generous portions of both types of fiber.

PROTEIN'S PLACE

Protein is a source of the amino acids which are so important to tissue growth and repair. However, most Americans get much more protein than we need or should have. The recommended goal is to limit protein to 15% to 20% of the total calories consumed.

Protein comes from two main sources: plants (vegetables) and animals. Vegetable protein is generally high in complex carbohydrates and fiber and low in fat. Animal protein is slightly more complete because it has a better balance of amino acids, but it's often loaded with fat (much of it saturated) and cholesterol. Some low-fat sources of animal protein are fish, most shellfish, and chicken or turkey without the skin. These are featured liberally in *Cooking Light '87* recipes. So are low-fat dairy products, which include the protein and calcium of dairy products with much less fat.

Certain cuts of red meat, like flank steak, are quite low in fat, especially if portions are kept moderate. Red meat is also a very good source of iron, a mineral that's essential for the healthy functioning of blood, and one that many Americans, particularly women, need more of than they get.

Foods are, after all, more than just mixtures of fat, carbohydrates, and protein. They're full of other nutrients you need for health: vitamins, minerals, and trace elements.

ADDITIONAL NUTRIENTS WE NEED

Calcium. This essential mineral is needed to keep bones strong and to maintain proper function of nerves and muscles. Calcium, preliminary research shows, may also lower high blood pressure and protect against colon cancer. Calcium is found in dairy products, green leafy vegetables, beans, tofu, and canned salmon, bones and all. Vitamin D, found in fortified milk, helps absorb calcium.

Iron. This mineral is a vital component to hemoglobin, the substance in red blood cells which transports oxygen to all parts of the body. Red meat, as well as some fish and poultry, beans, tofu, and seeds are good sources of iron.

Trace elements. Zinc, magnesium, copper, chromium, and selenium are essential in small amounts. They may keep our immune systems working (zinc); regulate blood pressure (magnesium); reduce blood cholesterol (copper); regulate blood sugar (chromium); and may protect against cancer (selenium).

Vitamins. These nutrients, essential for life, are needed by the body's enzymes for a multitude of functions, from getting energy from foods and regulating the nervous system (B vitamins) to maintaining healthy skin (vitamin A).

Vitamins are either fat-soluble (A, D, E) or water-soluble (C, the Bs). Fat-soluble vitamins are stored in our fat, so we don't need to get vitamin A every day. Water-soluble vitamins (C, the Bs), are needed every day.

Potassium and Sodium. These elements work together to regulate heartbeat, body fluid balance, and other functions. Most of us get too much sodium and too little potassium, a combination that may contribute to high blood pressure. Citrus fruits, bananas, raisins, carrots, and dark green leafy vegetables are good sources of potassium.

WEIGHING YOUR BEST

One key to controlling weight and staying healthy is to eat foods rich in nutrients but low in calories. Nutritionists call such foods nutrient dense. Potato chips, for example, do provide some nutrients, but lots of calories and fat, so they're not very nutrient dense. A carrot, on the other hand, gives you lots of vitamin A but hardly any calories.

One way to get nutritionally dense foods in our diet is to cut down on fats and increase complex carbohydrates. When we eat fat, much of it gets turned into body fat, but it's harder for our bodies to convert carbohydrates or protein into body fat.

The bottom line: If you eat a low-fat diet, it will be easier to control your weight, even if you eat the same amount of calories as before. Complex carbohydrates and fiber are also quite filling, and that helps curb appetite. So does aerobic exercise.

But beware of fad diets and crash diets. Some, such as the (once popular) liquid protein diets, are actually so unbalanced that they can cause serious health problems. Beware of any diet that focuses on one magic food, requires fasting, excludes major food groups like meat or milk, or restricts calories to under 1,000 calories per day.

Crash diets, ironically, don't even work in the long run. If someone promises you that if you eat only grapefruit for a week, you will lose weight — he's probably right. But you'll also probably regain the weight you lose rapidly after returning to a normal diet. One reason for this is that severe dieting slows down your metabolic rate, which is the rate at which you burn calories.

Nutritionists, therefore, recommend that you try to lose no more than two or three pounds a week on a diet. That way, you won't significantly slow down metabolism, and you're more likely to get the nutrients you need.

Diet alone isn't enough. To lose weight permanently, you've got to exercise regularly. When you do aerobic exercise, such as brisk walking, running, bicycling, tennis, swimming, rowing, or dancing, you burn calories. You also increase your metabolic rate, so you'll burn calories faster and continue to burn calories for hours later, not just when you're exercising. The result can be permanent, life-long weight control. And you'll feel great!

Fortunately, you don't have to be an Olympic athlete to get some joyful, healthy exercise. Even something as simple as walking a couple of miles every day can make a dramatic difference in the number of weekly calories you burn — and maybe even in how long you live.

READING THE *COOKING LIGHT* GRID

PRO 8.2 / FAT 1.7 / CARB 19.3 / FIB 0.2 / CHOL 4 / SOD 150 / POT 391

Accompanying each *Cooking Light '87* recipe is a grid (see above) that indicates the amount of selected nutrients in the recipe. The nutrients are: protein, in grams; fat, in grams; carbohydrates, in grams; fiber, in grams; cholesterol, in milligrams; sodium, in milligrams; and potassium, in milligrams. This nutrient information and the calorie count of each recipe were derived from a computer analysis based primarily on information from the U.S. Department of Agriculture. The values are as accurate as possible and reflect the standards below:

* All meats are trimmed of fat and skin before cooking.
* When a range is given for an ingredient (3 to 3½ cups flour), the lesser amount is calculated.
* Alcohol calories evaporate when heated, and this reduction is reflected in the calculations.
* When a marinade is used, the total amount of the marinade is calculated.
* Garnishes and other optional ingredients are not calculated.
* All fruits and vegetables listed in the ingredients are not peeled unless otherwise specified.

Whether you're counting calories or just trying to make your calories count, you will find the recipe grids a valuable source for monitoring your diet.

Other current information appears throughout *Cooking Light '87.* All information is based on the newest findings of the medical and scientific communities and has been compiled to keep you apprised of the latest from the world of food and fitness. Nutrition and fitness facts are flagged by the following symbols:

NUTRITION   FITNESS

A Daily Guide To The Grid Nutrients

Nutrients	Daily Nutrient Amounts*	× Calories Per Gram	= Calorie Range
PRO (Protein)	48 to 96 grams	4	192 to 384
FAT (Fat)	40 to 80 grams	9	360 to 720
CARB (Carbohydrate)	162 to 324 grams	4	648 to 1296
FIB (Fiber)	24 to 48 grams	0	0
CHOL (Cholesterol)	300 milligrams or less	0	0
SOD (Sodium)	1,100 to 3,300 milligrams	0	0
POT (Potassium)	1,875 to 5,625 milligrams	0	0

*Based on a range of 1200-2400 calories per day

The *Cooking Light* Kitchen

To cook light, you've got to buy light. Although it may never be easy to resist a chocolate bar, it's certainly easier to do so if you have no chocolate in the house but do have a bowl of apples or peaches to reach for instead.

SNACKING LIGHT

If you're in the habit of reaching for salty, fatty snacks like potato chips, try stocking your refrigerator with chopped raw vegetables as an alternative. Good choices include carrot sticks, celery, broccoli flowerets, zucchini strips, green pepper rings, cauliflower pieces, and even raw pea pods. Just prepare and store them in plastic bags in the refrigerator. They will be ready when you are for a quick snack or salad.

If giving up some of your favorite snack foods is too difficult for you, then look for ways to improve them nutritionally. Popcorn is a good example. Unsalted and unbuttered popcorn is an ideal snack. However, if this is too bland for you, simply try cutting back on the amount of butter and salt you would normally use. Nutritionally, you are still better off than eating the fully buttered, salted variety. If you substitute margarine for the butter, you will be cutting back on saturated fat.

PREPARING LIGHT

When you buy meats, choose lean cuts and then trim away all visible fats. For poultry, remove any visible fat and the skin before cooking. Remove fat from homemade soups, stews, and gravies by refrigerating them and then skimming off the congealed fat on top. You'll save 100 calories for each teaspoon. Reduce sodium from canned vegetables and tuna by rinsing with water before cooking.

When you cook, try steaming, boiling in a small amount of water, sautéeing, poaching, broiling, grilling, baking, rack-roasting, or stir-frying instead of deep-fat frying or pan-frying. Avoid boiling foods in large amounts of water that will deplete nutrients or roasting meat in a pan that is constructed to allow the meat to cook in fat.

By observing these cooking techniques, you'll serve meals that naturally are lower in fat and calories. And by cooking vegetables in just a little water or steaming them, you'll save water-soluble vitamins like vitamin C, as well.

SMART SUBSTITUTIONS

Smart substitutions are the essence of the *Cooking Light* style. Instead of using a cup of sour cream, with its unwanted calories and saturated fat, use plain low-fat yogurt for creamy sauces. You'll find the taste is very similar — but the differences in calories (466 vs 144) and grams of fat (40 vs 3.5) are significant.

When it is possible, use egg whites for cholesterol-loaded egg yolks, and use margarine, the softer the better, instead of butter. For hard shortening or lard, use vegetable oils or soft vegetable shortening. For vegetable oils used in cooking, use a vegetable spray whenever possible, but when you do need to use oil, use one that is monounsaturated, such as olive oil, or polyunsaturated, such as corn or safflower oil. Instead of Cheddar, Monterey Jack, or Swiss cheese, try part-skim mozzarella. Instead of regular hamburger, serve leaner ground chuck or the new ground turkey.

The following chart gives you examples of other substitutions and the calories and fat you save in using these "light" alternatives.

Light Substitutions		
FOOD	CALORIES	FAT IN GRAMS
1 cup whole milk	159	8.5
1 cup skim milk	86	.4
2 tablespoons cream cheese	99	9.9
2 tablespoons Neufchâtel	74	6.6
½ cup cream-style cottage cheese	108	4.7
½ cup 2% low-fat cottage cheese	102	2.2
½ cup canned fruit cocktail in heavy syrup	93	trace
½ cup canned fruit cocktail packed in water	39	trace
1 tablespoon mayonnaise	99	11.0
1 tablespoon reduced-calorie mayonnaise	40	4.0
1 tablespoon vegetable oil	121	13.6
2 seconds vegetable cooking spray	8	.8
1 chicken breast with skin, roasted	193	7.6
1 chicken breast without skin, roasted	142	3.1
Tuna packed in oil	571	40.7
Water-packed tuna	235	1.5

Exercise — The Perfect Partner

Exercise is the perfect partner to eating right, providing both short- and long-term benefits. Research studies show that regular exercise can help you reach and maintain ideal weight, improve the efficiency of your heart and cardiovascular system, strengthen your muscles and bones, reduce anxiety and lift your mood, lower your risk of adult-onset diabetes and perhaps certain types of cancer.

Just as your body requires a variety of foods to be adequately nourished, it also requires a variety of exercises in order for it to perform at peak efficiency. A good exercise program should combine activities which focus on the three types of exercise: aerobics, strength, and flexibility. An aerobic workout strengthens the heart and improves circulation, helps control weight by burning calories and raising metabolic rate, improves your body's ability to use insulin, and reduces the relative amount of cholesterol in the blood. By training the body to handle stress, aerobic exercise also reduces anxiety. Activities such as running, dancing, swimming, and brisk walking are considered aerobic.

Strength training promotes stronger muscles; because lean body mass burns more calories than body fat, a strength training program may also help in weight control. By strengthening the abdominal muscles that hold your back, it reduces back strain, too. Examples of strength training include weight training and calisthenics.

Flexibility exercises simply stretch the muscles and connective tissues. These exercises reduce the risk of injury, ease aches and pains, keep joints supple, and often improve posture.

An exercise program should also include some weight-bearing exercises (walking, running, playing tennis) to keep bones strong. When you put weight on your bones, they get denser and stronger. Even in women after menopause, when bones begin to lose mass, weight-bearing exercise may arrest bone loss. Regular weight-bearing exercise, researchers believe, is an important factor in preventing osteoporosis, a "brittle bone" disease.

EVERYDAY EXERCISES

Increasing everyday physical activity is one key to better health and longer life, perhaps even more so than vigorous sports, according to the finding of a major 16-year Stanford University School of Medicine study published in the *New England Journal of Medicine* last year. And you don't have to join an exercise class to get more exercise, although you may want to.

The prime predictor of longevity, researchers found, was how many extra calories the subjects burned in a week. We burn calories every minute, even when we are sleeping, but extra calories are those that we burn doing some additional activity, whether gardening or playing racquetball. Death rates were as much as one-third lower in those who burned an extra 2,000 calories a week compared to those who were almost entirely sedentary. Heart disease and respiratory conditions in particular were much less prevalent in the active persons.

Many of the extra calories expended, the researchers found, came from activities that aren't normally associated with sports and fitness. These activities are referred to as "background" exercises. For example: Ten minutes of moderate stair climbing burns about 67 calories; ten minutes of vigorous stair climbing burns about 150 calories. Shovel snow for 10 minutes and you'll burn nearly 100 calories. Garden for an hour, and you'll burn up to 345 calories. Saw wood by hand for 20 minutes, and you'll burn up an extra 115 calories.

Vigorous activity still has a place, of course. In an earlier study, the Stanford researchers found that whether you burned 500 calories a week or 2,000, those people who also include aerobic exercise vigorous enough to raise the heart rate to 70% - 75% of maximum have a reduced risk of getting coronary heart disease.

For many people, walking is the easiest way to increase activity. It's certainly background exercise, and one that is fairly easy to increase in the course of an average day. Its advantages and benefits are many. Walking is nearly injury-free; it is inexpensive. Walking is a weight-bearing exercise; it can be aerobic, and if done right, can improve strength and flexibility. You can set your own pace. (For tips on how to buy good walking shoes, see page 227.) Since walking a mile burns about 100 calories, you can burn 2000 calories a week by walking 20 miles, no matter what your pace.

Walk more often, and you will burn more calories and strengthen your bones; walk briskly for 20 minutes or more, and walking becomes an aerobic workout. (Try "healthwalking," demonstrated on pages 10 and 11, and you'll improve your posture and flexibility, strengthen your abdomen, and reduce back strain in the bargain.)

Before undertaking a program that would change your activity pattern, consult your physician. This is particularly important if you are over 40 or have diabetes, high blood pressure, heart disease, orthopedic problems, or any other medical condition that increases your risk while exercising.

Healthwalking Program

Good posture while walking will help circulation, give you energy, and reduce back strain. Keep your back straight, with stomach and buttocks pulled in. Look straight ahead, not down.

Walking is a pleasant activity that you can easily make aerobic. By walking briskly 20 minutes a day, 3 times a week, you'll be meeting the recommended minimum for aerobic fitness.

To get the circulation going, warm up by stretching or by walking at a normal pace for 3 to 5 minutes. (Save the real stretching for after your walk.) Then increase your pace, swinging arms and striding forward. Pace yourself. If you can carry on a normal conversation while walking, you're doing fine. How long and how far you walk is more important than how fast. As you get in better shape, increase your workout by walking longer, farther, and faster.

A cool down is important. A 5-minute leisurely walk will allow your pulse to slow down.

Stretching helps maintain good flexibility and should be a part of your walking program. On the right are a few stretches that you can do before or after walking. Each stretch should be slow and controlled and repeated 3 times with the last stretch held for 8 seconds.

Stride forward as far as is reasonably comfortable. As your hips stretch forward and backward, and side to side, you'll be tightening your abdominal muscles which also reduces back strain. Swing your arms for the full range of motion—90 degrees, if possible. This helps keep the body in balance and actually serves as a circulation pump; you'll be improving your upper-body muscle tone, too.

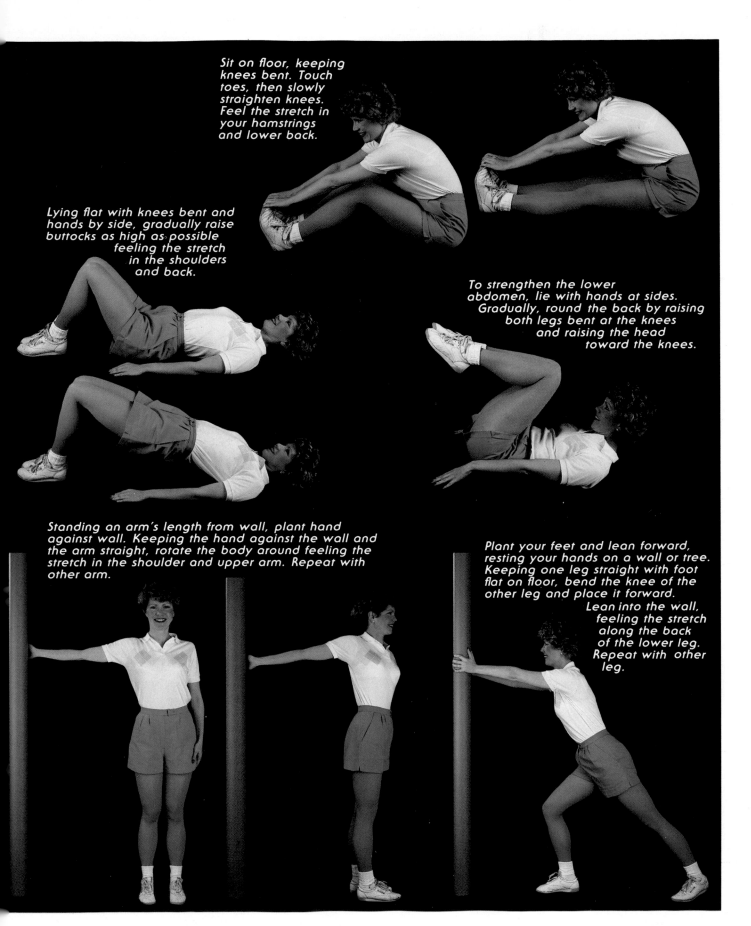

Sit on floor, keeping knees bent. Touch toes, then slowly straighten knees. Feel the stretch in your hamstrings and lower back.

Lying flat with knees bent and hands by side, gradually raise buttocks as high as possible feeling the stretch in the shoulders and back.

To strengthen the lower abdomen, lie with hands at sides. Gradually, round the back by raising both legs bent at the knees and raising the head toward the knees.

Standing an arm's length from wall, plant hand against wall. Keeping the hand against the wall and the arm straight, rotate the body around feeling the stretch in the shoulder and upper arm. Repeat with other arm.

Plant your feet and lean forward, resting your hands on a wall or tree. Keeping one leg straight with foot flat on floor, bend the knee of the other leg and place it forward. Lean into the wall, feeling the stretch along the back of the lower leg. Repeat with other leg.

Healthy American Meals

Many people consider an "all-American" meal to be a hamburger, French fries, and a creamy milkshake, and that is fine, occasionally. However, years of research indicate that a more balanced, varied diet that is lower in calories, fat, sugar, and protein, and higher in carbohydrates is healthier for everyone.

The United States Department of Agriculture and an increasing number of nutrition and health-related organizations, including the American Dietetic Association and the American Heart Association, have identified specific dietary guidelines for Americans. These guidelines are the following:

1. Eat a variety of foods.
2. Maintain desirable weight.
3. Avoid too much fat, saturated fat, and cholesterol.
4. Eat foods with adequate starch and fiber.
5. Avoid too much sugar.
6. Avoid too much sodium.
7. If you drink alcoholic beverages, do so in moderation.

The thirty menus in "Healthy American Meals" were developed along these guidelines. In each menu, calories derived from fat were limited to no more than 30 percent of the total meal, and from protein no more than 20 percent, while the carbohydrate content was raised to at least 50 percent.

And yet, we didn't overlook the fact that developing new food habits takes time. People eat foods that are familiar to them. In "Healthy American Meals" you may recognize the names of some of

Savor the fresh gifts of spring by serving Shrimp-Asparagus Salad, Italian Marinated Tomatoes, and Rye Breadsticks, featured in the Ladies' Spring Luncheon (menu begins on page 38).

your favorite dishes. We have applied the philosophy of *Cooking Light* to the foods and created fare which looks fabulous and tastes delicious, yet is lower in calories and higher in nutrition.

The Après-Swim Lunch menu is a good example of the favorite all-American meal gone "light." Grilled Veal Burgers, with ground veal replacing the more traditional ground beef, have a lower fat content. There's plenty of flavor in the burgers with the addition of marjoram and lemon rind, as well as in the zesty horseradish topping. Served on whole wheat hamburger buns for more flavor, texture, and fiber, these burgers are as nutritious as they are flavorful.

New Potato Salad with Green Goddess Dressing offers an alternative to the traditional French fries or potato salad. The high-calorie mayonnaise has been replaced with an equally satisfying combination of plain low-fat yogurt and reduced-calorie mayonnaise. When you spice it up to your own taste with chives, lemon juice, tarragon, and garlic powder, you have the perfect accompaniment to the Grilled Veal Burgers.

And what about dessert? Instead of a milkshake, high in calories, fat, and sugar, try Banana-Yogurt Freeze. By substituting flavorful, fresh bananas for some of the sugar, and plain low-fat yogurt and egg whites in place of the whole eggs and cream, you will have a dessert which will satisfy your taste for something sweet and provide you with the benefits of protein, calcium, and potassium. When you compare the Après-Swim Lunch menu at 606 calories per serving, with the traditional meal of about 840 calories, you can begin to see how the philosophy of *Cooking Light* can change your eating habits without dramatically changing your food preferences.

In planning these menus, we also took into consideration that people lead busy lives, and that, as a result, less and less time can be spent in the kitchen preparing food — nutritious or otherwise. With this time factor in mind, we developed menus that are quick and easy, using convenience products where appropriate and giving suggestions on how to prepare the meal in the most efficient way possible. In "Breakfast & Brunch" menus, for instance, there are simple make-ahead breakfasts such as Breakfast-on-the-Go. In "Light & Healthy" you will find delightful menus for an everyday lunch or a weekend picnic. The menus from "Quick & Easy" as well as from "Microwave It Light" provide just the help you need to get a nutritious family meal on the table. And for those special occasions when you would like to entertain, impress your family and friends with light, nutritious meals from "That's Entertaining."

If you keep sound nutritional principles in mind, such as those demonstrated in "Healthy American Meals," you won't have to sacrifice culinary pleasure. Instead, you may benefit from the loss of a few extra pounds, while you increase longevity and lower the risk of heart disease, stroke, diabetes, and certain forms of cancer. Most of all, you'll gain a real sense of well-being.

Dried shiitake mushrooms, with their rich flavor, are one of the ingredients that give this Shiitake Mushroom Omelet its zippy taste. The bran muffin is loaded with carbohydrates. And don't discount the parsley; it's a great source of Vitamin A (menu begins on page 20).

Breakfast & Brunch

Breakfast-On-The-Go

Carrot-Raisin Muffins
Apricot-Yogurt Smoothie

Serves 6
Total calories per serving: 246

Swiss Oatmeal
Basic Hot Chocolate

Serves 4
Total calories per serving: 333

In a hurry? Concerned about a nutritious breakfast? Here are two nutrient-packed meals to make and eat in a jiffy.

The first combines Carrot-Raisin Muffins (1 muffin per serving) with a calcium-rich beverage. The muffins may be made ahead, frozen, and then re-heated in the microwave.

The second breakfast features a high-fiber cereal, combining fruit, nuts and grains in a tasty blend. Basic Hot Chocolate is the flavorful, easy-to-make beverage.

CARROT-RAISIN MUFFINS

2½ cups wheat bran flakes cereal
1 cup skim milk
1 egg, beaten
3 tablespoons vegetable oil
1 cup all-purpose flour
1 tablespoon baking powder
3 tablespoons firmly packed brown sugar
1 teaspoon ground nutmeg
⅛ teaspoon salt
⅔ cup grated carrot
¼ cup raisins
Vegetable cooking spray

Combine cereal and milk in a large bowl; stir well. Let stand 3 minutes. Combine egg and oil in a small bowl; mix well. Add egg mixture to cereal mixture, stirring well.

Combine flour, baking powder, sugar, nutmeg, and salt, mixing well. Add to cereal mixture; stir just until blended. Stir in carrot and raisins.

Spoon batter into muffin pans coated with cooking spray, filling three-fourths full. Bake at 400° for 20 minutes or until golden brown. Yield: 1 dozen (138 calories each).

Note: Leftover muffins may be sealed in an airtight container and frozen for later use. To thaw, let stand at room temperature several hours or microwave 1 muffin at MEDIUM (50% power) for 1 minute or until thoroughly heated.

PRO 3.6 / FAT 4.3 / CARB 22.6 / FIB 1.8 / CHOL 23 / SOD 196 / POT 158

A quick energy way to start the day.

APRICOT-YOGURT SMOOTHIE

1 (16-ounce) can unsweetened apricot halves, chilled and drained
1 (16-ounce) carton vanilla low-fat yogurt
1 cup skim milk
2 teaspoons sugar
½ teaspoon vanilla extract
¼ teaspoon almond extract
Ground nutmeg

Combine first 6 ingredients in container of an electric blender, and process until smooth. Serve immediately or refrigerate until ready to serve. Garnish each serving with ground nutmeg sprinkled over top. Yield: 6 cups (108 calories per 1-cup serving).

PRO 5.8 / FAT 1.2 / CARB 19.2 / FIB 0.6 / CHOL 5 / SOD 72 / POT 373

Store Swiss Oatmeal in an airtight container for quick breakfasts or anytime you want a high-energy snack. Served with Yogurt-Brown Sugar Topping and Basic Hot Chocolate, this oatmeal is a good source of protein.

SWISS OATMEAL

1 cup regular oats, uncooked
½ cup wheat germ
½ cup raw bran
¼ cup unsalted sunflower seeds
1 cup raisins
1 cup dried apricots (5 ounces), chopped
¼ cup plus 1 tablespoon slivered almonds (2 ounces), toasted
Yogurt-Brown Sugar Topping
Ground cinnamon

Combine first 4 ingredients, and spread in a jellyroll pan. Bake at 350° for 10 minutes, stirring occasionally. Let cool completely. Combine oat mixture, raisins, apricots, and almonds. Store in an airtight container until ready to use.

To serve, place ½ cup oat mixture in individual bowls, and top with ¼ cup Yogurt-Brown Sugar Topping. Sprinkle each serving with ground cinnamon to garnish. Yield: 10 servings (216 calories per serving).

Yogurt-Brown Sugar Topping:

2½ cups plain low-fat yogurt
2 tablespoons plus 1½ teaspoons brown sugar
¾ teaspoon ground cinnamon

Combine all ingredients in a bowl, stirring until well blended. Yield: 2½ cups (11 calories per tablespoon).

Note: Yogurt-Brown Sugar Topping may be covered and stored in refrigerator for later use.

PRO 8.6 / FAT 6.3 / CARB 36.3 / FIB 3.6 / CHOL 3 / SOD 47 / POT 584

BASIC HOT CHOCOLATE

¼ cup Dutch process cocoa
2 tablespoons sugar
½ cup water
3½ cups skim milk
½ teaspoon vanilla extract

Combine cocoa and sugar in a large saucepan; stir until well blended. Stir in water; bring to a boil. Reduce heat to medium, and cook, stirring constantly, until cocoa and sugar dissolve. Reduce heat to low, and add milk; cook until thoroughly heated. Stir in vanilla. Pour into mugs, and serve immediately. Yield: 4 cups (117 calories per 1-cup serving).

PRO 8.2 / FAT 1.7 / CARB 19.3 / FIB 0.2 / CHOL 4 / SOD 150 / POT 391

A remarkable breakfast! Delicious, satisfying and only 376 calories a serving!

Sunday Morning Family Treat

When the family is all together on Sunday morning, take a little extra time to put together a special meal they're sure to enjoy.

Spicy French Toast is a delicious, light version of a classic. Our recipe is flavored with cinnamon, cloves, and vanilla extract. Calories and fat are kept low by using cooking spray in the skillet instead of butter or margarine.

Your morning will go smoother

**Summer Berry Medley
Spicy French Toast
Turkey Sausage Patties
Breakfast Pear Nog**

Serves 4
Total calories per serving: 376

if you shape and chill the patties for Turkey Sausage the day or night before. In the morning, all

you'll need to do is cook the patties about 10 minutes.

Another time-saving hint is to prepare Summer Berry Medley ahead and put the ingredients for the beverage in the refrigerator on Saturday evening. By starting with thoroughly chilled ingredients, the beverage will be just the right temperature immediately after it is processed in the blender.

SUMMER BERRY MEDLEY

1 cup fresh strawberry halves
½ cup fresh blackberries
½ cup orange sections
2 tablespoons unsweetened orange juice
1 tablespoon sifted powdered sugar
4 sprigs fresh mint

Combine strawberries, blackberries, orange sections, orange juice, and powdered sugar in a medium bowl; toss gently. Cover and refrigerate 1 hour or overnight.

Spoon fruit mixture into individual serving bowls; garnish with mint sprigs. Yield: 4 servings (51 calories per serving).

Note: Summer Berry Medley may be spooned over Spicy French Toast, if desired.

PRO 0.8 / FAT 0.4 / CARB 12.2 / FIB 2.3 / CHOL 0 / SOD 1 / POT 181

SPICY FRENCH TOAST

½ cup skim milk
2 eggs
3 tablespoons sifted powdered sugar
½ teaspoon ground cinnamon
¼ teaspoon ground cloves
½ teaspoon vanilla extract
Vegetable cooking spray
4 slices whole wheat bread

Combine milk, eggs, sugar, cinnamon, cloves, and vanilla in a shallow bowl, beating well.

Coat a large skillet with cooking spray; place over medium heat until hot. Dip 2 bread slices, one at a time, into egg mixture, coating well. Drain off excess; arrange bread slices in skillet, and cook over medium heat 4 minutes on each side or until lightly browned. Remove to a serving platter, and keep warm. Repeat with remaining bread slices. Yield: 4 servings (136 calories per serving.)

PRO 6.8 / FAT 3.6 / CARB 19.8 / FIB 1.4 / CHOL 138 / SOD 183 / POT 155

TURKEY SAUSAGE PATTIES

½ (1-pound) package raw ground turkey, thawed
1 egg white
1 teaspoon dried Italian seasoning
⅛ teaspoon salt
Vegetable cooking spray
2 teaspoons vegetable oil

Combine first 4 ingredients in a small bowl, mixing well. Shape mixture into 4 patties, and chill at least 1 hour.

Coat a large skillet with cooking spray; add oil. Place over medium-high heat until hot. Place patties in skillet; cook 5 minutes on each side or until done. Place patties on paper towels to drain; serve warm. Yield: 4 servings (93 calories per serving).

PRO 13.2 / FAT 3.9 / CARB 0.5 / FIB 0.1 / CHOL 37 / SOD 126 / POT 188

BREAKFAST PEAR NOG

2 cups pear nectar, chilled
1 (8-ounce) carton plain low-fat yogurt
¼ teaspoon almond extract

Combine all ingredients in container of an electric blender; process 30 seconds or until smooth. Serve immediately. Yield: 3 cups (96 calories per ¾-cup serving.)

PRO 3.0 / FAT 0.9 / CARB 18.2 / FIB 0.8 / CHOL 3 / SOD 46 / POT 148

Weekend Breakfast For Two

After your next Saturday or Sunday morning tennis game, revive your partner with a breakfast that's colorful, delicious, and serves two without leftovers. But perhaps the best news is that this nourishing menu provides a boost of energy at a cost of only 371 calories per serving.

Extra egg whites are added to two whole eggs to make the omelet hearty enough for two servings without increasing the cholesterol count.

Shiitake Mushroom Omelet
Bran Muffins for Two
Honeydew Melon with
Strawberry-Orange Sauce
Cinnamon-Raisin Tea

Serves 2
Total calories per serving: 371

The bran muffins and our special honeydew dish are both quick and easy, making them excellent choices for breakfast.

And don't think we omitted eggs from the list of muffin ingredients by mistake — unlike most quick breads, these muffins are made without an egg! And they're so tasty, you'll never miss the egg.

Prepare Strawberry-Orange Sauce for the honeydew and Cinnamon-Raisin Tea the evening before your planned meal. The flavors are best after chilling, and what's more, you'll be able to stay on the court a few extra minutes in the morning.

SHIITAKE MUSHROOM OMELET

½ cup dried shiitake mushrooms
1½ cups hot water
Vegetable cooking spray
2 teaspoons minced green onion
1 tablespoon sherry
1 teaspoon Worcestershire sauce
⅛ teaspoon pepper
2 eggs
2 egg whites
2 tablespoons skim milk
⅛ teaspoon white pepper
1 teaspoon chopped fresh parsley
Tomato roses (optional)

Soak mushrooms in hot water 45 minutes; drain. Coarsely chop, and set aside.

Coat a small skillet with cooking spray. Place over medium heat until hot. Add mushrooms and green onion; sauté until tender. Stir in sherry, Worcestershire sauce, and pepper; cook over medium heat 1 minute or until liquid is absorbed. Transfer mixture to a small bowl; set aside, and keep warm.

Combine eggs, egg whites, milk, and white pepper in a small bowl; beat well and set aside. Coat a 10-inch nonstick skillet or omelet pan with cooking spray; place over medium heat until hot enough to sizzle a drop of water. Pour

in egg mixture. As mixture begins to cook, gently lift edges of omelet with a spatula, and tilt pan to allow uncooked portions to flow underneath. When egg mixture is set, spoon reserved mushroom mixture over half of omelet; loosen omelet with spatula, and carefully fold in half. Carefully slide omelet onto a warm serving platter; garnish wrih chopped parsley. Cut omelet in half, and serve immediately. Garnish each serving with a tomato rose, if desired. Yield: 2 servings (142 calories per serving).

PRO 10.9 / FAT 5.7 / CARB 8.5 / FIB 0.9 / CHOL 274 / SOD 154 / POT 282

 These days, mushrooms are a popular ingredient in gourmet dishes. That's a healthy trend. They're rich in potassium, a good source of the B vitamin niacin and fiber, and very low in calories and sodium.

Shiitake (shee-TAH-kay) mushrooms, originally grown and savored in the Far East, have a light garlic-pine aroma. Shiitakes are usually available year round, but are most plentiful during spring and autumn. Because of their unusual taste, shiitakes should be allowed to star in any recipe where they are used.

What's a breakfast without fruit? Its
natural sweetness and fresh flavor
provide a wake-up perk without any
fat and few calories. Honeydew
Melon with Strawberry-Orange
Sauce is a delicious example.
Cinnamon-Raisin Tea is the tasty
2-calorie-per-cup beverage.

HONEYDEW MELON WITH STRAWBERRY-ORANGE SAUCE

½ cup fresh strawberries, washed and hulled
1 teaspoon sugar
1½ teaspoons Triple Sec or other orange-flavored
   liqueur
¼ teaspoon grated orange rind
6 (1-inch) slices honeydew melon
2 fresh strawberries (optional)

Combine ½ cup strawberries, sugar, Triple Sec,
and orange rind in container of an electric
blender; process until smooth. Chill thoroughly.

Arrange 3 melon slices on each serving plate,
and spoon sauce over top. Garnish each serving
with a strawberry, if desired. Yield: 2 servings
(95 calories per serving).

PRO 1.7 / FAT 0.7 / CARB 20.6 / FIB 1.8 / CHOL 0 / SOD 23 / POT 524

CINNAMON-RAISIN TEA

2⅓ cups boiling water
2 (3-inch) sticks cinnamon
2 tablespoons raisins
2 individual tea bags
Additional cinnamon sticks (optional)

Pour boiling water over cinnamon, raisins, and
tea bags; cover and let steep 5 minutes or until
desired strength. Remove tea bags. Cover and
let stand 8 hours or overnight.

To serve, heat to desired temperature. Remove cinnamon and raisins. Garnish with fresh
cinnamon sticks, if desired. Yield: 2 cups (2 calories per 1-cup serving).

PRO 0.0 / FAT 0.0 / CARB 0.0 / FIB 0.0 / CHOL 0 / SOD 0 / POT 0

BRAN MUFFINS FOR TWO

3 tablespoons morsels of wheat bran cereal
3 tablespoons skim milk
2 teaspoons margarine, melted
2 teaspoons honey
3 tablespoons all-purpose flour
½ teaspoon baking powder
Dash of salt
Vegetable cooking spray

Combine cereal and milk in a small bowl; stir
well, and let stand 2 minutes. Add margarine
and honey, stirring until blended. Combine flour,
baking powder, and salt in a small bowl. Add to
cereal mixture, and stir just until moistened.

Spoon batter into 2 muffin cups coated with
cooking spray. Bake at 400° for 20 minutes or
until golden brown. Yield: 2 muffins (132 calories each).

PRO 3.3 / FAT 4.2 / CARB 22.9 / FIB 2.6 / CHOL 0 / SOD 256 / POT 188

Special Occasion Brunch

Light Eggs Sardou
Bran English Muffins
Melon Ball Mélange
Spiced Coffee

Serves 6
Total calories per serving: 367

Who would think that the New Orleans favorite, Eggs Sardou, could be the star of a light brunch? Our version is topped with a sauce of reduced-calorie mayonnaise and low-fat yogurt to minimize fat and calories.

Bran English Muffins (1 muffin per serving) should be made ahead since the dough requires kneading and rising time. Store leftover muffins in an airtight container or freeze them for a quick breakfast during the week.

This brunch is guaranteed to make any occasion special.

LIGHT EGGS SARDOU

¼ pound fresh spinach, trimmed
1 (14-ounce) can artichoke bottoms, undrained
1 tablespoon skim milk
Dash of salt
6 eggs, poached
Tarragon Sauce
Paprika

Wash spinach and place in a Dutch oven (do not add water); cover and cook over high heat 3 to 4 minutes. Drain spinach well; place between paper towels, and squeeze until barely moist. Set aside.

Place artichoke bottoms with liquid in a small saucepan; cook over medium heat 5 minutes or until thoroughly heated. Drain well; set aside, and keep warm.

Combine spinach, skim milk, and salt in container of an electric blender; process until smooth.

Place 1 heated artichoke bottom on each of 6 individual serving plates. Place 1 tablespoon spinach mixture in each artichoke bottom. Place 1 poached egg on top of each bed of spinach. Cover each serving with 2 tablespoons warm Tarragon Sauce; sprinkle each serving with paprika, and serve immediately. Yield: 6 servings (150 calories per serving).

Note: Light Eggs Sardou may be served on a toasted English muffin half.

Tarragon Sauce:

¼ cup plus 2 tablespoons reduced-calorie
    mayonnaise
¼ cup plus 2 tablespoons plain low-fat yogurt
¼ teaspoon dried whole tarragon
Dash of white pepper

Combine all ingredients in a small saucepan; stir with a wire whisk until smooth. Cook over low heat, stirring constantly, 3 to 4 minutes or until thoroughly heated (do not allow mixture to boil). Yield: ¾ cup.

PRO 8.6 / FAT 9.9 / CARB 7.2 / FIB 0.7 / CHOL 280 / SOD 253 / POT 294

BRAN ENGLISH MUFFINS

1⅔ cups skim milk
2 tablespoons margarine
½ teaspoon salt
1½ cups wheat bran flakes cereal
1 package dry yeast
¼ cup warm water (105° to 115°)
3½ to 4¼ cups all-purpose flour
Vegetable cooking spray
1 teaspoon cornmeal

Combine milk, margarine, and salt in a small saucepan; cook over low heat until margarine melts. Add cereal, stirring well; let cool to 105° to 115°

Dissolve yeast in warm water in a large bowl; let stand 5 minutes. Stir lukewarm milk mixture into dissolved yeast. Gradually stir in 3½ cups flour. Knead in enough remaining flour to make a soft dough.

Place dough in a large bowl coated with cooking spray, turning to grease top. Cover and let rise in a warm place (85°), free from drafts, 1 hour or until doubled in bulk. Turn dough out onto a lightly floured surface; roll to ½-inch thickness. Cut into rounds with a 3-inch floured biscuit cutter. Cover and let rest on a floured surface 30 minutes.

Coat an electric skillet with cooking spray. Heat at medium (350°) until hot; sprinkle lightly with cornmeal. Transfer muffins to skillet; cook, partially covered, 12 minutes. Turn and cook, partially covered, an additional 12 minutes. Transfer to wire racks to cool completely. Split

muffins, and toast until lightly browned. Muffins may be stored in airtight containers. Yield: 16 muffins (137 calories each).

PRO 4.5 / FAT 1.8 / CARB 25.6 / FIB 1.4 / CHOL 1 / SOD 139 / POT 102

MELON BALL MÉLANGE

2 cups watermelon balls
2 cups honeydew balls
2 cups cantaloupe balls
½ cup unsweetened orange juice
¼ cup lime juice
1 tablespoon Triple Sec or other orange-flavored
    liqueur
1 tablespoon chopped fresh mint leaves
2 teaspoons grated orange rind
Additional fresh mint leaves (optional)

Combine watermelon, honeydew, and cantaloupe in a 13- x 9- x 2-inch baking dish. Combine orange juice, lime juice, Triple Sec, 1 tablespoon mint leaves, and orange rind in container of an electric blender; process until mint is finely chopped. Pour juice mixture over melon balls, stirring gently. Cover and chill 2 hours or overnight. Spoon into individual serving bowls; garnish with additional mint leaves, if desired. Yield: 6 servings (75 calories per serving).

PRO 1.5 / FAT 0.6 / CARB 16.8 / FIB 0.7 / CHOL 0 / SOD 13 / POT 426

SPICED COFFEE

⅔ cup whole Columbian coffee beans or ⅔ cup
    ground coffee
¾ teaspoon ground cardamom
½ teaspoon vanilla extract
½ teaspoon almond extract
6 cups water

Place coffee beans in container of a coffee grinder; process to a medium grind. Assemble drip coffee maker according to manufacturer's directions. Place ground coffee beans in paper filter of filter basket; sprinkle with cardamom and flavorings. Add water to coffee maker, and brew. Serve immediately. Yield: 6 cups (5 calories per 1-cup serving).

PRO 0.0 / FAT 0.0 / CARB 0.3 / FIB 0.0 / CHOL 0 / SOD 0 / POT 191

Country Morning

Breakfast in the country often results in too much cholesterol and too many calories. By using light cooking methods and ingredients, you and your guests can enjoy this hearty egg and biscuit breakfast for only 433 calories and 285 milligrams of cholesterol. That even includes an herby tomato side dish, a Bran-Buttermilk Biscuit, Peach Ambrosia, and a glass of skim milk as well. (Allow 1 cup milk per serving for correct calorie count.)

Poached Eggs with
Chile-Cheese Sauce
Herb-Baked Tomatoes
Bran-Buttermilk Biscuits
Peach Ambrosia
Skim Milk

Serves 6
Total calories per serving: 433

The ambrosia should be the first dish in your order of preparation. It needs an hour of chilling time for the Grand Marnier to penetrate the fruit. Then, with a sprinkling of coconut flakes, it's ready.

Poaching is certainly a healthful way to cook eggs. However, since many people think plain poached eggs are rather uninteresting, we topped these with a flavorful Chile-Cheese Sauce. Use extra-sharp Cheddar instead of a milder cheese in the sauce so that a very small amount provides plenty of cheese flavor.

POACHED EGGS WITH CHILE-CHEESE SAUCE

2 teaspoons margarine
2 teaspoons all-purpose flour
¼ cup plus 2 tablespoons skim milk
⅛ teaspoon salt
⅛ teaspoon paprika
Dash of red pepper
¼ cup (1 ounce) shredded extra-sharp Cheddar cheese
2 tablespoons chopped green chiles
6 eggs, poached
Additional paprika
Fresh parsley sprigs

Melt margarine in a small saucepan over low heat. Add flour, stirring until mixture is smooth.

Cook 1 minute, stirring constantly. Gradually add milk; cook over medium heat, stirring constantly, until mixture is thickened and bubbly. Stir in salt, ⅛ teaspoon paprika, red pepper, shredded cheese, and chopped green chiles; remove from heat, and continue to stir until cheese melts.

Place each poached egg in a 6-ounce ramekin or custard cup, and top with 1 tablespoon cheese sauce. Sprinkle each serving with additional paprika, and garnish with parsley sprigs. Serve immediately. Yield: 6 servings (119 calories per serving).

PRO 8.0 / FAT 8.5 / CARB 2.3 / FIB 0.1 / CHOL 279 / SOD 176 / POT 105

HERB-BAKED TOMATOES

3 medium tomatoes, cut into wedges
Vegetable cooking spray
⅓ cup whole wheat breadcrumbs
1 tablespoon chopped fresh parsley
2 teaspoons margarine, melted
¼ teaspoon garlic powder
¼ teaspoon ground coriander
¼ teaspoon ground cumin
¼ teaspoon pepper

Arrange tomato wedges in a 10- x 6- x 2-inch baking dish coated with cooking spray. Combine remaining ingredients in a small bowl, stirring well; sprinkle over tomatoes.

Bake, uncovered, at 425° for 5 minutes or until tomatoes are thoroughly heated and topping is lightly browned. Serve hot. Yield: 6 servings (39 calories per serving).

PRO 1.3 / FAT 1.6 / CARB 6.0 / FIB 0.9 / CHOL 0 / SOD 51 / POT 170

With its combination of fruits, enhanced by Grand Marnier and garnished with flaked coconut, Peach Ambrosia could be the perfect ending or beginning of any meal.

BRAN-BUTTERMILK BISCUITS

⅔ cup all-purpose flour
¾ teaspoon baking powder
¼ teaspoon baking soda
¼ teaspoon salt
2 tablespoons margarine
¼ cup crushed wheat bran flakes cereal
¼ cup plus 3 tablespoons buttermilk

Combine flour, baking powder, soda, and salt in a medium bowl; cut in margarine with a pastry blender until mixture resembles coarse meal. Set aside.

Combine crushed wheat bran flakes cereal and buttermilk in a small bowl, and let stand for 2 minutes. Add cereal mixture to reserved flour mixture, stirring until all dry ingredients are moistened.

Turn dough out onto a lightly floured surface, and knead 3 to 4 times. Roll dough to ½-inch thickness; cut into rounds with a 2-inch biscuit cutter. Place biscuits on an ungreased baking sheet. Bake at 425° for 12 minutes or until biscuits are golden brown. Yield: 6 biscuits (94 calories each).

PRO 2.4 / FAT 3.2 / CARB 13.8 / FIB 0.7 / CHOL 1 / SOD 231 / POT 54

PEACH AMBROSIA

4 medium-size ripe peaches, peeled and sliced
2 medium oranges, peeled and sectioned
1 medium-size ripe banana, sliced
1 tablespoon plus 1½ teaspoons Grand Marnier or other orange-flavored liqueur
1 tablespoon plus 1½ teaspoons lemon juice
2 tablespoons flaked coconut, toasted

Combine fruit in a large bowl; sprinkle with liqueur and lemon juice, and toss well. Cover and chill 1 hour.

Spoon fruit mixture into individual serving bowls, and sprinkle with coconut. Yield: 6 servings (95 calories per serving).

PRO 1.2 / FAT 1.0 / CARB 20.5 / FIB 3.1 / CHOL 0 / SOD 7 / POT 347

Tofu-Spinach Quiche is the energy-rich star of this Saturday brunch.

Saturday Brunch

Brunch is a fun way to entertain friends after your morning workouts. However, the usual main dishes for brunch, like eggs, sausage, bacon, and ham, are high in cholesterol, fat, and/or sodium. Not so with this Saturday Brunch; it's a deliciously light but nutrient-rich menu for you and your health-conscious friends to eat and enjoy.

The main dish, Tofu-Spinach Quiche, provides protein by combining only three eggs with nutritious tofu and other ingredients

Tofu-Spinach Quiche
Miniature Blueberry Muffins
Minted Fruit Compote
Cappuccino

Serves 8
Total calories per serving: 441

that are loaded with calcium — plain low-fat yogurt, evaporated skim milk, and Swiss cheese. The rice crust is significantly lower in fat than a regular pastry crust and adds a nice crunchy texture

to the quiche.

You may want to prepare the Minted Fruit Compote the night before. The orange and grapefruit sections and strawberries will better absorb the mint flavor, and your morning schedule will be easier.

While the Miniature Blueberry Muffins bake (2 muffins per serving), combine and heat ingredients for Cappuccino. There's only 1 teaspoon brandy per ¾-cup serving — enough to give this beverage a special flavor.

TOFU-SPINACH QUICHE

¾ cup (6 ounces) tofu
2 eggs
¾ cup evaporated skim milk
¼ cup plain low-fat yogurt
¼ teaspoon salt
⅛ teaspoon pepper
3 cups fresh spinach leaves
2 tablespoons water
¾ cup (3 ounces) shredded Swiss cheese
Rice Crust
Sweet red pepper rings (optional)
Fresh parsley sprigs (optional)

Wrap tofu with several layers of cheesecloth or paper towels; press lightly to remove excess liquid. Remove cheesecloth.

Combine tofu, eggs, milk, yogurt, salt, and pepper in container of an electric blender; process 10 seconds or until smooth.

Remove stems from spinach; wash leaves, and drain. Place spinach and water in a medium saucepan. Cover and cook over high heat 3 minutes or until spinach is tender. Drain spinach well; place between paper towels, and squeeze until barely moist. Chop spinach, and

stir into tofu mixture.

Sprinkle cheese over bottom of Rice Crust. Pour tofu mixture over cheese. Cover edge of crust with aluminum foil. Bake at 350° for 45 minutes or until set. Let quiche stand 10 minutes on a wire rack before serving. Garnish with sweet red pepper rings and parsley, if desired. Yield: 8 servings (197 calories per serving).

Rice Crust:

Vegetable cooking spray
2½ cups cooked parboiled rice (cooked without salt or fat)
1 tablespoon margarine, melted
1 egg, lightly beaten
¼ cup (1 ounce) shredded Swiss cheese

Coat a 9-inch pieplate well with cooking spray; set aside.

Combine rice, margarine, egg, and cheese, stirring until well blended. Press mixture evenly over bottom and up sides of pieplate. Yield: one 9-inch crust.

PRO 12.0 / FAT 8.6 / CARB 17.9 / FIB 1.1 / CHOL 117 / SOD 205 / POT 287

MINTED FRUIT COMPOTE

4 medium oranges, peeled, sectioned, and seeded
1½ cups pink grapefruit sections
1 cup sliced fresh strawberries
1 tablespoon chopped fresh mint
2 teaspoons sugar
Fresh mint sprigs

Combine orange, grapefruit, strawberries, chopped mint, and sugar in a large bowl; stir to mix. Cover and chill thoroughly.

To serve, spoon fruit mixture evenly into 8 stemmed dessert glasses. Garnish each with fresh mint sprigs. Serve chilled. Yield: 8 servings (43 calories per serving).

PRO 0.8 / FAT 0.2 / CARB 10.7 / FIB 1.3 / CHOL 0 / SOD 1 / POT 167

MINIATURE BLUEBERRY MUFFINS

1¾ cups all-purpose flour
2 teaspoons baking powder
½ teaspoon ground cinnamon
¼ teaspoon salt
1 cup fresh or frozen blueberries, thawed and patted dry
¾ cup skim milk
⅓ cup sugar
¼ cup vegetable oil
1 egg
1 teaspoon grated orange rind
1 teaspoon vanilla extract

Combine first 4 ingredients in a large bowl. Add blueberries, and toss gently to coat. Combine milk, sugar, oil, egg, orange rind, and vanilla; add to dry ingredients, stirring just until moistened.

Spoon batter into paper-lined miniature muffin pans, allowing 1 tablespoon batter per muffin. Bake at 400° for 20 minutes or until golden brown. Yield: 3 dozen (52 calories each).

Note: Leftover muffins may be sealed in an airtight container and frozen for later use. To thaw, let stand at room temperature several hours or microwave 2 muffins at MEDIUM (50% power) for 30 seconds or until thoroughly heated.

PRO 1.0 / FAT 1.7 / CARB 7.8 / FIB 0.4 / CHOL 8 / SOD 38 / POT 21

CAPPUCCINO

2⅔ cups skim milk
¾ cup plus 2 tablespoons instant nonfat dry milk powder
1 tablespoon plus 1 teaspoon sugar
1 tablespoon plus 1 teaspoon Dutch process cocoa
2⅔ cups hot espresso coffee
2 tablespoons plus 2 teaspoons brandy
Ground cinnamon

Combine first 4 ingredients in a medium saucepan. Place over medium heat; cook, stirring constantly, until sugar dissolves and mixture is thoroughly heated.

Combine half each of hot milk mixture, hot espresso, and brandy in container of an electric blender; process until mixture is well blended and frothy. Pour into individual mugs, and sprinkle each with cinnamon. Repeat procedure with remaining ingredients. Serve immediately. Yield: 6 cups (98 calories per 3/4-cup serving).

PRO 7.8 / FAT 0.5 / CARB 13.4 / FIB 0.0 / CHOL 4 / SOD 120 / POT 414

A sweet ending to a Gourmet Tailgate Picnic (menu begins on page 40), and it's only 29 calories a tablespoonful! Filled with pecans, raisins and grated orange rind, this Yogurt-Cheese Spread is delicious with any in-season fruit, and especially when served with White Wine Coolers.

Soup's On
And A Sandwich, Too

Soup and sandwich are just naturals for lunch at home or even if you're packing a lunch for work or school. This menu with the Fresh Lemon Cookies would be delightfully satisfying even as a light supper.

The Basil Tomato Soup is a delicious creamy blend of canned tomatoes, onion, skim milk, and basil. We tested the recipe with fresh basil, but if the fresh herb is not available you can substitute one-fourth as much dried whole basil for the same flavor. Basil is the perfect herb to use with any

Basil Tomato Soup
Tuna-Vegetable Pita Sandwiches
Fresh Lemon Cookies

Serves 4
Total calories per serving: 358

tomato recipe.

You'll enjoy Tuna-Vegetable Pita Sandwiches with this hot soup as well as by themselves for a light summer lunch. In this and other tuna recipes, we recom-

mend rinsing the tuna to reduce the sodium content. By rinsing tuna for one minute in a strainer under cold tap water and then letting it drain for one minute, the sodium content can be reduced by almost 80 percent.

The Fresh Lemon Cookies (allow 2 cookies per serving for correct calorie count) featured for dessert are a real treat to calorie counters. Since such a small amount of fat is used, calories for these flavorful cookies are only 42 each. Store leftover cookies in a cookie jar or tin.

BASIL TOMATO SOUP

1 (14-ounce) can whole Italian plum tomatoes, undrained
½ cup chopped onion
1 teaspoon dried whole basil or 1 tablespoon plus 1 teaspoon minced fresh basil
1 clove garlic, minced
¼ teaspoon salt
¼ teaspoon white pepper
1 tablespoon margarine
1 tablespoon plus 1½ teaspoons all-purpose flour
1½ cups skim milk
¼ cup chopped, peeled tomato
4 small leaves fresh basil

Combine first 6 ingredients in container of an electric blender, and process until smooth. Place tomato mixture in a medium saucepan; bring to a boil. Cover; reduce heat, and simmer 10 minutes.

Melt margarine in a small heavy saucepan over low heat; add flour, stirring until smooth. Cook 1 minute, stirring constantly. Gradually add milk; cook over low heat, stirring constantly, until thickened and bubbly.

Gradually stir white sauce into tomato mixture. Cook over low heat until thoroughly heated. Pour mixture into individual serving bowls. Garnish each with 1 tablespoon chopped tomato and 1 basil leaf. Serve hot. Yield: 4 servings (106 calories per serving).

PRO 5.2 / FAT 3.4 / CARB 14.9 / FIB 0.8 / CHOL 2 / SOD 416 / POT 500

 To stay slim, eat breakfast like a king, lunch like a prince, and dinner like a pauper, say nutritionists. Why? We burn up early calories during an active day, but most of the evening's calories aren't needed, so they turn to body fat.

Obese women, as reported by obesity experts, tend to skip breakfast, eat a light lunch, and consume 80% of daily calories in the evening. Such women, studies find, have a lower metabolic rate — they burn up calories slower — than people who eat three meals a day. But eating frequent small meals, plus aerobic exercise, keeps our metabolisms revved up.

Tuna salad sandwiches take on a new taste when packed into half rounds of pita bread. Serve with hot Basil Tomato Soup and Fresh Lemon Cookies.

TUNA-VEGETABLE PITA SANDWICHES

1 (6½-ounce) can chunk white tuna in water
1 medium cucumber, peeled and chopped
3 tablespoons chopped dill pickle
2 tablespoons minced onion
2 tablespoons chopped pimiento
1 hard-cooked egg, coarsely chopped
3 tablespoons plain low-fat yogurt
3 tablespoons reduced-calorie mayonnaise
4 (6-inch) whole wheat pita bread rounds, halved
4 leaves curly leaf lettuce

Place tuna in a colander; rinse under cold tap water 1 minute. Set colander aside to let tuna drain 1 minute. Combine tuna and next 5 ingredients in a medium bowl; toss gently. Combine yogurt and mayonnaise in a small bowl. Add to tuna mixture, and toss gently. Chill 1 hour or until serving time.

Spoon equal amounts of tuna mixture into each pita round half; add lettuce leaves, and serve immediately. Yield: 4 servings (168 calories per serving).

PRO 13.3 / FAT 4.1 / CARB 18.2 / FIB 3.7 / CHOL 96 / SOD 349 / POT 388

FRESH LEMON COOKIES

1 cup all-purpose flour
2 teaspoons baking powder
⅛ teaspoon salt
2 tablespoons margarine, softened
½ cup sugar
1 egg
1 tablespoon grated lemon rind
2 tablespoons lemon juice
Vegetable cooking spray

Combine flour, baking powder, and salt in a small bowl; set aside. Cream margarine in a medium bowl until light and fluffy. Gradually add sugar, beating well. Add egg, lemon rind, and lemon juice; beat well. Add flour mixture, and stir until blended.

Drop dough by heaping teaspoonfuls onto cookie sheets lightly coated with cooking spray. Bake at 350° for 10 minutes or until edges are lightly browned. Cool slightly on cookie sheets; remove to wire racks, and cool completely. Yield: 28 cookies (42 calories each).

PRO 0.7 / FAT 1.0 / CARB 7.5 / FIB 0.2 / CHOL 10 / SOD 45 / POT 9

Packed For Two

Ham-Vegetable Stacks
Tangy Cottage Cheese Dip
with
Assorted Fresh Vegetables
Whole Wheat Sugar Cookies
Fresh Pears
Fruited Iced Tea

Serves 2
Total calories per serving: 506

Whether it's a cozy picnic for two or just lunch at the office, this menu will be a welcome midday treat. To reduce calories in the sandwich, low-fat yogurt replaces mayonnaise.

Instead of using sour cream in the dip, we cut the fat content by substituting pureed low-fat cottage cheese. We calculated total calories with one-half carrot, but feel free to enjoy a variety of fresh raw vegetables as dippers.

Whole Wheat Sugar Cookies (1 cookie per serving) make a great picnic dessert. We've also added a pear (1 per serving) for extra fiber and complex carbohydrates.

A sure cure for the midday slump is this generous luncheon spread.

HAM-VEGETABLE STACKS

2 tablespoons plain low-fat yogurt
1 tablespoon minced sweet pickle
¾ teaspoon Dijon mustard
1 (2½-ounce) loaf French bread
2 (4/5-ounce) slices lean ham
2 ounces sliced Muenster cheese
1 leaf curly leaf lettuce
¼ medium cucumber, thinly sliced
3 slices tomato
½ cup alfalfa sprouts

Combine yogurt, pickle, and mustard. Slice bread in half lengthwise. Spread both cut sides of bread with yogurt mixture.

Layer remaining ingredients on bottom half of loaf in order given; cover with top half of loaf. Cut sandwich in half to serve. Yield: 2 servings (261 calories per serving).

Note: For picnic, add lettuce, cucumber, tomato, and alfalfa sprouts just before serving.

PRO 17.2 / FAT 11.5 / CARB 24.4 / FIB 3.1 / CHOL 41 / SOD 745 / POT 424

TANGY COTTAGE CHEESE DIP

1 (12-ounce) carton low-fat cottage cheese
1 tablespoon low-fat buttermilk
1 tablespoon minced onion
½ teaspoon dried whole dillweed
¼ teaspoon salt
⅛ teaspoon garlic powder
2 drops Worcestershire sauce

Combine all ingredients in container of an electric blender; process until smooth. Chill. Spoon dip into a serving bowl, and serve with assorted fresh vegetables. Yield: 1¾ cups. Serving size: 1 tablespoon (11 calories per serving).

PRO 1.7 / FAT 0.2 / CARB 0.5 / FIB 0.0 / CHOL 1 / SOD 71 / POT 14

WHOLE WHEAT SUGAR COOKIES

1 cup all-purpose flour
¾ cup whole wheat flour
1 teaspoon baking powder
⅓ cup margarine
⅓ cup sugar
1 egg
1 teaspoon vanilla extract
Vegetable cooking spray

Combine first 3 ingredients; set aside.
Cream margarine in a medium bowl; gradually add sugar, beating until light and fluffy. Add egg, beating well. Stir in vanilla. Add flour mixture, stirring until blended. Cover and chill dough thoroughly.

Turn dough out onto a lightly floured surface, and roll to ¼-inch thickness; cut with a 2-inch cookie cutter. Place on cookie sheets lightly coated with cooking spray. Bake at 375° for 8 minutes or until golden brown. Remove from cookie sheets, and cool completely on wire racks. Yield: 28 cookies (61 calories each).

PRO 1.2 / FAT 2.5 / CARB 8.5 / FIB 0.4 / CHOL 10 / SOD 40 / POT 20

FRUITED ICED TEA

1½ cups brewed orange pekoe tea
¼ cup plus 2 tablespoons unsweetened orange juice
2 tablespoons lemon juice
2 teaspoons sugar
Ice cubes
2 thin slices orange

Combine first 4 ingredients in a small pitcher; stir well. Chill thoroughly. Pour tea into 2 ice-filled 12-ounce glasses; garnish each with an orange slice. Yield: 2 cups (43 calories per 1-cup serving).

PRO 0.4 / FAT 0.0 / CARB 11.2 / FIB 0.0 / CHOL 0 / SOD 1 / POT 150

 More and more Americans are skipping lunch. A recent survey finds that 15 million of us skip it nine days out of ten. That's 63% more skippers than a decade ago.

But if you skip, you'll likely dip — in concentration later on in the day. True, eating a heavy meal in the middle of the day will make you groggy in the afternoon, but eating *nothing* will make you tired a few hours later as your body's energy supplies dwindle.

Researchers at the Medical Research Council in England have found that the best compromise is to eat a light, low-calorie lunch. It's not so heavy that you'll slump soon after eating, but it does have the nutrition that you'll need to stay alert through the afternoon.

For peak concentration, include lean protein, such as turkey in a sandwich or a low-fat yogurt. Studies show that eating carbohydrates without any protein can make you drowsy. This is good to remember when packing lunches for school-age youngsters and for hard-working adults.

Après-Swim Lunch

When the weather is sunny and it's more fun to be outside romping in the pool, lake or even the sprinkler, treat yourself and your family or friends to this easy make-ahead lunch.

These veal burgers are a delicious change of pace from the usual hamburger. Make the patties ahead of time and keep them refrigerated until your guests are present and the grill is hot. The patties will be grilled to perfection in just 14 minutes or so and are especially good with the creamy Horseradish Sauce.

The New Potato Salad and Ba-

**Grilled Veal Burgers
New Potato Salad with
Green Goddess Dressing
Banana-Yogurt Freeze**

Serves 6
Total calories per serving: 606

nana-Yogurt Freeze should also be started early in the morning or the day before. We recommend cooking the potatoes first, then slicing them. That way you'll preserve more water-soluble vitamins. The Green Goddess

Dressing is much lower in fat and calories than the traditional recipe, thanks to the use of low-fat yogurt and reduced-calorie mayonnaise.

Banana-Yogurt Freeze is a perfect light dessert for summer. It's easy to prepare, low in fat, and provides less than half the calories of ice cream.

To further reduce calories, offer sparkling mineral water to drink. There are several varieties available — some with a hint of lemon, lime, or orange. The orange-flavor would complement this menu.

GRILLED VEAL BURGERS

1½ pounds ground veal
¾ cup soft whole wheat breadcrumbs
1 egg, beaten
¼ cup skim milk
2 tablespoons finely chopped green onion
¼ teaspoon grated lemon rind
⅛ teaspoon salt
⅛ teaspoon dried whole marjoram, crushed
⅛ teaspoon freshly ground pepper
Horseradish Sauce
6 whole wheat hamburger buns, split
6 lettuce leaves

Combine first 9 ingredients in a large bowl; mix well. Shape mixture into 6 (¾-inch-thick) patties. Grill 5 to 6 inches over medium-hot coals for 7 minutes on each side or until desired degree of doneness.

Spread 1½ teaspoons Horseradish Sauce on cut side of each bun half. Place one lettuce leaf on bottom of each bun. Top each with a veal pattie. Cover with tops of buns. Yield: 6 servings (350 calories per serving).

Horseradish Sauce:

¼ cup plain low-fat yogurt
2 tablespoons reduced-calorie mayonnaise
1½ teaspoons prepared horseradish
⅛ teaspoon dry mustard

Combine all ingredients in a small bowl, mixing well; chill for 1 hour. Yield: ¼ cup plus 2 tablespoons.

PRO 24.9 / FAT 13.3 / CARB 32.7 / FIB 2.4 / CHOL 126 / SOD 268 / POT 509

 Calcium, found in low-fat yogurt and other dairy foods, is currently making news as an important element in preventing osteoporosis and lowering blood pressure. Because of this, calcium is being added to foods such as flours, cereals, fruit juices, and diet sodas. Unlike these non-dairy foods, however, fortified dairy products like yogurt have vitamin D, which helps our bodies absorb calcium. To make dairy foods an even better source of calcium, some manufacturers are adding extra calcium to milk, cottage cheese, and yogurt.

NEW POTATO SALAD WITH GREEN GODDESS DRESSING

6 medium-size red new potatoes
¼ cup reduced-calorie mayonnaise
3 tablespoons plain low-fat yogurt
1 tablespoon plus 1 teaspoon minced fresh parsley
1 tablespoon lemon juice
2 teaspoons minced chives
2 teaspoons vinegar
½ teaspoon dried whole tarragon
Dash of garlic powder
6 cherry tomatoes

Place potatoes in a medium saucepan; cover with water, and bring to a boil. Cover; reduce heat, and cook 20 minutes or until tender. Drain and slice potatoes into a serving bowl. Chill.

Combine next 8 ingredients in a small bowl. Spoon dressing over potatoes. Before serving, arrange cherry tomatoes on top of salad. Yield: 6 servings (147 calories per serving).

PRO 4.0 / FAT 3.0 / CARB 27.3 / FIB 1.3 / CHOL 4 / SOD 91 / POT 833

BANANA-YOGURT FREEZE

2 tablespoons sugar
2 tablespoons hot water
2 cups mashed, very ripe bananas
1 teaspoon lemon juice
1 (8-ounce) carton plain low-fat yogurt
2 egg whites, beaten

Combine sugar and water in a medium bowl, stirring until sugar dissolves. Add bananas, lemon juice, and yogurt; mix well. Pour mixture into a 9-inch square baking pan, and freeze until almost firm.

Spoon mixture into a large bowl, and add beaten egg whites. Beat at high speed of an electric mixer 10 minutes or until mixture is smooth and fluffy.

Return to pan, and freeze until firm. To serve, let stand at room temperature 10 minutes; spoon into individual serving bowls. Yield: 6 cups (109 calories per 1-cup serving).

PRO 3.8 / FAT 0.9 / CARB 23.3 / FIB 1.0 / CHOL 2 / SOD 44 / POT 380

Towel off and park the float while you enjoy Grilled Veal Burgers and New Potato Salad.

Picnic In The Park

Even if you're not a vegetarian, this meatless menu is one you'll enjoy eating just because it tastes so good.

Most of the protein is provided by beans and pasta in Garbanzo-Pasta Salad. Combining the vegetable proteins of these two foods (legumes and grain) creates a quality protein equal to the protein in an animal product.

The quality of protein is improved still further when an animal product such as milk, cheese, yogurt, or eggs is eaten at the same meal.

Garbanzo-Pasta Salad
Marinated Cucumbers
Herbed Whole Wheat Mini-Loaves
Spicy Wheat Cookies

Serves 4
Total calories per serving: 510

The combination of wheat flour and skim milk provides additional protein in Herbed Whole Wheat Mini-Loaves. You'll use only one mini-loaf in this four-serving menu; freeze the remaining loaves for later use.

Make Marinated Cucumbers a day ahead of your picnic so that flavor will be at its peak. They provide only 8 milligrams sodium per serving of one-half cucumber — a delightful alternative to regular dill pickles which scale in at around 1000 milligrams of sodium for one-half pickle.

For dessert, we suggest a spicy cookie made with whole wheat flour and wheat germ. (Allow 2 cookies per serving for correct calorie count.) Store leftovers for healthy snacking.

GARBANZO-PASTA SALAD

4 ounces spinach fusilli or corkscrew pasta
1 (15-ounce) can garbanzo beans, drained
½ cup chopped celery
⅓ cup chopped sweet red pepper
⅓ cup shredded carrot
2 tablespoons chopped fresh chives
3 tablespoons white wine vinegar
2 tablespoons reduced-calorie mayonnaise
1 tablespoon olive or vegetable oil
2 teaspoons Dijon mustard
¼ teaspoon salt
¼ teaspoon pepper
4 medium-size leaves Romaine lettuce (optional)
1 medium tomato, cut into wedges

Cook pasta according to package directions, omitting salt. Drain and cool.

Rinse garbanzo beans in a colander under cold running water 1 minute; set colander aside to let beans drain 1 minute.

Combine pasta, beans, celery, red pepper, carrot, and chives in a large bowl; toss lightly to mix well.

Combine vinegar, mayonnaise, oil, mustard, salt, and pepper in a small bowl; beat with a wire whisk until well blended. Pour over salad, and toss lightly to coat well. Cover and chill thoroughly.

Serve chilled salad on individual lettuce-lined plates, if desired. Arrange tomato wedges around each serving. Yield: 4 servings (200 calories per serving).

PRO 6.6 / FAT 8.5 / CARB 24.3 / FIB 5.3 / CHOL 41 / SOD 459 / POT 450

MARINATED CUCUMBERS

2 medium cucumbers
2 tablespoons chopped onion
2 tablespoons chopped celery
¼ cup vinegar
¼ cup lemon juice
2 tablespoons sugar
2 teaspoons grated, peeled gingerroot

Cut cucumbers in half; cut each half lengthwise into fourths. Combine cucumber, onion, and celery in a 10- x 6- x 2-inch baking dish. Combine vinegar, lemon juice, sugar, and gingerroot in a small bowl, stirring well. Pour marinade over vegetables in baking dish, and toss to coat. Cover and refrigerate 8 hours or overnight. Drain, and serve chilled. Yield: 4 servings (53 calories per serving).

PRO 1.1 / FAT 0.2 / CARB 13.3 / FIB 0.9 / CHOL 0 / SOD 8 / POT 267

An easy-to-pack lunch that will satisfy picnic appetites.

and knead 10 minutes or until smooth and elastic. Place in a large bowl coated with cooking spray, turning to grease top. Cover and let rise in a warm place (85°), free from drafts, 1½ hours or until doubled in bulk.

Punch dough down, and turn out onto a lightly floured surface; cover with inverted bowl, and let rest 15 minutes. Divide dough into thirds; shape each portion into a loaf. Place each loaf in a 5- x 3- x 2-inch loafpan coated with cooking spray. Let rise in a warm place, free from drafts, 30 minutes or until doubled in bulk.

Bake at 400° for 20 minutes or until loaves sound hollow when tapped. Remove loaves from pans, and cool on wire racks. Cut each loaf into 1¼-inch slices. Yield: 3 loaves (169 calories per slice).

PRO 5.5 / FAT 2.5 / CARB 31.9 / FIB 2.0 / CHOL 0 / SOD 232 / POT 176

HERBED WHOLE WHEAT MINI-LOAVES

2 cups whole wheat flour, divided
1½ cups all-purpose flour, divided
1 tablespoon sugar
1 package dry yeast
1 teaspoon salt
½ teaspoon dried whole basil
½ teaspoon dried whole oregano
⅛ teaspoon dried whole thyme
1 cup plus 2 tablespoons skim milk
2 tablespoons margarine
2 tablespoons molasses
Vegetable cooking spray

Combine 1 cup whole wheat flour, ½ cup all-purpose flour, sugar, yeast, salt, basil, oregano, and thyme in a large bowl; stir until well blended. Set aside.

Combine milk, margarine, and molasses in a small saucepan; cook over low heat until mixture is very warm (120° to 130°).

Gradually add milk mixture to flour mixture, beating at low speed of an electric mixer until blended. Increase speed to medium, and beat 2 minutes. Stir in enough remaining flour to make a stiff dough.

Turn dough out onto a lighty floured surface,

SPICY WHEAT COOKIES

¼ cup vegetable oil
¼ cup firmly packed brown sugar
1 egg white
2 tablespoons plus 2 teaspoons unsweetened
   orange juice
1 cup whole wheat flour
¼ cup unsweetened wheat germ
½ teaspoon baking soda
½ teaspoon ground cinnamon
¼ teaspoon ground nutmeg
⅛ teaspoon salt
⅛ teaspoon ground cloves
¼ cup raisins

Combine oil and sugar in a medium bowl. Add egg white and orange juice, stirring well. Combine flour, wheat germ, soda, cinnamon, nutmeg, salt, and cloves in a small bowl. Add flour mixture to oil mixture, stirring until blended. Stir in raisins.

Drop dough by rounded teaspoonfuls onto ungreased cookie sheets, 2 inches apart. Bake at 350° for 10 minutes or until lightly browned. Remove from cookie sheets, and cool on wire racks. Yield: 2½ dozen (44 calories each).

PRO 1.0 / FAT 2.0 / CARB 6.1 / FIB 0.5 / CHOL 0 / SOD 18 / POT 41

Ladies' Spring Luncheon

Shrimp-Asparagus Salad
Italian Marinated Tomatoes
Rye Breadsticks
Amaretto Chocolate
Mousse
White Wine

Serves 8
Total calories per serving: 474

The appearance of fresh asparagus and English peas is a sure sign that spring has arrived. Celebrate with a luncheon that features these two vegetables in an eye-catching shrimp salad.

Serve the salad with Italian Marinated Tomatoes and Rye Breadsticks (1 breadstick per serving). Since the recipe makes 40 breadsticks, store the remaining breadsticks in an airtight container at room temperature or in the freezer. They make a tasty addition to any meal.

Amaretto Chocolate Mousse will be a hit among your guests. They'll love the taste, especially knowing that each serving contains only 127 calories.

Toast the freshness of spring with a glass of wine for each guest (3½ ounces per serving).

SHRIMP-ASPARAGUS SALAD

1½ quarts water
2 pounds medium-size fresh unpeeled shrimp
1½ pounds fresh asparagus
1 cup shelled fresh English peas
1 pound Boston lettuce, separated into leaves
6 medium carrots, scraped and thinly sliced
1 cup julienned yellow pepper
2 cups thinly sliced cucumber
¼ cup plus 2 tablespoons catsup
¼ cup plus 2 tablespoons reduced-calorie mayonnaise
¼ cup minced dill pickle
¼ cup skim milk

Bring water to a boil in a large saucepan; add shrimp, and reduce heat. Cook 3 minutes. Drain and rinse with cold water. Peel and devein shrimp. Set shrimp aside in refrigerator.

Snap off tough ends of asparagus. Remove scales from stalks, if desired, using a knife or vegetable peeler. Cook asparagus, covered, in a small amount of boiling water 6 to 8 minutes or until crisp-tender; drain and chill. Cook peas, covered, in boiling water to cover 6 to 8 minutes or until crisp-tender; drain and chill.

Place lettuce leaves on 8 individual plates; arrange shrimp, asparagus, peas, carrots, yellow pepper, and cucumber on lettuce.

Combine catsup, mayonnaise, pickle, and milk in a small bowl, mixing well. Spoon 2 tablespoons dressing over each salad to serve. Yield: 8 servings (196 calories per serving).

PRO 21.0 / FAT 4.3 / CARB 19.8 / FIB 3.4 / CHOL 131 / SOD 470 / POT 899

Chilled and garnished with fresh strawberries, Amaretto Chocolate Mousse is a light dessert your guests will love — especially those who are watching their calories.

ITALIAN MARINATED TOMATOES

4 medium-size ripe tomatoes, sliced
¼ cup red wine vinegar
3 tablespoons water
2 tablespoons vegetable oil
1 tablespoon chopped fresh parsley
1 teaspoon dried Italian seasoning
1 teaspoon grated onion
1 clove garlic, minced
¼ teaspoon freshly ground black pepper

Arrange tomato slices in a large shallow container. Combine remaining ingredients in a small bowl, stirring well. Pour marinade over tomatoes; cover and chill 8 hours or overnight. Yield: 8 servings (47 calories per serving).

PRO 0.7 / FAT 3.6 / CARB 3.5 / FIB 0.6 / CHOL 0 / SOD 7 / POT 162

RYE BREADSTICKS

1½ cups rye flour
1½ cups all-purpose flour
1 package dry yeast
¾ teaspoon salt
1 cup very warm water (120° to 130°)
1 tablespoon vegetable oil
1 tablespoon molasses
1½ teaspoons caraway seeds
Vegetable cooking spray

Combine flour in a medium bowl. Combine 1½ cups flour mixture, yeast, and salt in a large bowl; set remaining flour aside. Add water, oil, molasses, and caraway seeds to flour mixture; beat at medium speed of an electric mixer 2 to 3 minutes or until smooth. Stir in enough remaining flour to make a stiff dough. Turn out

onto a lightly floured surface; knead 6 to 8 minutes or until smooth and elastic.

Divide dough into fourths; cut each fourth into 10 equal pieces. Shape each piece into an 8-inch rope. (Cover remaining dough while working to prevent drying.)

Place ropes 2 inches apart on baking sheets coated with cooking spray. Cover; let rise in a warm place (85°), free from drafts, 50 minutes. (Dough will not double in bulk.) Bake at 400° for 10 minutes or until lightly browned. Yield: 40 breadsticks (36 calories each).

PRO 0.9 / FAT 0.4 / CARB 6.9 / FIB 0.3 / CHOL 0 / SOD 44 / POT 20

AMARETTO CHOCOLATE MOUSSE

1 envelope unflavored gelatin
1½ cups skim milk, divided
2 egg yolks
¼ cup sugar
⅓ cup Dutch process cocoa
2 tablespoons Amaretto or other almond-flavored liqueur
4 egg whites
⅓ cup sugar
Strawberry halves (optional)

Combine gelatin and ½ cup milk in a medium saucepan, stirring well; let stand 1 minute. Cook over medium heat, stirring constantly, 1 minute or until gelatin dissolves.

Combine remaining 1 cup milk and egg yolks, beating well. Add yolk mixture, ¼ cup sugar, and cocoa to saucepan; stir well. Cook over medium heat, stirring constantly, 8 minutes or until smooth and thickened. Remove from heat; stir in Amaretto, and chill 20 minutes.

Beat egg whites (at room temperature) in a medium bowl until foamy. Gradually add ⅓ cup sugar, 1 tablespoon at a time, beating until stiff peaks form. Gradually add chilled chocolate mixture to beaten egg whites, folding gently.

Spoon mixture into a 1½-quart serving dish or 8 individual dessert dishes. Chill at least 2 hours. Garnish with strawberry halves, if desired. Yield: 8 servings (127 calories per serving).

PRO 5.8 / FAT 2.0 / CARB 19.8 / FIB 0.2 / CHOL 69 / SOD 53 / POT 172

Gourmet Tailgate Party

At the first sign of cooler weather, people across the country gather at football stadiums to watch their favorite teams play ball. Part of the fun of Saturday games is packing a hearty meal to eat beforehand. Instead of hotdogs and chips, try this gourmet approach to tailgating.

Light Chicken Terrine is the star of the menu, with Pasta-Pine Nut Salad and Parmesan Oatmeal Crackers as accompaniments. (Allow 4 crackers per serving for correct calorie count.)

Light Chicken Terrine
Pasta-Pine Nut Salad
Parmesan Oatmeal
Crackers
Fresh Fruit with
Yogurt-Cheese Spread
White Wine Coolers

Serves 10
Total calories per serving: 546

Make the terrine a day ahead so that it can chill thoroughly overnight. It would be best to transport the terrine to the meal site in a loafpan, and then invert it on a platter to serve.

Fresh fruit with a chunky Yogurt-Cheese Spread is the ideal dessert. (Calories are calculated with 1 apple per serving, but be sure to have a variety of fruit available for your guests.)

Sparkling orange-flavored mineral water is mixed with chilled white wine for our gourmet beverage. By diluting the wine with mineral water, calories and alcohol are cut almost in half.

LIGHT CHICKEN TERRINE

1 medium-size sweet red pepper, seeded and chopped
1 medium-size green pepper, seeded and chopped
¾ cup diced carrot
½ cup diced onion
1¼ pounds boneless chicken breasts, skinned
1 teaspoon chicken-flavored bouillon granules
½ teaspoon white pepper
½ teaspoon curry powder
½ teaspoon hot sauce
1 (13-ounce) can evaporated skim milk, divided
¼ cup dry white wine
1 egg
1 egg white
1 medium bunch Romaine lettuce
Vegetable cooking spray
Carrot curls (optional)

Steam peppers, diced carrot, and onion in a vegetable steamer over boiling water 10 minutes. Drain well on paper towels. Set aside.

Cut chicken into 1-inch pieces; set aside. Position knife blade in processor bowl; add bouillon granules, pepper, curry powder, hot sauce, and half of chicken. Process 1½ minutes or until smooth, scraping bowl once. Remove food pusher. Slowly pour ¾ cup evaporated milk, wine, and egg through food chute with the processor running, blending just until smooth. Spoon mixture into a large bowl. Repeat procedure with remaining chicken, evaporated milk, and egg white. Stir chicken mixtures together.

Coat bottom and sides of an 8½- x 4½- x 3-inch loafpan with cooking spray. Line bottom and sides of loafpan with Romaine leaves, dull side up. Allow leaves to hang over sides of pan. Spread half of chicken mixture in bottom and two-thirds up sides of pan. Spoon vegetables over center well of chicken mixture. Spread remaining chicken mixture over vegetables.

Cover pan tightly with aluminum foil; punch a hole in foil to allow steam to escape. Place loafpan in a 13- x 9- x 2-inch baking pan. Fill baking pan with hot water to a depth of 1½ inches. Bake at 350° for 1 hour and 15 minutes or until terrine is firm and center springs back after touching. Remove foil from loafpan, and allow terrine to cool. When warm to touch, pour off excess liquid. Cool completely. Unmold terrine onto a serving platter; cover with heavy-duty plastic wrap, and refrigerate overnight.

Let stand at room temperature 30 minutes. Slice with an electric knife. Garnish with carrot curls, if desired. Yield: 10 servings (122 calories per serving).

PRO 16.9 / FAT 2.3 / CARB 6.9 / FIB 0.5 / CHOL 64 / SOD 126 / POT 345

Toast your team with this winning gourmet spread of Light Chicken Terrine, Pasta-Pine Nut Salad, Parmesan Oatmeal Crackers and White Wine Coolers.

PASTA-PINE NUT SALAD

4 ounces fusilli
2 cups broccoli flowerets
1 medium-size green pepper, seeded and
   cut into julienne strips
¼ cup chopped green onion
3 ounces mozzarella cheese, cut into
   2- x ¼-inch strips
⅓ cup reduced-calorie Italian salad
   dressing
¼ cup white wine vinegar
2 tablespoons grated Parmesan cheese
¾ teaspoon dried whole basil or 1 tablespoon
   minced fresh basil
1 clove garlic, minced
8 leaves curly leaf lettuce
2 tablespoons pine nuts, toasted

Cook pasta according to package directions, omitting salt. Drain and let cool.

Cook broccoli in a vegetable steamer over boiling water 7 minutes or until crisp tender. Drain and let cool.

Combine pasta, broccoli, green pepper, green onion, and mozzarella in a large bowl. Combine salad dressing, vinegar, Parmesan, basil, and garlic in a small bowl, stirring well. Pour over pasta mixture; toss gently. Cover and chill 8 hours or overnight.

To serve, spoon mixture onto a lettuce-lined platter or bowl with a slotted spoon. Sprinkle with pine nuts. Yield: 10 servings (95 calories per serving).

PRO 5.1 / FAT 4.9 / CARB 9.0 / FIB 1.1 / CHOL 29 / SOD 136 / POT 184

PARMESAN OATMEAL CRACKERS

1½ cups quick-cooking oats, uncooked
1 cup all-purpose flour
¼ cup wheat germ
1 tablespoon plus 1½ teaspoons sugar
¾ teaspoon baking powder
¼ teaspoon salt
¼ cup margarine
¼ cup plus 3 tablespoons water
Vegetable cooking spray
2 tablespoons grated Parmesan cheese

Combine first 6 ingredients in a large bowl; mix well. Cut in margarine with a pastry blender until mixture resembles fine crumbs. Sprinkle with water, stirring just until dry ingredients are moistened.

Place mixture on a baking sheet coated with cooking spray; roll to ⅛-inch thickness. Cut into 2½- x 1-inch rectangles. Prick tops with a fork. Sprinkle with Parmesan cheese. Bake at 350° for 22 minutes or until crisp and browned.

Separate crackers; remove from baking sheet, and cool on wire racks. Store in a tightly covered container. Yield: 5 dozen (36 calories each).

PRO 1.1 / FAT 1.2 / CARB 5.3 / FIB 0.7 / CHOL 0 / SOD 26 / POT 22

 When it comes to alcohol, less is more. As a nation, we're drinking less total alcohol; in particular, we're swapping hard liquor for beer and wine. Even our beers and wines are lightening up: Low- and no-alcohol varieties are a growing segment of the market. Light white wines, such as the popular blush wine, White Zinfandel, are also naturally lower in alcohol than many other varieties.

What is a healthy limit of alcoholic drinks for those who drink? About two drinks a day, according to the newest guidelines from the American Heart Association. Over two drinks a day and blood pressure often rises.

Don't buy special spirits to drink light. Just make a beverage like our White Wine Cooler. Wine mixed with equal amounts of mineral water has half the alcohol and calories of straight wine. Add an extra zip to that cooler by using sparkling mineral water flavored with orange, lime, or lemon.

YOGURT-CHEESE SPREAD

1 (16-ounce) carton plain low-fat yogurt
2 tablespoons golden raisins, chopped
1 tablespoon chopped pecans, toasted
2 teaspoons sugar
1 teaspoon grated orange rind
Vegetable cooking spray

Line a colander or sieve with a double layer of cheesecloth that has been rinsed out and squeezed dry; allow cheesecloth to overlap at the sides. Stir yogurt until smooth; pour into sieve, and fold edges of cheesecloth over to cover yogurt. Place colander in a large pan; refrigerate 12 to 24 hours. Remove yogurt from colander, and set aside. Discard liquid.

Combine strained yogurt, raisins, pecans, sugar, and orange rind in a small bowl. Refrigerate until ready to serve. To serve, spoon into a serving bowl or desired container. Serve with assorted fresh fruit. Yield: 1 cup. Serving size: 1 tablespoon (29 calories per serving).

PRO 1.7 / FAT 0.8 / CARB 3.9 / FIB 0.0 / CHOL 2 / SOD 21 / POT 83

WHITE WINE COOLERS

5 cups Chablis or other dry white wine, chilled
6 (6½-ounce) bottles sparkling mineral water with orange, chilled
Orange rind strips

Combine wine and mineral water in a large pitcher. Pour into individual tall glasses; serve over ice, if desired. Garnish with strips of orange rind, and serve immediately. Yield: 10 cups (78 calories per 1-cup serving).

PRO 0.1 / FAT 0.0 / CARB 0.7 / FIB 0.0 / CHOL 0 / SOD 5 / POT 72

Relax with friends over a summer meal that's easy to put together. Refresh first with Apple-Mint Tea. Then serve chilled Carrot-Cabbage Coleslaw with Mesquite Grilled Pompano and Grilled Summer Vegetables, hot from the coals. (Dining Alfresco menu begins on page 54).

Easy Family Supper

Swiss Burger Steaks
Two-Squash Sauté
Carrot-Fruit Salad
Whole Wheat Corn Muffins
Apple Crumb Dessert with
Spiced Ice Milk

Serves 4
Total calories per serving: 641

Whole Wheat Corn Muffins, Carrot-Fruit Salad and Two-Squash Sauté.

Make this easy supper even easier by preparing the patties for Swiss Burger Steaks ahead of time. Refrigerate them until about 20 minutes before serving, and then cook in a skillet coated with vegetable cooking spray. Be sure to drain the cooked patties on paper towels to eliminate any excess fat.

Save time in preparing the fiber-rich Carrot-Fruit Salad by using the food processor to shred the carrots and slice the celery.

The muffin recipe makes just enough for 4 servings. While they're baking, you can quickly sauté-steam the zucchini and yellow squash together.

Just before you sit down to eat, pop the Apple Crumb Dessert into a 375° oven to bake for 35 minutes. You may want to make more than one recipe of the Spiced Ice Milk — it would be a refreshing dessert by itself on another night.

SWISS BURGER STEAKS

¾ pound ground chuck
½ cup soft whole wheat breadcrumbs
1 egg, lightly beaten
1 clove garlic, crushed
¼ teaspoon dry mustard
¼ teaspoon pepper
4 (½-ounce) slices low-fat Swiss cheese
Vegetable cooking spray
1 tablespoon chopped fresh parsley

Combine first 6 ingredients, mixing well. Divide into 8 thin patties. Place a slice of Swiss cheese on each of 4 patties; top with remaining patties, and seal edges.

Coat a skillet with cooking spray; place over medium heat until hot. Cook patties in skillet 8 minutes on each side or until desired degree of doneness. Drain well on paper towels. Place on a warm serving platter, and garnish with chopped parsley. Yield: 4 servings (217 calories per serving).

Note: Patties may be made ahead of time. Cover and refrigerate until time to cook.

PRO 23.9 / FAT 10.0 / CARB 7.0 / FIB 0.7 / CHOL 142 / SOD 278 / POT 355

TWO-SQUASH SAUTÉ

Vegetable cooking spray
1 teaspoon margarine
2½ cups julienned zucchini squash
2 cups julienned yellow squash
¼ teaspoon chicken-flavored bouillon granules
¼ teaspoon dried whole basil
⅛ teaspoon freshly ground black pepper

Coat a large skillet with cooking spray; add margarine, and place over medium heat until margarine melts. Add remaining ingredients; cover and cook 5 minutes or until crisp-tender, stirring occasionally. Yield: 4 servings (33 calories per serving).

PRO 1.7 / FAT 1.2 / CARB 5.3 / FIB 1.1 / CHOL 0 / SOD 39 / POT 331

CARROT-FRUIT SALAD

2 medium oranges, peeled, sectioned, and seeded
2 medium carrots, grated
1 medium-size Red Delicious apple, chopped
½ stalk celery, thinly sliced
¼ cup seedless raisins
2 tablespoons reduced-calorie mayonnaise
½ teaspoon lemon juice
Leaf lettuce

Combine first 5 ingredients in a medium bowl; toss lightly. Add mayonnaise and lemon juice, stirring until well blended. Chill mixture until serving time.

To serve, spoon mixture onto a lettuce-lined serving platter. Yield: 4 servings (112 calories per serving).

PRO 1.3 / FAT 2.4 / CARB 23.8 / FIB 3.3 / CHOL 2 / SOD 76 / POT 363

WHOLE WHEAT CORN MUFFINS

¼ cup whole wheat flour
¼ cup white cornmeal
2 teaspoons sugar
1 teaspoon baking powder
⅛ teaspoon salt
¼ cup skim milk
1 egg white
1 tablespoon vegetable oil
Vegetable cooking spray

Combine flour, cornmeal, sugar, baking powder, and salt; mix well. Add milk, egg white, and oil; stir just until blended.

Spoon batter into muffin pans coated with cooking spray, filling two-thirds full. Bake at 425° for 20 minutes or until lightly browned. Yield: 4 muffins (97 calories each).

PRO 3.1 / FAT 3.9 / CARB 12.9 / FIB 1.7 / CHOL 0 / SOD 169 / POT 87

APPLE CRUMB DESSERT WITH SPICED ICE MILK

1 tablespoon all-purpose flour
1 tablespoon sugar
¾ teaspoon grated lemon rind
4 medium-size cooking apples, cored and thinly sliced
2 tablespoons lemon juice
2 tablespoons all-purpose flour
2 tablespoons sugar
¼ teaspoon ground cinnamon
⅛ teaspoon ground ginger
Dash of ground mace
1 tablespoon margarine
Spiced Ice Milk

Combine 1 tablespoon flour, 1 tablespoon sugar, and lemon rind in a small bowl. Sprinkle apple slices with lemon juice; add to flour mixture, tossing gently. Spoon apple mixture into a 1-quart casserole.

Combine 2 tablespoons flour, 2 tablespoons sugar, cinnamon, ginger, and mace in a medium bowl. Cut in margarine with a pastry blender until mixture resembles coarse meal; sprinkle evenly over apple mixture in casserole. Bake at 375° for 35 minutes. Serve warm with Spiced Ice Milk. Yield: 4 servings (182 calories per serving).

Spiced Ice Milk:

1 cup vanilla ice milk, softened
¼ teaspoon apple pie spice

Combine softened ice milk and apple pie spice, stirring until smooth. Spoon mixture into a freezer container; cover and freeze until firm. Yield: 1 cup.

PRO 2.2 / FAT 4.9 / CARB 34.5 / FIB 2.3 / CHOL 5 / SOD 63 / POT 179

A Neighborly Supper

Lime Turkey Cutlets
Fettuccine with
Fresh Tomato Sauce
Italian Cauliflower Salad
Commercial Italian Bread
Peach Sauce Flambé

Serves 8
Total calories per serving: 563

Be prepared for last minute guests with this quick-to-fix supper menu.

Drop in guests from the neighborhood? Don't despair! The solution is to keep a supply of turkey breast cutlets in the freezer for just such an occasion. When needed, they can be thawed quickly and cooked in minutes for Lime Turkey Cutlets.

Serve the cutlets with an easy pasta side dish, cauliflower salad, and Italian bread (one ½-inch-thick slice per serving). Peach Sauce Flambé is easy to make yet spectacular to serve.

LIME TURKEY CUTLETS

⅓ cup all-purpose flour
½ teaspoon pepper
16 turkey breast cutlets (2 pounds)
Vegetable cooking spray
3 tablespoons margarine
½ cup water
½ teaspoon chicken-flavored bouillon granules
3 tablespoons lime juice
¼ teaspoon dried whole dillweed
1 tablespoon chopped parsley
Lime slices

Combine flour and pepper in a small bowl; dredge turkey lightly in flour mixture.

Coat a large non-aluminum skillet with cooking spray; add margarine, and place over medium heat until margarine melts. Add turkey, and cook 2 to 3 minutes on each side or until browned. Remove from skillet, and drain on paper towels. Wipe skillet dry with paper towels.

Combine water, bouillon granules, lime juice, and dillweed in skillet; add turkey. Cover; simmer over low heat 10 minutes or until turkey is tender. Remove to a warm platter. Sprinkle with parsley, and garnish with lime slices. Yield: 8 servings (195 calories per serving).

PRO 26.1 / FAT 7.2 / CARB 5.0 / FIB 0.2 / CHOL 59 / SOD 131 / POT 278

FETTUCCINE WITH FRESH TOMATO SAUCE

½ (16-ounce) package fettuccine
¾ cup loosely packed fresh basil leaves
1 clove garlic
3 tablespoons water
1½ cups peeled, seeded, diced tomato
2 tablespoons grated Parmesan cheese
⅛ teaspoon salt
⅛ teaspoon pepper
Fresh basil sprig

Cook fettuccine according to the package directions, omitting salt; drain and set aside.

Combine basil leaves, garlic, and water in container of an electric blender, and process until smooth. Combine basil mixture and tomato in a medium saucepan; cook over medium heat 2 to 4 minutes or until mixture is thoroughly heated, stirring constantly. Add fettuccine, Parmesan cheese, salt, and pepper; cook over low heat, tossing gently, until thoroughly heated. Garnish with a fresh basil sprig. Yield: 8 servings (108 calories per serving).

PRO 4.6 / FAT 1.7 / CARB 20.7 / FIB 1.3 / CHOL 1 / SOD 63 / POT 260

ITALIAN CAULIFLOWER SALAD

3½ cups thinly sliced cauliflower flowerets
¼ cup chopped sweet red pepper
¼ cup sliced celery
1 tablespoon chopped green onion
¼ cup plain low-fat yogurt
3 tablespoons reduced-calorie Italian salad dressing
8 leaves red leaf lettuce
Paprika

Combine cauliflower, red pepper, celery, and onion in a medium bowl.

Combine yogurt and salad dressing; pour over cauliflower mixture, and toss to coat. Cover and refrigerate until chilled. Arrange lettuce leaves on individual salad plates; spoon chilled vegetable mixture evenly over lettuce. Sprinkle each serving with paprika. Yield: 8 servings (21 calories per serving).

PRO 1.4 / FAT 0.2 / CARB 3.8 / FIB 0.6 / CHOL 0 / SOD 67 / POT 203

PEACH SAUCE FLAMBÉ

1½ (16-ounce) packages frozen unsweetened peaches, thawed
1 tablespoon plus 1½ teaspoons sugar
1 tablespoon plus 1½ teaspoons lemon juice
¼ cup Cointreau or other orange-flavored liqueur
1 quart vanilla ice milk

Combine first 3 ingredients in container of an electric blender; process until smooth.

Transfer peach mixture to a small saucepan, and cook over medium heat 5 minutes or until thoroughly heated.

Place Cointreau in a small, long-handled pan; heat just until warm. Ignite with a long match, and pour over peach mixture. Stir gently until flames die down. Serve immediately over ½-cup portions of ice milk. Yield: 8 servings (156 calories per serving).

PRO 3.1 / FAT 2.9 / CARB 27.0 / FIB 1.8 / CHOL 9 / SOD 53 / POT 297

 Turkey is fast becoming a year-round staple. In the first 8 months of last year, sales were up nearly 15%. It's a delicious source of protein and B vitamins, with fair amounts of iron, zinc and other trace elements.
Turkey's naturally low in fat, even lower than chicken. But trim it well — most of the fat's in the skin. A 3½-ounce serving of turkey with the skin, for example, has 8 grams of fat, but the same amount of white meat without skin has only 1 gram. Since fat has 9 calories per gram, that's a difference of 63 calories!

A no-hassle menu starring easy, elegant Crab Mornay.

Seafood Dinner For Two

Just because this menu is special enough for a romantic dinner doesn't mean you have to slave in the kitchen. In fact, this meal featuring Crab Mornay is one of our easiest to prepare. You can serve your guest a delicious elegant meal, and still relax and enjoy the evening.

Get a head start by preparing the salad and dessert several hours before mealtime. The salad is made by tossing cooked rice with celery, chives, sweet red pepper, and a tasty curry dress-

Crab Mornay
Tarragon Carrots and Broccoli
Curried Rice Salad
Commercial Rolls
Fresh Fruit with Cointreau-Yogurt Sauce

Serves 2
Total calories per serving: 583

ing. For dessert, both the Cointreau-Yogurt Sauce and the layers of fresh fruit should be prepared

and chilled, then combined just before serving.

Crab Mornay rates high in both taste and ease of preparation. First, assemble your ingredients. While the broccoli and carrots cook for your side dish, prepare and spoon the crab mixture into two ramekins. Two minutes before serving, broil the crab.

To complement dinner, we suggest commercial rolls (allow a 1-ounce roll for each serving), such as hard rolls which are made without extra butter.

CRAB MORNAY

¼ cup water
¼ cup Chablis or other dry white wine
½ teaspoon chicken-flavored bouillon granules
Dash of white pepper
½ cup sliced fresh mushrooms
1 tablespoon sliced green onion
¼ cup skim milk
1½ teaspoons cornstarch
¼ cup (1 ounce) shredded Swiss cheese
⅓ pound lump crabmeat
Paprika
Green onion fans

Combine first 4 ingredients in a small saucepan; bring to a boil. Add mushrooms and onion. Cover; reduce heat, and simmer 1 minute or until mushrooms are tender.

Combine milk and cornstarch, mixing well; add to mushroom mixture. Cook, stirring constantly, 2 minutes or until thickened. Remove from heat; add cheese, and stir until melted. Stir in crabmeat. Spoon into 2 (6-ounce) ramekins or custard cups. Sprinkle with paprika. Broil 2 minutes or until hot. Garnish with green onion fans. Yield: 2 servings (153 calories per serving).

PRO 18.7 / FAT 5.6 / CARB 6.5 / FIB 0.2 / CHOL 89 / SOD 309 / POT 304

 Calorie counters, take note of the six most popular food sources of calories: White bread, rolls, and crackers lead the list. Next: donuts, cookies, cakes. Third: alcoholic beverages. Fourth: whole milk. Fifth: beef steaks and roasts. Sixth: regular soft drinks.

TARRAGON CARROTS AND BROCCOLI

1 cup fresh broccoli flowerets
1 cup diagonally sliced carrots
½ teaspoon dried whole tarragon
1 teaspoon margarine

Cook broccoli in a vegetable steamer over boiling water 8 minutes or until crisp-tender. Set aside, and keep warm.

Cook carrots and tarragon in a small amount of boiling water 8 minutes or just until carrots are tender. Drain well.

Combine carrots, broccoli, and margarine in a small bowl; toss lightly until margarine melts. Yield: 2 servings (60 calories per serving).

PRO 2.2 / FAT 2.2 / CARB 9.3 / FIB 1.7 / CHOL 0 / SOD 59 / POT 380

CURRIED RICE SALAD

½ cup cooked parboiled rice (cooked without salt or fat)
¼ cup chopped celery
2 tablespoons minced chives
2 tablespoons finely chopped sweet red pepper
2 tablespoons reduced-calorie salad dressing
1 teaspoon vinegar
½ teaspoon curry powder
1 tablespoon slivered almonds, toasted
2 leaves Bibb lettuce

Combine first 4 ingredients in a small bowl. Combine salad dressing, vinegar, and curry powder in a small bowl, stirring until well blended. Add to rice mixture, and toss well. Cover and chill at least 2 hours.

To serve, stir in almonds, and spoon mixture over lettuce leaves. Yield: 2 servings (101 calories per serving.).

PRO 2.4 / FAT 4.4 / CARB 13.6 / FIB 1.0 / CHOL 8 / SOD 34 / POT 146

FRESH FRUIT
WITH COINTREAU-YOGURT SAUCE

¼ cup vanilla low-fat yogurt
1 tablespoon plus 1½ teaspoons Cointreau or other orange-flavored liqueur
½ cup sliced banana
Lemon juice
2 medium oranges, peeled, sectioned, and seeded
½ cup seedless green grapes
½ cup sliced fresh strawberries

Combine yogurt and liqueur in a small bowl; cover and chill 1 hour.

Toss banana slices with a small amount of lemon juice to prevent browning. Layer fruit in 2 (10-ounce) compotes or custard cups; cover and chill 1 hour or until serving time. To serve, spoon chilled yogurt sauce over fruit. Yield: 2 servings (196 calories per serving).

PRO 3.7 / FAT 1.3 / CARB 40.4 / FIB 4.5 / CHOL 2 / SOD 23 / POT 614

Special Late-Night Dinner

Marsala Veal with Olives
Lemon Linguine
Watercress Salad with
Creamy Garlic Dressing
Easy Fruit Sauce over
Angel Food Cake

Serves 6
Total calories per serving: 601

The key to preparing dinner after an early evening engagement is to choose simple recipes and have your ingredients ready ahead of time.

Marsala Veal, Lemon Linguine, and Easy Fruit Sauce are all easy, last-minute dishes. Actual cooking time for the veal is only about 5 minutes. And total preparation time for Lemon Linguine is less than 15 minutes.

Both Watercress Salad and Creamy Garlic Dressing (1 tablespoon per serving) can be chilling until serving time.

By spooning the fruit sauce over commercial angel food cake (1 slice per serving) even the dessert for this menu is quick and easy.

Marsala Veal, Lemon Linguine and Watercress Salad with Creamy Garlic Dressing.

MARSALA VEAL WITH OLIVES

1½ pounds veal cutlets (¼-inch thick)
¼ cup all-purpose flour
¼ to ½ teaspoon freshly ground black pepper
Vegetable cooking spray
1 tablespoon unsalted margarine
⅓ cup Marsala wine
¼ cup water
¼ teaspoon beef-flavored bouillon granules
⅓ cup sliced ripe olives

Place veal cutlets between 2 sheets of waxed paper, and flatten to ⅛-inch thickness, using a meat mallet or rolling pin; cut veal into 2-inch pieces. Combine flour and pepper; dredge veal in flour mixture. Coat a large skillet with cooking spray; add margarine, and place over medium-high heat until margarine melts. Add veal pieces, and cook 1 minute on each side or until lightly browned. Remove veal from skillet, and set aside.

Add wine, water, and bouillon granules to skillet; bring to a boil. Return veal to skillet, turning to coat; add olives. Reduce heat, and simmer 1 to 2 minutes or until sauce is thickened and veal is thoroughly heated. Yield: 6 servings (233 calories per serving).

PRO 23.1 / FAT 12.5 / CARB 5.7 / FIB 0.5 / CHOL 81 / SOD 178 / POT 383

LEMON LINGUINE

6 ounces linguine
¼ cup lemon juice
3 tablespoons skim milk
1 tablespoon margarine
⅛ teaspoon salt
¼ cup grated Parmesan cheese
1 tablespoon chopped fresh parsley
Lemon twists

Cook linguine in a large Dutch oven according to package directions, omitting salt. Drain and place in a serving bowl; toss with lemon juice. Set aside, and keep warm.

Combine milk, margarine, and salt in a small saucepan; cook over low heat until margarine melts. Add warm milk mixture to linguine in serving bowl. Sprinkle linguine with Parmesan cheese, and toss well. Garnish with chopped fresh parsley and lemon twists. Yield: 6 servings (142 calories per serving).

PRO 5.3 / FAT 3.3 / CARB 22.7 / FIB 0.7 / CHOL 3 / SOD 139 / POT 85

WATERCRESS SALAD

4 cups torn watercress
½ cup sliced fresh mushrooms
½ cup sliced canned hearts of palm
2 tablespoons chopped green onion
¼ teaspoon pepper

Combine all ingredients in a large salad bowl. Cover and chill. Serve with Creamy Garlic Dressing. Yield: 6 servings (17 calories per serving).

PRO 0.9 / FAT 0.1 / CARB 3.9 / FIB 0.8 / CHOL 0 / SOD 37 / POT 121

CREAMY GARLIC DRESSING

¾ cup low-fat cottage cheese
¾ cup skim milk
2 tablespoons vinegar
1 (0.8-ounce) envelope reduced-calorie Italian salad dressing mix
1 clove garlic, minced

Combine all ingredients in container of an electric blender; process until smooth. Cover and chill thoroughly. Serve with Watercress Salad or other green salad. Refrigerate leftover dressing. Yield: 1⅔ cups (13 calories per tablespoon).

PRO 1.3 / FAT 0.2 / CARB 1.6 / FIB 0.0 / CHOL 1 / SOD 247 / POT 28

EASY FRUIT SAUCE

1 (16-ounce) can unsweetened chunky mixed fruits, undrained
1 tablespoon cornstarch
⅓ cup unsweetened orange juice
½ teaspoon grated lemon rind
2 (3-inch) sticks cinnamon

Drain fruit, reserving liquid; set fruit aside. Combine reserved liquid, cornstarch, orange juice, and lemon rind in a small saucepan; stir with a wire whisk to dissolve cornstarch. Add cinnamon sticks, and cook over medium heat, stirring constantly, until thickened and bubbly. Remove from heat; discard cinnamon sticks. Stir in reserved fruit; serve warm over angel food cake. Yield: 6 servings (46 calories per serving).

PRO 0.5 / FAT 0.0 / CARB 11.7 / FIB 0.5 / CHOL 0 / SOD 3 / POT 98

Dinner With A Mexican Flavor

The Mexican-Style Chicken Roll-Ups take a few minutes to flatten and roll, but once they're dipped in milk and dredged in a breadcrumb mixture, the baking time is only 30 minutes. Each roll-up is served over shredded lettuce and topped with picante sauce and low-fat yogurt.

While the chicken bakes, you can cook the rice and steam the broccoli (allow 1 cup per serving for correct calorie count). The mangos should be prepared the

Mexican-Style Chicken Roll-Ups
Seasoned Rice
Steamed Broccoli
Minted Mangos
Kahlúa Soufflé

Serves 8
Total calories per serving: 535

night before so the flavors of mango and mint will blend.

Several hours before mealtime shape an aluminum foil collar around a soufflé dish and cook the custard mixture for the Kahlúa Soufflé; allow time for it to cool to room temperature.

During the last few minutes that the chicken is baking, beat the egg whites and fold them into the custard mixture. After removing the chicken roll-ups from the oven, reduce the temperature to 350°, and add the soufflé. It will be puffed and set, ready to serve for dessert.

MEXICAN-STYLE CHICKEN ROLL-UPS

8 boneless chicken breast halves (2 pounds), skinned
4 canned whole green chiles, halved and seeded
3 ounces Monterey Jack cheese, cut into 8 strips
¾ cup fine, dry breadcrumbs
1 tablespoon chili powder
1½ teaspoons ground cumin
¼ teaspoon salt
¼ teaspoon garlic powder
¼ cup skim milk
Vegetable cooking spray
4 cups shredded lettuce
½ cup commercial picante sauce
¼ cup plain low-fat yogurt

Trim excess fat from chicken. Place each chicken breast half between 2 sheets of waxed paper; flatten to ¼-inch thickness, using a meat mallet or rolling pin.

Place a green chile half and one strip of cheese in center of each chicken breast half; roll up lengthwise, tucking edges under. Secure with wooden picks.

Combine breadcrumbs, chili powder, cumin, salt, and garlic powder. Dip chicken rolls in milk; dredge in breadcrumb mixture, coating well. Place chicken in a 12- x 8- x 2-inch baking dish coated with cooking spray. Bake at 400° for 30 minutes or until chicken is done.

Place each chicken roll on ½ cup shredded lettuce; top each with 1 tablespoon picante sauce and 1½ teaspoons yogurt. Serve immediately. Yield: 8 servings (236 calories per serving).

PRO 30.7 / FAT 7.1 / CARB 10.6 / FIB 0.7 / CHOL 80 / SOD 405 / POT 392

SEASONED RICE

Vegetable cooking spray
½ cup chopped onion
½ cup chopped sweet red pepper
2½ cups water
1 teaspoon chicken-flavored bouillon granules
½ teaspoon ground cumin
⅛ teaspoon hot sauce
1 cup parboiled rice, uncooked

Coat a medium saucepan with cooking spray; place over medium heat until hot. Add onion and pepper; sauté 5 minutes or until tender.

Add water, bouillon granules, cumin, and hot sauce; bring to a boil, and stir in rice. Cover; reduce heat, and simmer 20 minutes or until rice is tender and liquid is absorbed. Yield: 8 servings (90 calories per serving).

PRO 1.9 / FAT 0.3 / CARB 20.2 / FIB 0.3 / CHOL 0 / SOD 51 / POT 78

Calorie counters take note: A single serving of this luscious Kahlúa Soufflé will add only 100 calories to your daily total.

MINTED MANGOS

4 (1¼-pound) fresh ripe mangos, peeled, seeded, and sliced
⅓ cup fresh mint leaves, cut into thin strips

Combine mangos and mint in a medium bowl; toss lightly to combine. Cover and refrigerate 8 hours or overnight. Serve chilled. Yield: 8 servings (84 calories per serving).

PRO 0.7 / FAT 0.4 / CARB 21.9 / FIB 1.4 / CHOL 0 / SOD 4 / POT 212

KAHLÚA SOUFFLÉ

Vegetable cooking spray
¼ cup sugar
¼ cup Dutch process cocoa
1 tablespoon cornstarch
¾ cup skim milk
2 tablespoons Kahlúa
3 egg yolks
4 egg whites
2 tablespoons sugar
¼ teaspoon cream of tartar

Cut a piece of aluminum foil long enough to fit around a 1½-quart soufflé dish, allowing a 1-inch overlap. Fold foil lengthwise into thirds. Lightly coat one side of foil with cooking spray; wrap foil around outside of dish, coated side against dish, allowing foil to extend 4 inches above rim to form a collar. Secure foil with string or freezer tape. Set aside.

Combine ¼ cup sugar, cocoa, and cornstarch in top of a double boiler; gradually stir in milk and Kahlúa. Bring water to a boil over medium heat; cook Kahlúa mixture until slightly thickened, stirring constantly.

Beat egg yolks slightly. Gradually stir about one-fourth of hot mixture into yolks; add to remaining hot mixture, stirring constantly. Cook 10 minutes over boiling water, stirring constantly with a wire whisk, until thickened. Remove from heat, and let cool to room temperature.

Beat egg whites (at room temperature) and cream of tartar until soft peaks form. Gradually add 2 tablespoons sugar, 1 tablespoon at a time, beating until stiff peaks form and sugar dissolves. Gently fold egg whites into Kahlúa mixture.

Pour into prepared soufflé dish. Place dish in a 13- x 9- x 2-inch baking pan; pour hot water into pan to a depth of ½ inch. Bake at 350° for 50 minutes or until puffed and set. Serve immediately. Yield: 8 servings (100 calories per serving).

PRO 4.0 / FAT 2.8 / CARB 13.9 / FIB 0.1 / CHOL 103 / SOD 66 / POT 88

It's cool, it's low-cal, and it's delicious: Frozen Cantaloupe Yogurt!

Dining Alfresco

Summer is simply not the time to spend hours over a hot kitchen stove. It's much more fun, and healthy, to be outdoors playing tennis, golf, or swimming. After your next game or outing, invite your fellow players over for supper from the grill.

Your guests can cool off and relax with a glass of Apple-Mint Tea while you grill the pompano and vegetables. Both dishes take very little time to prepare for grilling and both require medium coals. Start the pompano about 5

Apple-Mint Tea
Mesquite-Grilled Pompano
Grilled Summer
Vegetables
Carrot-Cabbage Coleslaw
Frozen Cantaloupe Yogurt

Serves 4
Total calories per serving: 654

minutes after you place the foil pouches of seasoned summer vegetables on the grill.

The Carrot-Cabbage Coleslaw

and Frozen Cantaloupe Yogurt should be prepared ahead so the salad will be thoroughly chilled and the yogurt mixture frozen by serving time. These make-aheads will help eliminate some last-minute hassles.

Your food processor can be a helpful time-saver with both recipes. Use the shredding disc for the cabbage and carrot and the grating disc for the apple. The knife blade is recommended to puree the cantaloupe mixture for the frozen yogurt.

APPLE-MINT TEA

1 quart-size tea bag
½ cup fresh mint leaves
2 tablespoons fresh lemon juice
2 cups boiling water
2 cups unsweetened apple juice
4 thin slices lemon
4 sprigs fresh mint

Combine first 3 ingredients in a pitcher; pour in water. Cover; let stand 5 minutes.

Remove and discard tea bag and mint leaves. Add apple juice. Serve over ice; garnish each glass with a lemon slice and mint sprig. Yield: 4 cups (63 calories per 1-cup serving).

PRO 0.3 / FAT 0.2 / CARB 15.7 / FIB 0.4 / CHOL 0 / SOD 7 / POT 197

MESQUITE-GRILLED POMPANO

4 mesquite chips
½ teaspoon grated orange rind
2 tablespoons unsweetened orange juice
1 tablespoon margarine, melted
½ teaspoon dried whole tarragon or 1½ teaspoons chopped fresh tarragon
4 pompano fillets (1 pound)
4 orange slices
Fresh tarragon sprigs

Soak mesquite chips in water to cover 30 minutes; set aside.

Combine orange rind and juice, margarine, and tarragon in a small bowl; stir well. Set mixture aside.

Drain chips; place directly on medium coals. Grill pompano 6 inches over coals 5 minutes on each side or until fish flakes easily when tested with a fork. Baste often with reserved orange juice mixture. Garnish each serving with an orange slice and a tarragon sprig. Yield: 4 servings (218 calories per serving).

PRO 21.4 / FAT 13.7 / CARB 1.0 / FIB 0.0 / CHOL 62 / SOD 89 / POT 238

GRILLED SUMMER VEGETABLES

4 medium-size new potatoes, cut into ¼-inch slices
2 medium zucchini squash, cut into ¼-inch slices
1 medium-size yellow squash, cut into ¼-inch slices
1 medium-size yellow pepper, seeded and cut into thin strips
1 medium onion, thinly sliced
½ teaspoon dried whole basil or 2 teaspoons chopped fresh basil
⅛ teaspoon freshly ground pepper

Cook new potatoes in boiling water to cover 5 minutes or just until tender; drain.

Arrange equal amounts of potato, zucchini squash, yellow squash, yellow pepper, and onion on four 12-inch squares of aluminum foil. Sprinkle each with equal amounts of basil and pepper. Fold foil over vegetables, sealing securely. Grill 6 inches over medium coals 15 minutes, turning once. Yield: 4 servings (160 calories per serving).

PRO 5.9 / FAT 0.7 / CARB 35.4 / FIB 3.0 / CHOL 0 / SOD 17 / POT 1264

CARROT-CABBAGE COLESLAW

1¼ cups shredded cabbage
¾ cup shredded carrot
¼ cup grated red apple
¼ cup drained unsweetened crushed pineapple
¼ cup reduced-calorie salad dressing
1 tablespoon lemon juice
Cabbage leaves

Combine first 6 ingredients in a medium bowl; toss well. Chill thoroughly. Spoon coleslaw into cabbage-lined bowls to serve. Yield: 4 servings (78 calories per serving).

PRO 0.8 / FAT 4.2 / CARB 10.7 / FIB 1.4 / CHOL 5 / SOD 99 / POT 210

FROZEN CANTALOUPE YOGURT

4 cups diced cantaloupe
3 tablespoons sugar
2 tablespoons lemon juice
2 teaspoons unflavored gelatin
¼ cup cold water
1 (8-ounce) carton vanilla low-fat yogurt

Combine cantaloupe, sugar, and lemon juice in a medium bowl; cover and refrigerate 30 minutes. Place mixture in container of an electric blender or food processor; process until smooth. Transfer mixture to a medium bowl.

Soften gelatin in cold water in a small saucepan for 1 minute. Cook over low heat, stirring constantly, 5 minutes or until gelatin dissolves. Add to cantaloupe mixture, stirring well. Add yogurt, stirring until smooth.

Pour mixture into an 8-inch square baking pan; freeze until almost firm. Transfer mixture to a large bowl; beat at high speed of an electric mixer until fluffy. Spoon mixture back into baking pan; freeze until firm. Scoop into individual serving dishes to serve. Yield: 4 cups (135 calories per 1-cup serving).

PRO 5.7 / FAT 1.3 / CARB 27.4 / FIB 0.5 / CHOL 3 / SOD 56 / POT 637

For a healthy life, you need a good diet, regular exercise, and a little relaxation. Medical scientists are discovering that training in relaxation techniques has profound health-promoting effects.

By blocking the body's hormonal response to stress, relaxation can lower blood pressure and cholesterol levels, slow the heart beat, bring relief to many patients with chronic pain, and even boost immunity to infection.

To achieve real relaxation, meditation, yoga, biofeedback, and prayer all work well. Relaxation expert Dr. Herbert Benson of Harvard advises: Sit quietly, breathe slowly, pay attention to breathing, and on each exhale utter a word, sound, phrase, or prayer. As thoughts arise, passively disregard them. Use this relaxation technique 15 minutes a day and notice the difference.

Behold a feast that's sumptuous in appearance but light in calories. Begin with fresh, tart Cranberry Punch followed by the elegant entrée, Spinach-Stuffed Turkey Breast. Tasty side dishes are Orange-Honey Carrots and Endive Salad with Pimiento Dressing (menu begins on page 67).

By The Pool

Teriyaki Flank Steak
Corn-Stuffed Tomatoes
Kiwi Green Salad
Whole Wheat French
Bread
Citrus Fruit Ice

Serves 6
Total calories per serving: 493

Since flank steak is one of the leanest cuts of meat, it's a great choice for a light dinner from the grill. The pineapple juice-based marinade helps to tenderize and flavor the meat.

Serve the steak with grilled stuffed tomatoes, a kiwifruit salad, and Whole Wheat French Bread (1 slice per serving). Citrus Fruit Ice, made the night before, is the refreshing dessert.

Relax with your guests by serving a light dinner from the grill.

TERIYAKI FLANK STEAK

1½ pounds beef flank steak
¼ cup plus 2 tablespoons unsweetened
   pineapple juice
¼ cup reduced-sodium soy sauce
2 tablespoons chopped green onion
2 tablespoons cider vinegar
2 tablespoons vegetable oil
1 tablespoon honey
1 teaspoon ground ginger
1 clove garlic, crushed
Green onion fans (optional)

Trim excess fat from steak; place steak in a shallow container. Combine next 8 ingredients, stirring well; pour marinade over steak. Cover and marinate in refrigerator overnight.

Remove steak from marinade, reserving marinade. Grill steak 5 inches over hot coals 5 to 7 minutes on each side or until desired degree of doneness, basting often with marinade.

To serve, thinly slice steak diagonally across the grain. Garnish with green onion fans, if desired. Yield: 6 servings (227 calories per serving).

PRO 28.0 / FAT 9.1 / CARB 6.9 / FIB 0.1 / CHOL 55 / SOD 440 / POT 356

CORN-STUFFED TOMATOES

6 medium tomatoes
2 cups fresh corn, cut from cob
½ cup water
¼ cup chopped green onion
Vegetable cooking spray
2 teaspoons minced fresh parsley
1 tablespoon chopped fresh basil
   or 1 teaspoon dried whole basil
¼ teaspoon freshly ground black pepper
Basil leaves (optional)

Cut off top of each tomato; scoop out pulp, leaving shells intact. Chop ½ cup pulp, and set aside; reserve remaining tomato pulp for use in other recipes. Invert tomato shells on paper towels to drain.

Combine corn, water, and green onion in a medium skillet coated with cooking spray; cook, uncovered, over medium heat 15 minutes or until water is absorbed. Stir in ½ cup tomato pulp, parsley, chopped basil, and pepper. Spoon mixture into tomato shells, and wrap each stuffed tomato in aluminum foil.

Grill foil-wrapped tomatoes 5 inches over hot coals 5 minutes or until thoroughly heated. Garnish with basil leaves, if desired. Serve hot. Yield: 6 servings (77 calories per serving).

PRO 2.7 / FAT 0.9 / CARB 17.9 / FIB 1.2 / CHOL 0 / SOD 17 / POT 331

KIWI GREEN SALAD

3 cups torn spinach leaves
3 cups torn Bibb lettuce leaves
2 medium kiwifruit, peeled and sliced
1 small onion, thinly sliced and separated into rings
3 tablespoons lemon juice
2 tablespoons honey
1 tablespoon vegetable oil
¼ teaspoon pepper

Combine first 4 ingredients in a large salad bowl. Combine lemon juice, honey, oil, and pepper in a glass jar; cover tightly, and shake vigorously. Pour over salad, and toss to coat. Serve immediately. Yield: 6 servings (73 calories per serving).

PRO 1.7 / FAT 2.5 / CARB 12.2 / FIB 2.1 / CHOL 0 / SOD 24 / POT 338

WHOLE WHEAT FRENCH BREAD

1 package dry yeast
2 teaspoons sugar
1½ cups warm water (105° to 115°)
1½ cups whole wheat flour, divided
2½ cups all-purpose flour
¾ teaspoon salt
Vegetable cooking spray
1 tablespoon water
2 teaspoons sesame seeds

Dissolve yeast and sugar in 1½ cups warm water in a large bowl; let stand 5 minutes. Add 1 cup whole wheat flour, stirring well. Place in a warm place (85°) for 10 minutes. (Bubbles will appear on surface.)

Add remaining ½ cup whole wheat flour, all-purpose flour, and salt; stir well. Shape dough into a ball, and place in a bowl coated with cooking spray, turning to grease top. Cover and let rise in a warm place (85°), free from drafts, 1 hour or until doubled in bulk.

Turn dough out onto a lightly floured surface; knead 5 minutes or until smooth and elastic. Roll dough out to a 20- x 10- x ½-inch rectangle. Roll dough up jellyroll fashion, starting at long side. Pinch long seam together, and tuck ends under. Brush with 1 tablespoon water; sprinkle loaf with sesame seeds.

Place loaf, seam side down, on a baking sheet coated with cooking spray. Let rise in a warm place 45 minutes or until doubled in bulk. Cut crosswise slashes in top of loaf with a sharp knife. Bake at 400° for 40 minutes or until loaf sounds hollow when tapped.

Remove loaf from baking sheet, and place on a cooling rack to cool completely. Cut into ½-inch slices. Yield: 40 (½-inch) slices (48 calories per slice).

PRO 1.6 / FAT 0.3 / CARB 10.0 / FIB 0.6 / CHOL 0 / SOD 44 / POT 30

CITRUS FRUIT ICE

1 pint fresh strawberries, washed, hulled, and sliced
1 (8½-ounce) can pear halves in light syrup, drained
1 cup unsweetened orange juice
2 tablespoons sugar
1 teaspoon grated lemon rind
2 tablespoons lemon juice

Position knife blade in food processor bowl; add all ingredients. Process until smooth. Spoon mixture into a 9-inch square baking pan. Freeze until almost firm. Remove from freezer; process in food processor. Return mixture to pan, and freeze until frozen. Yield: 6 servings (68 calories per serving).

PRO 0.8 / FAT 0.4 / CARB 16.8 / FIB 1.5 / CHOL 0 / SOD 1 / POT 195

Anniversary Dinner For Two

Marinated Vegetable
Salad
Herbed Lamb Chops
with Bordelaise Sauce
Sesame Orzo
Raspberry-Orange Alaskas

Serves 2
Total calories per serving: 712

Marinated Vegetable Salad is a delicious foretaste of things to come.

Get this special dinner off to a great start with an eye-catching appetizer salad. The ingredients for Marinated Vegetable Salad should be combined ahead of time and chilled overnight for optimum flavor.

The lamb chops should also be marinated ahead so that the meat will be more tender and flavorful. Serve the chops with our tasty light Bordelaise Sauce (2 tablespoons per serving).

Sesame Orzo is a very easy dish and is an interesting change of pace from the more traditional rice or pasta side dishes.

Our dessert, the spectacular Raspberry-Orange Alaskas, should be started well ahead of dinner so that the sherbet-yogurt filling will be firmly frozen. Just before serving, brown the meringue under the broiler.

MARINATED VEGETABLE SALAD

¼ pound fresh snow peas
4 cherry tomatoes, cut in half
1 medium carrot, scraped and thinly sliced
   diagonally
½ medium zucchini squash, thinly sliced diagonally
2 tablespoons vinegar
1 tablespoon vegetable oil
1½ teaspoons sugar
Dash of celery seeds
Dash of dry mustard
Dash of paprika
1 tablespoon feta cheese, crumbled

Cook snow peas in a vegetable steamer over boiling water 3 to 5 minutes or until crisp-tender. Cover and chill thoroughly.

Combine tomatoes, carrot, and zucchini in a 10- x 6- x 2-inch baking dish. Combine vinegar, oil, sugar, celery seeds, mustard, and paprika in a glass jar; cover tightly, and shake vigorously. Pour over vegetables; cover and marinate 8 hours or overnight in refrigerator, stirring occasionally.

To serve, arrange chilled snow peas on a serving platter; spoon marinated vegetables over top, using a slotted spoon. Sprinkle feta cheese over vegetables. Yield: 2 servings (136 calories per serving).

PRO 3.3 / FAT 7.9 / CARB 14.6 / FIB 2.1 / CHOL 3 / SOD 58 / POT 416

HERBED LAMB CHOPS

2 tablespoons red wine vinegar
1 tablespoon water
2 teaspoons minced onion
2 teaspoons reduced-sodium soy sauce
1 clove garlic, minced
¼ teaspoon dried whole rosemary, crushed
⅛ teaspoon dried whole thyme, crushed
Dash of pepper
2 (5-ounce) lamb chops (1-inch thick)

Combine first 8 ingredients in a shallow 1-quart casserole; mix well. Set aside.

Trim excess fat from lamb chops. Add lamb chops to marinade, turning to coat. Cover and marinate in refrigerator 4 hours.

Drain lamb chops, reserving marinade. Place lamb chops on a rack in a broiler pan. Broil 5 inches from heating element 6 minutes on each side or until done, basting frequently with marinade. Serve warm with Bordelaise Sauce. Yield: 2 servings (179 calories per serving).

PRO 26.4 / FAT 6.5 / CARB 1.5 / FIB 0.1 / CHOL 91 / SOD 259 / POT 290

BORDELAISE SAUCE

1 tablespoon margarine
1 tablespoon all-purpose flour
½ cup water
1 tablespoon plus 1½ teaspoons dry red wine
1½ teaspoons minced green onion
1½ teaspoons minced fresh parsley
1 bay leaf
½ teaspoon beef-flavored bouillon granules
⅛ teaspoon dried whole thyme
Dash of freshly ground black pepper

Melt margarine in a small saucepan over low heat; add flour, stirring until smooth. Cook 1 minute, stirring constantly. Gradually add water and wine, stirring until smooth. Stir in onion, parsley, bay leaf, bouillon granules, thyme, and pepper. Cook over medium-high heat, stirring constantly, until thickened and bubbly. Remove bay leaf. Serve sauce warm over lamb chops. Yield: ½ cup (18 calories per tablespoon).

PRO 0.2 / FAT 1.5 / CARB 1.1 / FIB 0.1 / CHOL 0 / SOD 46 / POT 8

SESAME ORZO

1 quart water
⅓ cup orzo
1 tablespoon grated Parmesan cheese
1 tablespoon skim milk
2 teaspoons sesame seeds, toasted
Dash of salt
⅛ teaspoon paprika

Bring water to a boil in a medium saucepan. Stir in orzo; continue to boil 10 minutes, stirring occasionally. Drain.

Return orzo to saucepan; add remaining ingredients, and toss well. Transfer to a serving dish. Serve immediately. Yield: 2 servings (163 calories per serving).

PRO 6.3 / FAT 2.8 / CARB 27.9 / FIB 1.4 / CHOL 2 / SOD 125 / POT 103

RASPBERRY-ORANGE ALASKAS

2 medium oranges
½ cup raspberry sherbet, softened
½ cup vanilla low-fat yogurt
1 egg white
⅛ teaspoon cream of tartar
⅛ teaspoon vanilla extract
1 tablespoon sugar

Cut a 1-inch slice from tops of oranges. Gently remove orange pulp, clipping the membranes, and being careful not to puncture bottoms of oranges. Strain pulp, reserving 3 tablespoons juice; discard pulp, and reserve remaining juice for use in other recipes.

Combine 3 tablespoons orange juice, sherbet, and yogurt; mix well. Freeze 4 hours or until almost firm, stirring several times. Beat sherbet mixture at high speed of an electric mixer 1 minute. Spoon into orange shells.

Beat egg white (at room temperature), cream of tartar, and vanilla until foamy. Gradually add sugar, beating until stiff peaks form. Spread meringue over top opening of each orange shell, making sure edges are sealed. Freeze up to 2 hours or until ready to serve.

Broil 6 inches from heating element 1 minute or until lightly browned. Serve immediately. Yield: 2 servings (198 calories per serving).

PRO 6.3 / FAT 1.4 / CARB 42.4 / FIB 2.6 / CHOL 3 / SOD 110 / POT 441

Let's Celebrate Spring

Spring is such a special time of year, it deserves a celebration. Welcome the season with a light dinner of spring favorites!

Fresh English peas are plentiful for only a short time, so take advantage of their delicate flavor while you can. The creaminess of Fresh Pea Soup may come as a surprise since not a drop of cream is used. Instead, the smooth consistency results from processing the tender cooked pea mixture in an electric blender or food processor.

Fresh Pea Soup
Pork Madeira
Steamed Asparagus
Dijon Potatoes with Leeks
Blue Cheese Green Salad
Strawberries with
Cointreau-Cream Sauce

Serves 4
Total calories per serving: 592

The main course for this feast is Pork Madeira — an outstanding entrée that is easy to prepare

and delicious as well.

New potatoes in a tasty Dijon sauce and steamed fresh asparagus (½ cup per serving) are the seasonal side dishes. Leave the red skins on the potatoes to add color and fiber to the menu.

Finally, what's a spring celebration without fresh strawberries? Top them with a tasty low-fat Cointreau sauce that starts with whipped evaporated skim milk, and you have a refreshing, attractive dessert with only 101 calories per serving.

FRESH PEA SOUP

1½ cups fresh shelled English peas
2 cups shredded lettuce
2 cups water
¼ cup chopped green onion
1 teaspoon chicken-flavored bouillon granules
¼ teaspoon white pepper
¼ teaspoon dried whole tarragon
⅓ cup skim milk

Combine all ingredients except milk in a large saucepan; bring to a boil. Cover; reduce heat, and simmer 25 minutes or until very tender.

Transfer mixture to container of an electric blender; add milk, and process until smooth. Pour into soup bowls; serve warm. Yield: 3 cups (59 calories per ¾-cup serving).

PRO 4.1 / FAT 0.4 / CARB 10.2 / FIB 2.3 / CHOL 0 / SOD 111 / POT 231

PORK MADEIRA

8 (1- to 1½-inch-thick) slices pork tenderloin (about 1 pound)
¼ teaspoon pepper
Vegetable cooking spray
1 cup thinly sliced fresh mushrooms
½ cup water
2 tablespoons Madeira or other dry, sweet golden wine
2 teaspoons minced fresh chives
1 teaspoon Worcestershire sauce
½ teaspoon beef-flavored bouillon granules
1 tablespoon cornstarch
1 tablespoon water

Sprinkle pork with pepper. Coat a large skillet with cooking spray; place over medium heat until hot. Add pork, and cook until browned on

both sides. Remove pork; drain on paper towels. Wipe skillet dry with a paper towel.

Coat skillet with cooking spray; place over medium heat until hot. Add mushrooms; sauté 2 minutes or until tender. Add pork, ½ cup water, Madeira, chives, Worcestershire sauce, and bouillon granules; bring to a boil. Cover; reduce heat, and simmer 10 minutes or until pork is tender. Remove pork to a warm serving platter.

Combine cornstarch and 1 tablespoon water, stirring well; stir into mixture in skillet. Cook over medium heat, stirring constantly, until mixture comes to a full boil. Boil 1 minute, stirring constantly. Spoon sauce over pork to serve. Yield: 4 servings (157 calories per serving).

PRO 24.9 / FAT 4.2 / CARB 3.5 / FIB 0.2 / CHOL 79 / SOD 128 / POT 543

DIJON POTATOES WITH LEEKS

Vegetable cooking spray
½ cup sliced leeks, cut into ¼-inch-thick slices
1½ pounds small new potatoes
1 cup water
½ cup Chablis or other dry white wine
1 tablespoon Dijon mustard
1½ teaspoons chicken-flavored bouillon granules
Freshly ground pepper

Coat a small skillet with cooking spray, and place over medium heat until hot. Add leeks, and sauté 3 minutes or until tender. Set aside.

Wash potatoes; cut into quarters. Combine potatoes, water, wine, mustard, and bouillon granules in a medium saucepan. Bring to a boil. Cover; reduce heat, and simmer 6 minutes. Uncover and simmer 15 minutes or until tender.

Add reserved leeks to potatoes; cook until thoroughly heated. Place in a serving bowl; sprinkle with pepper. Serve with a slotted spoon. Yield: 4 servings (145 calories per serving).

PRO 4.1 / FAT 0.6 / CARB 31.7 / FIB 1.5 / CHOL 0 / SOD 270 / POT 926

BLUE CHEESE GREEN SALAD

4 cups torn Bibb lettuce leaves
1 medium tomato, cut into wedges
1 medium carrot, scraped and thinly sliced
½ cup croutons
Blue Cheese Salad Dressing

Combine lettuce, tomato, carrot, and croutons in individual salad bowls. Serve each with 2 tablespoons Blue Cheese Salad Dressing. Yield: 4 servings (107 calories per serving).

Blue Cheese Salad Dressing:

¼ cup reduced-calorie mayonnaise
¼ cup (1 ounce) coarsely crumbled blue cheese
2 tablespoons skim milk
1½ teaspoons minced chives
1 teaspoon vinegar
Dash of hot sauce

Combine all ingredients in a bowl, mixing well. Cover; refrigerate until chilled. Yield: ½ cup (73 calories per 2-tablespoon serving).

PRO 3.5 / FAT 6.9 / CARB 8.7 / FIB 1.0 / CHOL 11 / SOD 247 / POT 316

Strawberries with Cointreau-Cream Sauce.

STRAWBERRIES WITH COINTREAU-CREAM SAUCE

1 quart fresh strawberries, washed, hulled, and chilled
⅓ cup evaporated skim milk
2 tablespoons sifted powdered sugar
2 tablespoons vanilla low-fat yogurt
2 teaspoons Cointreau or other orange-flavored liqueur
⅛ teaspoon grated orange rind
¼ teaspoon vanilla extract

Divide strawberries among 4 individual dessert dishes, reserving 4 strawberries for garnish. Set aside in refrigerator.

Freeze evaporated milk in a small bowl until ice crystals form around edges. Chill beaters. Add sugar to evaporated milk; beat at high speed of an electric mixer until stiff peaks form. Combine remaining ingredients; gently fold into whipped milk mixture until blended. Spoon equal amounts of sauce over individual servings of strawberries; garnish each with a reserved strawberry. Serve immediately. Yield: 4 servings (101 calories per serving).

PRO 3.0 / FAT 0.9 / CARB 20.5 / FIB 2.8 / CHOL 1 / SOD 31 / POT 331

Fireside Tray Dining

A fire in the fireplace is an inviting scene on cold winter evenings. Take advantage of the cozy fireside setting by inviting friends over to enjoy a special dinner in its circle of warmth.

Start the evening with steaming mugs of Hot Spiced Wine. Our recipe calls for diluting the Bordeaux with unsweetened orange juice and water. Cloves and cinnamon add a pleasant hint of spice.

The scallops, pasta, and salad

Hot Spiced Wine
Scallops Sauté
Angel Hair Pasta with
Pimiento
Spinach-Radicchio Salad
Commercial Breadsticks
Chocolate-Banana Parfait

Serves 4
Total calories per serving: 743

are all relatively easy to prepare, allowing you to spend time with

your guests. Angel Hair Pasta with Pimiento is especially quick since the pasta itself is done after only 30 seconds in boiling water.

To round out the menu, offer commercial breadsticks with the main course. (Allow 4 per serving for the correct calorie count.)

Chocolate-Banana Parfait is a delicious dessert that can be made a day ahead. Spoon the mixture into pretty parfait glasses or dessert dishes to make the dessert look its best.

HOT SPICED WINE

4 whole cloves
1 (3-inch) stick cinnamon
1 cup unsweetened orange juice
½ cup water
3 thin slices lemon
3 thin slices orange
2½ cups Bordeaux or other dry red wine
4 (3-inch) sticks cinnamon (optional)

Tie cloves and 1 cinnamon stick in a cheesecloth bag; place in a large non-aluminum saucepan. Add orange juice and water; bring to a boil. Reduce heat, and simmer, uncovered, 10 minutes. Remove from heat; add lemon and orange slices. Cover and let stand 15 minutes.

Add wine to saucepan; bring to a simmer (do not boil). Strain into mugs, discarding spices and fruit slices. Garnish with additional cinnamon sticks as stirrers, if desired. Serve warm. Yield: 4 cups (128 calories per 1-cup serving).

PRO 0.7 / FAT 0.1 / CARB 7.1 / FIB 0.0 / CHOL 0 / SOD 15 / POT 308

SCALLOPS SAUTÉ

1 pound fresh sea scallops
Vegetable cooking spray
1 tablespoon margarine
½ pound fresh snow peas
2 stalks celery, diagonally sliced
2 tablespoons Chablis or other dry white wine
1 tablespoon plus 1½ teaspoons lemon juice
¾ teaspoon dried whole dillweed or 2 teaspoons chopped fresh dill
¼ teaspoon freshly ground pepper
1 tablespoon chopped fresh parsley

Rinse scallops in cold water; drain and set scallops aside.

Coat a large skillet with cooking spray; add margarine, and place over medium-high heat until margarine melts. Add snow peas and celery; sauté 1 minute or until crisp-tender. Remove vegetables from skillet, using a slotted spoon; set aside.

Add scallops, wine, lemon juice, dillweed, and pepper to skillet. Bring mixture to a boil. Cover; reduce heat, and simmer 5 to 6 minutes or until scallops are done. Add reserved vegetables, and cook just until thoroughly heated. Sprinkle with chopped fresh parsley, and serve with a slotted spoon. Yield: 4 servings (152 calories per serving).

PRO 19.5 / FAT 3.3 / CARB 9.3 / FIB 1.1 / CHOL 40 / SOD 345 / POT 667

Surprise your friends with this especially interesting menu which is easily managed on a tray.

ANGEL HAIR PASTA WITH PIMIENTO

1 (4-ounce) jar sliced pimiento, undrained
¼ pound fresh angel hair pasta
2 tablespoons grated Parmesan cheese
1 tablespoon chopped chives
1 teaspoon olive oil
Dash of garlic powder

Drain pimiento, reserving 1 teaspoon juice; set aside.

Break pasta into thirds; cook in boiling water in a large saucepan 30 seconds or until tender but still firm. Drain well; place in a warm serving bowl with pimiento, 1 teaspoon pimiento juice, and remaining ingredients. Toss well to coat before serving. Yield: 4 servings (129 calories per serving).

PRO 4.7 / FAT 2.3 / CARB 22.1 / FIB 1.1 / CHOL 2 / SOD 50 / POT 85

SPINACH-RADICCHIO SALAD

¼ pound radicchio, washed
½ pound fresh spinach, washed and torn
½ cup thinly sliced fresh mushrooms
1 sweet red pepper, seeded and thinly sliced
8 pitted ripe olives, sliced
¼ cup red wine vinegar
2 tablespoons lemon juice
1 tablespoon plus 1½ teaspoons olive oil
¼ teaspoon freshly ground pepper
1 tablespoon plus 1 teaspoon grated Parmesan cheese

Combine radicchio, spinach, mushrooms, red pepper, and olives in individual salad bowls. Cover; chill until serving time.

Combine vinegar, lemon juice, olive oil, and pepper in a glass jar; cover tightly, and shake vigorously. Pour mixture evenly over salads. Sprinkle each salad with 1 teaspoon Parmesan cheese before serving. Yield: 4 servings (95 calories per serving).

PRO 3.1 / FAT 7.6 / CARB 5.3 / FIB 2.8 / CHOL 1 / SOD 140 / POT 464

CHOCOLATE-BANANA PARFAIT

3 tablespoons sugar
3 tablespoons Dutch process or unsweetened cocoa
2 teaspoons unflavored gelatin
1 cup skim milk
2 eggs, separated
1 teaspoon vanilla extract
2 medium-size ripe bananas, mashed

Combine sugar, cocoa, and gelatin in the top of a double boiler; gradually stir in milk. Cook over boiling water until sugar and gelatin dissolve, stirring occasionally.

Beat egg yolks lightly. Gradually add one-fourth of hot gelatin mixture to egg yolks; stir egg yolk mixture into gelatin mixture. Cook, stirring constantly, 2 minutes or until mixture is slightly thickened.

Pour mixture into a large bowl, and stir in vanilla; let cool to room temperature, stirring occasionally.

Beat egg whites (at room temperature) in a medium bowl until stiff peaks form. Gently fold beaten whites into gelatin mixture. Stir in banana. Spoon mixture into 4 individual dessert dishes. Chill until set. Yield: 4 servings (173 calories per serving).

PRO 7.8 / FAT 4.1 / CARB 28.8 / FIB 1.0 / CHOL 138 / SOD 98 / POT 396

 Running strengthens bones without increasing arthritic risk, found researchers at Stanford University School of Medicine. Comparing 41 long-distance runners, who averaged running 26 miles per week, with 41 volunteers who ran a little or not at all, they found that the long-distance runners had 40% denser bones, but no greater signs of arthritis.

Elegant Holiday Feast

Cranberry Punch
Spinach-Stuffed Turkey
Breast
Orange-Honey Carrots
Endive Salad with Pimiento
Dressing
Cloverleaf Wheat Rolls
Rum Bavarian Cream with
Raspberry Sauce

Serves 10
Total calories per serving: 649

Unlike most holiday menus, the dishes in this feast are light. Total calories for the whole meal are under 650 per serving.

The star of the menu, Spinach-Stuffed Turkey Breast, takes a little extra time to prepare, but the resulting appearance and taste are well worth the effort.

Orange-glazed carrots, and a unique salad of endive and pimiento, plus Cloverleaf Wheat Rolls (1 roll per serving) round out the main course.

When it comes to desserts,

Spinach-Stuffed Turkey Breast is enhanced by delicious accompaniments.

Rum Bavarian Cream is a masterpiece. By preparing it with evaporated skim milk, fat and calories are kept low. A sparkling red Raspberry Sauce tops this delightful creation.

CRANBERRY PUNCH

1 (12-ounce) package fresh cranberries
1 quart unsweetened apple juice
2 (3-inch) sticks cinnamon
¾ teaspoon whole allspice
1½ cups club soda, chilled
½ cup unsweetened orange juice, chilled

Wash and sort cranberries; drain well. Combine cranberries, apple juice, cinnamon, and allspice in a small Dutch oven. Bring to a boil. Cover; reduce heat, and simmer 5 minutes or until berries pop. Line a colander with 2 layers of cheesecloth; strain mixture into a large bowl, discarding pulp and spices. Chill cranberry liquid.

Just before serving, combine cranberry liquid, club soda, and orange juice, stirring until blended. Pour into individual cups over crushed ice, if desired. Yield: 6 cups (58 calories per ½-cup serving).

PRO 0.2 / FAT 0.2 / CARB 14.7 / FIB 0.6 / CHOL 0 / SOD 3 / POT 140

SPINACH-STUFFED TURKEY BREAST

Vegetable cooking spray
1 medium onion, finely chopped
½ cup chopped fresh mushrooms
1 clove garlic, minced
1 (10-ounce) package frozen chopped spinach
1 cup soft whole wheat breadcrumbs
2 tablespoons grated Parmesan cheese
1 egg, beaten
½ teaspoon dried whole thyme
½ teaspoon pepper
1 (3½-pound) boneless turkey breast
¾ teaspoon rubbed sage
¼ teaspoon salt
¼ teaspoon white pepper
¼ teaspoon paprika
Fresh thyme sprigs

Coat a small skillet with cooking spray; place over medium-high heat until hot. Add onion, mushrooms, and garlic to skillet; sauté until tender, and set aside.

Cook spinach according to package directions, omitting salt. Drain well, and place on paper towels; squeeze until barely moist. Combine spinach, breadcrumbs, Parmesan, egg, thyme, and ½ teaspoon pepper in a small bowl; stir until well blended. Set mixture aside.

Lay turkey breast flat, skin side up, on waxed paper. Carefully slice away tendons, skin, and excess fat, keeping meat intact. Turn turkey breast over carefully to keep center of turkey breast attached. Beginning at center of turkey breast, slice horizontally through thickest part of each side of breast almost to outer edge; flip the cut pieces of breast fillets over and out to enlarge breast surface area and to make a more even thickness. To fill in shallow area between breast halves, slice meat horizontally from thickest parts of breast, and lay slices in shallow area. Pound breast to ½-inch thickness.

Spread reserved spinach mixture over turkey breast, leaving a ½-inch border at sides. Roll up turkey, jellyroll fashion, starting at long side. Sew up seams, using a needle and thread, or secure with wooden picks, if necessary.

Combine sage, salt, white pepper, and paprika in a small bowl; stir well, and rub over outer surface of turkey.

Insert meat thermometer into turkey breast, making sure end touches meat. Place in a browning bag prepared according to package directions. Place in a shallow roasting pan. Bake at 350° for 1 hour or until meat thermometer registers 170°. Transfer to a serving platter; let stand 15 minutes. Remove thread or wooden picks. Slice with an electric knife. Garnish with thyme sprigs before serving. Yield: 10 servings (194 calories per serving).

PRO 30.5 / FAT 4.3 / CARB 7.5 / FIB 1.3 / CHOL 91 / SOD 217 / POT 445

ORANGE-HONEY CARROTS

2½ pounds carrots, scraped and cut into julienne strips
1 teaspoon grated orange rind
½ cup unsweetened orange juice
2 tablespoons honey
½ teaspoon ground ginger

Combine all ingredients in a large saucepan; cover and cook over medium heat 5 minutes. Uncover and cook an additional 10 to 15 minutes, stirring frequently, until carrot strips are crisp-tender. Yield: 10 servings (68 calories per serving).

PRO 1.3 / FAT 0.2 / CARB 16.4 / FIB 1.7 / CHOL 0 / SOD 40 / POT 393

ENDIVE SALAD WITH PIMIENTO DRESSING

¼ cup red wine vinegar
1 (2-ounce) jar sliced pimiento, undrained
2 tablespoons olive or vegetable oil
1 tablespoon water
1 teaspoon sugar
¼ teaspoon pepper
1 (6-ounce) head oak leaf or Bibb lettuce
3 ounces curly leaf lettuce leaves
4 small heads Belgian endive, separated into leaves

Combine first 6 ingredients in a small jar. Cover tightly, and shake vigorously. Chill dressing thoroughly.

Arrange lettuce leaves on individual salad plates. Stir dressing, and drizzle 1 tablespoon over each salad before serving. Yield: 10 servings (35 calories per serving).

PRO 0.6 / FAT 2.8 / CARB 2.0 / FIB 0.4 / CHOL 0 / SOD 8 / POT 137

CLOVERLEAF WHEAT ROLLS

1 package dry yeast
¼ cup warm water (105° to 115°)
1 cup skim milk, scalded
2 tablespoons sugar
1 tablespoon plus 1½ teaspoons shortening
½ teaspoon salt
1½ cups whole wheat flour, divided
1 cup bread flour, divided
Vegetable cooking spray

Dissolve yeast in warm water in a small bowl, stirring well; let stand 5 minutes. Combine milk, sugar, shortening, and salt in a large bowl; stir until shortening melts. Cool to 105° to 115°. Add dissolved yeast, 1 cup whole wheat flour, and ½ cup bread flour to milk mixture. Beat at medium speed of an electric mixer 3 minutes. Stir in enough remaining whole wheat flour and bread flour to make a soft dough.

Turn dough out onto a lightly floured surface; knead 10 minutes or until smooth and elastic. Place dough in a medium bowl coated with cooking spray, turning to grease top. Cover and let rise in a warm place (85°), free from drafts, 1½ hours or until doubled in bulk. Punch dough down; let dough rest 20 minutes.

Lightly coat muffin pans with cooking spray. Shape dough into 1-inch balls; place 3 balls in each muffin cup. Cover and let rise in a warm place, 1 hour or until almost doubled in bulk. Bake at 400° for 15 minutes or until golden brown. Yield: 1 dozen (114 calories each).

PRO 4.1 / FAT 1.8 / CARB 21.1 / FIB 1.4 / CHOL 0 / SOD 109 / POT 112

RUM BAVARIAN CREAM WITH RASPBERRY SAUCE

½ cup sugar
2 envelopes unflavored gelatin
1½ cups skim milk
½ cup light rum
4 eggs, separated
¾ teaspoon vanilla extract
1 cup evaporated skim milk, partially frozen
3 tablespoons sifted powdered sugar
Vegetable cooking spray
Raspberry Sauce
Fresh raspberries (optional)
Fresh mint sprigs (optional)

Combine ½ cup sugar, gelatin, 1½ cups skim milk, and rum in top of a double boiler; stir well to blend. Place over boiling water; reduce heat, and cook over simmering water 10 minutes or until gelatin dissolves. Gradually add one-fourth of hot mixture to egg yolks; stir into remaining hot mixture. Cook over simmering water, stirring constantly, 3 minutes or until mixture coats the back of a metal spoon. Remove from heat, and stir in vanilla. Transfer to a large bowl and chill, stirring at 30 minute intervals, until mixture mounds when dropped from a spoon.

Combine evaporated skim milk and powdered sugar in a small bowl that has been chilled. Beat at high speed of an electric mixer with chilled mixer blades until soft peaks form; gently fold into custard mixture.

Beat egg whites (at room temperature) in a small bowl until stiff peaks form; gently fold into custard mixture. Spoon mixture into a 2-quart mold coated with cooking spray. Cover and chill overnight.

Unmold Bavarian Cream onto a serving platter, and spoon Raspberry Sauce over top. Garnish platter with fresh raspberries and mint sprigs, if desired. Serve chilled. Yield: 10 servings (180 calories per serving).

Raspberry Sauce:

1 (10-ounce) package frozen raspberries in light syrup, thawed
1 tablespoon cornstarch
¼ cup plus 2 tablespoons unsweetened orange juice

Process raspberries through a food mill. Combine raspberry liquid and cornstarch in a small saucepan, stirring until well blended. Bring to a boil. Cover; reduce heat, and cook, stirring constantly, until smooth and thickened. Remove from heat, and stir in orange juice. Cover and chill thoroughly. Yield: ¾ cup.

PRO 7.2 / FAT 2.4 / CARB 25.9 / FIB 0.6 / CHOL 111 / SOD 78 / POT 218

Reassure your waist-watching guests with the low-calorie count of Smoked Turkey Pâté and Basil-Yogurt Dip with fresh vegetables.

Open House, Light-Style

Spiced Pineapple Cooler
or
Rum Cocktail
or
Gin Fizz Cocktail
Shrimp Vinaigrette
Smoked Turkey Pâté
with Melba Toast
Rounds
Basil-Yogurt Dip with
assorted Fresh Vegetables
Miniature Strawberry
Cheesecakes

Serves 18
Total calories per serving: 401

An open house menu usually brings to mind high-calorie drinks, rich finger foods, and fatty pâtés. However, this one is for health-conscious folks who try to eat light but still enjoy good food. Even the spirited beverages have been lightened.

Shrimp Vinaigrette wrapped with thin strips of carrot and Smoked Turkey Pâté will add visual appeal to the hors d'oeuvre table. Serve the pâté with a tray of melba rounds (allow 6 per serving for correct calorie count).

"Yogurt cheese" replaces sour cream or cream cheese as the base for Basil-Yogurt Dip. Total menu calories include one carrot per serving as a dipper; however, we urge you to include a colorful variety of fresh vegetables for your guests to enjoy.

Offer a tray of Miniature Strawberry Cheesecakes to satisfy the universal sweet tooth. This recipe is made light by using plain low-fat yogurt and Neufchâtel cheese. At only 135 calories each, these are sure to be a hit.

SPICED PINEAPPLE COOLER

7¼ cups unsweetened pineapple juice
4 (3-inch) sticks cinnamon
20 whole cloves
3 cups unsweetened orange juice
4¾ cups club soda, chilled
Crushed ice
Orange rind strips (optional)

Combine first 3 ingredients in a large non-aluminum saucepan. Bring to a boil. Cover; reduce heat, and simmer 20 minutes. Cool and strain mixture, discarding whole spices. Stir in orange juice; cover and chill thoroughly.

Add club soda before serving. Pour over ice. Garnish with orange rind strips, if desired. Yield: 13½ cups (74 calories per ¾-cup serving).

PRO 0.7 / FAT 0.1 / CARB 18.0 / FIB 0.1 / CHOL 0 / SOD 1 / POT 227

RUM COCKTAIL

½ cup club soda, chilled
1 tablespoon lime juice
1 teaspoon sugar
1 tablespoon plus 1½ teaspoons light rum
½ cup crushed ice

Combine all ingredients in a tall glass; stir well, and serve immediately. Yield: 1 serving (71 calories per serving).

PRO 0.1 / FAT 0.0 / CARB 5.5 / FIB 0.0 / CHOL 0 / SOD 0 / POT 17

GIN FIZZ COCKTAIL

2 tablespoons gin
1 tablespoon lemon juice
½ cup club soda, chilled
Crushed ice
1 strip lemon rind (optional)

Combine first 3 ingredients in an 8-ounce glass; stir gently. Add crushed ice. Garnish with lemon rind, if desired. Yield: 1 serving (72 calories per serving).

PRO 0.1 / FAT 0.0 / CARB 1.3 / FIB 0.0 / CHOL 0 / SOD 0 / POT 20

SHRIMP VINAIGRETTE

1 quart water
36 medium-size fresh shrimp (1½ pounds)
1 cup water
¼ cup plus 2 tablespoons white wine vinegar
2 tablespoons Dijon mustard
¾ teaspoon dried whole dillweed
¼ teaspoon ground ginger
2 cloves garlic, minced
48 (4-inch) strips thinly cut carrot

Bring 1 quart water to a boil in a large saucepan. Add shrimp, and reduce heat; cook 3 to 4 minutes. (Do not boil.) Drain; rinse in cold water. Peel and devein shrimp.

Combine 1 cup water, vinegar, mustard, dillweed, ginger, and garlic. Pour over shrimp in a large shallow container. Cover and marinate in refrigerator at least 4 hours.

To serve, wrap each shrimp with a strip of carrot; secure with wooden picks, and place on a serving platter. Yield: 18 servings. Serving size: 2 shrimp (31 calories per serving).

PRO 5.2 / FAT 0.4 / CARB 1.1 / FIB 0.1 / CHOL 43 / SOD 91 / POT 82

 Don't underestimate the power of the lowly garlic. Not only is it a tasty alternative to salt, it has theraputic powers as well. Garlic lowers cholesterol levels in the blood, and in Japan, it is officially recognized as a treatment for high blood pressure.

To avoid garlic breath, eat lots of parsley; parsley's chlorophyll acts as a natural breath freshener.

SMOKED TURKEY PÂTÉ

1½ pounds boneless smoked turkey breast,
  cut into cubes
½ (8-ounce) package Neufchâtel cheese,
  softened
3 tablespoons Chablis or other dry white
  wine
2 teaspoons finely grated onion
¼ teaspoon white pepper
¼ teaspoon celery seeds
⅛ teaspoon ground nutmeg
Vegetable cooking spray
Fresh parsley sprigs (optional)
Pimiento strips (optional)
Olive slice (optional)

Position knife blade in food processor bowl;
add first 7 ingredients, and process until smooth.
Spoon into a 2½-cup mold coated with cooking
spray. Cover and chill overnight.

Unmold onto a serving plate, and garnish with
parsley sprigs, if desired. Arrange pimiento strips
and olive slice over top of pâté, if desired. Serve
with melba toast rounds. Yield: 2½ cups. Serving
size: 1 tablespoon (32 calories per serving).

PRO 4.8 / FAT 1.2 / CARB 0.1 / FIB 0.0 / CHOL 13 / SOD 21 / POT 51

BASIL-YOGURT DIP

2 (16-ounce) cartons plain low-fat yogurt
½ cup minced fresh basil leaves
¼ cup grated Parmesan cheese
1 small clove garlic, minced
⅛ teaspoon freshly ground pepper

Line a large colander or sieve with a double
layer of cheesecloth that has been rinsed out
and squeezed dry; allow cheesecloth to overlap
at the sides. Stir yogurt until smooth; pour into
colander. Fold edges of cheesecloth over to
cover yogurt. Place in a large bowl to drain;
refrigerate 8 hours or overnight. Remove yogurt
from colander; set aside. Discard liquid.

Combine drained yogurt and remaining ingredients in a small bowl. Cover and chill at least 4
hours. Serve with assorted raw vegetables. Yield:
1½ cups. Serving size: 1 tablespoon (31 calories
per serving).

PRO 2.5 / FAT 0.9 / CARB 3.4 / FIB 0.2 / CHOL 3 / SOD 42 / POT 128

MINIATURE STRAWBERRY CHEESECAKES

1 (8-ounce) carton plain low-fat yogurt
18 vanilla wafers
1½ (8-ounce) packages Neufchâtel cheese,
  softened
1 (8-ounce) carton commercial sour cream
2 eggs
½ cup sugar
2 teaspoons vanilla extract
¼ teaspoon almond extract
9 fresh strawberries, halved lengthwise

Line a colander with a double layer of
cheesecloth that has been rinsed out and
squeezed dry; allow cheesecloth to overlap at
the sides. Stir yogurt until smooth; pour into colander. Place in a large bowl to drain; refrigerate
8 hours or overnight. Remove yogurt from colander; set aside. Discard liquid.

Line 18 (2½-inch) muffin pans with 2 paper
baking cups each. Place 1 wafer in bottom of
each liner.

Beat Neufchâtel cheese in a medium bowl
until creamy. Add drained yogurt, sour cream,
eggs, sugar, and flavorings; beat until smooth.
Spoon mixture evenly into muffin cups.

Bake at 325° for 20 to 25 minutes or until set
but centers are still creamy (do not overbake).
Remove muffin pans from oven to wire racks to
cool to room temperature.

Remove cakes from pans, and refrigerate until
thoroughly chilled. Garnish each with a strawberry half. Yield: 18 servings (135 calories per
serving).

PRO 3.8 / FAT 8.8 / CARB 10.2 / FIB 0.0 / CHOL 52 / SOD 115 / POT 78

*Enlist the aid of your microwave
oven in preparing this Dinner with
Special Guests so you can relax and
enjoy visiting with your company.
The cornish hens are stuffed with
herb-flavored rice and served with
Shredded Yellow Squash. Adding
color and spice to the meal is the
Tomato-Vegetable Aspic, unmolded
onto a bed of cucumber slices
(menu begins on page 80).*

Microwave It Light

Breakfast In The Creole Tradition

The microwave oven is a great time-saver — especially when it comes to breakfasts on busy mornings. Creole Eggs, Glazed Apples, and Cinnamon Hot Chocolate are all excellent dishes for the microwave.

The apples are especially easy. Be sure to leave the peeling on so you'll benefit from the extra fiber. Microwave the apples for only 5 to 6 minutes, set the dish

Creole Eggs
Glazed Apples
Cinnamon Hot Chocolate

Serves 4
Total calories per serving: 393

aside, and keep them warm. Then start the Creole Eggs.

After adding eggs to the tomato sauce, pierce the egg yolks; this allows excess steam to

escape which would otherwise cause the yolk to burst. Cook the eggs just until the whites are partially set; the standing time allows the whites to continue cooking without overcooking the yolks. Before serving, spoon eggs and sauce over muffins.

Microwave the milk mixture for Cinnamon Hot Chocolate, then call everyone to the table for a Creole-style breakfast.

CREOLE EGGS

¼ pound sliced fresh mushrooms
¼ cup chopped onion
¼ cup chopped green pepper
¼ cup water
2 (8-ounce) cans no-salt-added tomato sauce
¼ teaspoon salt
¼ teaspoon dried whole thyme
¼ teaspoon pepper
4 eggs
2 English muffins, split and toasted

Combine first 4 ingredients in a 10- x 6- x 2-inch baking dish; cover with heavy-duty plastic wrap, and microwave at HIGH for 3 to 4 minutes, stirring after 2 minutes. Drain well, and return to baking dish.

Combine tomato sauce, salt, thyme, and pepper in a small bowl; stir well, and add to sautéed vegetables. Cover with heavy-duty plastic wrap, and microwave at HIGH for 4 to 5 minutes or until mixture comes to a boil.

Break eggs, one at a time, into a 6-ounce custard cup. Gently slip each egg into sauce mixture, and pierce yolk with a wooden pick. Cover with heavy-duty plastic wrap, and microwave at MEDIUM-HIGH (70% power) for 5 to 6 minutes or until egg whites are partially set. Let stand, covered, 3 to 4 minutes. Carefully spoon eggs and sauce over English muffins. Yield: 4 servings (217 calories per serving).

PRO 10.6 / FAT 6.4 / CARB 29.3 / FIB 1.6 / CHOL 274 / SOD 409 / POT 676

GLAZED APPLES

⅓ cup unsweetened orange juice
1 teaspoon cornstarch
¼ teaspoon ground allspice
2 medium cooking apples, cored and sliced

Combine orange juice, cornstarch, and allspice in a 2-quart casserole, stirring until smooth.

Stir in apples. Cover with a glass lid or heavy-duty plastic wrap. Microwave at HIGH for 5 to 6 minutes or until thickened and apples are tender, stirring once. Serve warm. Yield: 4 servings (46 calories per serving).

PRO 0.3 / FAT 0.4 / CARB 11.4 / FIB 1.5 / CHOL 0 / SOD 1 / POT 106

Enjoy Creole Eggs, Glazed Apples, and Cinnamon Hot Chocolate for a fast but delicious breakfast.

CINNAMON HOT CHOCOLATE

2 tablespoons sugar
3 tablespoons Dutch process cocoa
2 tablespoons instant coffee powder
½ teaspoon ground cinnamon
4 cups skim milk
4 (3-inch) sticks cinnamon

Combine sugar, cocoa, coffee powder, ground cinnamon, and milk in a large bowl, stirring well. Cover with heavy-duty plastic wrap and microwave at HIGH for 6 to 8 minutes or until thoroughly heated, stirring after 4 minutes. Ladle chocolate into mugs; add 1 stick cinnamon to each, and serve immediately. Yield: 4 cups (130 calories per 1-cup serving).

PRO 9.4 / FAT 1.5 / CARB 22.2 / FIB 0.8 / CHOL 5 / SOD 158 / POT 502

 If you're exercising to lose a little weight, carbohydrates are most important. New research from the University of Massachusetts and elsewhere reveals that a calorie of fat is more fattening than a calorie of carbohydrates!

Why? Two reasons. It takes energy for the body to convert carbohydrates into body fat, so less fat is stored. But it's easier for our bodies to convert dietary fat directly into body fat. Result: fewer fat calories are lost in conversion — and more winds up as stored fat.

Secondly, other researchers have found that eating carbohydrates actually stimulates metabolism. The faster our metabolism, the more calories we burn off. Exercise also speeds up metabolism, which is another reason why it's an essential component in a weight-control program.

Bite into Cheesy Pita Salad Sandwiches to taste the melted cheese inside.

Lunch In A Hurry

The clock says it's noon, and your stomach says it's time for lunch. Here's a hearty soup-and-sandwich combo that can be made in a jiffy — thanks to the microwave oven!

Start by assembling the Microwave Pear Crunch and dividing the mixture among 4 custard cups. Set the cups aside until you're ready to eat lunch.

Next, get your ingredients together for Quick Vegetable-Beef

Quick Vegetable-Beef Soup
Cheesy Pita Salad Sandwiches
Microwave Pear Crunch

Serves 4
Total calories per serving: 441

Soup. While it cooks the final 9 to 10 minutes, you can prepare the ingredients for Cheesy Pita

Salad Sandwiches.

The pita bread rounds filled with Swiss cheese are microwaved for only 30 to 60 seconds. After the cheese melts, the sandwiches are stuffed with a medley of freshly chopped vegetables and served.

Finally, while you're enjoying the soup and sandwich, pop the pear crunch into the microwave for just 6 minutes, and it will be ready to serve.

QUICK VEGETABLE-BEEF SOUP

½ pound ground chuck
¼ cup chopped green pepper
¼ cup chopped onion
1 (14½-ounce) can stewed tomatoes, undrained
1 cup frozen mixed vegetables
1 cup water
¼ teaspoon dried whole basil
⅛ teaspoon garlic powder
½ teaspoon freshly ground pepper

Combine ground chuck, green pepper, and chopped onion in a 2-quart casserole; cover with heavy-duty plastic wrap, and microwave at HIGH for 4 minutes or until meat is no longer pink, stirring after 2 minutes. Drain well in a colander, and pat dry with paper towels. Wipe casserole dry with a paper towel. Return drained meat mixture to casserole.

Add remaining ingredients to meat mixture. Cover and microwave at HIGH for 9 to 10 minutes, stirring every 3 minutes. Ladle into individual serving bowls; serve hot. Yield: 4 cups (163 calories per 1-cup serving).

PRO 14.4 / FAT 5.3 / CARB 14.3 / FIB 1.2 / CHOL 40 / SOD 304 / POT 551

CHEESY PITA SALAD SANDWICHES

1 medium tomato, coarsely chopped
½ cup sliced cucumber
½ cup alfalfa sprouts
¼ cup chopped sweet red pepper
¼ cup chopped green pepper
¼ cup chopped celery
⅛ teaspoon coarsely ground pepper
¼ cup reduced-calorie Italian salad dressing
½ cup (2 ounces) shredded Swiss cheese
2 (6-inch) whole wheat pita bread rounds, cut in half crosswise

Combine first 8 ingredients in a medium bowl; toss well. Set aside.

Divide Swiss cheese evenly into pocket bread halves; cover with paper towels, and microwave at MEDIUM-HIGH (70% power) for 30 seconds to 1 minute or until cheese melts.

Open sandwiches, and stuff with equal amounts of vegetable mixture. Serve immediately. Yield: 4 servings (139 calories per serving).

PRO 6.2 / FAT 4.6 / CARB 17.6 / FIB 1.9 / CHOL 14 / SOD 310 / POT 246

MICROWAVE PEAR CRUNCH

2 teaspoons slivered almonds
3 medium-size ripe pears, chopped
2 teaspoons lemon juice
¼ teaspoon almond extract
1 tablespoon all-purpose flour
1 tablespoon firmly packed dark brown sugar
1 tablespoon margarine
2 tablespoons regular oats, uncooked

Place almonds in a custard cup. Cover with heavy-duty plastic wrap, and microwave at HIGH for 1 to 1½ minutes or until almonds are toasted; set aside.

Combine pears, lemon juice, and almond extract in a medium bowl, tossing well. Divide among 4 (6-ounce) custard cups or individual baking dishes; set aside.

Combine flour and sugar; cut in margarine with a pastry blender until mixture resembles coarse meal. Stir in oats and reserved almonds. Divide among custard cups.

Microwave at HIGH for 6 minutes or until pears are tender, rotating cups after 3 minutes. Yield: 4 servings (139 calories per serving).

PRO 1.4 / FAT 4.3 / CARB 25.9 / FIB 3.5 / CHOL 0 / SOD 36 / POT 192

Italian-Style Chicken Dinner

Chicken Mozzarella
Spaghetti Squash with
Summer Vegetables
Wilted Lettuce Salad
Commercial Italian Bread
Pineapple Dessert Sauce
over Ice Milk

Serves 8
Total calories per serving: 593

Chicken Mozzarella combines conventional and microwave cooking. After dredging in a breadcrumb mixture, the chicken is browned in a skillet. The final cooking is completed in 10 minutes in the microwave oven.

Serve the chicken and squash with the salad and Italian bread (two ½-inch-thick slices per serving). The dessert is an easy microwave sauce over ice milk.

Enjoy the ease of preparing this microwave dinner.

CHICKEN MOZZARELLA

½ cup whole wheat breadcrumbs
¼ cup wheat germ
8 boneless chicken breast halves (2 pounds), skinned
½ cup skim milk
Vegetable cooking spray
2 teaspoons sesame or vegetable oil
1 (8-ounce) can no-salt-added tomato sauce
1 tablespoon minced fresh parsley
1 teaspoon dried whole basil
1 teaspoon dried whole oregano
⅛ teaspoon pepper
1 clove garlic, minced
½ cup (2 ounces) shredded mozzarella cheese

Combine breadcrumbs and wheat germ; set mixture aside.

Trim excess fat from chicken. Place chicken between 2 sheets of waxed paper, and flatten to ¼-inch thickness, using a meat mallet or rolling pin. Dip chicken in milk; dredge in breadcrumb mixture. Coat a large skillet wih cooking spray; add oil, and place over medium heat until hot. Add chicken to skillet, and cook until browned on both sides. Drain on paper towels.

Pour one-third of tomato sauce in bottom of a 13- x 9- x 2-inch baking dish coated with cooking spray. Place chicken breasts in dish. Pour half of remaining tomato sauce over chicken; sprinkle with parsley, basil, oregano, pepper, garlic, and cheese. Top with remaining tomato sauce.

Microwave, uncovered, at HIGH for 8 to 10 minutes; rearrange chicken after 4 minutes. Cover with heavy-duty plastic wrap, and let stand 2 minutes. Yield: 8 servings (209 calories per serving).

PRO 29.7 / FAT 6.3 / CARB 7.9 / FIB 0.7 / CHOL 76 / SOD 135 / POT 294

SPAGHETTI SQUASH WITH SUMMER VEGETABLES

1 (3-pound) spaghetti squash
¼ cup water
½ teaspoon chicken-flavored bouillon granules
¼ cup hot water
2 medium zucchini squash, sliced
1 medium-size yellow squash, sliced
1 medium carrot, scraped and grated
½ cup chopped green pepper
¼ cup sliced green onion
3 tablespoons chopped fresh parsley
3 tablespoons grated Parmesan cheese
¼ teaspoon pepper

Wash spaghetti squash, and cut in half lengthwise; remove and discard seeds. Place squash, cut side down, in a 13- x 9- x 2-inch baking dish; add ¼ cup water to dish. Cover with heavy-duty plastic wrap, and microwave at HIGH for 20 to 22 minutes, rotating and rearranging at 8 minute intervals. Let stand, covered, 5 minutes. Drain spaghetti squash, and cool. Remove 4 cups spaghetti-like strands using a fork, and set aside. Reserve any remaining spaghetti squash for use in other recipes.

Combine bouillon granules and ¼ cup hot water in a 12- x 8- x 2-inch baking dish; stir until bouillon granules are dissolved, and set aside. Combine zucchini squash, yellow squash, carrot, green pepper, green onion, and reserved 4 cups spaghetti squash in a large bowl. Toss well to combine ingredients, and transfer to baking dish containing bouillon mixture. Sprinkle chopped parsley, Parmesan cheese, and pepper evenly over squash mixture.

Cover vegetable mixture with heavy-duty plastic wrap, and microwave at HIGH for 6 to 8 minutes, stirring at 3 minute intervals. Let stand, covered, 2 minutes. Yield: 8 servings (47 calories per serving).

PRO 2.1 / FAT 0.9 / CARB 8.5 / FIB 1.8 / CHOL 1 / SOD 78 / POT 260

WILTED LETTUCE SALAD

4 cups torn red leaf lettuce
4 cups torn iceberg lettuce
¾ cup sliced fresh mushrooms
¾ cup oil-free Italian salad dressing

Combine first 3 ingredients in a large salad bowl; toss lightly, and set aside.

Place dressing in a 2-cup glass measure. Cover with heavy-duty plastic wrap, and microwave at HIGH for 1 to 2 minutes or until mixture boils. Immediately pour over lettuce mixture, tossing until well coated. Serve immediately. Yield: 8 servings (38 calories per serving).

PRO 0.8 / FAT 3.1 / CARB 2.2 / FIB 0.5 / CHOL 12 / SOD 31 / POT 87

PINEAPPLE DESSERT SAUCE OVER ICE MILK

1 (20-ounce) can unsweetened crushed pineapple, undrained
1 teaspoon cornstarch
1 tablespoon Grand Mariner or other orange-flavored liqueur
2 tablespoons flaked coconut
¼ teaspoon grated orange rind
1 quart vanilla ice milk

Drain pineapple, reserving ¼ cup juice in a 1-quart glass measure. Set pineapple aside.

Add cornstarch to reserved juice, stirring until well blended. Stir in pineapple and liqueur. Microwave at HIGH for 1 to 2 minutes; stir well, and microwave at HIGH for 3 to 4 minutes or until thickened. Stir in coconut and orange rind; to serve, spoon ¼-cup portions of warm pineapple sauce over ½-cup portions of ice milk. Yield: 8 servings (133 calories per serving).

PRO 2.8 / FAT 3.6 / CARB 22.6 / FIB 0.7 / CHOL 9 / SOD 57 / POT 199

Dinner With Special Guests

It's difficult to prepare dinner after a busy workday — especially if it's for a special occasion. This is another of the many times when a microwave oven can really come in handy.

Streamline the evening's work by preparing and refrigerating the salad a day ahead. You can even prepare the strawberry sauce for Dressed-Up Pears a day early since the sauce needs time to chill thoroughly and thicken.

Stuffed Cornish Hens are a

Stuffed Cornish Hens
Shredded Yellow Squash
Tomato-Vegetable Aspic
Commercial Whole Wheat
Rolls
Dressed-Up Pears

Serves 4
Total calories per serving: 542

great microwave entrée. Total microwaving time for the two hens is only about 19 minutes

compared to one hour or more in a conventional oven.

You can cook Shredded Yellow Squash during the standing time for the hens. It will be done in only two to three minutes and does not require standing time. It can be served directly from your microwave oven.

Even with commercial whole wheat rolls (allow 1 roll per serving), calories for this menu are under 550. What a treat for almost any special evening!

STUFFED CORNISH HENS

1½ cups cooked parboiled rice (cooked without salt or fat)
2 tablespoons minced fresh parsley
¼ teaspoon grated lemon rind
1 tablespoon plus 1½ teaspoons lemon juice
1 tablespoon plus 1½ teaspoons minced green onion
½ teaspoon chicken-flavored bouillon granules
¼ teaspoon celery seeds
¼ teaspoon pepper
2 (1¼-pound) Cornish hens, completely thawed and skinned
½ cup Chablis or other dry white wine
¼ cup water
1 teaspoon Worcestershire sauce
½ teaspoon poultry seasoning
¼ teaspoon chicken-flavored bouillon granules
¼ teaspoon paprika
⅛ teaspoon garlic powder

Combine first 8 ingredients in a medium bowl, stirring well; set aside.

Remove giblets from hens; reserve for use in another recipe. Rinse hens with cold water, and pat dry. Stuff hens with reserved rice mixture. Close cavities, and secure with wooden picks;

truss. Twist the wing tips behind backs.

Place hens, breast side down, on a microwave rack. Place rack inside a 13- x 9- x 2-inch baking dish.

Combine Chablis, water, Worcestershire sauce, poultry seasoning, ¼ teaspoon bouillon granules, paprika, and garlic powder in a small bowl; pour one-third of mixture over hens. Cover hens with a tent of waxed paper; microwave at HIGH for 10 minutes.

Turn hens breast side up, and give each a half turn on rack. Pour half of remaining wine mixture over hens. Cover with waxed paper tent; microwave at HIGH for 3 minutes.

Pour remaining wine mixture over hens; cover with waxed paper tent. Microwave at HIGH an additional 6 minutes or until juices run clear when hens are pierced with a fork between leg and thigh. Microwave meat thermometer should register 185° when inserted in meaty area between leg and thigh. Cover with aluminum foil, and let stand 4 to 6 minutes. Split hens in half with an electric knife and serve. Yield: 4 servings (272 calories per serving).

PRO 30.8 / FAT 7.7 / CARB 18.0 / FIB 0.7 / CHOL 90 / SOD 173 / POT 344

SHREDDED YELLOW SQUASH

1 pound yellow squash, coarsely shredded
1 teaspoon margarine
¼ teaspoon dried whole oregano
⅛ teaspoon garlic powder
⅛ teaspoon chicken-flavored bouillon granules

Combine all ingredients in a 1½-quart casserole. Cover and microwave at HIGH for 2 to 3 minutes or until vegetables are crisp-tender and mixture is thoroughly heated, stirring after 1½ minutes. Yield: 4 servings (32 calories per serving).

PRO 1.4 / FAT 1.2 / CARB 5.1 / FIB 1.3 / CHOL 0 / SOD 26 / POT 224

TOMATO-VEGETABLE ASPIC

2 cups tomato juice
2 sprigs fresh parsley
1 bay leaf
¼ teaspoon dried whole basil
1 envelope unflavored gelatin
¼ cup cold water
1 tablespoon lemon juice
2 to 3 drops of hot sauce
¼ cup finely chopped cucumber
¼ cup finely chopped celery
¼ cup finely chopped sweet red pepper
1 tablespoon minced onion
Vegetable cooking spray
24 very thin slices cucumber

Combine first 4 ingredients in a 2-quart mixing bowl. Cover with heavy-duty plastic wrap and microwave at HIGH for 5 to 6 minutes or until boiling; stir well. Cover and microwave at HIGH an additional 2 minutes. Strain, discarding herbs.

Soften gelatin in cold water 1 minute; add to hot tomato juice mixture, stirring until gelatin dissolves. Stir in lemon juice and hot sauce. Chill until the consistency of unbeaten egg white.

Stir in chopped cucumber, celery, sweet red pepper, and onion. Pour into 4 (6-ounce) molds coated with cooking spray. Chill overnight. Arrange cucumber slices on individual plates. Unmold chilled aspic onto cucumber slices to serve. Yield: 4 servings (37 calories per serving).

PRO 2.8 / FAT 0.2 / CARB 7.5 / FIB 1.1 / CHOL 0 / SOD 452 / POT 541

A hint of orange liqueur flavors Dressed-Up Pears.

DRESSED-UP PEARS

1 cup halved fresh strawberries
2 tablespoons water
2 teaspoons cornstarch
1 tablespoon Triple Sec or other orange-flavored liqueur
8 canned unsweetened pear halves, chilled
Zest of 1 orange

Place strawberries in container of an electric blender; process until pureed. Transfer strawberries to a small bowl, and set aside. Combine water and cornstarch in a small bowl, stirring until blended. Add cornstarch mixture and Triple Sec to strawberries; stir until well blended. Cover with heavy-duty plastic wrap, and microwave at HIGH for 4 to 5 minutes or until sauce thickens and boils. Chill thoroughly.

Divide sauce among 4 individual dessert plates with slightly raised edges; place two pear halves on top of sauce in each plate. Garnish with orange zest before serving. Yield: 4 servings (128 calories per serving).

PRO 0.9 / FAT 0.8 / CARB 30.3 / FIB 4.8 / CHOL 0 / SOD 0 / POT 268

Easy Dinner For Two

A special dinner for two can be ready in minutes with this microwave menu featuring Shish Kabobs. By marinating the lamb for at least 8 hours, you'll have an easier before-dinner schedule. What's more, the meat will be more tender and flavorful.

Our Curried Rice recipe takes only about 20 minutes to cook in the microwave, and the blend of flavors makes it especially good to serve with Shish Kabobs.

While the microwave oven can be used to cook rice, it is also a good way to reheat al-

Shish Kabobs
Curried Rice
Green Salad with
Dijon-Vinaigrette Dressing
Bananas Foster over
Ice Milk

Serves 2
Total calories per serving: 547

ready cooked rice. Just add a small amount of water to cold cooked rice; cover and microwave at MEDIUM-HIGH (70% power) until thoroughly heated.

The result is rice that looks and tastes freshly cooked.

Serve the Shish Kabobs and rice with a green salad (allow 1 cup salad greens per serving for correct calorie count) and 2 tablespoons Dijon-Vinaigrette Dressing per serving.

After you've enjoyed the main course, excuse yourself to whip up an elegant dessert for two — Bananas Foster over Ice Milk. It will take only a few minutes. As with many flaming desserts, this one is impressive in appearance as well as taste.

SHISH KABOBS

½ pound lean boneless lamb
2 tablespoons white wine vinegar
2 tablespoons water
1 tablespoon dry sherry
2 teaspoons chopped fresh parsley
1 teaspoon sugar
¾ teaspoon dried whole rosemary, crushed
⅛ teaspoon garlic salt
⅛ teaspoon pepper
1 small green pepper, seeded and cut into 8 pieces
6 medium-size fresh mushrooms
4 cherry tomatoes

Trim excess fat from lamb; cut into 1-inch cubes. Place lamb in a 9-inch square baking dish. Combine vinegar, water, sherry, parsley, sugar, rosemary, garlic salt, and pepper in a small bowl, stirring well; pour over lamb. Cover and refrigerate 8 hours or overnight.

Place green pepper on a microwave-safe plate; cover and microwave at HIGH for 2 minutes. Drain lamb, discarding marinade. Alternate lamb and vegetables on four 10-inch wooden skewers. Place skewers on a microwave-safe roasting rack; cover with waxed paper. Microwave at MEDIUM (50% power) for 5 to 6

minutes; rearrange kabobs. Microwave 5 to 6 minutes or until desired degree of doneness. Yield: 2 servings (216 calories per serving).

PRO 26.1 / FAT 6.8 / CARB 10.8 / FIB 1.7 / CHOL 85 / SOD 201 / POT 681

CURRIED RICE

⅓ cup water
2 tablespoons chopped green onion
⅓ cup water
⅓ cup parboiled rice, uncooked
½ teaspoon chicken-flavored bouillon granules
¼ teaspoon curry powder
Dash of pepper
Green onion fans (optional)

Combine ⅓ cup water and onion in a 1-quart casserole. Cover and microwave at HIGH for 1 to 1½ minutes. Add ⅓ cup water, rice, bouillon granules, curry powder, and pepper; stir well. Cover and microwave at HIGH for 2½ to 3 minutes or until water boils; stir well. Cover; microwave at MEDIUM (50% power) for 10 to 12 minutes or until liquid is absorbed. Let stand 4 minutes. Garnish with green onion fans, if desired. Yield: 2 servings (115 calories per serving).

PRO 2.3 / FAT 0.3 / CARB 25.9 / FIB 0.3 / CHOL 0 / SOD 99 / POT 74

DIJON-VINAIGRETTE DRESSING

1 tablespoon water
2 tablespoons white wine vinegar
1 tablespoon vegetable oil
2 teaspoons Dijon mustard
1 clove garlic, crushed
1 to 2 drops of hot sauce

Combine water, vinegar, vegetable oil, mustard, garlic, and hot sauce in a glass jar; cover tightly, and shake vigorously. Serve immediately over salad greens. Yield: ¼ cup (23 calories per tablespoon).

PRO 0.0 / FAT 2.4 / CARB 0.3 / FIB 0.0 / CHOL 0 / SOD 50 / POT 6

BANANAS FOSTER OVER ICE MILK

¼ cup unsweetened apple juice
1 tablespoon lemon juice
⅛ teaspoon ground cinnamon
1 medium banana, split lengthwise and halved
2 tablespoons light rum
1 cup vanilla ice milk

Combine apple juice, lemon juice, and cinnamon in a 1-quart casserole, stirring well. Add banana, turning to coat well. Cover with plastic wrap and microwave at HIGH for 1½ to 2 minutes or until thoroughly heated; set aside, and keep warm.

Place rum in a 1-cup glass measure, and microwave at HIGH for 15 to 30 seconds or until heated. (Do not boil.) Pour over banana, and ignite with a long match; baste banana with mixture until flames die. Serve immediately over ½-cup portions of ice milk. Yield: 2 servings (163 calorie per serving).

PRO 3.2 / FAT 3.1 / CARB 32.8 / FIB 0.9 / CHOL 9 / SOD 54 / POT 415

An elegant but easy dinner features Shish Kabobs, Curried Rice and salad with Dijon-Vinaigrette Dressing.

Family Celebration

Sole en Papillote with
Garden Vegetables
Herbed-Parsley Rice
Fruit Salad with
Citrus Dressing
Microwave Vanilla Custard

Serves 4
Total calories per serving: 512

Whatever the occasion, family celebrations deserve an extra-special meal. And when the entrée is prepared and served in parchment paper, the menu will certainly be special.

Remember when cooking the sole that the least amount of overcooking can result in dry, tough fish. Fish is done when it flakes easily. Be sure to allow for the extra cooking that occurs during standing time.

Save last-minute hassles by making both the salad dressing and custard a day ahead.

Celebrate any occasion by serving Sole en Papillote with Garden Vegetables.

SOLE EN PAPILLOTE WITH GARDEN VEGETABLES

1 tablespoon margarine
1 medium-size sweet red pepper, seeded and sliced
2 medium carrots, cut into julienne strips
⅔ cup fresh broccoli flowerets
1 clove garlic, crushed
4 sole fillets (1 pound)
2 teaspoons lemon juice
¼ teaspoon paprika
⅛ teaspoon pepper

Place margarine in a 1-quart casserole. Microwave at HIGH for 20 seconds or until melted.

Add red pepper, carrots, broccoli, and garlic; cover and microwave at HIGH for 2 to 3 minutes or until crisp tender, stirring once; set aside.

Cut four 16- x 12-inch pieces of parchment paper; cut each into a large heart shape. Fold in half; open out flat. Place a fillet along center fold on each sheet of paper. Sprinkle fillets with lemon juice, paprika, and pepper.

Top each fillet with equal amounts of vegetable mixture. Fold paper edges over to seal securely. Place 2 pouches on a microwave-safe 12-inch platter. Microwave at HIGH for 3 to 4 minutes; set aside. Repeat with remaining pouches. Transfer pouches to serving plates. Cut openings in pouches before serving. Yield: 4 servings (135 calories per serving).

PRO 20.0 / FAT 4.0 / CARB 4.3 / FIB 0.8 / CHOL 57 / SOD 136 / POT 553

HERBED-PARSLEY RICE

1 medium onion, chopped
2 tablespoons water
1 teaspoon margarine
1¼ cups hot water
⅔ cup parboiled rice, uncooked
1 teaspoon chicken-flavored bouillon granules
¼ teaspoon dried whole basil
¼ teaspoon dried whole thyme
¼ teaspoon pepper
½ cup chopped fresh parsley

Combine onion, 2 tablespoons water, and margarine in a 2-quart casserole. Cover with heavy-duty plastic wrap, and microwave at HIGH for 1½ to 2 minutes or until onion is tender. Add hot water, rice, bouillon granules, basil, thyme, and pepper; stir well. Cover with heavy-duty plastic wrap, and microwave at HIGH for 4 to 5 minutes. Reduce power to MEDIUM (50% power), and microwave an additional 12 to 14 minutes or until liquid is absorbed. Stir in parsley; let stand, covered, 8 minutes. Fluff with a fork, and serve immediately. Yield: 4 servings (145 calories per serving).

PRO 2.9 / FAT 1.3 / CARB 29.9 / FIB 1.2 / CHOL 0 / SOD 112 / POT 127

FRUIT SALAD WITH CITRUS DRESSING

1 (8-ounce) can unsweetened pineapple tidbits, undrained
1½ teaspoons cornstarch
¼ cup unsweetened orange juice
¼ teaspoon grated lemon rind
Dash of ground cinnamon
1 cup seedless red grapes, halved
1 medium banana, peeled and sliced
1 kiwifruit, peeled and sliced
1 teaspoon lemon juice
4 orange cups
Bibb lettuce leaves

Drain pineapple, reserving ¼ cup juice in a 2-cup glass measure. Set pineapple aside.

Add cornstarch to reserved juice, stirring until well blended. Stir in orange juice, lemon rind, and cinnamon. Microwave at HIGH for 1½ to 2 minutes or until mixture begins to boil; stir. Microwave at HIGH for an additional 30 seconds to 1 minute or until thickened. Cool; cover and chill thoroughly.

Combine reserved pineapple, grapes, banana, kiwifruit, and lemon juice in a medium bowl; toss gently. Spoon equal amounts of fruit into orange cups; place each cup on a lettuce leaf. Serve with 2 tablespoons dressing per serving. Yield: 4 servings (104 calories per serving).

PRO 1.3 / FAT 0.6 / CARB 25.7 / FIB 2.5 / CHOL 0 / SOD 4 / POT 380

 Microwave cooking saves nutrients. In one study, broccoli cooked six minutes in a microwave had 116 mg of vitamin C. When boiled, the broccoli had only 77 mg.

MICROWAVE VANILLA CUSTARD

2 cups skim milk
3 tablespoons sugar
1 egg, beaten
1 tablespoon sugar
1 tablespoon plus 1 teaspoon cornstarch
½ teaspoon vanilla extract
4 fresh strawberries

Combine milk and 3 tablespoons sugar in a 2-quart glass measure. Microwave at HIGH for 5 to 6 minutes or just until mixture begins to boil, stirring at 3 minute intervals.

Combine egg and 1 tablespoon sugar in a small bowl; beat well, using a wire whisk. Gradually add cornstarch, beating constantly. Gradually stir one-fourth of hot milk mixture into egg mixture; add to remaining milk mixture, stirring constantly. Microwave at HIGH for 2 to 3 minutes or until thickened, stirring every 30 seconds. Remove from microwave, and stir 3 minutes. Stir in vanilla.

Spoon mixture into 4 dessert dishes; chill until set. Garnish each with a strawberry. Yield: 4 servings (128 calories per serving)

PRO 5.8 / FAT 1.7 / CARB 22.2 / FIB 0.3 / CHOL 81 / SOD 81 / POT 243

Light Recipes

Achieving a healthful style of eating doesn't mean you have to throw away your cookbooks and treasured family recipes or ignore your acquired food preferences and habits. Nor does it mean you must clean out your kitchen pantry and freezer, spend a bundle of money to restock, and shop only in health food stores, thus making the quest for nutritional well-being a full time pursuit and occupation. It isn't nearly as complicated and time consuming as that. Slow down, take stock of your present food habits, and be realistic. Move ahead by incorporating sound nutritional knowledge into what you're already doing. Aim for gradual change in the areas where you find change to be necessary. The key is to begin adapting favorite recipes and food preferences to the techniques and ingredients you know to be nutritionally sound and sensible.

If you have a taste for something, go ahead and satisfy your craving, but before you prepare the recipe, take the time to step back and look at it from a nutritional point of view. Keep in mind practices you know will improve your nutritional well-being, such as lowering the amount of fat, sodium, and sugar you are consuming. Ask yourself if it's really necessary to sauté the onions and garlic in butter, or will vegetable cooking spray do just as well. Do the muffins you plan to make really need that much sugar, or will less sugar and some raisins do the trick?

Any food contains basic nutritional elements, whether they are calories, fats, carbohydrates, proteins, vitamins, minerals, and/or trace elements. In general, the less we do to refine or alter a food, the

A sampling of light recipes that look as delicious as they are nutritious: Special Romaine Salad (page 165), Stuffed Eggplant Rolls (page 126), and Peach Meringues with Fresh Strawberry Sauce (page 212).

more nutrients we will obtain from it. When looking at recipes, remember that recipes which use fresh ingredients and simple cooking techniques will provide more nutritional benefits than recipes which call for highly refined foods and more lengthy cooking techniques.

As you begin looking at recipes with a "nutritional eye," you'll find yourself making many ingredient substitutions that will greatly increase the nutritional impact and food value of the recipes without sacrificing great taste and eye appeal. The more you think along these lines, the easier it will become to lighten recipes. Instead of a bagel with cream cheese for breakfast, think whole wheat bagel with light cream cheese or Neufchâtel cheese. Top your pizza with part-skim mozzarella cheese instead of whole milk mozzarella, and make your pizza crust with whole wheat flour. If a recipe calls for a high-fat dairy product such as whole milk or half-and-half, try substituting skim milk. Use plain low-fat yogurt instead of sour cream. If you are planning chili for supper tonight, try substituting ground turkey for the ground beef, and zip it up with additional ground cumin and oregano instead of salt.

Creating a light recipe doesn't necessarily mean giving up on convenience foods. Today, available in the marketplace are reduced-calorie salad dressings made with decreased amounts of oil, as well as low-sugar fruit spreads, reduced-calorie mayonnaises, low-fat cheeses, and many other convenience items that will help you make gradual changes in your diet. Use *Cooking Light* recipes as a reliable reference when you want to lighten a recipe of your own. All the little changes you make in your diet now may pay off in big health benefits later.

It's all a matter of making the right choices. *Cooking Light* delivers a wealth of recipes to get you started down the right path. If you make healthy eating part of your lifestyle, there will rarely be an occasion in which you'll feel you can't eat as healthfully as you'd like. Entertaining a special group of people? Start off with our Cassis Spritzers and Caviar-Stuffed Pea Pods, Chicken Pâté, or creamy Artichoke Bisque. For an impressive entrée, serve Roast Beef With Garlic-Basil Purée or Chicken Breasts Stuffed With Herb Cheese. Add Buttermilk Wheat Rolls or Pecan-Brown Rice Pilaf to round out the meal. For an elegant finale, serve Peach Meringues With Fresh Strawberry Sauce or a simple, richly flavored cup of Cardamom Coffee. Your guests will hardly feel cheated!

Cooking Light has recipes to suit every taste. A light recipe does not mean a recipe that is bland and boring. In the mood for something spicy? Try Creole-Blackened Bass or Chicken Fajitas. Something more oriental in mind? How about Egg Drop Soup and Stir-Fried Beef and Broccoli. Try getting your family involved in choosing recipes and planning menus too. By showing them that nutritious can be delicious, you'll be encouraging a healthy pattern of eating for the whole family.

Put your guests in a party mood with Cassis Spritzers (page 96) and Caviar-Stuffed Pea Pods (page 90).

Appetizers & Beverages

ARTICHOKE NIBBLES

Vegetable cooking spray
1 teaspoon margarine
2 tablespoons minced onion
1 clove garlic, minced
1 (14-ounce) can artichoke hearts, drained
   and finely chopped
3 eggs, beaten
¾ cup (3 ounces) shredded extra sharp
   Cheddar cheese
¾ cup (3 ounces) shredded Monterey Jack
   cheese
3 tablespoons whole wheat flour
¼ teaspoon dried whole tarragon,
   crushed
¼ teaspoon dried whole chervil,
   crushed
⅛ teaspoon curry powder

Coat a medium skillet with cooking spray; add margarine, and place over medium heat until melted. Add onion and garlic; sauté until tender.

Combine onion mixture, artichoke hearts, eggs, cheese, flour, tarragon, chervil, and curry powder, mixing well. Pour mixture into an 8-inch square baking pan coated with cooking spray. Bake at 325° for 25 minutes or until set. Cut into squares, and serve hot. Yield: 25 appetizers. Serving size: 1 square (47 calories each).

PRO 2.9 / FAT 3.1 / CARB 2.0 / FIB 0.2 / CHOL 41 / SOD 58 / POT 47

MARINATED JICAMA

1 (1-pound) jicama, peeled and cut into
   3- x ½-inch strips
¼ cup vinegar
2 tablespoons vegetable oil
¼ teaspoon chili powder
¼ teaspoon red pepper
1 clove garlic, peeled and halved

Combine all ingredients in a shallow dish. Cover and refrigerate 3 to 4 hours. Drain, discarding garlic, and serve. Yield: 80 appetizers. Serving size: 1 strip (6 calories each).

PRO 0.1 / FAT 0.4 / CARB 0.6 / FIB 0.0 / CHOL 0 / SOD 0 / POT 10

CAVIAR-STUFFED PEA PODS

2 ounces Neufchâtel cheese, softened
¼ cup low-fat cottage cheese
½ teaspoon grated lemon rind
1½ teaspoons lemon juice
16 large, fresh snow pea pods
2 teaspoons red, black, or golden caviar
Leaf lettuce (optional)

Combine first 4 ingredients in container of an electric blender; process until smooth.

String pea pods, and carefully open curved side of pod. Remove peas from each pod. Pipe 1 teaspoon cheese mixture into each pod. Place ⅛ teaspoon caviar on top of cheese mixture. Arrange pods on a lettuce-lined serving plate, if desired. Chill thoroughly before serving. Yield: 16 appetizers. Serving size: 1 pod (20 calories each).

PRO 1.4 / FAT 1.3 / CARB 0.8 / FIB 0.1 / CHOL 7 / SOD 52 / POT 23

Pleasing appetizers prepare both the body and mind for a coming feast. The very act of tasting, smelling, even thinking about food stimulates appetite and prepares us for digestion, scientists find. Our mouths produce saliva; our stomachs, enzymes. And our brains get the message that a taste treat is on the way.

Novelty is perhaps the best appetizer. We crave variety, finds Johns Hopkins University psychologist Dr. Barbara Rolls. Give someone as much of one food as desired, and he'll eat a certain amount and no more.

But then surprise him with a new food — a sweet one after a sour one, even one that's different in color or size — and suddenly he's hungry again. It's the "always room for dessert" syndrome, scientifically demonstrated.

So if you have company, prepare a nice varied selection of low-calorie appetizers such as those presented here. A pleasing variety will prepare your guests' minds and bodies for the main course.— without filling them up.

If you're on a diet, on the other hand, try not to have too many different kinds of snack foods around. There's no reason to tempt an appetite when you're trying to control it.

PINEAPPLE-CARROT ROUNDS

1 cup grated carrot
1 (8-ounce) can unsweetened crushed pineapple, drained
3 tablespoons reduced-calorie mayonnaise
⅛ teaspoon ground cardamom
28 melba toast rounds

Combine first 4 ingredients in a medium bowl; mix well. Cover and refrigerate until thoroughly chilled. Spread mixture on melba toast rounds; place on a serving plate. Serve immediately. Yield: 28 appetizers. Serving size: 1 melba toast round (27 calories each).

PRO 0.6 / FAT 0.4 / CARB 4.4 / FIB 0.2 / CHOL 1 / SOD 49 / POT 31

ZUCCHINI TEA SANDWICHES

1 medium zucchini squash, peeled and cut into 36 (⅛-inch-thick) slices
½ cup vinegar
½ cup water
6 ice cubes
¼ cup part-skim ricotta cheese
2 tablespoons reduced-calorie mayonnaise
1 teaspoon minced onion
½ teaspoon minced fresh watercress
⅛ teaspoon dried whole chervil
⅛ teaspoon dried whole savory
1 teaspoon lemon juice
Dash of hot sauce
9 slices thinly-sliced whole wheat bread
Pimiento slices (optional)

Combine first 4 ingredients in a medium bowl. Let stand 30 minutes; drain well. Discard liquid. Set zucchini aside.

Combine ricotta cheese, mayonnaise, onion, watercress, chervil, savory, lemon juice, and hot sauce in a small bowl. Cover and chill.

Remove crust from bread. Cut four 1½-inch rounds from each bread slice. Spread ½ teaspoon ricotta mixture on bread rounds. Top each with a zucchini slice; garnish with pimiento slices, if desired. Yield: 3 dozen appetizers. Serving size: 1 sandwich (10 calories each).

PRO 0.4 / FAT 0.4 / CARB 1.1 / FIB 0.1 / CHOL 1 / SOD 18 / POT 19

SPINACH-WRAPPED CHICKEN WITH ORIENTAL DIP

4 chicken breast halves (1 pound 10 ounces), skinned
1¾ cups water
2 tablespoons reduced-sodium soy sauce
1 tablespoon Worcestershire sauce
9 ounces large fresh spinach leaves, trimmed and washed
Leaf lettuce (optional)
Oriental Dip

Trim excess fat from chicken. Combine water, soy sauce, and Worcestershire sauce in a large skillet. Bring to a boil, and add chicken. Cover; reduce heat, and simmer 20 minutes or until chicken is tender. Remove chicken from skillet, and cool; discard liquid. Bone chicken; cut meat into 1-inch cubes.

Pick out largest spinach leaves; place a few at a time on a steaming rack over boiling water. Cover and steam 1 minute or until leaves are slightly wilted.

Place 1 cube of chicken on each spinach leaf. Roll over once; fold leaf in on both sides, and continue rolling around chicken cube. Secure end of leaf with a wooden pick. Repeat procedure with remaining chicken cubes and spinach leaves.

Cover and chill thoroughly. Serve chicken on a lettuce-lined serving plate, if desired; serve with Oriental Dip. Yield: 50 appetizers. Serving size: 1 appetizer plus 2 teaspoons sauce (22 calories each).

Oriental Dip:

½ cup plain low-fat yogurt
½ cup reduced-calorie mayonnaise
1 tablespoon sesame seeds, toasted
2 tablespoons reduced-sodium soy sauce
2 tablespoons Worcestershire sauce
1½ teaspoons ground ginger

Combine all ingredients in a small bowl, and mix well. Cover mixture and refrigerate at least 4 hours. Yield: about 2¼ cups. Serving size: 2 teaspoons.

PRO 2.6 / FAT 1.0 / CARB 0.8 / FIB 0.2 / CHOL 7 / SOD 80 / POT 58

MARINATED SHRIMP

3 cups water
1 pound fresh medium shrimp, uncooked
1 medium onion, finely chopped
1 clove garlic, minced
¼ cup plus 2 tablespoons reduced-calorie Italian salad dressing
3 tablespoons Chablis or other dry white wine
3 tablespoons lemon juice
¼ teaspoon pepper
¼ teaspoon hot sauce

Bring water to a boil; add shrimp, and cook 3 minutes. Drain well, and chill. Peel and devein shrimp; set aside.

Combine remaining ingredients in a large bowl; mix well. Add shrimp to marinade, tossing gently. Cover and refrigerate 8 hours or overnight, stirring occasionally.

Remove shrimp from marinade; transfer to a serving bowl, and serve with cocktail picks. Yield: 60 appetizers. Serving size: 1 shrimp (7 calories each).

PRO 1.1 / FAT 0.1 / CARB 0.5 / FIB 0.0 / CHOL 9 / SOD 22 / POT 18

AMARETTO CREAM DIP

⅔ cup low-fat cottage cheese
3 tablespoons sifted powdered sugar
3 tablespoons Neufchâtel cheese, softened
1 tablespoon Amaretto or other almond-flavored liqueur

Combine all ingredients in container of an electric blender; process until smooth. Spoon into a small bowl; cover and chill thoroughly. Serve with fresh fruit dippers. Yield: ¾ cup. Serving size: 1 tablespoon (32 calories per serving).

PRO 2.1 / FAT 1.1 / CARB 2.8 / FIB 0.0 / CHOL 4 / SOD 65 / POT 17

 Running isn't the only sport that lifts depression. Weight lifting can be just as effective, find researchers at the University of Rochester Medical Center in New York.

In a study of 40 depressed women divided into 3 groups, 1 group ran, 1 group lifted weights, and 1 group remained sedentary. The 2 active groups exercised for 30 minutes, 3 times a week, and both groups reported a definite "lifting of the blues." Researchers concluded that it was not just fitness that lifted spirits as much as doing something to help oneself.

HERB CHEESE DIP

1 (8-ounce) package Neufchâtel cheese, softened
⅔ cup low-fat cottage cheese
1 tablespoon finely chopped fresh parsley
1 clove garlic, minced
2 teaspoons skim milk
1 teaspoon red wine vinegar
½ teaspoon Worcestershire sauce
⅛ teaspoon dried whole marjoram
⅛ teaspoon dried whole thyme
⅛ teaspoon dried whole basil
⅛ teaspoon ground savory

Combine all ingredients in a small bowl; beat at medium speed of an electric mixer until fluffy. Cover and chill thoroughly. Transfer to a serving bowl; serve with melba toast rounds or unsalted crackers. Yield: 1⅔ cups. Serving size: 1 tablespoon (27 calories per serving).

PRO 1.6 / FAT 2.1 / CARB 0.5 / FIB 0.0 / CHOL 7 / SOD 57 / POT 18

CHUNKY FRUIT DIP

1 cup low-fat cottage cheese
½ (8-ounce) package Neufchâtel cheese, softened
2 tablespoons skim milk
½ cup finely chopped apple
2 teaspoons lemon juice
¼ cup golden raisins, chopped
½ teaspoon grated orange rind

Position knife blade in food processor bowl; add first 3 ingredients, and process until smooth. Set aside.

Combine apple and lemon juice in a medium bowl, tossing gently. Add cheese mixture and remaining ingredients to apple mixture; stir well. Cover and chill thoroughly.

Serve chilled mixture as a dip with fresh fruit. Yield: 2 cups. Serving size: 1 tablespoon (21 calories per serving).

PRO 1.4 / FAT 1.0 / CARB 1.7 / FIB 0.1 / CHOL 3 / SOD 43 / POT 24

CURRY VEGETABLE DIP

1 (8-ounce) package Neufchâtel cheese, softened
½ cup low-fat cottage cheese
3 tablespoons skim milk
2 teaspoons curry powder
2 teaspoons Worcestershire sauce
2 teaspoons finely grated onion
Dash of hot sauce

Position knife blade in food processor bowl; add all ingredients, and process until smooth. Spoon dip into a bowl; cover and chill thoroughly. Serve with fresh raw vegetables. Yield: 2 cups. Serving size: 1 tablespoon (23 calories per serving).

PRO 1.3 / FAT 1.8 / CARB 0.6 / FIB 0.0 / CHOL 6 / SOD 47 / POT 19

PICO DE GALLO WITH CHIPS

3 medium tomatoes, peeled and finely chopped
2 green onions, finely chopped
1 (4-ounce) can chopped green chiles, drained
2 tablespoons chopped fresh cilantro
1 tablespoon chopped jalapeño pepper
1 teaspoon vinegar
1 teaspoon vegetable oil
Crispy Chips

Combine all ingredients except Crispy Chips in a medium bowl; mix well. Cover and chill thoroughly. Serve with Crispy Chips. Yield: 3 cups. Serving size: 1 chip plus 2 teaspoons sauce (17 calories per serving).

Crispy Chips:

8 (6-inch) corn tortillas
2 teaspoons vegetable oil
1 teaspoon chili powder

Lightly brush one side of each tortilla with oil; sprinkle with chili powder. Stack tortillas, and cut into 8 wedges. Arrange wedges in a single layer on baking sheets; bake at 400° for 10 minutes or until wedges are crisp and lightly browned. Serve warm or cool. Store in an airtight container. Yield: 64 chips.

PRO 0.5 / FAT 0.4 / CARB 3.1 / FIB 0.1 / CHOL 0 / SOD 13 / POT 17

TORTELLINI WITH BASIL SAUCE

1 (9-ounce) package refrigerated spinach tortellini with chicken and prosciutto
1 (8-ounce) can tomato sauce
1 clove garlic, pressed
½ teaspoon dried whole basil, crushed
¼ teaspoon dried whole oregano, crushed
1 tablespoon grated Parmesan cheese

Cook tortellini according to package directions, omitting salt. Drain and keep warm.
Combine tomato sauce, garlic, basil, and oregano in a small saucepan; bring to a boil. Cover; reduce heat, and simmer 5 minutes. Stir in Parmesan cheese. Transfer sauce to a serving bowl, and surround with tortellini to dip in warm sauce. Yield: 35 appetizers. Serving size: 1 tortellini (16 calories per serving).

PRO 1.1 / FAT 0.6 / CARB 1.7 / FIB 0.0 / CHOL 8 / SOD 71 / POT 49

CHICKEN PÂTÉ

1½ cups finely chopped cooked chicken breast
½ (8-ounce) package Neufchâtel cheese, softened
3 tablespoons chopped onion
2 tablespoons dry sherry
2 tablespoons reduced-calorie mayonnaise
2 teaspoons lemon juice
¼ teaspoon hot sauce
⅛ teaspoon ground nutmeg
Vegetable cooking spray
Paprika
Fresh parsley sprigs (optional)

Combine chicken, Neufchâtel, onion, sherry, mayonnaise, lemon juice, hot sauce, and nutmeg in container of an electric blender; process until smooth. Transfer mixture to a 2-cup mold coated with cooking spray. Cover mixture, and chill overnight.
Unmold onto a serving plate; sprinkle with paprika. Garnish with parsley sprigs, if desired. Serve with melba toast rounds or unsalted crackers. Yield: 1¾ cups. Serving size: 1 tablespoon (28 calories per serving).

PRO 2.8 / FAT 1.5 / CARB 0.3 / FIB 0.0 / CHOL 10 / SOD 30 / POT 27

CARAWAY RYE WAFERS

¾ cup all-purpose flour
½ cup rye flour
¼ cup whole wheat flour
1 tablespoon sugar
¼ teaspoon baking powder
¼ teaspoon salt
1 teaspoon caraway seeds
¼ cup margarine
¼ cup cold water
Vegetable cooking spray
1 tablespoon skim milk
1 tablespoon caraway seeds

Combine first 7 ingredients in a medium bowl. Cut in margarine with a pastry blender until mixture resembles coarse meal. Sprinkle water over flour mixture, stirring until dry ingredients are moistened.

Turn dough out onto a lightly floured surface; knead 4 to 5 times. Roll dough to ⅛-inch thickness; cut into rounds with a 2-inch cookie cutter. Place on baking sheets coated with cooking spray. Brush each wafer with milk; sprinkle evenly with 1 tablespoon caraway seeds. Bake at 375° for 10 to 12 minutes or until edges of wafers are lightly browned. Yield: 44 appetizers. Serving size: 1 wafer (25 calories each).

PRO 0.5 / FAT 1.1 / CARB 3.4 / FIB 0.2 / CHOL 0 / SOD 28 / POT 9

LEMON-MINT TEA

1 cup boiling water
6 lemon-flavored tea bags
2 tablespoons fresh mint leaves, crushed
1 (6-ounce) can frozen lemonade concentrate, thawed and undiluted
1 cup freshly squeezed orange juice
7½ cups cold water
Fresh mint sprigs

Combine first 3 ingredients in a large container; cover and steep 5 minutes. Discard tea bags. Stir in lemonade concentrate, orange juice, and cold water. Cover and chill overnight; strain before serving. Pour over ice cubes in serving glasses; garnish with mint sprigs. Yield: 10 cups (45 calories per 1-cup serving).

PRO 0.2 / FAT 0.0 / CARB 11.4 / FIB 0.0 / CHOL 0 / SOD 1 / POT 62

MINTY GRAPE TEA

1½ cups boiling water
3 lemon-flavored, caffeine-free tea bags
2 tablespoons fresh mint leaves
1 (24-ounce) bottle unsweetened grape juice, chilled
1½ cups club soda, chilled
6 sprigs fresh mint

Combine boiling water, tea bags, and mint leaves; cover and steep 7 minutes. Discard tea bags and mint; cover and chill.

Add grape juice and club soda to tea just before serving. Pour over ice cubes in serving glasses, and garnish with fresh mint sprigs. Serve immediately. Yield: 6 cups (81 calories per 1-cup serving).

PRO 0.5 / FAT 0.0 / CARB 20.0 / FIB 0.0 / CHOL 0 / SOD 4 / POT 150

ORANGE-CINNAMON COFFEE

1 medium orange, thinly sliced
2 (3-inch) sticks cinnamon
½ cup ground coffee
6 orange rind twists
6 (3-inch) sticks cinnamon

Combine first 3 ingredients in basket of a drip coffee maker or electric percolator. Fill pot to the 6-cup mark with water. Prepare coffee according to manufacturer's instructions. Place an orange rind twist and a cinnamon stick in each cup. Pour coffee into each cup. Serve hot. Yield: 6 cups (14 calories per 1-cup serving).

PRO 0.2 / FAT 0.1 / CARB 3.3 / FIB 0.6 / CHOL 0 / SOD 0 / POT 189

CARDAMOM COFFEE

2 quarts freshly brewed hot coffee
12 cardamom seeds, crushed
1 medium orange, thinly sliced and seeded

Combine all ingredients in a small Dutch oven; bring to a boil. Cover; reduce heat, and simmer 5 minutes. Strain and serve hot. Yield: 2 quarts (17 calories per 1-cup serving).

PRO 0.3 / FAT 0.1 / CARB 3.6 / FIB 0.6 / CHOL 0 / SOD 3 / POT 146

GAZPACHO FIZZ

1 (15-ounce) can no-salt-added tomato sauce
1½ cups tomato juice
2 stalks celery, chopped
2 green onions, chopped
1 medium cucumber, peeled and seeded
2 tablespoons lime juice
¼ teaspoon hot sauce
1 (10-ounce) bottle club soda, chilled

Combine first 7 ingredients in container of an electric blender; process until smooth. Cover and chill thoroughly. Stir in club soda just before serving. Pour into glasses. Yield: 6 cups (47 calories per 1-cup serving).

PRO 1.6 / FAT 0.1 / CARB 11.1 / FIB 1.7 / CHOL 0 / SOD 252 / POT 681

STRAWBERRY-CIDER COOLER

2 cups fresh strawberries, washed and hulled
2 cups sparkling cider, chilled
1 cup club soda, chilled

Place strawberries in container of an electric blender; process until smooth. Press strawberries through a sieve lined with two layers of cheesecloth; lift cheesecloth from sieve, and squeeze to drain remaining juice. Discard seeds. Transfer juice to a large pitcher; stir in cider and soda. Yield: 4 cups (95 calories per 1-cup serving).

PRO 0.1 / FAT 0.1 / CARB 23.5 / FIB 0.3 / CHOL 0 / SOD 4 / POT 248

FRUIT JUICE COOLER

4 (6½-ounce) bottles sparkling mineral water, chilled
2 (12-ounce) cans peach nectar, chilled
1 cup unsweetened orange juice, chilled
½ cup unsweetened grapefruit juice, chilled
¼ cup lemon juice, chilled
Orange rind strips

Combine first 5 ingredients in a large pitcher; mix well. Pour over ice cubes in serving glasses; garnish with strips of orange rind. Yield: 8 cups (70 calories per 1-cup serving).

PRO 0.6 / FAT 0.2 / CARB 17.7 / FIB 0.1 / CHOL 0 / SOD 7 / POT 126

Warm up party spirits with Hot Cranberry Punch.

HOT CRANBERRY PUNCH

2½ cups unsweetened pineapple juice
2 cups cranberry juice cocktail
1¾ cups water
3 (3-inch) sticks cinnamon
¼ cup firmly packed brown sugar
1 tablespoon whole cloves
1½ teaspoons whole allspice

Combine first 3 ingredients in water reservoir of a 10-cup electric coffee maker. Place basket in glass carafe. Combine remaining ingredients in basket, omitting paper filter. (Tie spices in cheesecloth, if necessary.) Cover coffee maker with top. Brew according to manufacturer's instructions. Serve hot. Yield: 6 cups (54 calories per ½-cup serving).

PRO 0.2 / FAT 0.1 / CARB 13.4 / FIB 0.1 / CHOL 0 / SOD 2 / POT 88

BANANA-MANGO SMOOTHIE

1 cup chopped ripe mango
1 cup fresh pineapple chunks
1 medium banana, cut into fourths
2 cups low-fat buttermilk
2 tablespoons honey
1 teaspoon lime juice
½ teaspoon vanilla extract

Combine all ingredients in container of an electric blender; process until smooth. Chill thoroughly. Yield: 4½ cups (128 calories per ¾-cup serving).

PRO 3.4 / FAT 1.1 / CARB 28.4 / FIB 1.4 / CHOL 3 / SOD 87 / POT 365

The mango, a sweet tropical fruit that's increasingly popular in the United States, is a valuable source of carotenoids, the building blocks of vitamin A.

An average mango provides enough to produce about 8,000 international units (IU) of vitamin A — nearly double an adult's entire daily requirement (5,000 IU)! Vitamin A helps us see at night, keeps our skin healthy and increases our resistance to infections.

Carotenoids are especially helpful in protecting the body from dangerous chemicals called free oxygen radicals (FORs). These arise from normal body processes, including aging, but especially from smoking, solar radiation, pollution, and eating cured meats.

SHANGHI MARY

1 cup no-salt-added tomato juice
1 cup Bloody Mary mix
2 teaspoons lemon juice
½ teaspoon reduced-sodium soy sauce
⅛ teaspoon garlic powder
⅛ teaspoon ground ginger
Celery stalks (optional)

Combine first 6 ingredients in a small pitcher; mix well. Cover and chill thoroughly. Pour over ice cubes in serving glasses; garnish with celery stalks, if desired. Yield: 2 cups (50 calories per 1-cup serving).

PRO 2.2 / FAT 0.2 / CARB 12.4 / FIB 0.8 / CHOL 0 / SOD 504 / POT 682

MOCK SANGRIA

1 (25.4-ounce) bottle sparkling pink Catawba, chilled
3 cups cranapple juice, chilled
3 tablespoons lime juice, chilled
1 tablespoon instant powdered tea
1 (10-ounce) bottle club soda, chilled
Orange slices
Lime slices
Lemon slices

Combine first 5 ingredients in a serving pitcher just before serving; stir until well blended. Float orange, lime, and lemon slices in pitcher to garnish. Pour over ice in serving glasses, and serve immediately. Yield: 8 cups (116 calories per 1-cup serving).

PRO 0.4 / FAT 0.1 / CARB 29.3 / FIB 0.1 / CHOL 0 / SOD 7 / POT 207

CASSIS SPRITZER

1 tablespoon crème de cassis
½ teaspoon lime juice
¾ cup club soda, chilled
Lime slices (optional)

Combine crème de cassis and lime juice in a wine glass; add club soda. Stir lightly; garnish with lime slices, if desired. Yield: ¾ cup (21 calories per ¾-cup serving).

Note: Kahlúa may be substituted for crème de cassis.

PRO 0.0 / FAT 0.0 / CARB 1.4 / FIB 0.0 / CHOL 0 / SOD 1 / POT 14

Surprise your family with one of these homemade breads: (clockwise from top) Cranberry-Oatmeal Muffins (page 98), Granola Loaf (page 104), and Cardamom Coffee Braid (page 105).

Breads, Grains & Pastas

CHEDDAR-WHOLE WHEAT POPOVERS

1 egg, beaten
1 egg white, lightly beaten
¼ cup plus 2 tablespoons whole wheat flour
2 tablespoons all-purpose flour
½ cup skim milk
1 tablespoon margarine, melted
⅛ teaspoon salt
Vegetable cooking spray
2 tablespoons (½ ounce) shredded extra-sharp
  Cheddar cheese

Combine first 7 ingredients in a medium bowl; beat with an electric mixer just until smooth.

Place a muffin pan coated with cooking spray in oven at 450° for 2 minutes or until a drop of water sizzles when dropped in pan. Remove pan from oven; pour 1 tablespoon batter into each cup. Sprinkle each with 1 teaspoon cheese; fill cups three-fourths full with remaining batter. Bake at 450° for 20 minutes; remove from oven, and prick each popover with tines of a fork. Bake an additional 5 minutes. Remove from muffin pans, and serve immediately. Yield: 6 popovers (85 calories each).

PRO 4.2 / FAT 3.8 / CARB 8.7 / FIB 0.6 / CHOL 49 / SOD 118 / POT 86

BRAN-ORANGE BISCUITS

¾ cup low-fat buttermilk
½ cup shreds of wheat bran cereal
½ cup whole wheat flour
½ cup all-purpose flour
1 teaspoon baking powder
1 teaspoon sugar
¼ teaspoon baking soda
⅛ teaspoon salt
1 teaspoon grated orange rind
3 tablespoons shortening
Vegetable cooking spray

Combine buttermilk and cereal in a small bowl; set aside. Combine next 7 ingredients in a medium bowl, mixing well. Cut in shortening with a pastry blender until mixture resembles coarse meal. Add reserved cereal mixture, stirring with a fork just until dry ingredients are moistened.

Turn dough out onto a floured surface; knead 4 to 5 times. Roll dough to ½-inch thickness; cut with a 2-inch biscuit cutter. Place on a baking sheet coated with cooking spray. Bake at 400° for 12 minutes or until biscuits are lightly browned. Serve warm. Yield: 16 biscuits (55 calories each).

PRO 1.5 / FAT 2.3 / CARB 7.8 / FIB 1.0 / CHOL 0 / SOD 69 / POT 61

CRANBERRY-OATMEAL MUFFINS

1 cup whole wheat flour
¾ cup all-purpose flour
¾ cup regular oats, uncooked
⅓ cup firmly packed brown sugar
2 teaspoons baking powder
½ teaspoon ground cinnamon
⅛ teaspoon salt
1 teaspoon grated orange rind
¼ cup margarine
1 egg, beaten
1 cup skim milk
¾ cup fresh or frozen cranberries, coarsely chopped
Vegetable cooking spray

Combine first 8 ingredients in a large bowl; stir until well blended. Cut in margarine with a pastry blender until mixture resembles coarse meal. Make a well in center of mixture. Combine egg and milk in a small bowl; stir until well blended. Add to dry ingredients, stirring just until moistened; gently fold in cranberries.

Spoon batter into muffin pans coated with cooking spray, filling two-thirds full. Bake at 400° for 20 minutes or until lightly browned. Remove from muffin pans, and serve hot. Yield: 14 muffins (136 calories each).

PRO 3.6 / FAT 4.3 / CARB 21.5 / FIB 1.6 / CHOL 20 / SOD 120 / POT 112

PEACH YOGURT MUFFINS

2 cups whole wheat flour
¼ cup firmly packed brown sugar
2 teaspoons baking powder
½ teaspoon baking soda
½ teaspoon ground cinnamon
¼ teaspoon salt
¼ teaspoon ground nutmeg
Dash of ground mace
1 egg, beaten
⅓ cup skim milk
¼ cup vegetable oil
1 (8-ounce) carton peach low-fat yogurt
⅓ cup finely chopped dried peaches
Vegetable cooking spray

Combine flour, sugar, baking powder, soda, cinnamon, salt, nutmeg, and mace in a medium bowl, stirring well. Make a well in center of mixture. Combine egg, milk, oil, yogurt, and peaches; add to dry ingredients, stirring just until moistened.

Spoon batter into muffin pans coated with cooking spray, filling two-thirds full. Bake at 400° for 20 minutes or until golden. Yield: 14 muffins (140 calories each).

PRO 3.7 / FAT 4.9 / CARB 21.9 / FIB 1.4 / CHOL 20 / SOD 116 / POT 159

SPICED BRAN LOAF

½ cup shreds of wheat bran cereal
1 cup low-fat buttermilk
1 egg, beaten
¼ cup honey
3 tablespoons vegetable oil
1 cup whole wheat flour
1 cup all-purpose flour
1 teaspoon baking powder
1 teaspoon baking soda
1 teaspoon ground cinnamon
¼ teaspoon salt
¼ teaspoon ground nutmeg
Vegetable cooking spray

Combine cereal and buttermilk in a small bowl; let stand 5 minutes. Stir in egg, honey, and oil; mix well.

Combine next 7 ingredients in a large bowl. Add bran mixture to flour mixture, stirring just until dry ingredients are moistened. Spoon batter into an 8½- x 4½- x 3-inch loafpan coated with cooking spray. Bake at 350° for 45 minutes or until a wooden pick inserted in center comes out clean. Yield: 1 loaf or 17 (½-inch) slices (107 calories per slice).

PRO 3.0 / FAT 3.1 / CARB 18.0 / FIB 1.6 / CHOL 17 / SOD 121 / POT 94

 We have long known that eating whole grains and fresh fruits were good for us because they provided *insoluble fiber* (bulk) to our diets. Research is finding that *soluble fiber* found in certain grains and fruits actually lowers the level of cholesterol in the diet.

Oatmeal is a good example. When we eat oatmeal the soluble fiber found in the bran of the oatmeal forms a gel that binds with cholesterol, allowing it to pass harmlessly out of the system. Studies indicate that the soluble fiber in barley and pectin, another type of fiber found in apples and pears, may have similar effects.

ORANGE-PINEAPPLE BREAD

1½ cups whole wheat flour
1 cup all-purpose flour
2 teaspoons baking powder
¼ teaspoon baking soda
¼ teaspoon salt
¼ cup firmly packed brown sugar
¼ cup vegetable oil
1 egg, beaten
2 teaspoons grated orange rind
½ cup unsweetened orange juice
1 (8-ounce) can unsweetened crushed pineapple, undrained
Vegetable cooking spray

Combine first 5 ingredients, and set aside.

Combine brown sugar, oil, and egg; mix well. Stir in orange rind, juice, and pineapple. Stir in dry ingredients, blending until smooth.

Spoon batter into an 8½- x 4½- x 3-inch loafpan coated with cooking spray. Bake at 350° for 1 hour or until a wooden pick inserted in center comes out clean. Yield: 1 loaf or 17 (½-inch) slices (121 calories per slice).

PRO 2.7 / FAT 3.8 / CARB 19.8 / FIB 1.1 / CHOL 16 / SOD 81 / POT 96

BANANA-OATMEAL PANCAKES

¾ cup regular oats, uncooked
1½ cups skim milk
2 eggs, beaten
2 tablespoons vegetable oil
1 medium-size ripe banana,
  mashed
1¼ cups all-purpose flour
1 teaspoon baking powder
¼ teaspoon salt
Vegetable cooking spray

Combine oats and milk in a medium bowl; let stand 5 minutes. Add eggs, oil, and banana to the oat and milk mixture; beat well.

Combine flour, baking powder, and salt in a large bowl; add oat mixture to dry ingredients, and stir just until blended.

For each pancake, pour 2 tablespoons batter onto hot griddle or skillet coated with cooking spray. Cook over medium heat, turning pancakes when tops are bubbly and edges are browned. Repeat procedure until all batter is used. Yield: 20 (4-inch) pancakes (75 calories each).

PRO 2.6 / FAT 2.3 / CARB 10.9 / FIB 0.8 / CHOL 28 / SOD 61 / POT 79

GINGERED APPLESAUCE WAFFLES

1 cup whole wheat flour
2 teaspoons sugar
½ teaspoon baking powder
½ teaspoon baking soda
¾ teaspoon ground ginger
1½ cups low-fat buttermilk
½ cup unsweetened applesauce
2 tablespoons vegetable oil
1 egg, separated
Vegetable cooking spray

Combine flour, sugar, baking powder, soda, and ginger in a medium bowl, stirring well; set aside.

Combine buttermilk, applesauce, oil, and egg yolk in a small bowl; mix well, and gradually add to dry ingredients, stirring until smooth.

Beat egg white (at room temperature) in a small bowl until stiff peaks form; gently fold into batter.

Coat a waffle iron with cooking spray; allow waffle iron to preheat. Pour 1¼ cups batter onto hot waffle iron, spreading batter to edges. Bake 3 minutes or until steaming stops. Repeat procedure until all batter is used. Yield: 16 (4-inch) waffles (60 calories each).

PRO 2.2 / FAT 2.4 / CARB 7.9 / FIB 0.6 / CHOL 18 / SOD 49 / POT 74

BUTTERMILK-WHEAT ROLLS

1½ cups whole wheat flour
2 packages dry yeast
½ teaspoon baking soda
½ teaspoon salt
1¼ cups low-fat buttermilk
½ cup water
¼ cup margarine
2 tablespoons honey
2½ cups all-purpose flour
Vegetable cooking spray

Combine whole wheat flour, yeast, soda, and salt in a large bowl. Set aside.

Combine buttermilk, water, margarine, and honey in a saucepan; place over low heat until very warm (120° to 130°). Gradually add milk mixture to dry ingredients, beating at low speed of an electric mixer until blended. Beat 3 minutes at medium speed; stir in all-purpose flour.

Turn dough out onto a lightly floured surface; knead 5 minutes or until smooth and elastic. Shape dough into a ball. Place in a bowl coated with cooking spray, turning to grease top. Cover and let rise in a warm place (85°), free from drafts, 40 minutes or until doubled in bulk.

Punch dough down, and shape into 1½-inch balls; place balls on a 15- x 10- x 1-inch jellyroll pan coated with cooking spray. Cover and let rise in a warm place (85°), free from drafts, 30 minutes or until doubled in bulk. Bake at 400° for 12 minutes or until golden brown. Yield: 28 rolls (84 calories each).

PRO 2.5 / FAT 2.0 / CARB 14.4 / FIB 0.8 / CHOL 0 / SOD 80 / POT 63

Lower bagels, a few at a time, into boiling water; cook 3 minutes on each side.

After cooking bagels, transfer them to a baking sheet. Brush with egg and water; sprinkle with caraway seeds.

Whole Wheat-Onion Bagels — cooled and ready to eat.

WHOLE WHEAT-ONION BAGELS

1 package dry yeast
1 cup warm water (105° to 115°)
3 tablespoons instant minced onion
1 tablespoon vegetable oil
1½ cups whole wheat flour
½ teaspoon salt
1¼ cups all-purpose flour
Vegetable cooking spray
3½ quarts water
1 egg
1 tablespoon water
1 tablespoon caraway seeds

Dissolve yeast in warm water in a large bowl; let stand 5 minutes. Add onion and oil, stirring well. Stir in whole wheat flour and salt; gradually stir in all-purpose flour. Turn dough out onto a lightly floured surface; knead 1 minute. Cover and let rest 10 minutes. Knead an additional 7 to 10 minutes or until smooth and elastic. Place dough in a large bowl coated with cooking spray, turning to grease top. Cover and let rise in a warm place (85°), free from drafts, 1½ hours or until doubled in bulk.

Punch dough down, and divide into 12 equal portions. Shape each portion into a smooth ball; punch a hole in the center of each ball, using floured fingers. Gently pull dough away from center, making a 1½-inch hole. Place shaped bagels on a baking sheet coated with cooking spray.

Bring 3½ quarts water to a boil in a large Dutch oven. Lower bagels, a few at a time, into gently boiling water; cook 3 minutes on each side. Transfer bagels to a baking sheet coated with cooking spray, using a slotted spoon. Combine egg and 1 tablespoon water; beat well, and gently brush over bagels. Sprinkle with caraway seeds. Bake at 450° for 20 minutes or until golden brown. Cool on wire racks. Yield: 1 dozen (127 calories each).

PRO 4.5 / FAT 2.2 / CARB 23.2 / FIB 1.7 / CHOL 23 / SOD 107 / POT 111

 Despite its name, buttermilk is actually low in fat. It's made from skim or 1 percent milk and can be substituted for whole milk in pancakes and baked goods.

HONEY-WHEAT CRESCENTS

1 package dry yeast
½ cup warm water (105° to 115°)
2 tablespoons honey, divided
3 tablespoons margarine
½ teaspoon salt
½ cup skim milk, scalded
1 egg, beaten
2 cups whole wheat flour
1½ cups all-purpose flour
Vegetable cooking spray

Dissolve yeast in ½ cup warm water and 1 teaspoon honey; stir well. Set aside, and let stand 5 minutes.

Combine remaining 1 tablespoon plus 2 teaspoons honey, margarine, and salt in a large bowl; add scalded milk, stirring until margarine melts. Let cool to lukewarm (105° to 115°). Add yeast mixture and egg, stirring well. Gradually add whole wheat flour, beating well. Add enough all-purpose flour to make a soft dough.

Place dough in a bowl coated with cooking spray, turning to grease top. Cover and let rise in a warm place (85°), free from drafts, 1 hour or until doubled in bulk.

Punch dough down; turn out onto a lightly floured surface. Let rest 10 minutes. Divide dough in half. Roll half of dough into a circle 10 inches in diameter and ¼-inch thick. Cut into 12 wedges. Roll each wedge up tightly, beginning at wide end. Place on baking sheets coated with cooking spray, point side down; curve into crescents. Repeat rolling and shaping procedure with remaining dough. Cover and let rise in a warm place, free from drafts, 45 minutes or until doubled in bulk. Bake at 400° for 10 minutes or until lightly browned. Yield: 2 dozen (89 calories each).

PRO 2.8 / FAT 2.0 / CARB 15.5 / FIB 1.0 / CHOL 12 / SOD 73 / POT 64

CINNAMON-OATMEAL ROLLS

1¾ to 2 cups all-purpose flour, divided
½ cup regular oats, uncooked
1 package dry yeast
1 tablespoon sugar
¼ teaspoon salt
¼ cup water
¼ cup skim milk
1 tablespoon margarine
1 egg
Vegetable cooking spray
¼ cup firmly packed brown sugar
1 teaspoon ground cinnamon
1 tablespoon margarine, melted

Combine ½ cup flour, oats, yeast, 1 tablespoon sugar, and salt in a large bowl; set aside.

Combine water, milk, and 1 tablespoon margarine in a small saucepan; cook over medium heat until very warm (120° to 130°). Add to dry ingredients; beat at medium speed of an electric mixer 2 minutes, scraping bowl occasionally. Add ½ cup flour and egg; beat at high speed an additional 2 minutes. Stir in enough remaining flour to make a soft dough.

Turn dough out onto a lightly floured surface; knead 8 to 10 minutes or until smooth and elastic. Place dough in a large bowl coated with cooking spray, turning to grease top. Cover and let rise in a warm place (85°), free from drafts, 1 hour or until doubled in bulk. Punch dough down. Turn dough out onto a lightly floured surface; cover and let rest 10 minutes.

Combine brown sugar and cinnamon; set aside.

Roll dough into a 12- x 9-inch rectangle on a lightly floured surface. Brush with melted margarine; sprinkle with reserved sugar mixture. Roll up jellyroll fashion, starting at long end; pinch ends and seam to seal. Cut into 1-inch slices. Place slices, cut sides down, in a 9-inch square baking pan coated with cooking spray. Cover and let rise in a warm place, free from drafts, 45 minutes or until doubled in bulk. Bake at 400° for 15 minutes or until golden brown. Cool in pan 5 minutes. Remove from pan, and serve warm. Yield: 1 dozen (135 calories each).

PRO 3.5 / FAT 2.9 / CARB 23.7 / FIB 1.1 / CHOL 23 / SOD 83 / POT 75

RAISIN AND RYE BUNS

¾ cup raisins
1 package dry yeast
1½ cups warm water (105° to 115°)
2 tablespoons firmly packed brown sugar
2 tablespoons dark molasses
2 tablespoons margarine, melted and cooled
¼ teaspoon salt
2¼ cups all-purpose flour
2 cups rye flour
Vegetable cooking spray

Place raisins in a bowl of water; let stand 5 minutes. Drain; set aside. Dissolve yeast in 1½ cups warm water in a bowl; let stand 5 minutes. Add sugar, molasses, margarine, salt, and all-purpose flour; beat well. Stir raisins and rye flour into mixture to form a soft dough.

Turn dough out onto a lightly floured surface; knead 8 to 10 minutes or until smooth and elastic. Place dough in a large bowl coated with cooking spray, turning to grease top. Cover and let rise in a warm place (85°), free from drafts, 1½ hours or until doubled in bulk.

Coat two 9-inch cakepans with cooking spray; set aside. Punch dough down; shape dough into 26 (1½-inch) balls, and place in prepared pans. Cover and let rise in a warm place, free from drafts, 45 minutes or until doubled in bulk. Bake at 400° for 20 minutes or until golden brown. Yield: 26 rolls (96 calories each).

PRO 2.1 / FAT 1.1 / CARB 19.6 / FIB 0.9 / CHOL 0 / SOD 36 / POT 81

WHOLE WHEAT-POTATO BREAD

1 medium potato, peeled and diced
2 packages dry yeast
2 tablespoons margarine, softened
2 tablespoons firmly packed brown sugar
1 teaspoon salt
1 cup skim milk
1 egg
3 cups whole wheat flour, divided
3 cups all-purpose flour
Vegetable cooking spray

Cook potato in a small saucepan in a small amount of boiling water 10 minutes or until tender. Drain, reserving cooking liquid. Mash potato in a small bowl, reserving ¾ cup; set aside. Add enough water to cooking liquid to yield 1 cup. Let liquid cool to lukewarm (105° to 115°).

Dissolve yeast in reserved potato liquid in a large bowl; let stand 5 minutes. Add margarine, and stir well. Stir in reserved mashed potato, brown sugar, salt, milk, egg, and 1 cup whole wheat flour. Gradually stir in remaining whole wheat flour. Stir in enough all-purpose flour to make a stiff dough.

Turn dough out onto a lightly floured surface, and knead about 8 to 10 minutes or until smooth and elastic. Place in a bowl coated with cooking spray, turning to grease top. Cover and let rise in a warm place (85°), free from drafts, 1 hour or until doubled in bulk.

Punch dough down, and divide in half; shape each half into a loaf. Place loaves in two 9- x 5- x 3-inch loafpans coated with cooking spray. Cover and let rise in a warm place, free from drafts, 30 minutes or until doubled in bulk. Bake at 375° for 30 to 35 minutes or until loaves sound hollow when tapped. Remove bread from pans; cool completely on wire racks before slicing. Yield: 2 loaves or 36 (½-inch) slices (98 calories per slice).

PRO 3.4 / FAT 1.2 / CARB 19.0 / FIB 1.2 / CHOL 8 / SOD 84 / POT 104

 To obtain the maximum nutritional benefits wheat has to offer, use whole wheat flour whenever possible. Whole wheat is exactly what the name implies; it is a milled form of the whole grain, which includes the inner seed or germ, the starchy layer or endosperm, and the outside bran and hull. When the hull, bran, and germ are removed during the refining process to produce white flour, up to 80% of the nutrients are lost. Refined white flour is normally enriched, but with only 4 nutrients — thiamine, riboflavin, niacin, and iron. Therefore, the less wheat is refined, the more nutrients it retains.

There are several types of nutrient-rich whole wheat flour. Stone ground wheat flour is the most nutritious, having been processed the least, followed by stone ground graham flour, whole wheat flour, and whole wheat pastry flour.

PUMPERNICKEL BREAD

3 cups medium rye flour, divided
1½ to 2¼ cups all-purpose flour,
  divided
1 cup whole wheat flour
¼ cup shreds of wheat bran
  cereal
¼ cup yellow cornmeal
2 packages dry yeast
2 tablespoons cocoa
¾ teaspoon salt
2 cups water
¼ cup molasses
1 tablespoon vegetable oil
2 teaspoons caraway seeds
Vegetable cooking spray

Combine 1 cup rye flour, 1 cup all-purpose flour, whole wheat flour, cereal, cornmeal, yeast, cocoa, and salt in a large bowl; mix well. Set aside.

Combine water, molasses, and oil in a small saucepan; cook over medium heat until very warm (120° to 130°). Remove from heat. Gradually add liquid mixture to flour mixture, beating at low speed of a heavy-duty electric mixer 2 minutes. Add remaining 2 cups rye flour, and beat at medium speed 3 minutes. Stir in caraway seeds. Add enough remaining all-purpose flour to make a stiff dough. (Dough will be sticky.)

Turn dough out onto a lightly floured surface; knead 1 minute. Cover and let rest 10 minutes. Knead about 8 to 10 minutes or until smooth and elastic. Place in a bowl coated with cooking spray, turning to grease top. Cover and let rise in a warm place (85°), free from drafts, 1 hour or until doubled in bulk.

Punch dough down, and divide in half. Shape each half into a round loaf; place loaves on a baking sheet coated with cooking spray. Cover and let rise in a warm place, free from drafts, 45 minutes or until doubled in bulk. Cut an "X," ¼-inch deep, in top of each loaf. Cut a piece of aluminum foil long enough to fit around one loaf. Divide in half lengthwise; fold both halves into thirds lengthwise. Wrap foil around loaf. Secure foil with freezer tape. Repeat procedure with second loaf. Bake at 375° for 45 minutes or until loaves sound hollow when tapped. Re-

move foil, and place loaves on wire racks. Cool loaves completely before slicing. Yield: 2 loaves or 32 wedges (84 calories per wedge).

PRO 2.4 / FAT 0.7 / CARB 17.3 / FIB 1.1 / CHOL 0 / SOD 63 / POT 84

GRANOLA LOAF

1 cup whole wheat flour
1 package dry yeast
½ teaspoon salt
1 cup skim milk
½ cup water
3 tablespoons honey
2 tablespoons margarine
1 egg
¼ cup all-natural granola cereal
2 tablespoons unsalted sunflower kernels, toasted
2 teaspoons grated orange rind
2 to 2½ cups all-purpose flour
Vegetable cooking spray

Combine whole wheat flour, yeast, and salt in a large bowl; set aside.

Combine milk, water, honey, and margarine in a small saucepan; cook over medium heat until very warm (120° to 130°). Add milk mixture and egg to reserved flour mixture; beat at low speed of an electric mixer until well blended. Beat at medium speed an additional 3 minutes. Stir in cereal, sunflower kernels, orange rind, and enough all-purpose flour to make a soft dough.

Turn dough out onto a lightly floured surface; knead about 8 to 10 minutes or until smooth and elastic. Place dough in a large bowl coated with cooking spray, turning to grease top. Cover and let rise in a warm place (85°), free from drafts, 1 hour or until doubled in bulk.

Punch dough down. Turn dough out onto a lightly floured surface; knead 4 to 5 times. Shape dough into a loaf. Place in a 9- x 5- x 3-inch loaf pan coated with cooking spray. Cover and let rise in a warm place, free from drafts, 40 minutes or until doubled in bulk. Bake at 375° for 30 minutes or until loaf sounds hollow when tapped. Transfer loaf to a wire rack immediately; cool before slicing. Yield: 1 loaf or 18 (½-inch) slices (123 calories per slice).

PRO 3.9 / FAT 2.7 / CARB 21.4 / FIB 1.1 / CHOL 15 / SOD 96 / POT 89

CARDAMOM COFFEE BRAID

1 package dry yeast
½ cup warm water (105° to 115°)
1 egg, beaten
1 cup skim milk, scalded
3 tablespoons sugar
1 tablespoon margarine
½ teaspoon salt
½ teaspoon ground cardamom
3 to 3½ cups bread flour
Vegetable cooking spray
1 egg yolk
1 tablespoon water

Dissolve yeast in warm water in a large bowl; let stand 5 minutes. Stir in egg.

Add sugar, margarine, salt, and cardamom to scalded milk, stirring well. Cool to lukewarm (105° to 115°). Add to yeast mixture, stirring well. Gradually stir in enough flour to make a soft dough.

Turn dough out onto a lightly floured surface, and knead 5 minutes or until smooth and elastic. Place dough in a large bowl coated with cooking spray, turning to grease top. Cover and let rise in a warm place (85°), free from drafts, 1½ hours or until doubled in bulk.

Punch dough down; turn out onto a lightly floured surface. Divide dough into 6 equal portions; shape each portion into a 14-inch rope. Braid 3 ropes together, pinching ends to seal. Place braided loaf on a baking sheet coated with cooking spray, tucking ends under. Repeat procedure with remaining ropes to make second loaf.

Cover and let rise in a warm place, free from drafts, 45 minutes or until doubled in bulk. Combine egg yolk and water; beat well, and gently brush over loaves. Bake at 350° for 25 minutes or until loaves sound hollow when tapped. Cool on wire racks. Yield: 2 loaves or 24 (1-inch) slices (73 calories per slice).

PRO 2.5 / FAT 1.1 / CARB 13.0 / FIB 0.4 / CHOL 23 / SOD 64 / POT 41

SPICED COUSCOUS

Vegetable cooking spray
1 green onion, minced
2 medium tomatoes, peeled, seeded, and chopped
1 cup water
1 teaspoon margarine
½ teaspoon ground cumin
¼ teaspoon salt
¼ teaspoon curry powder
⅛ teaspoon ground cinnamon
¾ cup couscous, uncooked
3 tablespoons chopped fresh parsley

Coat a medium skillet with cooking spray; place over medium heat until hot. Add onion and tomatoes; sauté 3 minutes, stirring frequently. Set aside, and keep warm.

Combine next 6 ingredients in a saucepan. Cover and bring to a boil; remove from heat. Add couscous; cover and let stand 5 minutes or until liquid is absorbed. Add vegetables and parsley; toss lightly. Serve warm. Yield: 6 servings (94 calories per serving).

PRO 3.2 / FAT 1.0 / CARB 18.0 / FIB 1.0 / CHOL 0 / SOD 108 / POT 143

Spiced Couscous, low in fat and calories, is a quick and easy dish to prepare.

BARLEY AND MUSHROOM BAKE

Vegetable cooking spray
2 teaspoons margarine
2 cups thinly sliced fresh mushrooms
1 cup chopped onion
1 cup barley, uncooked
Vegetable cooking spray
2½ cups hot water
2 teaspoons beef-flavored bouillon granules
⅛ teaspoon pepper
2 tablespoons chopped fresh parsley

Coat a large skillet with cooking spray; add margarine. Place over medium heat until margarine melts. Add mushrooms and onion; sauté until tender. Add barley, and sauté 4 minutes or until barley is lightly browned. Remove from heat. Transfer to a 1½-quart baking dish coated with cooking spray.

Add water, bouillon granules, and pepper to barley mixture. Cover and bake at 350° for 1 hour and 15 minutes, stirring at 15-minute intervals. Remove from oven, and gently stir in parsley. Yield: 8 servings (109 calories per serving).

PRO 2.7 / FAT 1.5 / CARB 22.2 / FIB 1.9 / CHOL 0 / SOD 129 / POT 147

GREEN BEAN-BULGUR TOSS

1 (9-ounce) package frozen green beans, thawed
1 cup bulgur wheat, uncooked
2 cups water
¾ teaspoon chicken-flavored bouillon granules
⅛ teaspoon ground ginger
⅛ teaspoon pepper
1 cup sliced fresh mushrooms
½ cup sliced water chestnuts
½ cup thinly sliced green onion
2 tablespoons reduced-sodium soy sauce

Drain green beans; cut each green bean in half crosswise. Set aside.

Combine bulgur, water, bouillon granules, ginger, and pepper in a medium saucepan. Bring to a boil. Cover; reduce heat, and simmer 15 minutes. Stir in green beans and remaining ingredients; simmer an additional 5 minutes or until liquid is absorbed and bulgur is tender. Yield: 8 servings (101 calories per serving).

PRO 3.6 / FAT 0.5 / CARB 21.5 / FIB 1.5 / CHOL 0 / SOD 188 / POT 178

GRITS COMBO

Vegetable cooking spray
¾ cup chopped green onion
¼ cup chopped sweet red pepper
2 medium tomatoes, peeled and chopped
⅛ teaspoon pepper
3 cups water
¼ teaspoon salt
¾ cup regular grits, uncooked

Coat a medium skillet with cooking spray; place over medium heat until hot. Add onion and red pepper; sauté 3 minutes or until tender. Add tomatoes and pepper. Bring to a boil; reduce heat, and simmer, uncovered, 20 minutes, stirring occasionally.

Combine water and salt in a medium saucepan; bring to a boil. Add grits; cook 10 to 15 minutes, stirring frequently, until thickened. Remove from heat; stir in tomato mixture, and serve immediately. Yield: 6 servings (82 calories per serving).

PRO 2.3 / FAT 0.3 / CARB 18.0 / FIB 0.9 / CHOL 0 / SOD 100 / POT 151

MEXICAN CHEESE GRITS

2¼ cups water
¼ teaspoon salt
¾ cup quick-cooking grits, uncooked
½ cup (2 ounces) shredded sharp Cheddar cheese
1 (4-ounce) can chopped green chiles, drained
1 (2-ounce) jar diced pimiento, drained
1 clove garlic, crushed
¼ teaspoon hot sauce
1 egg, beaten
Vegetable cooking spray

Combine water and salt in a medium saucepan; bring to a boil. Stir in grits. Cover; reduce heat to low, and cook 5 minutes, stirring occasionally. Remove from heat, and add cheese, stirring until cheese melts; stir in chiles, pimiento, garlic, and hot sauce. Gradually stir one-fourth of hot grits mixture into egg; stir egg mixture into remaining grits mixture. Spoon into a 1-quart baking dish coated with cooking spray. Bake at 350° for 30 minutes or until set. Yield: 6 servings (125 calories per serving).

PRO 5.1 / FAT 4.2 / CARB 16.3 / FIB 0.3 / CHOL 56 / SOD 191 / POT 83

MEXICAN HOMINY

Vegetable cooking spray
2 cups chopped, peeled tomato
1 cup chopped onion
1 (15-ounce) can hominy, drained
½ teaspoon chili powder
⅛ teaspoon garlic powder
⅛ teaspoon salt
⅛ teaspoon pepper
¼ cup (1 ounce) shredded Monterey
  Jack cheese

Coat a medium skillet with cooking spray; place over medium heat until hot. Add tomato and onion, and sauté 5 minutes or until onion is tender; remove from heat. Add hominy, chili powder, garlic powder, salt, and pepper; stir well. Spoon mixture into a 1-quart baking dish coated with cooking spray. Bake, uncovered, at 350° for 25 minutes; sprinkle with cheese, and bake an additional 5 minutes or until cheese melts. Yield: 6 servings (66 calories per serving).

PRO 2.9 / FAT 1.8 / CARB 11.2 / FIB 1.2 / CHOL 4 / SOD 204 / POT 210

BREAKFAST OATMEAL SPECIAL

1 cup skim milk
1 cup unsweetened apple juice
1 cup quick-cooking oats, uncooked
1 medium cooking apple, chopped
¼ cup dates, chopped
2 teaspoons honey
¼ teaspoon ground cinnamon
¼ teaspoon grated orange rind
Dash of ground cloves
3 tablespoons wheat germ

Combine milk and apple juice in a 1½-quart saucepan; bring to a boil. Add oats, apple, and dates; cook, stirring frequently, 1 minute. Remove from heat, and stir in honey, cinnamon, orange rind, and cloves. Cover and let stand 3 minutes.

Stir oatmeal; spoon into individual serving bowls. Sprinkle each serving with 1½ teaspoons wheat germ. Yield: 6 servings (134 calories per serving).

PRO 4.6 / FAT 1.7 / CARB 28.1 / FIB 3.2 / CHOL 1 / SOD 23 / POT 265

ITALIAN RICE

Vegetable cooking spray
½ cup chopped onion
½ cup chopped green pepper
1 clove garlic, minced
2¼ cups water
¼ cup Chablis or other dry white wine
1½ teaspoons chicken-flavored bouillon granules
¾ teaspoon dried whole oregano
¾ teaspoon dried whole basil
⅛ teaspoon pepper
1 cup parboiled rice, uncooked
2 tablespoons chopped fresh parsley
2 tablespoons grated Parmesan cheese

Coat a large saucepan with cooking spray; place over medium heat until hot. Add onion, green pepper, and garlic; sauté until tender. Stir in next 6 ingredients. Cover; bring to a boil. Stir in rice. Cover; reduce heat, and simmer 20 minutes or until rice is tender and liquid is absorbed. Remove from heat; stir in parsley and cheese. Yield: 8 servings (98 calories per serving).

PRO 2.4 / FAT 0.7 / CARB 20.9 / FIB 0.3 / CHOL 1 / SOD 98 / POT 95

JALAPEÑO RICE CASSEROLE

2⅔ cups water
½ teaspoon chicken-flavored bouillon granules
1 cup parboiled rice, uncooked
½ cup plain low-fat yogurt
2 tablespoons reduced-calorie creamy Italian salad dressing
1 jalapeño pepper, seeded and chopped
1 tablespoon chopped fresh parsley
Vegetable cooking spray
⅓ cup (1⅓ ounces) shredded Monterey Jack cheese

Combine water and bouillon granules in a medium saucepan; bring to a boil. Stir in rice. Cover; reduce heat, and simmer 25 minutes or until liquid is absorbed. Remove from heat; stir in yogurt, salad dressing, pepper, and parsley.

Spoon into a 1-quart baking dish coated with cooking spray. Bake, uncovered, at 350° for 20 minutes. Top with cheese; bake 5 minutes. Yield: 6 servings (150 calories per serving).

PRO 4.8 / FAT 2.5 / CARB 27.3 / FIB 0.1 / CHOL 6 / SOD 204 / POT 114

SPINACH-RICE CASSEROLE

1 (10-ounce) package frozen chopped spinach,
  thawed
Vegetable cooking spray
1 medium-size sweet red pepper, seeded
  and finely chopped
½ cup chopped onion
2 eggs
⅓ cup skim milk
1 teaspoon chicken-flavored bouillon granules
⅛ teaspoon ground nutmeg
⅛ teaspoon pepper
1 cup hot cooked parboiled rice (cooked
  without salt or fat)

Drain thawed spinach; squeeze out excess
moisture between paper towels, and set aside.

Coat a medium skillet with cooking spray;
place over medium heat until hot. Add red pepper and onion; sauté until tender. Set aside.

Combine eggs, milk, bouillon granules, nutmeg, and pepper in a medium bowl; stir until
well blended. Add reserved spinach, sautéed
vegetables, and rice; mix well.

Spoon mixture into a 1-quart baking dish
coated with cooking spray. Bake, uncovered, at
350° for 35 minutes. Yield: 6 servings (83 calories per serving).

PRO 4.9 / FAT 2.3 / CARB 11.5 / FIB 1.5 / CHOL 92 / SOD 130 / POT 264

CALICO WILD RICE

2 tablespoons raisins
¼ cup hot water
½ cup wild rice, uncooked
1½ cups water
Vegetable cooking spray
1 medium carrot, scraped and shredded
1 medium apple, chopped
¼ cup chopped celery
¼ cup chopped green pepper
1½ cups water
1½ teaspoons chicken-flavored bouillon
  granules
¼ teaspoon dried whole sage
⅛ teaspoon pepper
¾ cup parboiled rice, uncooked

Combine raisins and hot water in a small
bowl; let stand 5 minutes or until raisins are
plump. Drain and set aside.

Wash wild rice in a strainer under cold running water; drain. Combine wild rice and 1½
cups water in a medium saucepan; bring to a
boil. Cover; reduce heat to low, and simmer 45
minutes or until rice is tender. Set aside.

Coat a medium skillet with cooking spray;
place over medium heat until hot. Add carrot,
apple, celery, and green pepper; sauté until
crisp-tender. Set aside.

Combine 1½ cups water, bouillon granules,
sage, and pepper in a medium saucepan; bring
to a boil. Add parboiled rice. Cover; reduce
heat, and simmer 20 minutes or until liquid is
absorbed. Remove from heat; stir in reserved
raisins, wild rice, and sautéed vegetables. Cover
and let stand 5 minutes. Serve hot or cold. Yield:
12 servings (82 calories per serving).

PRO 1.9 / FAT 0.3 / CARB 18.6 / FIB 0.7 / CHOL 0 / SOD 54 / POT 96

PECAN-BROWN RICE PILAF

Vegetable cooking spray
½ cup chopped green onion
2½ cups water
1½ teaspoons chicken-flavored bouillon
  granules
½ teaspoon dried whole thyme
⅛ teaspoon pepper
1 cup brown rice, uncooked
¼ cup coarsely chopped pecans, toasted
2 tablespoons chopped fresh parsley
Fresh parsley sprigs (optional)

Coat a large saucepan with cooking spray;
place over medium heat until hot. Add onion,
and sauté until tender. Stir in next 4 ingredients;
cover and bring to a boil. Add rice, and remove
from heat.

Place rice mixture in a 1½-quart baking dish
coated with cooking spray; cover and bake at
350° for 50 minutes or until liquid is absorbed.
Stir in pecans and chopped parsley; garnish with
parsley sprigs, if desired. Yield: 8 servings (112
calories per serving).

PRO 2.2 / FAT 3.1 / CARB 19.3 / FIB 2.0 / CHOL 0 / SOD 74 / POT 86

CURRIED BROWN RICE

Vegetable cooking spray
½ cup chopped onion
2½ cups water
1 teaspoon chicken-flavored bouillon granules
¼ cup chopped dried apricots
1 teaspoon curry powder
1 cup brown rice, uncooked
2 tablespoons chopped fresh parsley
Fresh parsley sprigs (optional)

Coat a medium saucepan with cooking spray. Place over medium heat until hot; add onion, and sauté until tender.

Combine onion, water, bouillon granules, apricots, and curry in a medium saucepan; cover and bring to a boil. Add rice. Cover; reduce heat, and simmer 50 minutes or until liquid is absorbed. Stir in chopped parsley. Transfer to a serving platter, and garnish with parsley sprigs, if desired. Yield: 6 servings (129 calories per serving).

PRO 2.8 / FAT 0.8 / CARB 28.0 / FIB 2.5 / CHOL 0 / SOD 71 / POT 185

Spinach Noodles with Sautéed Vegetables is surrounded by a variety of pasta.

SPINACH NOODLES WITH SAUTÉED VEGETABLES

6 ounces spinach noodles
Vegetable cooking spray
1 medium onion, coarsely chopped
1 clove garlic, crushed
1 medium-size yellow squash, thinly sliced
1 medium zucchini squash, thinly sliced
1 cup fresh corn, cut from cob
1 tablespoon chopped fresh parsley
¾ teaspoon dried whole basil
¾ teaspoon dried whole oregano
¼ teaspoon salt
¼ teaspoon freshly ground pepper
2 medium tomatoes, peeled and chopped

Cook spinach noodles according to package directions, omitting salt; drain. Transfer to a serving platter, and keep warm.

Coat a large skillet with cooking spray; place over medium heat until hot. Add onion and garlic; sauté 3 minutes or until tender. Add next 8 ingredients; sauté 4 minutes or until vegetables are tender. (Do not overcook.) Stir in tomatoes. Serve vegetables over warm spinach noodles. Yield: 10 servings (77 calories per serving).

PRO 3.0 / FAT 1.5 / CARB 14.1 / FIB 1.1 / CHOL 23 / SOD 74 / POT 251

DILLED RIGATONI

½ (8-ounce) package Neufchâtel cheese, softened
¼ cup hot water
2 teaspoons chopped green onion
1 teaspoon lemon juice
½ teaspoon dried whole dillweed
¼ teaspoon salt
½ (16-ounce) package rigatoni

Beat Neufchâtel cheese in a medium bowl until fluffy. Gradually add hot water, beating until smooth. Stir in green onion, lemon juice, dillweed, and salt; set aside.

Cook rigatoni according to package directions, omitting salt; drain well. Add rigatoni to reserved Neufchâtel mixture, tossing gently. Serve immediately. Yield: 8 servings (142 calories per serving).

PRO 5.0 / FAT 3.7 / CARB 21.9 / FIB 0.7 / CHOL 11 / SOD 131 / POT 76

CHILLED ORIENTAL CORKSCREW TOSS

1 cup fusilli
3 tablespoons reduced-sodium soy sauce
2 teaspoons sesame oil
1 teaspoon honey
¼ teaspoon dry mustard
⅛ teaspoon ground ginger
1 (6-ounce) package frozen snow peas, thawed
   and drained
8 cherry tomatoes, halved
½ cup sliced water chestnuts
½ cup sliced fresh mushrooms
1 green onion, sliced

Cook fusilli according to package directions, omitting salt; drain. Set aside.

Combine soy sauce, oil, honey, dry mustard, and ginger; stir with a wire whisk until well blended. Combine reserved fusilli and soy sauce mixture in a large bowl; toss well. Add remaining ingredients, and toss gently. Cover and refrigerate 2 hours. Yield: 6 servings (89 calories per serving).

PRO 3.1 / FAT 1.8 / CARB 15.0 / FIB 1.2 / CHOL 0 / SOD 296 / POT 208

MEDITERRANEAN LINGUINE

6 ounces whole wheat linguine
Vegetable cooking spray
1 cup sliced fresh mushrooms
1 medium-size green pepper, seeded and cut into
   thin strips
1 medium-size sweet red pepper, seeded and cut
   into thin strips
1 clove garlic, minced
1 (14-ounce) can artichoke hearts, drained and
   quartered
½ cup reduced-calorie Italian salad dressing
3 tablespoons sliced, pitted ripe olives
1 tablespoon chopped fresh parsley
½ cup (2 ounces) shredded mozzarella cheese

Cook linguine according to package directions, omitting salt; drain. Transfer to a large bowl, and keep warm.

Coat a large skillet with cooking spray; place over medium heat until hot. Add mushrooms, green pepper, red pepper, and garlic; sauté

until crisp-tender. Add artichokes, salad dressing, olives, and parsley; stir well, and heat thoroughly. Add to reserved linguine; toss gently. Sprinkle with mozzarella cheese, and serve immediately. Yield: 12 servings (91 calories per serving).

PRO 3.7 / FAT 1.9 / CARB 15.6 / FIB 1.8 / CHOL 4 / SOD 139 / POT 186

BROCCOLI VERMICELLI

4 ounces vermicelli
1 teaspoon vegetable oil
2 cups broccoli flowerets
⅓ cup chopped onion
½ cup (2 ounces) shredded Swiss cheese
2 tablespoons grated Parmesan cheese
¼ teaspoon salt
⅛ teaspoon garlic powder
⅛ teaspoon dried whole thyme
⅛ teaspoon ground nutmeg

Cook vermicelli according to package directions, omitting salt; drain. Toss with oil in a large bowl, and keep warm.

Cook broccoli and onion, covered, in a small amount of boiling water 5 minutes or until crisp-tender. Drain well.

Add broccoli, onion, cheese, salt, garlic powder, thyme, and nutmeg to reserved vermicelli. Toss gently until cheese melts. Transfer to a serving bowl, and serve immediately. Yield: 6 servings (132 calories per serving).

PRO 6.7 / FAT 4.2 / CARB 16.9 / FIB 1.2 / CHOL 10 / SOD 162 / POT 161

Fish and shellfish are excellent food choices for dieters concerned about fat and calories. Here, shrimp and snow peas nestled in rice create an elegant entrée of Shrimp Sauté (page 121).

Fish & Shellfish

MONTEREY BAKED BASS

1 cup sliced fresh mushrooms
¼ cup sliced green onion
1 pound bass fillets
2 tablespoons Chablis or other dry white wine
1 teaspoon dried whole marjoram
2 teaspoons lemon juice
¼ teaspoon freshly ground black pepper
¼ cup (1 ounce) grated Monterey Jack cheese
¼ cup crushed low-salt round buttery crackers

Sprinkle mushrooms and green onion over the bottom of a 12- x 8- x 2-inch baking dish. Rinse fillets with cold water, and pat dry. Arrange fillets over vegetables. Sprinkle remaining ingredients over fillets. Cover and bake at 400° for 10 minutes. Uncover and bake an additional 15 minutes or until fillets flake easily when tested with a fork. Yield: 4 servings (187 calories per serving).

PRO 24.2 / FAT 6.7 / CARB 5.6 / FIB 0.4 / CHOL 68 / SOD 139 / POT 424

BLACKENED BASS

1 pound bass fillets (½-inch thick)
2 tablespoons water
1 tablespoon hot sauce
2 teaspoons onion powder
2 teaspoons garlic powder
2 tablespoons paprika
1 teaspoon dried whole thyme, crushed
1 teaspoon dried whole oregano, crushed
2 teaspoons pepper
1 to 2 teaspoons red pepper
Vegetable cooking spray
1 tablespoon margarine

Rinse fillets with cold water; leave damp, and place in a shallow dish.

Combine 2 tablespoons water and hot sauce in a small bowl; pour over fillets. Cover and marinate in refrigerator 2 hours, turning once.

Combine next 7 ingredients. Remove fillets from marinade, discarding marinade; dredge in spices to coat well.

Coat a large cast-iron skillet with cooking spray; add margarine, and place over high heat until margarine melts. Add fillets, and cook 2 to 3 minutes on each side, turning carefully. (This procedure may be done outside, if desired, to avoid the small amount of smoke that is created. Fillets should look charred.) Yield: 4 servings (169 calories per serving).

PRO 22.6 / FAT 6.5 / CARB 5.3 / FIB 1.2 / CHOL 62 / SOD 141 / POT 434

BROILED CATFISH MARGARITA

1 (8-ounce) can tomato sauce
⅓ cup unsweetened orange juice
2 tablespoons chili powder
3 tablespoons lime juice
2 tablespoons tequila
1 tablespoon Triple Sec
½ teaspoon pepper
⅛ teaspoon hot sauce
2 pounds catfish fillets
1 tablespoon lime juice
¼ teaspoon garlic powder
Vegetable cooking spray
Lime slices

Combine first 8 ingredients in a medium saucepan; bring to a boil. Reduce heat; simmer 5 minutes. Set aside, and keep warm.

Rinse fillets with cold water, and pat dry. Brush fillets with 1 tablespoon lime juice; sprinkle with garlic powder. Place on rack of a broiler pan coated with cooking spray. Broil 4 to 5 inches from heating element 7 to 8 minutes or until fillets flake easily when tested with a fork. Transfer to a serving platter. Serve with reserved sauce; garnish with lime slices. Yield: 8 servings (153 calories per serving).

PRO 20.7 / FAT 3.9 / CARB 5.6 / FIB 0.6 / CHOL 62 / SOD 260 / POT 549

Spinach and flounder, flavored with thyme, roll up to make Herbed Flounder Pinwheels. Top with a vegetable sauce to make the pinwheels even tastier.

DILLED COD KIEV

½ (8-ounce) package Neufchâtel cheese, softened
1 tablespoon lemon juice
¾ teaspoon dried whole dillweed or 1 tablespoon chopped fresh dillweed
¼ teaspoon Worcestershire sauce
⅛ teaspoon garlic powder
⅛ teaspoon hot sauce
6 cod fillets (1½ pounds)
¼ teaspoon pepper
1 egg
1 tablespoon skim milk
¼ cup seasoned, dry breadcrumbs
Vegetable cooking spray

Combine first 6 ingredients in a small bowl; stir until well blended. Shape mixture into a roll, 1½ inches in diameter; wrap in waxed paper. Freeze 30 minutes or until set.

Rinse fillets with cold water, and pat dry. Sprinkle fillets with pepper. Cut cheese mixture into 6 equal portions. Place one portion of cheese mixture near narrow end of each fillet; roll up jellyroll fashion, and secure with a wooden pick.

Combine egg and milk in a small bowl; beat well. Dip rolls in egg mixture; dredge in breadcrumbs to coat lightly. Place rolls, seam side down, in a 12- x 8- x 2-inch baking dish coated with cooking spray. Cover rolls and refrigerate for 1 hour.

Bake at 425° for 10 minutes or until fillets flake easily when tested with a fork. Yield: 6 servings (170 calories per serving).

PRO 23.5 / FAT 5.9 / CARB 4.3 / FIB 0.0 / CHOL 117 / SOD 201 / POT 487

HERBED FLOUNDER PINWHEELS

3 cups fresh spinach leaves, chopped
1 egg, beaten
¼ cup soft breadcrumbs
¼ teaspoon dried whole thyme
Dash of pepper
4 flounder fillets (1 pound)
1½ teaspoons cornstarch
2 tablespoons water
1 (6-ounce) can vegetable cocktail juice
Fresh parsley sprigs

Place spinach in a vegetable steamer. Place over boiling water, and steam just until wilted; drain well, and chop. Combine spinach, egg, breadcrumbs, thyme, and pepper in a small bowl; set aside. Rinse fillets with cold water, and pat dry. Spoon one-fourth of mixture in center of each fillet; roll up jellyroll fashion, beginning at narrow end, and place seam side down in an 8-inch square baking dish. Cover and bake at 375° for 15 to 20 minutes. Transfer rolls to a serving platter, and keep warm.

Combine cornstarch and water in a small saucepan, stirring until smooth. Stir in cocktail juice. Cook over medium heat until thickened and bubbly. Pour sauce over fish rolls. Garnish with fresh parsley, and serve immediately. Yield: 4 servings (147 calories per serving).

PRO 22.5 / FAT 2.7 / CARB 7.7 / FIB 1.6 / CHOL 125 / SOD 326 / POT 727

GROUPER KABOBS

1 (20-ounce) can unsweetened pineapple chunks, undrained
¼ cup reduced-sodium soy sauce
¼ cup dry sherry
1 tablespoon firmly packed brown sugar
1 teaspoon ground ginger
1 teaspoon dry mustard
1 clove garlic, minced
2 pounds grouper fillets, cut into 1-inch cubes
1 medium-size green pepper, seeded and cut into 1-inch pieces
1 medium-size sweet red pepper, seeded and cut into 1-inch pieces
Vegetable cooking spray
4 cups hot cooked parboiled rice (cooked without salt or fat)

Drain pineapple, reserving ⅓ cup juice. Set pineapple chunks aside.

Combine ⅓ cup reserved pineapple juice, soy sauce, sherry, brown sugar, ginger, mustard, and garlic in a jar; cover tightly, and shake vigorously. Set aside. Rinse fillets with cold water, and pat dry. Place fish in a large shallow container. Pour pineapple juice mixture over fish; cover and marinate in refrigerator 8 hours.

Remove fish from marinade, reserving marinade. Alternate fish cubes, reserved pineapple chunks, and green and red pepper pieces on 8 skewers. Coat grill with cooking spray. Grill kabobs 6 inches over medium coals 15 minutes or until fish flakes easily when tested with a fork, turning and basting often with reserved pineapple juice marinade.

Remove from grill, and transfer to a serving platter. Serve immediately over hot cooked rice. Yield: 8 servings (160 calories per serving plus 93 calories per ½ cup cooked rice).

PRO 24.9 / FAT 1.1 / CARB 32.5 / FIB 1.7 / CHOL 62 / SOD 364 / POT 519

CAJUN-STYLE HADDOCK

1 (14½-ounce) can stewed tomatoes, undrained
2 medium stalks celery, chopped
1 medium onion, finely chopped
½ medium-size green pepper, seeded and chopped
1 clove garlic, minced
1 bay leaf
¾ teaspoon dried whole thyme, crushed
½ teaspoon pepper
¼ teaspoon salt
¼ teaspoon hot sauce
1½ pounds haddock fillets
Vegetable cooking spray

Combine first 10 ingredients in a medium saucepan, stirring well. Bring to a boil. Cover; reduce heat, and simmer 25 minutes, stirring occasionally.

Rinse fillets with cold water, and pat dry. Arrange fillets in a 12- x 8- x 2-inch baking dish coated with cooking spray. Bake, uncovered, at 400° for 15 minutes or until fillets flake easily when tested with a fork. Remove bay leaf from sauce mixture, and discard. Serve immediately. Yield: 6 servings (126 calories per serving).

PRO 22.0 / FAT 0.4 / CARB 7.9 / FIB 0.8 / CHOL 68 / SOD 356 / POT 599

 The "no-pain, no-gain" theory of physical fitness is out. No longer is it recommended that you must exercise until it hurts. The new standards suggest that a moderate amount of exercise is enough to make you feel better and may be enough to help you live longer.

The secret is life-long regularity. Pick a form of exercise you enjoy, one that you look forward to doing and that you can stick with over the years.

Take swimming, for instance. It's a favorite activity for many and a great family sport. Because water is buoyant yet offers resistance, vigorous swimming provides a good cardiovascular workout. However, any vigorous activity in the water is good: running, bobbing, jumping or just walking. A moderate goal would be a 20- to 30-minute water workout every other day.

BAKED HALIBUT WITH ARTICHOKE HEARTS

Vegetable cooking spray
¼ cup chopped green onion
2 tablespoons chopped fresh parsley
1 (14-ounce) can artichoke hearts, drained and chopped
3 tablespoons grated Parmesan cheese
3 tablespoons reduced-calorie mayonnaise
1 tablespoon lemon juice
½ teaspoon garlic powder
¼ teaspoon red pepper
8 halibut steaks (2 pounds)

Coat a medium skillet with cooking spray; place over medium heat until hot. Add onion and parsley, and sauté until tender. Stir in next 6 ingredients, and set aside.

Rinse halibut with cold water, and pat dry. Place halibut steaks in a large aluminum foil-lined shallow roasting pan. Spoon artichoke mixture evenly over steaks. Bake, uncovered, at 375° for 10 minutes or until steaks flake easily when tested with a fork. Yield: 8 servings (149 calories per serving).

PRO 24.1 / FAT 3.7 / CARB 4.2 / FIB 0.4 / CHOL 60 / SOD 158 / POT 610

POLYNESIAN SEA FILLETS

4 (¾-inch-thick) orange roughy fillets (1 pound)
2 tablespoons teriyaki sauce
1 tablespoon vegetable oil
2 green onions, chopped
2 teaspoons minced fresh gingerroot
½ teaspoon grated orange rind
Vegetable cooking spray
Green onion fans (optional)

Rinse fillets with cold water, and pat dry; place in a single layer in a shallow baking dish. Combine teriyaki sauce, oil, chopped onion, gingerroot, and orange rind; mix well, and pour over fillets. Turn fillets in marinade to coat well. Cover and marinate in refrigerator at least 1 hour, turning fish occasionally.

Coat rack of a broiler pan with cooking spray. Remove fillets from marinade, discarding marinade. Arrange fillets on rack, and broil 6 inches from heating element 5 minutes or until fillets flake easily when tested with a fork.

Carefully transfer fillets to a serving platter, and garnish with green onion fans, if desired. Yield: 4 servings (218 calories per serving).

PRO 22.1 / FAT 12.7 / CARB 2.2 / FIB 0.2 / CHOL 62 / SOD 405 / POT 378

PEPPERED PERCH

4 pan-dressed freshwater perch (1½ pounds)
½ cup Chablis or other dry white wine
¼ cup lemon juice
2 tablespoons reduced-sodium soy sauce
1 tablespoon Worcestershire sauce
2 cloves garlic, minced
Vegetable cooking spray
Cracked black pepper
Lemon slices

Rinse fish with cold water, and pat dry. Place fish in a 12- x 8- x 2-inch baking dish. Combine wine, lemon juice, soy sauce, Worcestershire sauce, and garlic in a small mixing bowl; pour marinade over fish. Cover and refrigerate 4 hours, turning fish twice.

Coat rack of a broiler pan with cooking spray. Remove fish from marinade, reserving marinade; place fish on rack. Broil 4 inches from heating element 5 minutes. Turn fish, and sprinkle with cracked pepper. Broil an additional 8 minutes or until fish flakes easily when tested with a fork; baste occasionally with reserved marinade. Transfer to a serving platter, and garnish with lemon slices. Yield: 4 servings (236 calories per serving).

PRO 33.7 / FAT 6.8 / CARB 3.5 / FIB 0.0 / CHOL 94 / SOD 415 / POT 560

BARBECUED REDFISH

1 (1½-pound) redfish fillet
Vegetable cooking spray
3 tablespoons Dijon mustard
3 tablespoons reduced-calorie Italian salad dressing
2 tablespoons tarragon vinegar
2 teaspoons margarine, melted
⅛ teaspoon pepper
Dash of Worcestershire sauce
Dash of hot sauce

Rinse fillet with cold water, and pat dry. Cut fillet into six 4-ounce portions; place in a wire grilling basket coated with cooking spray. Set aside. Combine remaining ingredients in a small bowl, stirring well. Brush mustard mixture over fish in grilling basket.

Grill fish 6 inches over medium coals 7 minutes on each side or until fish flakes easily when tested with a fork; baste frequently with remaining sauce during grilling. Yield: 6 servings (124 calories per serving).

PRO 20.4 / FAT 3.1 / CARB 1.4 / FIB 0.0 / CHOL 62 / SOD 397 / POT 321

SALMON STEAKS WITH LEMON DILL SAUCE

4 (½-inch-thick) salmon steaks (1 pound)
1 medium onion, sliced
1 cup boiling water
1 tablespoon lemon juice
1 teaspoon chicken-flavored bouillon granules
1 teaspoon dried whole dillweed
1 tablespoon margarine
1 tablespoon all-purpose flour
¼ cup evaporated skim milk
1 tablespoon lemon juice

Rinse salmon with cold water, and pat dry. Place salmon steaks in a 12- x 8- x 2-inch baking dish; arrange onion slices over salmon. Combine water, 1 tablespoon lemon juice, bouillon granules, and dillweed; pour over salmon. Cover and bake at 350° for 15 to 18 minutes or until steaks flake easily when tested with a fork. Drain, reserving ¼ cup cooking liquid; discard onion. Transfer salmon steaks to a serving platter, and keep warm.

Melt margarine in a small heavy saucepan over low heat; add flour, stirring until smooth. Cook, stirring constantly, 1 minute. Gradually add milk, ¼ cup reserved cooking liquid, and 1 tablespoon lemon juice. Cook over medium heat, stirring constantly, until thickened and bubbly. Spoon sauce over salmon before serving. Yield: 4 servings (181 calories per serving).

PRO 24.1 / FAT 7.1 / CARB 3.5 / FIB 0.1 / CHOL 40 / SOD 126 / POT 403

SALMON CROQUETTES

1 (15½-ounce) can salmon, drained and flaked
2 tablespoons grated onion
1 egg, beaten
⅛ teaspoon pepper
Dash of hot sauce
3 tablespoons fine, dry breadcrumbs
Vegetable cooking spray
1 tablespoon vegetable oil

Place salmon in a colander, and rinse under cold tap water 1 minute; set colander aside to let salmon drain 1 minute.

Combine salmon, onion, egg, pepper, and hot sauce in a medium bowl; stir well. Divide mixture into 6 equal portions; shape each portion into a croquette. Roll each in breadcrumbs.

Coat a medium skillet with cooking spray. Add oil; place over medium heat until hot. Add croquettes, and cook 8 minutes or until golden brown, turning once. Drain on paper towels. Yield: 6 servings (109 calories per serving).

PRO 11.9 / FAT 5.3 / CARB 2.8 / FIB 0.1 / CHOL 64 / SOD 42 / POT 183

GRILLED SHARK

¼ cup plus 2 tablespoons reduced-calorie Italian salad dressing
¼ cup water
1½ teaspoons dried whole basil
1½ teaspoons chopped fresh parsley
1½ teaspoons lemon juice
1½ teaspoons dry sherry
⅛ teaspoon garlic powder
6 (½-inch-thick) shark steaks (1½ pounds)
Vegetable cooking spray
Lemon slices

Combine first 7 ingredients; stir with a wire whisk until well blended. Rinse steaks with cold water; pat dry. Brush shark steaks with dressing mixture, and place on a hot grill coated with cooking spray. Grill 3 to 4 inches over medium coals 6 to 8 minutes on each side or until fish flakes easily when tested with a fork. Baste often with dressing mixture. Transfer to a serving platter, and garnish with lemon slices. Yield: 6 servings (186 calories per serving).

PRO 20.0 / FAT 10.2 / CARB 1.9 / FIB 0.0 / CHOL 62 / SOD 197 / POT 389

POACHED RED SNAPPER WITH CAPER SAUCE

1 pound red snapper fillets
¼ teaspoon white pepper
1 cup water
2 medium stalks celery, cut into julienne strips
2 medium carrots, scraped and cut into julienne strips
1 medium onion, chopped
Caper Sauce

Rinse fillets with cold water; pat dry. Sprinkle fillets with white pepper, and set aside.

Pour 1 cup water into a 10-inch skillet. Cook over medium heat until water starts to "quiver." (Do not boil.) Add snapper fillets and vegetables. Cover; reduce heat to low, and cook 8 minutes or until fillets flake easily when tested with a fork. (Do not allow water to boil.)

Transfer fillets and vegetables to individual plates, and spoon equal amounts of Caper Sauce over each serving; serve immediately. Yield: 4 servings (219 calories per serving).

Caper Sauce:

½ cup reduced-calorie mayonnaise
3 tablespoons water
2 teaspoons lemon juice
1 teaspoon capers, drained
⅛ teaspoon white pepper

Combine all ingredients in a small saucepan; stir until smooth. Cook over low heat, stirring constantly, 3 minutes or until thoroughly heated. Yield: about ¾ cup.

PRO 23.8 / FAT 9.2 / CARB 9.6 / FIB 1.0 / CHOL 72 / SOD 495 / POT 603

Lighten up your cookout with Grouper Kabobs (page 114), and Grilled Shark (page 116).

SNAPPER DIJON

4 (½-inch-thick) red snapper fillets (1 pound)
¼ teaspoon pepper
¼ cup Dijon mustard
1 tablespoon vinegar
1 tablespoon water
½ teaspoon dried whole thyme
Dash of ground ginger
1 medium tomato, chopped

Cut four (15-inch) pieces of heavy-duty aluminum foil. Rinse fillets with cold water; pat dry. Place a fillet just off center of each piece of foil; sprinkle with pepper. Combine mustard, vinegar, water, thyme, and ginger, stirring well; pour evenly over fillets. Top with chopped tomato.

Fold foil over fillets, and securely seal; place on a baking sheet. Bake at 450° for 10 minutes or until fillets flake easily when tested with a fork. Remove fillets from foil, and serve. Yield: 4 servings (129 calories per serving).

PRO 23.7 / FAT 1.8 / CARB 3.9 / FIB 0.7 / CHOL 62 / SOD 218 / POT 508

SOLE SCALLOPINI

4 sole fillets (1 pound)
¼ cup plus 2 tablespoons fine, dry breadcrumbs
¼ teaspoon pepper
¼ teaspoon dried whole oregano
Vegetable cooking spray
1 (14½-ounce) can stewed tomatoes, undrained
½ teaspoon dried whole oregano

Rinse fillets with cold water, and pat dry. Combine breadcrumbs, pepper, and ¼ teaspoon oregano in a shallow dish; dredge fillets in breadcrumb mixture.

Transfer fillets to a 10- x 6- x 2-inch baking dish coated with cooking spray. Bake at 400° for 20 minutes or until fish flakes easily when tested with a fork. Remove from oven; set aside, and keep warm.

Combine stewed tomatoes and ½ teaspoon oregano in container of an electric blender. Process until mixture is pureed. Pour into a small saucepan; cook, uncovered, over medium-high heat 5 minutes or until thickened, stirring frequently. Spoon sauce over fish, and serve. Yield: 4 servings (158 calories per serving).

PRO 21.2 / FAT 1.6 / CARB 13.8 / FIB 0.5 / CHOL 57 / SOD 420 / POT 631

CITRUS SOLE

2 pounds sole fillets
1 medium-size pink grapefruit
¼ teaspoon grated orange rind
2 medium oranges
2 tablespoons Chablis or other dry white wine
1 teaspoon dried whole tarragon, crushed
½ teaspoon garlic powder
¼ teaspoon paprika

Rinse fillets with cold water; pat dry. Place in a 13- x 9- x 2-inch baking dish; set aside.

Section grapefruit over a bowl to catch juice; set sections aside, and reserve ½ cup juice. Add orange rind to grapefruit juice; set aside. Section oranges over bowl to catch juice; set sections aside, and reserve ½ cup juice.

Combine reserved grapefruit juice mixture, reserved orange juice, wine, tarragon, garlic powder, and paprika, stirring well. Pour over fillets. Bake, uncovered, at 400° for 15 minutes or until fish flakes easily when tested with a fork; baste occasionally with pan juices during cooking. Remove from oven, and carefully transfer fillets to a serving platter; top with reserved grapefruit and orange sections. Yield: 8 servings (117 calories per serving).

PRO 19.4 / FAT 1.0 / CARB 6.0 / FIB 0.2 / CHOL 57 / SOD 89 / POT 497

SWORDFISH VERACRUZ

4 swordfish steaks (1 pound)
¼ teaspoon pepper
Vegetable cooking spray
2 teaspoons margarine
½ cup chopped onion
1 clove garlic, crushed
1 medium tomato, chopped
2 tablespoons chopped green chiles
1 tablespoon Chablis or other dry white wine
1 tablespoon white wine vinegar
¼ teaspoon salt

Rinse swordfish with cold water, and pat dry. Sprinkle with pepper. Coat a skillet with cooking spray; add margarine, and place over medium heat until margarine melts. Add fish to skillet, and cook until browned on both sides; place in a 10- x 6- x 2-inch baking dish.

Wipe skillet with a paper towel, and coat with cooking spray. Place over medium heat until hot. Add onion and garlic, and sauté until tender. Add tomato, chiles, wine, vinegar, and salt; bring to a boil. Remove from heat, and spoon mixture over steaks. Bake, uncovered, at 450° for 10 minutes or until steaks flake easily when tested with a fork. Remove steaks from dish to a warm platter, using a slotted spoon. Yield: 4 servings (169 calories per serving).

PRO 22.4 / FAT 6.6 / CARB 3.9 / FIB 0.5 / CHOL 62 / SOD 243 / POT 637

OVEN-FRIED TROUT

1 pound trout fillets
1 tablespoon olive or vegetable oil
¼ teaspoon salt
⅛ teaspoon garlic powder
⅛ teaspoon pepper
⅓ cup cornflake crumbs
Vegetable cooking spray
Lemon slices
Fresh parsley sprigs

Rinse fillets with cold water, and pat dry. Brush fillets with oil, and sprinkle with salt, garlic powder, and pepper; dredge in cornflake crumbs.

Arrange fillets in a single layer in a 12- x 8- x 2-inch baking dish coated with cooking spray. Bake, uncovered, at 500° for 10 minutes or until fillets flake easily when tested with a fork. Carefully transfer to a serving platter, and garnish with lemon slices and parsley. Serve immediately. Yield: 4 servings (248 calories per serving).

PRO 21.3 / FAT 14.8 / CARB 6.3 / FIB 0.9 / CHOL 62 / SOD 308 / POT 341

DEVILED TUNA

2 (6½-ounce) cans light water-packed tuna
Vegetable cooking spray
1 teaspoon margarine
1 cup finely chopped celery
½ cup finely chopped onion
2 slices whole wheat bread, cut into cubes and divided
¼ cup reduced-calorie mayonnaise
1 teaspoon prepared horseradish
½ teaspoon dry mustard
¼ teaspoon salt
¼ teaspoon pepper

Place tuna in a colander, and rinse under cold tap water 1 minute; set colander aside to let tuna drain 1 minute.

Coat a large skillet with cooking spray; add margarine, and place over medium heat until margarine melts. Add celery and onion; sauté until tender. Remove from heat; stir in tuna and ¾ cup bread cubes. Add mayonnaise, horseradish, mustard, salt, and pepper; mix well.

Divide mixture evenly into 6 baking shells or 6-ounce custard cups coated with cooking spray. Sprinkle remaining bread cubes on top. Bake at 350° for 15 minutes. Yield: 6 servings (125 calories per serving).

PRO 15.2 / FAT 4.1 / CARB 6.6 / FIB 0.7 / CHOL 35 / SOD 246 / POT 246

 Fish oils are wonders. Omega 3 fatty acids, a special type of polyunsaturated fat found primarily in fatty northern ocean fish, such as salmon, mackerel, tuna, and bluefish, are virtual health tonics.

In the early 1970s, scientists who studied Eskimos wondered how they ate prodigious amounts of whale blubber and fatty fish yet almost never got heart diseases. Answer: Omega 3 fatty acids, which lab studies in the late '70s and early '80s show can dramatically lower blood cholesterol and reduce the tendency of the blood to form damaging clots.

Last year, a major study of Dutch men, reported in the *New England Journal of Medicine*, found that those who eat as little as two fish meals a week have half the rate of heart disease of those who eat no fish at all. But that's just a start. New studies find that Omega 3s, which affect powerful hormone-like blood substances called prostaglandins, have far-reaching benefits. They do the following:

*Improve infant development. When pregnant monkeys are fed fish oil, breast-milk levels of DHA, a fatty acid needed by infants for brain and eye development, go up. Moral: If you're breast feeding, include some fish in your diet.

*Reduce arthritic inflammation. A small study of patients with rheumatoid arthritis found that those fed a generally low-fat diet that's high in Omega 3s, have a small but significant reduction in symptoms such as morning soreness.

*Reduce cancer risk. Animals fed a carcinogen and a diet high in Omega 3s get significantly fewer tumors than animals that eat no fish, find researchers at Rockefeller University and elsewhere. Without Omega 3s, tumors develop.

And even though these are "fatty" fish, compared to other main dishes, they're low in fat and calories. A 3-ounce serving of salmon has only 5 grams of fat and 140 calories, while a regular hamburger of same serving has 18 grams of fat and 245 calories.

STEAMED BLUE CRABS

2 (3½-ounce) packages shrimp and crab boil
3 cups vinegar
2 (12-ounce) cans flat light beer
3 dozen live blue crabs

Combine shrimp and crab boil, vinegar, and beer in a very large stockpot with a steaming rack; bring to a boil. Place crabs on rack; cover and steam 20 minutes or until crabs turn red in color. Drain crabs well, and serve immediately. Yield: 3 dozen crabs or 6 servings (127 calories per serving).

PRO 15.1 / FAT 1.6 / CARB 10.9 / FIB 0.0 / CHOL 85 / SOD 188 / POT 201

OYSTER MÉLANGE

½ cup water
1 cup sliced fresh mushrooms
½ cup diced sweet red pepper
¼ cup diced shallot
¼ cup sliced green onion
¼ cup diced celery
½ cup water
2 teaspoons cornstarch
1 teaspoon chicken-flavored bouillon granules
¼ teaspoon salt
¼ teaspoon pepper
⅛ teaspoon red pepper
2 (12-ounce) containers Select oysters, drained
¼ cup chopped fresh parsley
2½ cups hot cooked parboiled rice (cooked without salt or fat)

Combine ½ cup water, mushrooms, sweet red pepper, shallot, green onion, and celery in a medium saucepan; bring to a boil. Cover; reduce heat, and simmer 10 minutes.

Combine ½ cup water and cornstarch, stirring until blended. Stir in bouillon granules, salt, and pepper. Add to vegetable mixture, stirring well;

SEASONED CRAB CAKES

1 pound fresh crabmeat, drained and flaked
½ cup seasoned, dry breadcrumbs
1 medium carrot, scraped and grated
2 teaspoons chopped fresh parsley
2 teaspoons reduced-calorie mayonnaise
1½ teaspoons Worcestershire sauce
2 eggs, beaten
½ teaspoon dry mustard
¼ teaspoon pepper
Vegetable cooking spray

Combine all ingredients except cooking spray in a medium bowl; stir well. Shape crabmeat mixture into 6 patties. Cover and chill 1 hour.

Coat a large skillet with cooking spray. Place over medium heat until hot. Add crabmeat patties, and cook until golden brown on both sides, turning once. Yield: 6 servings (141 calories per serving).

Note: Crab cakes may be served with Zesty Seafood Sauce (page 186), if desired.

PRO 16.4 / FAT 4.2 / CARB 8.4 / FIB 0.2 / CHOL 168 / SOD 272 / POT 226

bring to a boil. Add oysters; simmer 5 minutes or until oyster edges curl. Remove from heat, and stir in chopped parsley.

Serve immediately over hot cooked rice. Yield: 5 servings (94 calories per serving plus 93 calories per ½ cup cooked rice).

PRO 11.9 / FAT 2.3 / CARB 29.0 / FIB 1.4 / CHOL 54 / SOD 282 / POT 346

LINGUINE WITH CLAM SAUCE

6 ounces uncooked linguine
2 (6½-ounce) cans minced clams, rinsed and drained
½ pound fresh mushrooms, sliced
2 cloves garlic, minced
1 tablespoon margarine, melted
½ cup chopped fresh parsley
¼ cup dry white wine
⅛ teaspoon salt
¾ teaspoon pepper
¼ cup grated Parmesan cheese

Cook linguine according to package directions, omitting salt; drain. Set aside; keep warm.

Place clams in a colander, and rinse 1 minute; set colander aside to let clams drain.

Sauté mushrooms and garlic in margarine in a large skillet until tender. Stir in clams, parsley, wine, salt, and pepper; simmer, uncovered, until thoroughly heated.

Combine linguine, clam sauce, and Parmesan cheese; toss well. Transfer to a platter, and serve. Yield: 4 servings (264 calories per serving).

PRO 14.7 / FAT 6.1 / CARB 37.4 / FIB 1.7 / CHOL 27 / SOD 253 / POT 416

GRILLED SCALLOP KABOBS

1 (8-ounce) can unsweetened pineapple chunks, undrained
2 tablespoons sesame seeds
2 tablespoons lime juice
1 tablespoon reduced-sodium soy sauce
1 tablespoon honey
¼ teaspoon ground ginger
1 pound sea scallops
1 medium-size green pepper, seeded and cut into ¾-inch pieces

Drain pineapple, reserving juice; set aside.

Combine pineapple juice, sesame seeds, lime juice, soy sauce, honey, and ginger in a dish.

Rinse scallops with cold water, and pat dry. Add scallops to pineapple juice mixture; stir until well coated. Cover and refrigerate 3 to 4 hours, stirring frequently.

Remove scallops from marinade, reserving marinade. Alternate scallops, pineapple chunks, and green pepper on 4 skewers. Grill kabobs 4 inches over medium-hot coals 5 minutes on each side or until scallops are done, basting frequently with marinade. Yield: 4 servings (169 calories per serving).

PRO 18.9 / FAT 2.7 / CARB 17.4 / FIB 0.6 / CHOL 40 / SOD 437 / POT 585

SHRIMP SAUTÉ

½ cup Chablis or other dry white wine
1 pound medium shrimp, peeled and deveined
6 green onions, chopped
¼ pound snow peas
¾ teaspoon dried whole basil
1 teaspoon chopped fresh parsley
1 bay leaf
⅛ teaspoon garlic salt
2 tablespoons water
1½ teaspoons cornstarch
1 teaspoon lime juice
1 tablespoon reduced-sodium soy sauce
⅛ teaspoon freshly ground pepper
2 cups hot cooked parboiled rice (cooked without salt or fat)

Combine wine and shrimp in a large skillet; cover and cook over medium heat 5 minutes, stirring occasionally. Add green onion, snow peas, basil, parsley, bay leaf, and garlic salt; cover and cook 5 minutes, stirring occasionally.

Combine water and cornstarch in a small bowl; add lime juice, soy sauce, and pepper. Add cornstarch mixture to shrimp, stirring well; bring to a boil, and cook until slightly thickened, stirring constantly. Remove and discard bay leaf.

Serve immediately over hot cooked rice. Yield: 4 servings (106 calories per serving plus 93 calories per ½ cup cooked rice).

PRO 18.6 / FAT 0.9 / CARB 27.5 / FIB 1.6 / CHOL 128 / SOD 334 / POT 338

SHRIMP-STUFFED MACARONI SHELLS

18 jumbo macaroni shells
¼ cup all-purpose flour
½ cup skim milk
1¼ cups water
1 teaspoon chicken-flavored bouillon
   granules
1 tablespoon tomato paste
Vegetable cooking spray
1 teaspoon margarine
1 pound fresh medium shrimp, peeled
   and deveined
1 teaspoon minced garlic
1 (16-ounce) carton low-fat cottage
   cheese
1 egg
2 tablespoons grated Parmesan
   cheese
2 tablespoons chopped fresh
   parsley
1 teaspoon minced chives
⅛ teaspoon pepper
Paprika

Cook macaroni shells according to the package directions, omitting salt; drain well, and set aside.

Place flour in a small saucepan; add milk in a slow stream, stirring with a wire whisk until smooth. Add water, bouillon granules, and tomato paste. Bring to a boil; reduce heat, and simmer 2 minutes or until thickened. Set sauce aside, and keep warm.

Coat a large skillet with cooking spray; add margarine, and place over high heat until melted. Add shrimp, and saute 1 minute. Reduce heat to medium; add garlic, and cook 1 minute or until shrimp are done. Remove from heat, and chop shrimp.

Combine chopped shrimp, garlic, cottage cheese, egg, Parmesan, parsley, chives, and pepper in a large bowl; mix well. Stuff macaroni shells with shrimp mixture.

Pour half of reserved sauce into a 13- x 9- x 2-inch baking dish; add stuffed shells. Cover and bake at 350° for 30 minutes. Bring remaining sauce to a boil, and pour over shells to serve. Sprinkle with paprika. Yield: 6 servings (287 calories per serving).

PRO 28.3 / FAT 4.6 / CARB 31.3 / FIB 0.9 / CHOL 146 / SOD 520 / POT 352

SEAFOOD-STUFFED PEPPERS

4½ cups water
1½ pounds fresh medium shrimp
8 medium-size green peppers
Vegetable cooking spray
1 teaspoon margarine
1 stalk celery, chopped
4 green onions, chopped
1 clove garlic, minced
¾ pound lump crabmeat
1 cup cooked parboiled rice (cooked without salt or
   fat)
1 slice whole wheat bread, torn into small pieces
½ cup (2 ounces) shredded mozzarella cheese
¼ cup grated Parmesan cheese
2 tablespoons chopped fresh parsley
⅛ teaspoon pepper
Dash of hot sauce

Bring 4½ cups water to a boil; add shrimp, and reduce heat. Cook 3 minutes. Drain well, and rinse with cold water. Peel and devein shrimp; chop coarsely, and set aside.

Cut a slice from the top of each pepper; remove seeds. Place peppers in boiling water; boil 5 minutes. Drain and set aside.

Coat a large skillet with cooking spray; add margarine, and place over medium heat until margarine melts. Add celery, onion, and garlic; sauté 5 minutes or until tender. Remove from heat. Add chopped shrimp and remaining ingredients; stir well.

Spoon ¾ cup seafood mixture into each pepper; arrange peppers, cut side up, in a 12- x 8- x 2-inch baking dish. Bake at 350° for 30 minutes or until thoroughly heated. Yield: 8 servings (208 calories per serving).

PRO 21.6 / FAT 6.3 / CARB 17.7 / FIB 2.5 / CHOL 103 / SOD 220 / POT 567

Create a new family favorite with Tortilla Torte (page 128) surrounded by lettuce. This meatless main dish has hearty flavor that's sure to please everyone.

BROCCOLI-CORN QUICHE

2 cups finely chopped fresh broccoli
1 cup low-fat cottage cheese
3 eggs
2 tablespoons all-purpose flour
¼ teaspoon salt
⅛ teaspoon pepper
2 drops of hot sauce
¼ cup finely chopped onion
1 (8¾-ounce) can whole kernel corn,
  drained
1 cup (4 ounces) shredded Swiss cheese
Vegetable cooking spray

Place broccoli in a small saucepan; add a small amount of water. Bring to a boil. Cover; reduce heat, and simmer 5 minutes. Drain thoroughly; place broccoli on paper towels, and squeeze until barely moist. Set broccoli aside.

Combine cottage cheese, eggs, flour, salt, pepper, and hot sauce in container of an electric blender; cover and process until smooth.

Combine egg mixture, broccoli, onion, corn, and cheese in a large bowl. Pour into a 9-inch quiche dish or pieplate coated with cooking spray. Bake at 350° for 30 minutes or until a knife inserted off-center comes out clean. Let stand 10 minutes before serving. Cut into wedges, and serve warm. Yield: 6 servings (201 calories per serving).

PRO 16.8 / FAT 9.1 / CARB 14.5 / FIB 1.6 / CHOL 157 / SOD 354 / POT 276

CAULIFLOWER-TOMATO FRITTATA

Vegetable cooking spray
1 tablespoon vegetable oil
1 medium head cauliflower, cut into flowerets
  and coarsely chopped
½ cup chopped onion
1 medium tomato, peeled and chopped
2 tablespoons chopped ripe olives
6 eggs, beaten
¼ cup grated Parmesan cheese
1 tablespoon chopped fresh parsley
½ teaspoon dried Italian seasoning
¼ teaspoon salt
¼ teaspoon pepper
4 egg whites

Coat a 12-inch ovenproof skillet with cooking spray; add oil. Place over medium-high heat until hot. Add cauliflower and onion; sauté until tender. Add tomato and olives; stir well, and set aside.

Combine 6 eggs, Parmesan, parsley, Italian seasoning, salt, and pepper in a large bowl; beat well. Beat egg whites (at room temperature) until stiff but not dry; fold into egg mixture. Pour over vegetable mixture. Cover and cook over medium heat 10 minutes or until egg mixture is almost set. Broil frittata 6 inches from heating element 2 minutes or until lightly browned. Cut into wedges, and serve immediately. Yield: 6 servings (149 calories per serving).

PRO 11.0 / FAT 9.6 / CARB 5.1 / FIB 0.8 / CHOL 277 / SOD 290 / POT 308

CHEESY RICE SOUFFLÉ

2 tablespoons margarine
3 tablespoons all-purpose flour
¾ cup skim milk
¾ cup (3 ounces) shredded extra-sharp Cheddar
  cheese
¼ teaspoon dry mustard
⅛ teaspoon red pepper
3 egg yolks, beaten
1 cup cooked brown rice (cooked without salt or fat)
4 egg whites
Vegetable cooking spray

Melt margarine in a small heavy saucepan over low heat; add flour, stirring until smooth. Cook 1 minute, stirring constantly (mixture will be dry). Gradually add milk; cook over medium heat, stirring constantly with a wire whisk, until smooth and thickened. Add cheese, mustard, and red pepper; stir until cheese melts. Gradually stir one-fourth of hot mixture into beaten egg yolks; add to remaining hot mixture, stirring constantly. Gently fold in rice. Beat egg whites (at room temperature) until stiff but not dry; gently fold into cheese mixture.

Spoon mixture into a 1½-quart soufflé dish coated on bottom with cooking spray. Bake at 325° for 40 minutes or until puffed and golden. Serve immediately. Yield: 4 servings (291 calories per serving).

PRO 14.1 / FAT 17.4 / CARB 18.9 / FIB 1.2 / CHOL 227 / SOD 283 / POT 193

What's more spectacular than a main-dish roll? A Spinach-Mushroom Soufflé Roll that's nutritious too.

SPINACH-MUSHROOM SOUFFLÉ ROLL

Vegetable cooking spray
3 tablespoons margarine
¼ cup all-purpose flour
Dash of red pepper
1 cup skim milk
¼ cup plus 2 tablespoons grated
   Parmesan cheese, divided
4 egg yolks
5 egg whites
¼ teaspoon cream of tartar
Spinach-Mushroom Filling
Cherry tomatoes
Fresh parsley sprigs

Coat a 15- x 10- x 1-inch jellyroll pan with cooking spray. Line with waxed paper; coat waxed paper with cooking spray.

Melt margarine in a large, heavy saucepan over low heat; add flour and red pepper, stirring until smooth. Cook 1 minute, stirring constantly. Gradually add milk; cook over medium heat, stirring constantly, until thickened and bubbly.

Remove from heat; stir in ¼ cup Parmesan cheese, stirring until cheese melts.

Place egg yolks in a large bowl; beat at high speed of an electric mixer until thick and lemon colored. Gradually stir in one-fourth of hot cheese mixture; add remaining hot mixture, beating well.

Combine egg whites (at room temperature) and cream of tartar; beat at high speed of an electric mixer until stiff peaks form. Fold one-third of egg whites into cheese mixture; carefully fold in remaining egg whites.

Pour mixture evenly into jellyroll pan. Bake at 350° for 15 minutes or until puffed and firm to the touch. (Do not overcook.)

Loosen edges of soufflé with a metal spatula, but do not remove from pan; place on a wire rack. Let cool 10 minutes.

Sprinkle remaining 2 tablespoons Parmesan cheese in a 15- x 10-inch rectangle on pastry cloth. Quickly invert jellyroll pan onto pastry cloth; remove pan, and carefully peel waxed paper from soufflé. Spoon Spinach-Mushroom Filling over surface, spreading to edges.

Starting at long side, roll up soufflé jellyroll fashion, using pastry cloth to help support soufflé. Gently smooth and shape roll.

Carefully slide roll, seam side down, onto a serving platter. Cut into 1¼-inch slices; garnish with tomatoes and parsley. Serve immediately. Yield: 6 servings (211 calories per serving).

Spinach-Mushroom Filling:

1 (10-ounce) package frozen chopped spinach
Vegetable cooking spray
½ cup diced fresh mushrooms
2 tablespoons finely chopped onion
½ cup (2 ounces) shredded mozzarella cheese
¼ cup plain low-fat yogurt
⅛ teaspoon ground nutmeg

Cook spinach according to package directions, omitting salt; drain. Place on paper towels, and squeeze until barely moist.

Coat a small skillet with cooking spray; place over medium-high heat until hot. Add mushrooms and onion, and sauté 3 minutes or until tender; drain. Combine spinach, mushroom mixture, and remaining ingredients in a small bowl; stir well. Yield: about 1 cup.

PRO 12.6 / FAT 13.5 / CARB 10.3 / FIB 1.2 / CHOL 194 / SOD 318 / POT 341

CHILES RELLENOS CASSEROLE

2 (4-ounce) cans chopped green chiles, drained
1 cup (4 ounces) shredded Monterey Jack cheese
½ cup (2 ounces) shredded sharp Cheddar cheese
Vegetable cooking spray
4 eggs, separated
¼ cup skim milk
1 tablespoon all-purpose flour
⅛ teaspoon pepper
Seasoned Tomato Sauce

Layer green chiles and cheese in a 2-quart casserole coated with cooking spray. Set aside.

Combine yolks, milk, flour, and pepper; beat until well blended. Beat egg whites (at room temperature) until stiff peaks form; fold into yolks. Pour over cheese. Bake at 350° for 25 minutes or until puffed and golden brown. Spoon 2 tablespoons sauce over each serving. Yield: 6 servings (192 calories per serving).

Seasoned Tomato Sauce:

Vegetable cooking spray
¼ cup chopped green onion
1 clove garlic, minced
1 (8-ounce) can no-salt-added tomato sauce
¼ teaspoon chili powder
¼ teaspoon dried whole oregano
Dash of hot sauce

Coat a skillet with cooking spray; place over medium heat until hot. Add onion and garlic; sauté until tender. Stir in remaining ingredients; cover and simmer 10 minutes. Yield: ¾ cup.

PRO 12.1 / FAT 12.6 / CARB 6.9 / FIB 0.7 / CHOL 208 / SOD 251 / POT 302

VEGETARIAN CABBAGE ROLLS

1 medium cabbage
Vegetable cooking spray
1 medium onion, chopped
2 cups cooked brown rice (cooked without salt or fat)
¼ cup unsalted sunflower kernels, toasted
½ cup (2 ounces) shredded extra-sharp Cheddar cheese
1 (8-ounce) can tomato sauce
2 teaspoons Worcestershire sauce
¼ teaspoon pepper

Remove dark outer leaves from cabbage. Core cabbage. Place cabbage in a large bowl of hot water until leaves are easily separated. Remove 8 large leaves; reserve remaining cabbage for other uses. Cook leaves in boiling water 6 to 8 minutes or just until tender. Drain and set aside.

Coat a medium skillet with cooking spray; place over medium heat until hot. Add onion, and sauté until tender. Combine onion, rice, sunflower kernels, and cheese in a medium bowl; mix well.

Place ⅓ cup rice mixture in center of each cabbage leaf; fold sides in over rice mixture, and roll up each leaf. Secure each cabbage roll with a wooden pick. Place cabbage rolls in a large skillet.

Combine tomato sauce, Worcestershire sauce, and pepper in a small bowl; mix well. Pour over cabbage rolls in skillet. Bring to a boil. Cover; reduce heat, and simmer 15 minutes. Remove cabbage rolls to a serving platter, and serve immediately. Yield: 4 servings (258 calories per serving).

PRO 9.8 / FAT 10.0 / CARB 35.0 / FIB 4.0 / CHOL 15 / SOD 472 / POT 606

STUFFED EGGPLANT ROLLS

1 medium eggplant
1 egg, slightly beaten
¼ cup skim milk
½ cup whole wheat flour
Vegetable cooking spray
2 teaspoons vegetable oil
1½ cups part-skim ricotta cheese
¼ cup grated Parmesan cheese
2 tablespoons chopped fresh parsley
⅛ teaspoon salt
Italian-Style Sauce
1 cup (4 ounces) shredded part-skim mozzarella cheese

Peel eggplant, and cut lengthwise into twelve ⅛-inch-thick slices. Press each slice between paper towels to remove excess moisture.

Combine egg and milk in a small bowl; mix well. Dip eggplant slices in egg mixture; dredge in flour.

Coat a large heavy skillet with cooking spray; add oil. Place over medium heat until hot. Add eggplant slices to skillet; cook until browned on both sides. Drain on paper towels. (Remove skillet from heat during cooking, and recoat skillet as needed.)

Combine ricotta cheese, Parmesan cheese, parsley, and salt in a medium bowl. Spread 2 tablespoons cheese mixture on each eggplant slice. Starting at short side, roll up each slice, jellyroll fashion.

Spoon ½ cup Italian-Style Sauce in a 12- x 8- x 2-inch baking dish. Arrange eggplant rolls in sauce, seam side down; top with remaining sauce. Cover and bake at 375° for 20 minutes. Uncover; sprinkle with mozzarella cheese, and bake an additional 5 minutes. Serve hot. Yield: 6 servings (263 calories per serving).

Italian-Style Sauce:

Vegetable cooking spray
½ cup chopped onion
1 (15-ounce) can no-salt-added tomato sauce
2 tablespoons red wine
½ teaspoon dried whole oregano
½ teaspoon dried whole basil
¼ teaspoon garlic powder

Coat a skillet with cooking spray; place over medium-high heat until hot. Add onion; sauté until onion is tender. Stir in remaining ingredients; bring to a boil. Cover; reduce heat, and simmer 30 minutes. Yield: about 1½ cups.

PRO 17.5 / FAT 11.7 / CARB 23.4 / FIB 2.6 / CHOL 79 / SOD 313 / POT 663

VEGETABLE-TOFU CASSEROLE

1 pound tofu
Vegetable cooking spray
1 medium onion, coarsely chopped
2 cups cauliflower flowerets
2 cups broccoli flowerets
1 medium carrot, scraped and sliced
1 cup sliced fresh mushrooms
1 clove garlic, minced
1 tablespoon plus 1½ teaspoons margarine
2 tablespoons all-purpose flour
1 cup skim milk
1 cup (4 ounces) grated Swiss cheese, divided
1 teaspoon dried whole basil
½ teaspoon dried whole marjoram
¼ teaspoon salt
⅛ teaspoon white pepper
2 tablespoons unsalted sunflower kernels, toasted

Wrap tofu with several layers of cheesecloth or paper towels; press lightly to remove excess liquid. Remove cheesecloth; cut tofu into ½-inch cubes, and set aside.

Coat a large nonstick skillet with cooking spray; place over medium-high heat until hot. Add onion, cauliflower, broccoli, carrot, mushrooms, and garlic; sauté until vegetables are crisp-tender. Remove from heat, and add tofu, tossing gently; set aside.

Melt margarine in a small saucepan over low heat; add flour, stirring until smooth. Cook 1 minute, stirring constantly. Gradually add milk; cook over medium heat, stirring constantly with a wire whisk, until thickened and bubbly. Add ½ cup Swiss cheese, basil, marjoram, salt, and pepper; stir until cheese melts.

Place vegetable mixture in a 2-quart casserole coated with cooking spray. Spoon cheese sauce evenly over top. Bake at 350° for 20 minutes. Remove from heat, and sprinkle with remaining ½ cup cheese and sunflower kernels; bake an additional 5 minutes or until cheese melts. Yield: 6 servings (227 calories per serving).

PRO 15.9 / FAT 13.1 / CARB 14.2 / FIB 1.5 / CHOL 18 / SOD 227 / POT 485

Vegetable-Tofu Casserole, sprinkled with toasted sunflower kernels, will travel well to your next covered-dish supper.

CHILE-CHEESE CASSEROLE

2 (16-ounce) cans red kidney beans, drained
1½ cups part-skim ricotta cheese
1 cup (4 ounces) shredded Monterey Jack
  cheese
1 (4-ounce) can chopped green chiles, drained
¼ cup chopped green onion
2 eggs, beaten
4 (6-inch) corn tortillas
Vegetable cooking spray
1 teaspoon vegetable oil
¼ cup chopped green pepper
1 clove garlic, minced
1 (14½-ounce) can no-salt-added whole tomatoes,
  undrained and coarsely chopped
1 (8-ounce) can no-salt-added tomato sauce
2 teaspoons chili powder
½ cup (2 ounces) shredded extra-sharp Cheddar
  cheese

Place kidney beans in a colander, and rinse under cold tap water 1 minute; set colander aside to let beans drain 1 minute.

Combine cheeses, chiles, green onion, and eggs in a medium bowl, mixing well; set aside.

Cut each tortilla into 8 wedges; place on an ungreased baking sheet. Bake at 350° for 10 minutes or until crisp. Set aside.

Coat a large skillet with cooking spray; add oil, and place over medium-high heat until hot. Add green pepper and garlic; sauté until tender. Stir in kidney beans, tomatoes, tomato sauce, and chili powder; bring to a boil. Reduce heat, and simmer, uncovered, 15 minutes.

Spread half of ricotta cheese mixture in a 2-quart casserole coated with cooking spray. Arrange 8 tortilla wedges on cheese mixture; spread half of bean mixture evenly over tortillas. Repeat layers with remaining cheese mixture, 8 tortilla wedges, and remaining bean mixture. Cover and bake at 350° for 30 minutes. Remove from heat, and sprinkle with Cheddar cheese; bake, uncovered, an additional 5 minutes. Serve with remaining tortilla wedges. Yield: 8 servings (330 calories per serving).

PRO 19.9 / FAT 13.3 / CARB 33.7 / FIB 10.7 / CHOL 101 / SOD 414 / POT 616

TORTILLA TORTE

1 (15-ounce) can pinto beans
Vegetable cooking spray
½ cup chopped onion
1 clove garlic, minced
¼ teaspoon ground cumin
¼ cup commercial picante sauce
1 (4-ounce) can chopped green chiles, drained
4 (8-inch) whole wheat flour tortillas
¾ cup (3 ounces) shredded Monterey Jack
  cheese
2 tablespoons sliced ripe olives
2 cups shredded lettuce
1 medium tomato, chopped
Hot green pepper slices (optional)

Place pinto beans in a colander, and rinse under cold tap water 1 minute; set colander aside to let beans drain 1 minute.

Coat a large skillet with cooking spray; place over medium heat until hot. Add onion and garlic to skillet; sauté until tender. Stir in reserved pinto beans and cumin; reduce heat. Cook, un-

covered, 30 minutes or until mixture is a thick paste, stirring occasionally and mashing beans with a wooden spoon. Set mixture aside, and keep warm.

Combine picante sauce and green chiles, and set aside.

Wrap tortillas in aluminum foil, and bake at 350° for 10 minutes or until thoroughly heated.

Place a tortilla on a baking sheet lightly coated with cooking spray. Top with one-third of bean mixture, one-third of picante sauce mixture, ¼ cup cheese, and 2 teaspoons olives. Repeat layers twice; top with remaining tortilla. Cover with foil, and bake at 350° for 15 minutes or until thoroughly heated. Transfer to a serving platter. Arrange shredded lettuce around torte. Top lettuce with chopped tomato, and garnish with hot green pepper slices, if desired. Cut into wedges to serve. Yield: 4 servings (269 calories per serving).

PRO 13.0 / FAT 8.7 / CARB 36.5 / FIB 10.3 / CHOL 17 / SOD 409 / POT 462

GARBANZO SAUCE OVER BROWN RICE

1 (16-ounce) can garbanzo beans
Vegetable cooking spray
2 teaspoons vegetable oil
1 medium onion, coarsely chopped
2 cloves garlic, minced
1 medium-size green pepper, seeded and chopped
1 tablespoon chopped fresh parsley
2 (8-ounce) cans no-salt-added tomato sauce
½ teaspoon dried whole oregano
¼ teaspoon dried whole basil
¼ teaspoon pepper
2 cups hot cooked brown rice (cooked without salt or fat)
½ cup (2 ounces) shredded extra-sharp Cheddar cheese
1 tablespoon plus 1 teaspoon grated Parmesan cheese

Place garbanzo beans in a colander, and rinse under cold tap water for 1 minute; let garbanzo beans drain in colander for 1 minute. Set beans aside.

Coat a large skillet with cooking spray; add vegetable oil, and place over medium heat until hot. Add chopped onion, garlic, chopped green pepper, and parsley; sauté until tender. Add reserved garbanzo beans, tomato sauce, oregano, basil, and pepper. Cover; reduce heat, and simmer 30 minutes. Serve over hot cooked brown rice. Sprinkle Cheddar cheese and grated Parmesan cheese over top. Yield: 4 servings (207 calories per serving plus 102 calories per ½ cup cooked brown rice).

PRO 11.6 / FAT 9.1 / CARB 45.6 / FIB 6.7 / CHOL 16 / SOD 298 / POT 844

CUBAN BLACK BEANS WITH BROWN RICE

1 (16-ounce) package dried black beans
2 cups water
Vegetable cooking spray
2 teaspoons olive oil
1 cup chopped onion
1 medium-size green pepper, seeded and chopped
1 bay leaf
1 dried red pepper pod
1 clove garlic, minced
1 teaspoon salt
1½ quarts water
4 cups hot cooked brown rice (cooked without salt or fat)
1 (8-ounce) carton plain low-fat yogurt
¼ cup chopped green onion

Sort and wash beans; place in a medium saucepan. Add 2 cups water; bring to a boil. Cover; remove from heat, and let stand 1 hour. Drain beans, and set aside.

Coat a large skillet with cooking spray; add oil, and place over medium heat until hot. Add onion and green pepper, and sauté until tender. Add bay leaf, red pepper, garlic, and salt; cook one minute, stirring constantly. Remove from heat, and set aside.

Add 1½ quarts water to reserved beans in saucepan, and bring to a boil. Reduce heat, and simmer, uncovered, 1 hour. Stir in onion mixture, and continue to simmer, uncovered, 1½ hours or until beans are tender. (Add additional water, if necessary.)

Remove and discard bay leaf and red pepper pod. Serve ¾ cup black beans over ½ cup brown rice. Top with 2 tablespoons yogurt, and sprinkle green onion over top. Yield: 8 servings (232 calories per serving plus 102 calories per ½ cup cooked brown rice).

PRO 16.7 / FAT 3.1 / CARB 61.2 / FIB 16.7 / CHOL 2 / SOD 330 / POT 780

 Vegetarians, studies show, have significantly lower blood pressure, lower levels of blood cholesterol, and, consequently, less heart disease than meat-eaters.

Probably the healthiest approach, say scientists, is to be a "semi-vegetarian" — one who eats less red meat and more vegetables, fruits, and grains. While no diet can guarantee you'll be risk-free, semi-vegetarians have less chance of getting heart disease than those who eat meat daily.

CANNELLINI PILAF

1 cup brown rice, uncooked
1 (15-ounce) can cannellini beans
Vegetable cooking spray
1 tablespoon vegetable oil
⅓ cup unsalted sunflower kernels
2 medium carrots, scraped and grated
1 medium onion, chopped
1 medium-size yellow squash, thinly sliced
1 cup broccoli flowerets
1 medium tomato, chopped
1 clove garlic, minced
½ cup (2 ounces) shredded extra-sharp Cheddar
  cheese
½ teaspoon dried whole oregano
¼ teaspoon salt
¼ teaspoon dried whole thyme
¼ teaspoon dried whole rosemary, crushed
¼ teaspoon pepper
¼ cup grated Parmesan cheese
1 tablespoon chopped fresh parsley

Cook brown rice according to package directions, omitting salt and fat. Set aside.

Drain cannellini beans in a colander, and rinse under cold tap water 1 minute; set colander aside to let beans drain 1 minute.

Coat a large skillet with cooking spray; add oil. Place over medium heat until hot. Add sunflower kernels, and cook until lightly toasted, stirring constantly. Add next 6 ingredients to skillet; sauté until crisp-tender. Add brown rice, cannellini beans, Cheddar cheese, oregano, salt, thyme, rosemary, and pepper, tossing lightly. Sprinkle with Parmesan cheese and parsley. Serve warm or cold. Yield: 6 servings (301 calories per serving).

PRO 11.5 / FAT 11.4 / CARB 39.2 / FIB 6.3 / CHOL 13 / SOD 321 / POT 513

 Say "Cheese" and — Smile! Besides calcium, cheese offers teeth protection. Mouth bacteria feed on carbohydrates, especially sweets, producing acids that eat away at tooth enamel. But cheese, especially Cheddar, Swiss and Monterey Jack, inhibits acid production, find researchers at the University of Minnesota School of Dentistry. Cheese also stimulates saliva flow, which protects teeth.

LENTIL PASTICCIO

1 cup elbow macaroni, uncooked
¾ cup dry lentils
¾ cup chopped onion
1 medium carrot, finely chopped
1 clove garlic, minced
1¾ cups water
1 (8-ounce) can tomato sauce
2 tablespoons chopped fresh parsley
¼ teaspoon ground cinnamon
1 tablespoon margarine
1 tablespoon plus 1½ teaspoons all-purpose flour
1 cup skim milk
¼ cup grated Parmesan cheese
¼ teaspoon salt
⅛ teaspoon pepper
1 egg, beaten
Vegetable cooking spray

Cook macaroni according to package directions, omitting salt; set aside.

Sort and wash lentils; drain. Combine lentils, onion, carrot, garlic, and water in a medium saucepan. Bring to a boil; cover, reduce heat, and simmer 35 minutes. (Do not overcook lentils.) Remove from heat. Stir in tomato sauce, parsley, and cinnamon; set aside.

Melt margarine in a saucepan over low heat; add flour, stirring until smooth (mixture will be dry). Cook 1 minute, stirring constantly. Gradually add milk; cook over medium heat, stirring constantly, until thickened and bubbly. Remove from heat. Stir in Parmesan cheese, salt, and pepper; stir until cheese melts. Cool to room temperature. Add egg; stir well.

Layer half each of macaroni and lentil mixture in a 10- x 6- x 2-inch baking dish coated with cooking spray. Repeat layers; pour Parmesan cheese mixture evenly over top. Bake at 350° for 55 minutes or until lightly browned. Let stand 10 minutes before serving. Yield: 6 servings (263 calories per serving).

PRO 14.0 / FAT 4.6 / CARB 42.0 / FIB 2.3 / CHOL 49 / SOD 395 / POT 581

The classic entrée for a buffet or holiday meal — Roast Beef with Horseradish Sauce (page 132). Prepared the light way, it's both nutritious and delicious.

ROAST BEEF WITH GARLIC-BASIL PUREE

1½ cups water
6 cloves garlic, unpeeled
¼ cup packed chopped fresh basil
Dash of salt
1 (3-pound) beef eye-of-round roast
Vegetable cooking spray

Bring water to a boil in a medium saucepan; add garlic. Cover; reduce heat to medium-high, and cook 30 minutes. Drain well. Peel garlic. Combine garlic, basil, and salt in a food processor; process until smooth. Set aside.

Trim excess fat from roast. Rub garlic puree over entire surface of meat. Coat rack of a broiler pan with cooking spray. Place roast on rack. Insert meat thermometer into thickest part of roast; cover with aluminum foil, and bake at 450° for 20 minutes. Uncover and bake an additional 25 to 30 minutes or until meat thermometer registers 140° (rare) or 160° (medium).

Let roast stand at room temperature 15 minutes before cutting across grain into thin slices. Yield: 12 servings (210 calories per serving).

PRO 24.2 / FAT 11.4 / CARB 1.2 / FIB 0.2 / CHOL 77 / SOD 64 / POT 358

ROAST BEEF WITH HORSERADISH SAUCE

1 (5½-pound) beef eye-of-round roast
3 cloves garlic, sliced
1½ cups Burgundy or other dry red wine
2 tablespoons lemon juice
1 tablespoon Worcestershire sauce
½ teaspoon salt
2 teaspoons pepper
Plum tomato wedges
Fresh tarragon sprigs
Horseradish Sauce

Trim excess fat from roast. Make small slits in roast; stuff each slit with a slice of garlic. Place roast in a 13- x 9- x 2-inch baking dish. Combine wine, lemon juice, Worcestershire sauce, salt, and pepper; pour over roast. Cover and refrigerate overnight, turning roast occasionally.

Remove roast from marinade; discard marinade. Place roast on a rack in a shallow roasting pan; insert meat thermometer, if desired. Cover with aluminum foil, and bake at 450° for 20 minutes; uncover and bake 35 minutes or until meat thermometer registers 140° (rare).

Transfer roast to a warm serving platter; let stand 15 minutes before cutting across grain into thin slices. Garnish with plum tomato wedges and tarragon sprigs. Serve with 1 tablespoon Horseradish Sauce per serving. Yield: 18 servings (275 calories per serving).

Horseradish Sauce:

½ cup plain low-fat yogurt
½ cup reduced-calorie mayonnaise
2 tablespoons grated fresh horseradish
½ teaspoon sugar
½ teaspoon white pepper
½ teaspoon dry mustard
1½ teaspoons tarragon vinegar

Combine all ingredients; stir well. Cover; chill thoroughly. Yield: 1 cup plus 2 tablespoons.

PRO 29.8 / FAT 15.8 / CARB 1.5 / FIB 0.0 / CHOL 97 / SOD 116 / POT 413

BEEFED-UP RATATOUILLE

1 (1½-pound) beef rump roast
Vegetable cooking spray
1 medium onion, chopped
1 clove garlic, crushed
1 teaspoon vegetable oil
4 medium tomatoes, peeled, seeded, and chopped
2 medium zucchini squash, sliced
1 medium-size green pepper, seeded and chopped
1 small eggplant, peeled and cubed
1 cup sliced fresh mushrooms
½ teaspoon salt
¼ teaspoon dried whole basil, crushed
¼ teaspoon dried whole oregano, crushed
¼ teaspoon dried whole thyme, crushed
½ cup (2 ounces) shredded part-skim mozzarella cheese

Trim excess fat from roast, and cut roast into cubes. Coat a large skillet with cooking spray; place over medium heat until hot. Add beef, onion, and garlic; cook beef until browned on all sides, stirring frequently. Cover; reduce heat, and simmer 20 minutes, stirring occasionally.

Remove beef mixture from skillet; drain well on paper towels, and set aside.

Wipe skillet clean with a paper towel. Coat skillet with cooking spray; add oil, and place over medium heat until hot. Add remaining ingredients, except cheese; sauté 1 to 2 minutes. Add reserved beef mixture. Cover; reduce heat, and simmer 15 minutes or until tender. Sprinkle with cheese, and serve immediately. Yield: 8 servings (217 calories per serving).

PRO 21.8 / FAT 10.6 / CARB 9.0 / FIB 1.7 / CHOL 62 / SOD 224 / POT 647

Steak on a Stick's special ingredient is light beer.

STEAK ON A STICK

2 pounds lean boneless beef sirloin steak
1 (12-ounce) can light beer
1 clove garlic, pressed
½ teaspoon seasoned salt
⅛ teaspoon pepper

Trim excess fat from steak, and cut steak into 1-inch cubes. Place cubes in a 12- x 8- x 2-inch baking dish; set aside. Combine remaining ingredients, stirring well; pour over steak. Cover and refrigerate overnight.

Remove steak from marinade, reserving marinade; thread onto 8 short skewers. Grill 5 inches over medium coals 14 minutes or until done, turning once; baste often with marinade. Yield: 8 servings (157 calories per serving).

PRO 27.0 / FAT 4.5 / CARB 0.2 / FIB 0.0 / CHOL 55 / SOD 172 / POT 318

GRILLED SIRLOIN WITH RED PEPPER PUREE

1 (1-pound) lean boneless beef sirloin steak (about ¾-inch thick)
Vegetable cooking spray
4 medium-size sweet red peppers
⅓ cup chopped green onion
¼ cup water
2 tablespoons dry white wine
1 teaspoon beef-flavored bouillon granules
Fresh parsley sprigs

Trim excess fat from steak. Coat grill with cooking spray. Grill steak 4 to 6 inches over hot coals 8 minutes on each side or until desired degree of doneness. Set aside, and keep warm.

Cut three-fourths of one red pepper into thin strips; set aside. Seed and chop remaining red peppers. Set aside.

Coat a skillet with cooking spray. Place over medium heat until hot; add reserved pepper strips, and sauté until tender. Remove from skillet, and set aside.

Add chopped peppers, green onion, water, wine, and bouillon granules to skillet. Cover; reduce heat, and simmer 15 minutes. Cool slightly. Transfer pepper mixture to container of an electric blender or food processor; process until pureed. Strain mixture; return to skillet to heat thoroughly.

Cut steak into 4 equal portions. Spoon one-fourth of red pepper puree onto a serving plate; top with 1 steak portion. Garnish with reserved red pepper strips and parsley. Repeat procedure with remaining ingredients. Serve immediately. Yield: 4 servings (191 calories per serving).

PRO 28.1 / FAT 5.1 / CARB 7.4 / FIB 1.2 / CHOL 55 / SOD 171 / POT 549

STIR-FRIED BEEF AND BROCCOLI

1 (¾-pound) beef flank steak
2 tablespoons reduced-sodium soy sauce
2 teaspoons cornstarch
3 cups broccoli flowerets
Vegetable cooking spray
1 tablespoon vegetable oil
½ cup chopped onion
¾ teaspoon ground ginger or 1 tablespoon minced fresh gingerroot
3 tablespoons water

Trim excess fat from steak, and cut steak into ⅛-inch-thick slices. Combine steak, soy sauce, and cornstarch, stirring well; set aside.

Cook broccoli in boiling water 2 minutes; drain and set aside.

Coat a wok or large skillet with cooking spray; add oil. Heat at medium until hot. Add onion and ginger; stir-fry 30 seconds. Add reserved steak mixture; stir-fry 2 minutes. Add reserved broccoli and 3 tablespoons water; stir-fry 1 minute. Yield: 4 servings (199 calories per serving).

PRO 21.8 / FAT 8.6 / CARB 8.9 / FIB 1.4 / CHOL 80 / SOD 368 / POT 615

MARINATED FLANK STEAK

1 (2-pound) beef flank steak
¼ cup plus 2 tablespoons lemon juice
¼ cup plus 2 tablespoons reduced-sodium soy sauce
1 tablespoon dry mustard
1 tablespoon vegetable oil
Vegetable cooking spray

Trim excess fat from steak, and place steak in a large shallow dish. Combine lemon juice, soy sauce, dry mustard, and oil; mix well, and pour over steak. Cover and refrigerate overnight, turning occasionally.

Remove steak from marinade, reserving marinade. Coat rack of a broiler pan with cooking spray. Place steak on rack. Broil 3 to 4 inches from heating element 7 to 9 minutes on each side or to desired degree of doneness, basting often with marinade. Cut diagonally across grain into thin slices to serve. Yield: 8 servings (173 calories per serving).

PRO 27.5 / FAT 5.6 / CARB 1.5 / FIB 0.0 / CHOL 55 / SOD 197 / POT 333

GRILLED ROUND STEAK WITH TOMATILLO SAUCE

1½ pounds beef top round steak (about ¾-inch thick)
¾ cup Burgundy or other dry red wine
2 tablespoons lime juice
1 tablespoon Worcestershire sauce
½ teaspoon seasoned salt
Dash of pepper
1 clove garlic, minced
Vegetable cooking spray
Tomatillo Sauce

Trim excess fat from steak. Place steak in a large shallow baking dish. Combine next 6 ingredients in a small bowl; mix well, and pour over steak. Cover and refrigerate 24 hours, turning steak occasionally.

Remove steak from marinade. Coat grill with cooking spray. Grill 5 to 6 inches over hot coals 5 to 7 minutes on each side or until desired degree of doneness. Transfer steak to a cutting board; cut steak across grain into ¼-inch-thick slices. Serve immediately with equal amounts of Tomatillo Sauce per serving. Yield: 6 servings (215 calories per serving).

Tomatillo Sauce:

½ pound fresh tomatillos
1 small onion, chopped
1 clove garlic, peeled
½ cup loosely packed cilantro leaves
1 tablespoon vegetable oil
½ teaspoon sugar
½ teaspoon salt

Remove stems and outer husks of tomatillos; rinse well. Combine all ingredients in container of an electric blender; process until smooth. Transfer tomatillo mixture to a medium saucepan, and bring to a boil. Reduce heat, and simmer, uncovered, 10 minutes. Serve hot. Yield: about 1 cup.

PRO 27.7 / FAT 6.9 / CARB 4.4 / FIB 0.5 / CHOL 55 / SOD 441 / POT 504

 Take five, after exercise. Five minutes of slower movement allows blood pressure to readjust gradually, protecting the heart against a sudden drop in blood supply.

SPEEDY SKILLET STEAKS

2 tablespoons all-purpose flour
¼ teaspoon salt
¼ teaspoon dried thyme
¼ teaspoon dried chervil
⅛ teaspoon pepper
4 beef cube steaks (about 1 pound)
Vegetable cooking spray
2 tablespoons dry white wine
2 tablespoons water
½ cup chopped green onion
1 large ripe tomato, cut into
   wedges

Combine first 5 ingredients; dredge steaks in flour mixture. Coat a large skillet with cooking spray. Add steaks, and cook over medium heat 5 minutes on each side. Drain on paper towels, and wipe skillet clean. Return steaks to skillet; add wine, water, and onion. Cover and simmer 6 minutes or until steaks are tender. Add tomato wedges to skillet; cover and simmer 2 minutes or until thoroughly heated. Yield: 4 servings (190 calories per serving).

PRO 28.2 / FAT 4.7 / CARB 7.5 / FIB 1.1 / CHOL 55 / SOD 204 / POT 490

BEEF-SPINACH CRÊPES

1 (10-ounce) package frozen chopped spinach
½ pound ground chuck
¼ cup chopped onion
¼ cup chopped celery
¼ cup shredded carrot
1 egg, beaten
2 tablespoons grated Parmesan cheese
2 tablespoons Chablis or other dry white wine
½ teaspoon dried whole basil
¼ teaspoon dried whole oregano
Crêpes (recipe follows)
Vegetable cooking spray
2 tablespoons margarine
2 tablespoons all-purpose flour
1 cup skim milk
¼ cup Chablis or other dry white wine
⅛ teaspoon salt
⅛ teaspoon white pepper
½ cup (2 ounces) shredded part-skim mozzarella
   cheese

Cook spinach according to package directions, omitting salt; drain well. Place between paper towels, and squeeze until barely moist. Set aside.

Combine ground chuck, onion, celery, and carrot in a medium skillet; cook over medium heat 5 minutes or until meat is browned, stirring to crumble meat. Drain in a colander; pat with paper towels to remove excess grease.

Combine reserved spinach, meat mixture, egg, Parmesan cheese, 2 tablespoons wine, basil, and oregano in a medium bowl; stir well. Spoon ¼ cup mixture in center of each crêpe; roll up. Place crêpes, seam side down, in a 12- x 8- x 2-inch baking dish coated with cooking spray; set aside.

Melt margarine in a small saucepan over low heat; add flour, stirring until smooth. Cook 1 minute, stirring constantly. Gradually add milk and ¼ cup wine; cook over medium heat, stirring constantly, until thickened and bubbly. Remove from heat; add salt, pepper, and cheese, stirring until cheese melts. Spoon sauce over crêpes. Bake, uncovered, at 375° for 15 minutes or until bubbly. Yield: 4 servings (376 calories per 2-crêpe serving).

Crêpes:

½ cup all-purpose flour
¾ cup skim milk
1 egg
Vegetable cooking spray

Combine flour, milk, and egg in container of an electric blender; process until smooth. Refrigerate batter for 1 hour. (This allows flour particles to swell and soften so crêpes are light in texture.)

Coat bottom of a 6-inch crêpe pan with cooking spray; place pan over medium heat until hot. Pour 2 tablespoons batter into pan. Tilt pan quickly in all directions so batter covers bottom of pan. Cook 1 minute. Lift edge of crêpe to test for doneness. Crêpe is ready for flipping when it can be shaken loose from pan. Flip crêpe, and cook 30 seconds. Place on a paper towel to cool. Stack cooled crêpes between layers of waxed paper to prevent sticking. Repeat procedure until all batter is used. Yield: 8 (6-inch) crêpes.

PRO 27.6 / FAT 17.0 / CARB 28.0 / FIB 2.4 / CHOL 189 / SOD 430 / POT 754

EASY HOT CHILI

Vegetable cooking spray
1 pound ground chuck
¼ cup chopped onion
1 (8-ounce) can tomato sauce
1 cup water
1 (10-ounce) can tomatoes and green chilies,
 drained
2 tablespoons all-purpose flour
2 tablespoons chili powder
¼ teaspoon ground cumin (optional)

Coat a large skillet with cooking spray. Add meat and onion; cook until browned, stirring to crumble meat. Drain well; pat with paper towels to remove excess grease. Wipe pan drippings from skillet. Return meat to skillet; stir in tomato sauce, water, and tomatoes and chiles.

Combine flour, chili powder, and cumin, if desired. Stir into beef mixture. Cover and simmer 20 minutes, stirring occasionally. Yield: 4 servings (243 calories per serving).

PRO 25.5 / FAT 10.3 / CARB 11.7 / FIB 1.3 / CHOL 80 / SOD 345 / POT 794

CALF'S LIVER
WITH VEGETABLE GARNISH

2 tablespoons fine, dry breadcrumbs
¼ teaspoon pepper
⅛ teaspoon garlic powder
1½ pounds thinly sliced calf's liver
Vegetable cooking spray
2 tablespoons finely chopped green onion
2 tablespoons finely chopped tomato
2 tablespoons (½ ounce) shredded sharp Cheddar
 cheese
1 tablespoon minced fresh cilantro

Combine first 3 ingredients, stirring well; dredge liver in mixture. Coat a large skillet with cooking spray; place over medium heat until hot. Add liver; cook 5 minutes on each side or until browned. Drain; transfer to a warm platter.

Combine remaining ingredients in a small bowl; toss well. Spoon 1 tablespoon mixture onto each slice of liver; serve immediately. Yield: 6 servings (179 calories per serving).

PRO 22.7 / FAT 6.2 / CARB 6.7 / FIB 0.1 / CHOL 343 / SOD 114 / POT 345

 Red meat is getting leaner. That's good news for healthy eaters. Red meat is a good source of protein, B vitamins and iron, say many nutritionists, but it usually has too much fat, especially the saturated kind that's particularly bad for hearts.

Just last year, the United States Department of Agriculture (USDA) introduced a new designation, "Lite." By definition, Lite beef comes from livestock that's at least 25% leaner than regular animals — for that grade. That means that a Choice ground round that's Lite has 25% less fat than a regular Choice ground round.

To produce Lite beef, some producers are introducing breeds rarely seen in this country. Chianina steer, a tall breed imported from Italy to Texas, stores little fat as it grows. It has qualified for a Lite designation and is being marketed as "Key-Lite" beef.

Even if you can't find Lite beef in your market, you can dramatically reduce the amount of fat your family gets at dinner by buying lean cuts, and serving moderate portions flanked by grains and vegetables. A moderate portion is from 2 to 4 ounces of meat per person, more than enough concentrated protein in a single meal. The recipes in this book call for no more than 4 ounces of meat per serving before cooking.

Some lean cuts: round steak, round roast, sirloin, flank steak, fresh ham steak, pork loin chops, lamb leg, loin lamb chops, veal steak, veal chops and veal cutlets.

VEAL SCALLOPINI
WITH ZUCCHINI AND TOMATO

1 pound veal cutlets (¼-inch thick)
2 tablespoons all-purpose flour
½ teaspoon dried whole basil
⅛ teaspoon salt
⅛ teaspoon pepper
Vegetable cooking spray
1 tablespoon olive or vegetable oil
1 medium tomato, peeled and chopped
1 medium zucchini, thinly sliced
1 clove garlic, minced
1 tablespoon lemon juice
1 tablespoon water
1 teaspoon capers

Trim excess fat from veal cutlets; cut veal into serving-size pieces. Place veal between 2 sheets of waxed paper; flatten to ⅛-inch thickness, using a meat mallet or rolling pin. Combine flour, basil, salt, and pepper; dredge veal in flour mixture.

Coat a large skillet with cooking spray; add oil. Place over medium-high heat until hot. Add veal, and cook 4 to 5 minutes on each side or until browned. Drain on paper towels, reserving pan drippings in skillet. Transfer veal to a serving platter; keep warm.

Add tomato, zucchini, and garlic to skillet; sauté 2 minutes or until tender. Spoon mixture over veal. Add lemon juice and water to skillet; bring to a boil, scraping browned bits from bottom of pan. Stir in capers. Spoon mixture over veal to serve. Yield: 4 servings (239 calories per serving).

PRO 23.8 / FAT 12.7 / CARB 7.0 / FIB 0.3 / CHOL 81 / SOD 401 / POT 555

VEAL WITH PEPPERCORN SAUCE

1½ pounds veal cutlets
¼ teaspoon salt
⅛ teaspoon pepper
Vegetable cooking spray
1½ teaspoons margarine
¼ cup chopped onion
¾ cup water
¼ cup Chablis or other dry white wine
1 tablespoon lemon juice
1 teaspoon chicken-flavored bouillon granules
1 teaspoon crushed green peppercorns
½ teaspoon Worcestershire sauce
3 cups hot cooked vermicelli (cooked without salt)
2 teaspoons cornstarch
1 tablespoon water
Fresh parsley sprigs

Trim excess fat from veal cutlets. Place cutlets between two sheets of waxed paper; flatten to ⅛-inch thickness, using a meat mallet or rolling pin. Cut into ½-inch strips; sprinkle with salt and pepper. Set aside.

Coat a large skillet with cooking spray; add margarine. Place over medium-high heat until margarine melts. Add chopped onion, and sauté 2 minutes or until tender. Add reserved veal cutlets; cook, stirring frequently, until evenly browned. Add ¾ cup water, wine, lemon juice, bouillon granules, peppercorns, and Worcestershire sauce; bring to a boil. Cover; reduce heat, and simmer 10 minutes.

Place vermicelli on a serving platter; arrange veal over vermicelli, using a slotted spoon. Combine cornstarch and 1 tablespoon water, stirring to blend; add to pan juices. Cook, stirring constantly, 3 minutes or until thickened. Spoon over veal. Garnish with parsley, and serve immediately. Yield: 6 servings (194 calories per serving plus 105 calories per ½ cup cooked vermicelli).

PRO 26.0 / FAT 10.5 / CARB 23.4 / FIB 1.1 / CHOL 81 / SOD 280 / POT 448

SAVORY VEAL CHOPS

4 (5-ounce) loin veal chops (about ¾-inch thick)
½ teaspoon dried Italian seasoning
⅛ teaspoon pepper
Vegetable cooking spray
2 teaspoons vegetable oil
¼ cup water
¼ cup Chablis or other dry white wine
½ teaspoon chicken-flavored bouillon granules
1 clove garlic, crushed
1 small onion, thinly sliced
2 cups sliced fresh mushrooms
½ teaspoon dried whole rosemary, crushed
1 tablespoon chopped fresh parsley

Trim excess fat from veal chops. Sprinkle veal chops with Italian seasoning and pepper. Coat a large skillet with cooking spray; add oil, and place over medium-high heat until hot. Add veal to skillet, and cook 3 to 4 minutes on each side or until browned. Remove veal from skillet, and drain on paper towels; set aside. Wipe skillet dry with a paper towel. Add water, wine, bouillon granules, and garlic to skillet. Bring to a boil, stirring to dissolve bouillon; reduce heat, and simmer 2 minutes.

Place onion in bottom of a 12- x 8- x 2-inch baking dish; top with veal chops. Pour wine mixture over chops. Sprinkle with mushrooms and rosemary. Cover and bake at 350° for 25 minutes or until veal chops are tender. Sprinkle with parsley, and serve immediately. Yield: 4 servings (251 calories per serving).

PRO 24.5 / FAT 14.4 / CARB 5.0 / FIB 0.6 / CHOL 89 / SOD 122 / POT 644

A perfect one-dish supper: Veal Meatballs over Noodles.

VEAL MEATBALLS OVER NOODLES

1 pound ground veal
¼ cup fine, dry breadcrumbs
2 tablespoons chopped fresh parsley
2 tablespoons skim milk
1 egg
1 clove garlic, crushed
½ teaspoon pepper
¼ teaspoon salt
Vegetable cooking spray
1 teaspoon vegetable oil
1 cup sliced fresh mushrooms
1 tablespoon all-purpose flour
¾ cup skim milk
¼ cup plain low-fat yogurt
2 teaspoons Worcestershire sauce
¼ teaspoon pepper
1 (5-ounce) package medium egg noodles
1 teaspoon poppy seeds

Combine first 8 ingredients in a large bowl; mix well. Shape into eighteen 1½-inch balls.

Coat a large skillet with cooking spray; add oil, and place over medium-high heat until hot. Add meatballs, and cook 5 to 6 minutes on all sides or until browned. Remove meatballs; drain on paper towels, reserving pan drippings.

Add mushrooms to skillet; sauté until tender. Remove mushrooms, and set aside.

Combine flour and milk in skillet, stirring until smooth. Cook over medium heat, stirring constantly, until thickened. (Do not boil.) Stir in yogurt, Worcestershire sauce, and pepper. Add meatballs and mushrooms; cook over low heat until thoroughly heated. (Do not boil.)

Cook noodles according to package directions, omitting salt; drain and place on a serving platter. Sprinkle with poppy seeds. Spoon meatball mixture over noodles. Yield: 6 servings (278 calories per serving).

PRO 21.8 / FAT 9.5 / CARB 25.0 / FIB 0.3 / CHOL 123 / SOD 252 / POT 446

CHILE-SAUCED VEAL CHOPS

4 (5-ounce) loin veal chops (about ¾-inch thick)
Vegetable cooking spray
1 clove garlic, minced
2 green onions, finely chopped
1 (4-ounce) can chopped green chiles, drained
1 cup unsweetened orange juice
¾ teaspoon dried whole oregano
1 bay leaf
¼ teaspoon red pepper flakes
⅛ teaspoon salt
1 teaspoon cornstarch
¼ cup water

Trim excess fat from veal chops. Coat a large skillet with cooking spray; place over medium-high heat until hot. Add veal chops, and cook 4 minutes on each side or until lightly browned.

Remove chops from skillet; drain on paper towels. Place chops in an 8-inch square baking dish lightly coated with cooking spray; set aside.

Wipe skillet dry with a paper towel. Coat skillet with cooking spray; place over medium heat until hot. Add garlic, onions, and chiles; sauté until tender. Stir in orange juice, oregano, bay leaf, red pepper flakes, and salt. Bring to a boil; reduce heat, and simmer 3 minutes. Combine cornstarch and water; add to skillet. Cook over medium heat, stirring constantly, until mixture comes to a full boil. Boil 1 minute, stirring constantly. Remove from heat; spoon over chops. Cover; bake at 350° for 45 minutes or until veal is tender. Discard bay leaf. Yield: 4 servings (249 calories per serving).

PRO 23.9 / FAT 12.0 / CARB 9.5 / FIB 0.4 / CHOL 89 / SOD 175 / POT 621

GRILLED LEG OF LAMB

1 (7½-pound) lean leg of lamb, boned and
   butterflied
1 (8-ounce) bottle reduced-calorie French salad
   dressing
2 bay leaves, crushed
1 teaspoon peppercorns, crushed
1 teaspoon fines herbes

Trim excess fat from leg of lamb. Combine next 4 ingredients in a large dish or roasting pan. Place leg of lamb in marinade, turning to coat well. Cover and refrigerate 8 hours or overnight, turning occasionally. Remove leg of lamb, reserving marinade.

Insert 2 long skewers through meat at right angles, making an X, or place meat in a wire broiler basket. (Skewers help prevent curling during cooking.) Grill over medium coals 2 hours and 15 minutes for medium-rare or until desired degree of doneness; turn lamb every 15 minutes, and baste frequently with reserved marinade.

Transfer leg of lamb to a warm serving platter. Let stand 10 minutes before cutting across grain into thin slices. Yield: 15 servings (213 calories per serving).

PRO 32.6 / FAT 8.0 / CARB 0.4 / FIB 0.0 / CHOL 113 / SOD 229 / POT 342

LAMB STEAKS VÉRONIQUE

4 (¾-inch-thick) lean lamb sirloin steaks (1¼
   pounds)
Vegetable cooking spray
½ teaspoon salt
¼ teaspoon ground nutmeg
⅛ teaspoon pepper
¼ cup dry vermouth
½ cup skim milk
1 egg yolk, beaten
½ teaspoon chicken-flavored bouillon granules
⅓ cup sliced seedless green grapes
⅓ cup sliced seedless red grapes

Trim excess fat from steaks. Coat a skillet with cooking spray, and place over medium-high heat until hot. Add steaks, and cook until browned on both sides.

Combine salt, nutmeg, and pepper; sprinkle both sides of steaks with seasoning mixture. Reduce heat to medium-low; cook, uncovered, 5 minutes on each side or until desired degree of doneness. Remove steaks; place on a warm platter, and keep warm.

Drain skillet, and wipe dry with a paper towel (reserve any cooked-on pieces in pan). Add vermouth and stir, scraping bottom of pan. Stir in milk, egg yolk, and bouillon granules. Cook over low heat 20 minutes, stirring constantly, until sauce thickens. Stir in grapes. Cook just until thoroughly heated. Spoon sauce over steaks. Yield: 4 servings (223 calories per serving).

PRO 26.4 / FAT 7.9 / CARB 7.2 / FIB 0.5 / CHOL 155 / SOD 422 / POT 363

SAUTÉED LAMB CHOPS

4 (1¼-inch-thick) lean lamb rib chops (1¼
   pounds)
Pepper
Vegetable cooking spray
1 teaspoon vegetable oil
¼ cup chopped onion
1 teaspoon cornstarch
1 cup water, divided
1 teaspoon beef-flavored bouillon
   granules
1 teaspoon Worcestershire sauce

Trim excess fat from lamb chops. Sprinkle lamb chops with pepper. Coat a large skillet with cooking spray; add oil, and place over medium heat until hot. Add chops; cook 5 minutes on each side or until golden brown. Drain on paper towels; set aside, and keep warm. Wipe skillet dry with a paper towel.

Coat skillet with cooking spray. Add onion, and sauté until tender. Combine cornstarch with 1 tablespoon water; add to skillet with remaining water, bouillon granules, and Worcestershire sauce; stir until bouillon granules dissolve. Add lamb chops; bring to a boil. Reduce heat, and simmer 3 to 5 minutes or until sauce is thickened and lamb is thoroughly heated. Yield: 4 servings (178 calories per serving).

PRO 24.6 / FAT 7.4 / CARB 1.8 / FIB 0.1 / CHOL 86 / SOD 188 / POT 284

SPICY GRILLED LAMB CHOPS

2 tablespoons Chablis or other dry white wine
2 tablespoons lemon juice
1 tablespoon water
1 tablespoon margarine, melted
1 teaspoon dried whole cilantro or 1 tablespoon minced fresh coriander
1 small clove garlic, minced
1½ teaspoons chili powder
¼ teaspoon pepper
¼ teaspoon hot sauce
4 (1¼-inch-thick) lean lamb loin chops (1¼ pounds)

Combine first 9 ingredients in a small bowl; mix well. Set aside.

Trim excess fat from lamb chops. Grill lamb chops 5 to 6 inches over medium coals 8 to 10 minutes on each side or until desired degree of doneness, basting frequently with sauce. Yield: 4 servings (197 calories per serving).

PRO 24.6 / FAT 9.2 / CARB 1.8 / FIB 0.2 / CHOL 86 / SOD 108 / POT 291

CURRIED LAMB

Vegetable cooking spray
1 teaspoon vegetable oil
1 cup sliced celery
½ cup chopped onion
¾ pound lean boneless lamb, cut into ½-inch cubes
2 teaspoons curry powder
½ teaspoon salt
⅛ teaspoon ground cloves
½ cup water
¼ cup skim milk
1½ teaspoons cornstarch
2 cups hot cooked parboiled rice (cooked without salt or fat)
1 medium tomato, cut into wedges

Coat a large skillet with cooking spray; add oil, and place over medium-high heat until hot. Add celery and onion; sauté 3 minutes or until crisp-tender. Remove vegetables from skillet; set aside. Wipe skillet dry with a paper towel.

Coat skillet with cooking spray. Add lamb, and cook, stirring frequently, 2 minutes or until browned. Remove lamb, and drain on paper towels; wipe skillet dry with a paper towel.

Coat skillet with cooking spray. Return lamb to skillet. Stir in reserved vegetable mixture, curry, salt, and cloves; cook over medium heat 1 minute. Combine water, milk, and cornstarch in a small bowl; stir until well blended. Gradually pour milk mixture into skillet, stirring well; bring to a boil. Cook over high heat, stirring constantly, 1 minute. Reduce heat to low, and simmer 5 minutes. Serve over hot cooked rice, and garnish with tomato wedges. Yield: 4 servings (152 calories per serving plus 93 calories per ½ cup cooked rice).

PRO 20.9 / FAT 6.0 / CARB 25.3 / FIB 1.3 / CHOL 64 / SOD 375 / POT 383

GRECIAN-STYLE STUFFED ZUCCHINI

4 medium zucchini squash
Vegetable cooking spray
½ pound lean ground lamb
2 medium tomatoes, peeled and chopped
¼ cup chopped onion
1 clove garlic, crushed
2 tablespoons chopped fresh parsley
¼ teaspoon salt
Dash of pepper
Dash of ground cinnamon
1 cup (4 ounces) shredded mozzarella cheese

Cook whole zucchini squash in boiling water to cover 5 minutes; drain. Slice in half lengthwise; scoop out pulp, leaving ¼-inch shell. Chop pulp, and set aside. Place shells in a 12- x 8- x 2-inch baking dish coated with cooking spray; set aside.

Coat a medium skillet with cooking spray; place over medium heat until hot. Add lamb to skillet, and cook until browned, stirring to crumble; drain well in a colander. Wipe skillet dry with a paper towel, and return lamb to skillet. Add reserved zucchini pulp, tomatoes, onion, garlic, parsley, salt, pepper, and cinnamon to lamb. Cook over medium-low heat 10 minutes, stirring frequently. Remove from heat, and stir in cheese. Spoon mixture into reserved zucchini shells; bake at 350° for 15 minutes or until thoroughly heated. Yield: 8 servings (140 calories per serving).

PRO 16.1 / FAT 6.5 / CARB 4.7 / FIB 0.7 / CHOL 54 / SOD 160 / POT 426

LAMB PATTIES WITH PAPRIKA-DILL SAUCE

1 pound lean ground lamb
½ teaspoon seasoned salt
½ teaspoon Worcestershire sauce
¼ teaspoon pepper
Vegetable cooking spray
½ cup water
½ teaspoon chicken-flavored bouillon granules
½ teaspoon paprika
1 clove garlic, minced
1 medium onion, thinly sliced and separated
  into rings
½ cup plain low-fat yogurt
2 teaspoons cornstarch
1 teaspoon dried whole dillweed

Combine first 4 ingredients; mix well. Shape into 4 patties, ¼-inch thick. Coat rack of a broiler pan with cooking spray; place patties on rack, and broil 3 inches from heating element 6 minutes or until desired degree of doneness, turning once. Drain on paper towels. Transfer to a serving platter, and keep warm.

Combine water, bouillon granules, paprika, and garlic in a saucepan; stir well. Add onion, and bring to a boil. Cover; reduce heat, and simmer 5 minutes or until onion is tender. Combine yogurt and cornstarch in a small bowl; add a small amount of hot bouillon mixture to yogurt mixture, stirring well. Add to remaining bouillon mixture in saucepan. Cook, stirring constantly, until thickened and thoroughly heated. (Do not allow to boil.) Remove from heat, and stir in dillweed. Pour sauce over lamb patties. Yield: 4 servings (196 calories per serving).

PRO 26.1 / FAT 6.7 / CARB 6.6 / FIB 0.4 / CHOL 87 / SOD 354 / POT 396

DIJON-MARINATED PORK ROAST

1 (3½-pound) lean boneless pork loin roast, rolled
  and tied
½ cup vinegar
¼ cup Chablis or other dry white wine
3 tablespoons Dijon mustard
½ teaspoon dried whole rosemary, crumbled
¼ teaspoon white pepper
¼ teaspoon dried whole thyme

Unroll roast, and trim excess fat. Retie roast, and place in a shallow baking dish. Combine remaining ingredients, and pour over roast. Cover and marinate in refrigerator 8 hours or overnight, turning occasionally.

Remove roast from marinade, reserving marinade. Place roast on rack of a roasting pan, and insert a meat thermometer, if desired. Bake, uncovered, at 350° for 2½ hours or until meat thermometer registers 170°. Baste frequently with marinade. Let roast stand at room temperature 10 minutes before serving. Yield: 12 servings (229 calories per serving).

PRO 30.5 / FAT 10.3 / CARB 1.0 / FIB 0.0 / CHOL 93 / SOD 186 / POT 418

ZESTY SMOKED PORK ROAST

1 cup vinegar
1 (8-ounce) can tomato sauce
1 tablespoon dried onion flakes
1 tablespoon dry mustard
2 tablespoons firmly packed brown sugar
2 tablespoons Worcestershire sauce
1 teaspoon hot sauce
1 clove garlic, minced
¼ teaspoon red pepper
Vegetable cooking spray
1 (5-pound) lean pork loin roast

Combine first 9 ingredients in a saucepan, stirring well. Bring to a boil; reduce heat, and simmer, uncovered, 10 minutes, stirring occasionally. Remove from heat; set aside.

Prepare charcoal fire in smoker, and let burn 10 to 15 minutes. Place water pan in smoker; fill with ¼ cup sauce and 2 quarts water.

Coat food rack with cooking spray, and place in smoker. Trim excess fat from roast. Place roast on food rack. Baste roast generously on all sides with sauce. Insert meat thermometer, being careful not to touch bone or fat. Cover with smoker lid; cook 4 hours. Uncover; baste roast with sauce. Cover and cook 5 to 7 hours or until meat thermometer registers 170°, basting with sauce every hour. Refill water pan with sauce and water as needed. Transfer roast to a serving platter; let stand 10 minutes before serving. Yield: 10 servings (273 calories per serving).

PRO 34.6 / FAT 11.4 / CARB 6.7 / FIB 0.2 / CHOL 104 / SOD 255 / POT 579

The aroma of Pork Medallions with Fennel announces an especially tasty entrée.

PORK MEDALLIONS WITH FENNEL

1 (1¼-pound) pork tenderloin, cut into 8 slices
Vegetable cooking spray
1 teaspoon margarine
½ cup water
¼ cup Chablis or other dry white wine
½ teaspoon beef-flavored bouillon granules
½ teaspoon fennel seeds, crushed
¼ teaspoon pepper
1 teaspoon cornstarch
1 tablespoon water
Fresh fennel

Trim excess fat from pork. Coat a large skillet with cooking spray; add margarine. Place over medium heat until margarine melts. Add pork, and cook 5 to 6 minutes, turning to brown evenly. Remove pork from skillet; drain well.

Wipe skillet dry with a paper towel. Add ½ cup water, wine, bouillon granules, fennel seeds, and pepper to skillet. Bring to a boil; add pork. Cover; reduce heat, and simmer 5 minutes or until pork is tender.

Transfer pork to a serving platter; keep warm. Dissolve cornstarch in 1 tablespoon water. Add to pan juices, stirring to blend. Bring to a boil; reduce heat, and simmer until thickened. Pour over pork; garnish with fresh fennel. Yield: 6 servings (134 calories per serving.)

PRO 21.5 / FAT 4.3 / CARB 0.9 / FIB 0.0 / CHOL 69 / SOD 97 / POT 416

GINGERED GRILLED PORK CHOPS

4 lean center loin pork chops (1½ pounds)
3 tablespoons reduced-sodium soy sauce
¼ cup lemon juice
1 tablespoon grated gingerroot
¼ teaspoon garlic powder
Vegetable cooking spray

Trim excess fat from chops; place chops in a shallow baking dish. Combine next 4 ingredients in a small bowl; pour over pork chops. Cover and marinate in refrigerator 8 hours or overnight, turning occasionally.

Remove pork chops from marinade, reserving marinade. Arrange pork chops on a grill coated with cooking spray. Grill 5 to 6 inches over medium coals 20 minutes or until pork chops are tender, basting frequently with marinade. Yield: 4 servings (218 calories per serving).

PRO 25.1 / FAT 11.0 / CARB 2.9 / FIB 0.0 / CHOL 77 / SOD 495 / POT 332

PORK CHOPS DIJON

4 (½-inch-thick) lean center loin pork chops (1½ pounds)
Vegetable cooking spray
1 medium green onion, minced
¼ cup Chablis or other dry white wine
¼ cup water
¼ teaspoon chicken-flavored bouillon granules
⅛ teaspoon pepper
2 tablespoons Dijon mustard
½ teaspoon cornstarch
2 teaspoons chopped fresh chives

Trim excess fat from chops. Coat a large skillet with cooking spray; place over medium heat until hot. Add chops, and cook until browned on both sides. Remove chops, and drain well on a paper towel; set aside. Wipe skillet dry with a paper towel.

Coat skillet with cooking spray. Add onion to skillet; sauté 1 minute or until tender. Add wine, water, bouillon granules, and pepper; cook over medium heat, stirring constantly, 1 minute. Return reserved pork chops to skillet; cover and cook over low heat 30 minutes or until pork chops are tender.

Transfer chops to a serving platter, and keep warm. Combine mustard and cornstarch, stirring until smooth; stir mustard mixture into a small amount of pan juices, using a wire whisk; add to remaining pan juices in skillet, and bring to a boil. Reduce heat and cook, stirring constantly, until mixture thickens.

Remove from heat, and spoon sauce over pork chops. Sprinkle with chives, and serve immediately. Yield: 4 servings (217 calories per serving).

PRO 24.1 / FAT 11.6 / CARB 1.9 / FIB 0.0 / CHOL 77 / SOD 306 / POT 338

MANDARIN PORK CHOPS

6 (½-inch-thick) lean center loin pork chops
   (2¼ pounds)
¼ teaspoon pepper
Vegetable cooking spray
½ cup water
¼ cup chopped onion
½ teaspoon chicken-flavored bouillon
   granules
½ teaspoon curry powder
1 (10¼-ounce) can unsweetened mandarin
   oranges, undrained
1 teaspoon lemon juice
1 teaspoon cornstarch
1 medium-size green pepper, seeded
   and cut into strips

Trim excess fat from pork chops. Sprinkle pork chops with pepper. Coat an electric skillet with cooking spray; allow to heat at medium for 2 minutes. Add pork chops, and cook until browned on both sides. Remove pork chops,

and drain on paper towels; wipe skillet dry with a paper towel. Return pork chops to skillet. Combine water, onion, bouillon granules, and curry powder; pour over pork chops. Bring to a boil; cover, reduce heat, and simmer 45 minutes or until pork chops are tender. Transfer to a platter, and keep warm.

Drain mandarin oranges, reserving liquid; set oranges aside. Combine reserved liquid, lemon juice, and cornstarch in a small bowl. Add juice mixture and green pepper to skillet. Cook, stirring constantly, until mixture is thickened. Stir in mandarin oranges. Spoon sauce over pork chops to serve. Yield: 6 servings (227 calories per serving).

PRO 24.4 / FAT 11.2 / CARB 5.4 / FIB 0.4 / CHOL 77 / SOD 95 / POT 415

PORK CHOPS PAPRIKA

6 (½-inch-thick) lean center loin pork chops (2¼
   pounds)
Vegetable cooking spray
1 cup sliced fresh mushrooms
1 cup chopped green onion
1½ teaspoons paprika
¼ teaspoon salt
¼ teaspoon garlic powder
¼ teaspoon pepper
1 cup water
1 (8-ounce) carton plain low-fat yogurt

Trim excess fat from pork chops. Coat a large skillet with cooking spray. Place over medium heat until hot. Add pork chops, and cook until browned on both sides. Remove pork chops, and drain on paper towels; set aside. Wipe skillet dry with a paper towel.

Coat skillet with cooking spray. Add mushrooms and onion, and sauté until tender. Return pork chops to skillet. Add paprika, salt, garlic powder, pepper, and water to skillet. Cover; reduce heat, and simmer 40 minutes or until pork chops are tender. Transfer chops to a serving platter, and keep warm. Stir yogurt into mixture in skillet; cook until thoroughly heated. (Do not boil.) Serve yogurt sauce over pork chops. Yield: 6 servings (238 calories per serving).

PRO 26.7 / FAT 11.8 / CARB 5.0 / FIB 0.7 / CHOL 79 / SOD 184 / POT 492

HONEY-GLAZED CANADIAN BACON

8 (¼-inch-thick) slices Canadian bacon
Vegetable cooking spray
1 tablespoon honey
2 teaspoons vinegar
1 teaspoon Dijon mustard
Dash of ground cloves

Place Canadian bacon slices in a large skillet coated with cooking spray. Combine remaining ingredients, and drizzle over bacon. Cover and cook over medium heat 15 minutes, turning once. Place bacon on a warmed serving platter, and spoon any remaining glaze over slices. Yield: 4 servings (107 calories per serving).

PRO 11.7 / FAT 4.1 / CARB 5.6 / FIB 0.0 / CHOL 28 / SOD 836 / POT 202

SWISS-HAM-ASPARAGUS CRÊPES

24 thin spears fresh asparagus (about ¾ pound)
½ cup water
1 tablespoon unsalted margarine
2 tablespoons all-purpose flour
1 cup skim milk
½ cup (2 ounces) shredded Swiss cheese
1 cup finely chopped lean cooked ham
2 teaspoons instant minced onion
½ teaspoon Dijon mustard
⅛ teaspoon pepper
Crêpes (recipe follows)
Vegetable cooking spray
¼ cup grated Parmesan cheese
Paprika

Snap off tough ends of asparagus. Remove scales from stalks, using a knife or vegetable peeler, if desired.

Arrange spears in a large skillet; add ½ cup water, and bring to a boil. Cover; reduce heat, and simmer 6 to 8 minutes or until crisp-tender. Drain and set aside.

Melt margarine in a small saucepan over low heat; add flour, stirring until smooth (mixture will be dry). Cook 1 minute, stirring constantly. Gradually stir in milk; cook over medium heat, stirring constantly with a wire whisk, until mixture is thickened and bubbly. Remove from heat; stir in Swiss cheese, ham, onion, mustard, and pepper, stirring until cheese melts.

Place 2 asparagus spears in center of each crêpe. Spoon 2 tablespoons ham mixture over asparagus; roll up, and place seam side down in a 13- x 9- x 2-inch baking dish coated with cooking spray. Sprinkle with Parmesan cheese and paprika. Broil 4 to 5 inches from heating element 2 minutes or until golden. Yield: 6 servings (258 calories per 2-crêpe serving).

Crêpes:

2 eggs
1 cup skim milk
¾ cup all-purpose flour
2 teaspoons vegetable oil
⅛ teaspoon salt
Vegetable cooking spray

Combine first 5 ingredients in container of an electric blender; process 30 seconds or until smooth. Refrigerate batter 1 hour. (This allows flour particles to swell and soften so crêpes are light in texture.)

Coat bottom of a 6-inch crêpe pan or nonstick skillet with cooking spray; place pan over medium heat just until hot, not smoking.

Pour 2 tablespoons batter into pan. Tilt pan quickly in all directions so batter covers pan in a thin film; cook 1 minute. Lift edge of crêpe to test for doneness. Crêpe is ready for flipping when it can be shaken loose from pan. Flip crêpe, and cook 30 seconds on other side. (This side is rarely more than spotty brown and is the side on which the filling is placed.)

Place crêpes on a towel to cool. Stack cooled crêpes between layers of waxed paper to prevent sticking. Repeat procedure with remaining batter. Yield: 12 (6-inch) crêpes.

PRO 17.7 / FAT 10.7 / CARB 22.8 / FIB 1.2 / CHOL 117 / SOD 497 / POT 437

Turkey Cutlets with Dijon Pecan Sauce (page 156) makes the ideal entrée for a small dinner party. It's elegant in both appearance and taste but so easy to prepare. Serve it with a green vegetable and a salad, and your main course is complete.

ROASTED CHICKEN AND VEGETABLES

1 (3½-pound) broiler-fryer, skinned
1 medium cooking apple, cut into wedges
½ cup water
2 tablespoons lemon juice
2 tablespoons chopped fresh parsley
1 tablespoon prepared mustard
1 teaspoon chicken-flavored bouillon
  granules
1 teaspoon ground ginger
½ teaspoon ground cinnamon
½ teaspoon pepper
2 medium-size sweet potatoes, peeled and cut into
  thirds
3 medium onions, quartered

Remove giblets and neck from chicken, and reserve for other uses. Trim excess fat from chicken. Place apple wedges in cavity of chicken. Close cavity with skewers, and truss. Lift wingtips up and over back, tucking under bird securely. Place chicken, breast side up, on a rack in a roasting pan; set aside.

Combine water, lemon juice, parsley, mustard, bouillon granules, ginger, cinnamon, and pepper; brush over entire surface of chicken. Arrange sweet potatoes and onions around chicken. Cover and bake at 350° for 1½ hours or until drumsticks move up and down easily and juices run clear. Discard apple wedges.

Remove chicken and vegetables to a serving platter; serve immediately. Yield: 6 servings (272 calories per serving).

PRO 29.3 / FAT 7.6 / CARB 21.0 / FIB 2.0 / CHOL 84 / SOD 187 / POT 486

CRISPY OVEN-FRIED CHICKEN

1 egg, lightly beaten
1 tablespoon water
1 cup crispy rice cereal, crushed
¼ cup buttermilk baking mix
1 tablespoon instant minced onion
¼ teaspoon garlic powder
¼ teaspoon seasoned salt
¼ teaspoon pepper
1 (3½-pound) broiler-fryer, cut up and skinned
Vegetable cooking spray
Green onion fans (optional)
Carrot flowers (optional)

Combine egg and water in a shallow bowl; mix well, and set aside.

Combine crushed cereal, baking mix, minced onion, garlic powder, seasoned salt, and pepper in a shallow bowl; stir until well blended, and set aside.

Trim excess fat from chicken; dip chicken in egg mixture, and dredge in cereal mixture, coating well. Arrange chicken in a 15- x 10- x 1-inch jellyroll pan coated with cooking spray. Bake, uncovered, at 350° for 1 hour or until tender. Transfer to a serving platter, and garnish with green onion fans and carrot flowers, if desired. Yield: 6 servings (242 calories per serving).

PRO 29.2 / FAT 8.9 / CARB 9.4 / FIB 0.3 / CHOL 129 / SOD 284 / POT 266

 Grilling, indoors or out, summer or winter, is a delicious way to cook with little fat. But don't burn your steaks! Burnt meat is not only unappetizing, it's also unhealthy, says the National Cancer Institute (NCI). Charring creates substances in the fat that may even be cancer-causing.

To grill without charring, the NCI has some advice: Raise the grill up high above the coals or flame, and cook foods more slowly. Better yet: Wrap foods in foil, or place them in a pan, before grilling. That way, you get all the juices of the meat, with none of the charring.

ZESTY BARBECUED CHICKEN

1 (3½-pound) broiler-fryer, cut up and skinned
1 (8-ounce) can tomato sauce
½ teaspoon grated lemon rind
¼ cup lemon juice
1 tablespoon firmly packed brown sugar
2 tablespoons vinegar
1 tablespoon Worcestershire sauce
1 teaspoon prepared mustard
¼ teaspoon red pepper
¼ teaspoon pepper
1 clove garlic, crushed

Trim excess fat from chicken; place chicken in a 12- x 8- x 2-inch baking dish, and set aside.

Combine remaining ingredients in a small saucepan. Bring to a boil. Cover; reduce heat, and simmer 20 minutes. Pour barbecue sauce over chicken. Cover and marinate in refrigerator overnight, turning chicken occasionally.

Remove chicken from sauce, reserving sauce. Place chicken, bone side down, on grill over medium coals. Grill 45 minutes to 1 hour, turning and basting with sauce every 15 minutes. Yield: 6 servings (207 calories per serving).

PRO 28.0 / FAT 7.0 / CARB 7.2 / FIB 0.3 / CHOL 84 / SOD 284 / POT 459

CURRIED CHICKEN SKILLET DINNER

6 chicken breast halves (about 2½ pounds), skinned
⅛ teaspoon pepper
Vegetable cooking spray
1 medium cooking apple, peeled and chopped
1 medium onion, chopped
½ cup chopped celery
1 clove garlic, minced
1 cup water
¼ cup raisins
2 teaspoons curry powder
2 teaspoons grated orange rind
1 teaspoon chicken-flavored bouillon granules
⅛ teaspoon crushed red pepper
¼ cup unsweetened orange juice
1 tablespoon cornstarch
Fresh parsley sprigs

Trim excess fat from chicken, and sprinkle with pepper. Coat an electric skillet with cooking spray; allow to heat at medium for 2 minutes. Add chicken to skillet, and cook 4 minutes on each side or until browned. Remove chicken; drain on paper towels, and set aside.

Wipe skillet with a paper towel; recoat with cooking spray. Add apple, onion, celery, and garlic to skillet. Cook at medium heat, stirring constantly, until vegetables are tender. Stir in water and the next 5 ingredients; return chicken to skillet. Bring to a boil. Cover; reduce heat, and simmer 40 minutes or until chicken is tender, basting chicken occasionally. Remove chicken to a serving platter, and keep warm.

Combine orange juice and cornstarch, stirring until blended; stir into skillet. Bring to a boil, and cook 1 minute or until slightly thickened. Pour sauce over chicken; garnish with parsley. Yield: 6 servings (195 calories per serving).

PRO 27.8 / FAT 3.5 / CARB 12.7 / FIB 1.3 / CHOL 74 / SOD 140 / POT 388

CREOLE CHICKEN EN PAPILLOTE

Vegetable cooking spray
½ cup chopped onion
½ cup chopped green onion
½ cup chopped celery
½ cup chopped green pepper
2 cloves garlic, minced
1 (16-ounce) can tomatoes, undrained and chopped
1 (6-ounce) can tomato paste
¼ cup water
½ teaspoon dried whole basil
½ teaspoon dried whole thyme
½ teaspoon red pepper
½ teaspoon hot sauce
1 bay leaf
6 boneless chicken breast halves (1½ pounds), skinned
Parchment paper

Coat a large skillet with cooking spray; place over medium-high heat until hot. Add onions, celery, green pepper, and garlic; sauté until tender. Add tomatoes, tomato paste, water, basil, thyme, red pepper, hot sauce, and bay leaf. Bring to a boil; reduce heat, and simmer, uncovered, 20 minutes. Discard bay leaf; set sauce aside.

Trim excess fat from chicken breast halves. Place chicken between 2 sheets of waxed paper; flatten to ¼-inch thickness, using a meat mallet or rolling pin.

Cut six 15- x 14-inch pieces of parchment paper or aluminum foil; fold each piece of paper in half lengthwise, creasing the fold firmly. Cut each paper to form a large heart shape; place paper hearts on 2 baking sheets, and open out flat.

Place a chicken breast half on each parchment paper heart near crease. Spoon sauce in equal portions over each breast half. Fold paper edges over to seal securely; starting with rounded edge of heart, pleat and crimp edges of each heart to make an airtight seal.

Bake at 450° for 15 minutes or until pouches are puffed and browned. Place on individual serving plates; cut an opening in each pouch just before serving. Yield: 6 servings (191 calories per serving).

PRO 28.0 / FAT 3.6 / CARB 12.0 / FIB 6.3 / CHOL 70 / SOD 216 / POT 748

YOGURT-MARINATED CHICKEN

6 chicken breast halves (about 2½ pounds), skinned
1 (8-ounce) carton plain low-fat yogurt
¼ cup lemon juice
1 tablespoon Worcestershire sauce
1 teaspoon paprika
½ teaspoon pepper
¼ teaspoon garlic powder
¼ teaspoon celery salt
¾ cup soft whole wheat breadcrumbs
Vegetable cooking spray

Trim excess fat from chicken; place chicken in a single layer in a 13- x 9- x 2-inch baking dish. Combine next 7 ingredients; pour over chicken, turning to coat well. Cover and refrigerate 8 hours or overnight, turning occasionally.

Remove chicken from marinade, discarding marinade. Dredge chicken in breadcrumbs.

Arrange chicken in a 13- x 9- x 2-inch baking dish coated with cooking spray. Bake at 375° for 45 minutes or until chicken is tender. Yield: 6 servings (190 calories per serving).

PRO 29.9 / FAT 4.0 / CARB 7.4 / FIB 0.4 / CHOL 77 / SOD 236 / POT 375

LEMON CHICKEN CUTLETS

6 boneless chicken breast halves (1½ pounds), skinned
¼ teaspoon salt
¼ teaspoon pepper
Vegetable cooking spray
1 tablespoon margarine
¼ cup dry sherry
¼ cup chopped onion
2 tablespoons grated lemon rind
2 tablespoons lemon juice
1 cup water
1 teaspoon chicken-flavored bouillon granules
¼ cup water
2 tablespoons all-purpose flour
¼ cup grated Parmesan cheese
¼ teaspoon paprika
2 tablespoons chopped fresh parsley

Trim excess fat from chicken. Place chicken between 2 sheets of waxed paper; flatten to ¼-inch thickness, using a meat mallet or rolling pin. Sprinkle with salt and pepper; set aside.

Coat a large skillet with cooking spray; add margarine, and place over medium heat until margarine melts. Add chicken to skillet, and cook 3 minutes on each side or until lightly browned. Transfer chicken to a 13- x 9- x 2-inch baking dish coated with cooking spray, reserving liquid in skillet.

Add sherry, onion, lemon rind, and lemon juice to skillet; cook over medium heat 5 minutes or until onion is tender. Add 1 cup water and bouillon granules to skillet. Combine ¼ cup water and flour, stirring well; add to liquid in skillet. Cook over medium heat, stirring constantly, 5 minutes or until thickened and bubbly. Spoon sauce over chicken; sprinkle with Parmesan cheese, paprika, and parsley. Bake at 350° for 15 minutes or until thoroughly heated. Yield: 6 servings (188 calories per serving).

PRO 27.6 / FAT 6.0 / CARB 4.6 / FIB 0.2 / CHOL 73 / SOD 309 / POT 258

A topping of picante sauce, yogurt, and green chilies adds to the robust flavor of Chicken Fajitas.

CHICKEN FAJITAS

2 pounds boneless chicken breast halves, skinned
¼ cup white wine vinegar
¼ cup lime juice
2 tablespoons Worcestershire sauce
2 tablespoons chopped onion
2 cloves garlic, minced
1 teaspoon dried whole oregano
¼ teaspoon ground cumin
Vegetable cooking spray
8 (8-inch) flour tortillas
½ cup commercial picante sauce, divided
½ cup plain low-fat yogurt, divided
¼ cup chopped green chilies, divided

Trim excess fat from chicken. Place chicken between 2 sheets of waxed paper; flatten to ¼-inch thickness, using a meat mallet or rolling pin. Place chicken in a 13- x 9- x 2-inch baking dish. Combine vinegar, lime juice, Worcestershire sauce, onion, garlic, oregano, and cumin; pour over chicken. Cover and refrigerate 4 hours.

Remove chicken from marinade, discarding marinade; arrange chicken on a grill coated with cooking spray. Grill 6 inches over medium-hot coals 8 minutes, turning once. Slice chicken across the grain into ½-inch-wide strips.

Wrap tortillas in aluminum foil; bake at 325° for 15 minutes. Arrange strips of chicken just off center of each tortilla; roll up tortillas. Top each with 1 tablespoon picante sauce, 1 tablespoon yogurt, and 1½ teaspoons green chilies. Yield: 8 servings (308 calories per serving).

PRO 30.1 / FAT 5.6 / CARB 33.7 / FIB 0.4 / CHOL 71 / SOD 224 / POT 346

CHILLED CHICKEN WITH DILL SAUCE

8 boneless chicken breast halves (2 pounds), skinned
½ cup reduced-calorie Italian salad dressing
2 tablespoons water
1 tablespoon lime juice
1 tablespoon white wine vinegar
1 clove garlic, crushed
Vegetable cooking spray
Lime wedges
Dill Sauce

Trim excess fat from chicken. Place each piece between 2 sheets of waxed paper; flatten to ¼-inch thickness, using a meat mallet or rolling pin. Place chicken in a 13- x 9- x 2-inch baking dish. Combine next 5 ingredients in a small bowl; pour over chicken. Cover and refrigerate 2 hours.

Remove chicken from marinade, discarding marinade. Coat grill with cooking spray. Grill chicken 6 inches over medium coals 8 minutes, turning once.

Arrange chicken on a serving platter; garnish with lime wedges. Serve either warm or chilled with 1½ tablespoons Dill Sauce per serving. Yield: 8 servings (160 calories per serving).

Dill Sauce:

½ cup plain low-fat yogurt
¼ cup low-fat cottage cheese
1½ teaspoons lime juice
1½ teaspoons chopped green onion
½ teaspoon dried whole dillweed
⅛ teaspoon white pepper

Combine all ingredients in container of an electric blender; process until smooth. Cover and chill thoroughly. Yield: 1 cup.

PRO 27.5 / FAT 3.3 / CARB 3.3 / FIB 0.0 / CHOL 72 / SOD 236 / POT 264

Q: What's the best time to exercise — morning, noon or evening? A: Any time. Most people find that exercising the same time every day — or every other day — is the easiest way to build fitness into a busy life. Whenever you exercise, you'll get the same benefits of reducing stress, strengthening your heart, and making weight control easier.

But exercise has another benefit, one that's particularly welcome before dinner time: It reduces appetite. The reason: body heat. Exercise increases our internal temperature slightly. That's healthy; it may even help ward off colds.

The temperature regulation center in the brain is right next to the appetite control center, say researchers at the Human Performance Lab at Ball State University. When one part of the brain (temperature) is working overtime, it tends to inhibit the adjoining part (appetite).

Result: appetite is suppressed, at least for the hour or so following exercise.

CHICKEN IN ASPIC

6 boneless chicken breast halves (1½ pounds), skinned
1 cup water
1 teaspoon chicken-flavored bouillon granules
1 teaspoon dried whole basil
1 teaspoon peppercorns
2 teaspoons lemon juice
1 medium onion, sliced
2 envelopes unflavored gelatin
½ cup water
2 (12-ounce) cans tomato juice
2 teaspoons lemon juice
1 teaspoon onion powder
¼ teaspoon white pepper
24 fresh green beans
2 medium carrots, scraped and diagonally sliced

Trim excess fat from chicken; set aside.

Combine 1 cup water, bouillon granules, basil, peppercorns, and 2 teaspoons lemon juice in a large skillet; stir until well blended. Add onion and chicken; cook over medium heat until water starts to "quiver." (Do not boil.) Cover; reduce heat to low, and cook 8 minutes. (Do not let mixture boil.) Drain and cool chicken, discarding peppercorns and onion; cover and refrigerate chicken until chilled.

Combine gelatin and ½ cup water in a large saucepan; stir well, and let stand 1 minute. Add tomato juice, 2 teaspoons lemon juice, onion powder, and white pepper, stirring well. Bring to a boil, stirring constantly; remove from heat, and stir until gelatin dissolves. Transfer to a large mixing bowl. Cover and chill until mixture reaches consistency of unbeaten egg white (about 1 hour).

Cut green beans in half lengthwise; cut again in half crosswise. Arrange green beans and carrots in a steaming rack; place over boiling water. Cover and steam 5 minutes or until crisp-tender. Drain and chill.

Cut each chicken breast half into uniform slices, and arrange on a salad plate with a slightly raised edge. Place equal portions of steamed green beans and carrots around chicken slices. Pour ½ cup gelatin mixture over each serving. Cover and chill until gelatin is set. Yield: 6 servings (193 calories per serving).

PRO 29.6 / FAT 3.3 / CARB 11.3 / FIB 1.5 / CHOL 70 / SOD 548 / POT 793

CHICKEN BREASTS STUFFED WITH HERB CHEESE

½ (8-ounce) package Neufchâtel cheese, softened
1 tablespoon chopped fresh parsley
½ teaspoon lemon-pepper seasoning
¼ teaspoon dried whole basil
¼ teaspoon dried whole oregano
Dash of garlic powder
8 boneless chicken breast halves (2 pounds), skinned
1 egg, beaten
2 tablespoons water
½ cup fine, dry breadcrumbs

Combine Neufchâtel cheese, parsley, lemon-pepper seasoning, basil, oregano, and garlic powder in a small bowl; stir well. Set mixture aside.

Trim excess fat from chicken. Place each piece of chicken between 2 sheets of waxed paper; flatten to ¼-inch thickness, using a meat mallet or rolling pin.

Place equal portions of cheese mixture in center of each piece of chicken; roll up jellyroll fashion. Tuck in sides; secure with wooden picks.

Combine egg and water in a small bowl; stir well. Dip each roll in egg mixture; dredge in breadcrumbs. Place rolls in a 12- x 8- x 2-inch baking dish. Bake at 400° for 30 minutes. Remove wooden picks to serve. Yield: 8 servings (208 calories per serving).

PRO 28.7 / FAT 7.3 / CARB 5.2 / FIB 0.0 / CHOL 116 / SOD 173 / POT 250

ORANGE-GLAZED CHICKEN KABOBS

2 tablespoons reduced-sodium soy sauce
1 tablespoon honey
2 teaspoons cornstarch
1 teaspoon grated orange rind
¾ cup unsweetened orange juice
¼ teaspoon ground ginger
1 pound boneless chicken breast halves, skinned
8 whole water chestnuts
3 green onions, cut into 2-inch pieces
12 medium-size fresh mushrooms
Vegetable cooking spray

Combine first 6 ingredients in a non-aluminum saucepan. Bring to a boil; reduce heat, and cook over low heat, stirring constantly, 1 minute or until mixture thickens. Set aside to cool.

Trim excess fat from chicken; cut chicken into 1-inch pieces, and place in a 12- x 8- x 2-inch baking dish. Pour reserved mixture over chicken; cover and marinate in refrigerator overnight.

Remove chicken from marinade, reserving marinade. Alternate chicken pieces and vegetables on 4 skewers. Coat grill with cooking spray. Grill kabobs 6 inches over medium coals 15 minutes or until done, turning and basting often with marinade. Yield: 4 servings (220 calories per serving).

PRO 28.1 / FAT 3.3 / CARB 18.8 / FIB 0.8 / CHOL 70 / SOD 358 / POT 614

CHICKEN ASPARAGUS STIR-FRY

1½ pounds boneless chicken breast halves, skinned
¼ cup water
2 tablespoons reduced-sodium soy sauce
2 tablespoons dry sherry
¼ teaspoon garlic powder
¼ teaspoon chicken-flavored bouillon granules
¼ teaspoon ground ginger
2 teaspoons cornstarch
Vegetable cooking spray
1 pound fresh asparagus spears, cut into 1-inch pieces
1 medium onion, thinly sliced
½ pound fresh mushrooms, sliced
2 medium tomatoes, unpeeled and cut into wedges
3 cups hot cooked parboiled rice (cooked without salt or fat)

Trim excess fat from chicken; cut chicken into ¼-inch strips, and place in a shallow container. Combine next 6 ingredients; stir well. Pour mixture over chicken; cover and refrigerate 30 minutes. Drain chicken, reserving marinade. Combine marinade and cornstarch, stirring until smooth. Set aside.

Coat a nonstick wok or large skillet with cooking spray; allow to heat at medium-high (325°) for 2 minutes. Add chicken to wok; stir-fry 3 to 4 minutes. Remove chicken from wok, and drain on paper towels; set aside. Wipe pan drippings from wok with a paper towel.

Coat wok with cooking spray. Add asparagus and onion to wok; stir-fry at medium-high (325°)

3 minutes. Add mushrooms; stir-fry 2 minutes. Return chicken to wok. Pour reserved marinade mixture over chicken and vegetables, stirring well. Add tomatoes; cook 2 to 3 minutes or until sauce thickens. Serve over hot rice. Yield: 6 servings (190 calories per serving plus 93 calories per ½ cup cooked rice).

PRO 31.8 / FAT 3.6 / CARB 30.6 / FIB 2.3 / CHOL 70 / SOD 280 / POT 759

LEMON CHICKEN STIR-FRY

1½ pounds boneless chicken breast halves, skinned
¼ cup boiling water
2 tablespoons light soy sauce
1 teaspoon grated lemon rind
¼ cup lemon juice
¼ teaspoon chicken-flavored bouillon granules
1 tablespoon sugar
1 tablespoon cornstarch
Vegetable cooking spray
1 teaspoon vegetable oil
3 medium carrots, scraped and cut into julienne strips
4 green onions, cut into 2-inch pieces
1 medium-size green pepper, seeded and cut into strips
1 medium-size red pepper, seeded and cut into strips
3 cups hot cooked parboiled rice (cooked without salt or fat)

Trim excess fat from chicken; cut chicken into 1-inch pieces, and place in a shallow container. Combine next 5 ingredients, stirring to dissolve bouillon granules; pour over chicken, turning to coat well. Cover and refrigerate 30 minutes.

Drain chicken, reserving marinade. Combine marinade with sugar and cornstarch, stirring until smooth. Set aside.

Coat a wok or skillet with cooking spray; add oil. Allow to heat at medium-high (325°) for 2 minutes. Add carrots, onion, and peppers; stir-fry 3 minutes. Remove vegetables from wok.

Add chicken to wok; stir-fry 5 minutes. Add marinade and vegetables; cook at medium-high (325°), stirring constantly, until thickened. Serve over rice. Yield: 6 servings (191 calories per serving plus 93 calories per ½ cup cooked rice).

PRO 28.8 / FAT 4.1 / CARB 31.4 / FIB 1.9 / CHOL 70 / SOD 287 / POT 467

PINEAPPLE-GRILLED CHICKEN

6 chicken thighs (2 pounds), skinned
1 (8-ounce) can unsweetened pineapple tidbits,
   undrained
¼ cup reduced-sodium soy sauce
⅓ cup dry sherry
1 tablespoon firmly packed brown sugar
1 teaspoon dry mustard
Vegetable cooking spray
¼ cup water
2 teaspoons cornstarch

Trim excess fat from chicken; place chicken in a 12- x 8- x 2-inch baking dish, and set aside.

Drain pineapple, reserving juice; set pineapple aside. Combine pineapple juice, soy sauce, sherry, sugar, and mustard in a small bowl; stir well. Reserve ¼ cup marinade; pour remaining marinade over chicken. Cover and refrigerate 2 hours.

Remove chicken from marinade, reserving marinade in baking dish. Coat grill with cooking spray. Grill chicken 6 inches over medium coals 40 minutes or until chicken is tender, turning and basting with marinade in baking dish every 10 minutes. Transfer to a serving platter, and keep warm.

Place reserved ¼ cup marinade in a small saucepan. Combine water and cornstarch; stir into marinade. Bring to a boil over medium heat. Boil 1 minute or until mixture is thickened, stirring constantly; stir in reserved pineapple, and cook just until thoroughly heated. Spoon sauce over chicken to serve. Yield: 6 servings (196 calories per serving).

PRO 18.9 / FAT 7.6 / CARB 8.2 / FIB 0.1 / CHOL 65 / SOD 451 / POT 219

FRUITED CHICKEN THIGHS

6 chicken thighs (2 pounds), skinned
½ cup unsweetened apple juice
½ cup unsweetened orange juice
¼ cup lemon juice
¼ cup raisins
¼ cup chopped dried apricots
¼ cup chopped pitted prunes
¼ teaspoon ground ginger
1 medium onion, thinly sliced and separated
   into rings

Trim excess fat from chicken; place chicken in a 12- x 8- x 2-inch baking dish. Combine apple juice, orange juice, and lemon juice; pour over chicken. Cover and refrigerate 2 hours.

Drain chicken, reserving marinade; add raisins, apricots, prunes, and ginger to marinade, stirring well. Arrange onion rings over chicken; pour marinade mixture over chicken. Cover and bake at 350° for 1 hour.

Transfer chicken, onion, and fruit to a serving platter, using a slotted spoon; discard cooking liquid to serve. Yield: 6 servings (227 calories per serving).

PRO 19.0 / FAT 7.9 / CARB 20.8 / FIB 1.0 / CHOL 65 / SOD 72 / POT 529

HERBED CHICKEN THIGHS WITH VEGETABLE-WINE SAUCE

8 chicken thighs (2½ pounds), skinned
½ teaspoon dried whole thyme
½ teaspoon dried whole rosemary, crushed
¼ teaspoon dried whole basil
¼ teaspoon pepper
1 cup Chablis or other dry white wine
3 tablespoons all-purpose flour
3 tablespoons water
¼ cup shredded carrot
¼ cup shredded zucchini squash
2 tablespoons sliced green onion
Vegetable cooking spray

Trim excess fat from chicken; place chicken in a 13- x 9- x 2-inch baking dish. Sprinkle with thyme, rosemary, basil, and pepper. Pour wine around chicken. Cover and bake at 350° for 45 minutes. Uncover and bake 15 minutes.

Remove chicken to a warm platter, using a slotted spoon. Combine flour and water to form a smooth paste. Place cooking juices in a small saucepan; stir in flour paste. Cook over medium heat, stirring constantly, until thickened and bubbly. Remove from heat.

Coat a small skillet with cooking spray; place over medium-high heat until hot. Add carrots, zucchini, and onion; sauté until tender. Stir sautéed vegetables into sauce. Spoon sauce evenly over chicken to serve. Yield: 8 servings (116 calories per serving).

PRO 16.4 / FAT 3.2 / CARB 4.4 / FIB 0.3 / CHOL 67 / SOD 73 / POT 245

Enjoy Herbed Chicken Thighs with Vegetable-Wine Sauce; it's low in calories but rich in flavor.

ITALIAN-STYLE CHICKEN AND PEPPERS

½ cup fine, dry breadcrumbs
½ teaspoon dried Italian seasoning
¼ teaspoon dried whole basil
¼ teaspoon salt
⅛ teaspoon pepper
4 chicken thighs (1½ pounds), skinned
1 egg, lightly beaten
Vegetable cooking spray
1 teaspoon olive or vegetable oil
1 medium-size green pepper, seeded and cut into
    1-inch-wide strips
1 medium-size red pepper, seeded and cut into
    1-inch-wide strips
1 clove garlic, minced
¼ cup Burgundy or other dry red wine
1 tablespoon red wine vinegar
1 tablespoon grated Parmesan cheese

Combine first 5 ingredients in a small bowl; stir well, and set aside.

Trim excess fat from chicken. Dip chicken in egg; dredge in breadcrumb mixture.

Coat a large skillet with cooking spray; add oil. Place skillet over medium-high heat until hot. Add chicken to skillet; cook 2 to 3 minutes on each side or until lightly browned. Remove from skillet, and arrange in a 9-inch square baking dish coated with cooking spray. Cover and bake at 350° for 1 hour. Remove to a warm platter; set aside, and keep warm.

Wipe pan drippings from skillet with a paper towel; coat skillet with cooking spray. Add pepper strips and garlic to skillet; sauté until tender. Stir in wine and vinegar; simmer 2 minutes. Spoon mixture over chicken, and sprinkle with Parmesan cheese. Yield: 4 servings (263 calories per serving).

PRO 24.3 / FAT 12.2 / CARB 12.9 / FIB 0.6 / CHOL 144 / SOD 350 / POT 337

LIGHT CHICKEN PUFF

⅓ cup reduced-calorie mayonnaise
2 tablespoons all-purpose flour
1 cup skim milk
2 tablespoons grated Parmesan cheese
¼ teaspoon salt
¼ teaspoon pepper
3 eggs, separated
3 cups chopped, cooked chicken or turkey breast
    (skinned before cooking and cooked without salt)
½ cup chopped green onion
¼ cup chopped celery
¼ cup chopped green pepper
1 (2-ounce) jar diced pimiento, drained
Vegetable cooking spray

Combine mayonnaise and flour in a large heavy saucepan; stir until smooth. Cook over low heat 1 minute, stirring constantly. Gradually add milk; cook over medium heat, stirring constantly, until thickened and bubbly. Remove from heat. Stir in cheese, salt, and pepper.

Beat egg yolks until thick and lemon colored. Gradually stir one-fourth of hot cheese sauce into yolks; add to remaining sauce, stirring constantly. Add chicken, onion, celery, green pepper, and pimiento; mix well.

Beat egg whites (at room temperature) in a medium bowl until stiff, but not dry; gently fold into chicken mixture. Spoon mixture into a 9-inch square baking dish coated with cooking spray. Bake at 350° for 35 minutes or until puffed and golden brown. Serve immediately. Yield: 6 servings (231 calories per serving).

PRO 27.6 / FAT 9.5 / CARB 7.2 / FIB 0.6 / CHOL 203 / SOD 343 / POT 359

POPPY SEED CHICKEN CASSEROLE

1 cup sliced fresh mushrooms
2 tablespoons margarine, melted
2 tablespoons all-purpose flour
1 cup skim milk
½ teaspoon chicken-flavored bouillon granules
1 (8-ounce) carton plain low-fat yogurt
2 tablespoons dry vermouth
1 (8-ounce) can sliced water chestnuts, drained
3 cups chopped, cooked chicken or turkey breast
  (skinned before cooking and cooked without salt)
¼ cup fine, dry breadcrumbs
2 teaspoons margarine, melted
2 teaspoons poppy seeds

Sauté mushrooms in 2 tablespoons margarine in a medium skillet until tender. Remove mushrooms; set aside, reserving liquid in skillet. Add flour to skillet, stirring until smooth. Cook over low heat 1 minute, stirring constantly. Gradually add milk and bouillon granules; cook over medium heat, stirring constantly with a wire whisk, until thickened. Stir in mushrooms, yogurt, vermouth, water chestnuts, and chicken.

Spoon chicken mixture into a 1½-quart casserole. Combine breadcrumbs and 2 teaspoons margarine; sprinkle over chicken mixture. Sprinkle with poppy seeds.

Bake at 350° for 20 minutes or until thoroughly heated. (Do not overcook.) Yield: 6 servings (248 calories per serving).

PRO 26.6 / FAT 9.0 / CARB 14.2 / FIB 0.4 / CHOL 63 / SOD 227 / POT 430

WILD RICE AND CHICKEN CASSEROLE

1 (6-ounce) package long-grain and wild rice
  mix
2 tablespoons unsalted margarine
2 tablespoons all-purpose flour
1 cup skim milk
¼ cup Chablis or other dry white wine
Vegetable cooking spray
½ cup sliced fresh mushrooms
½ cup sliced green onion
4 cups chopped, cooked chicken or turkey breast
  (skinned before cooking and cooked without salt)
1 (2-ounce) jar diced pimiento, drained
2 tablespoons chopped fresh parsley

Cook rice mix according to package directions, omitting fat; set aside.

Melt margarine in a small heavy saucepan over low heat; add flour, stirring until smooth. Cook 1 minute, stirring constantly. Gradually add milk; cook over medium heat, stirring constantly, until thickened and bubbly. Remove from heat, and stir in wine. Set aside.

Coat a small skillet with cooking spray; place over medium heat until hot. Add mushrooms and onion, and sauté 2 to 3 minutes or until tender.

Combine sautéed vegetables, rice, sauce, chicken, pimiento, and parsley, stirring well. Spoon mixture into a 2-quart casserole coated with cooking spray. Bake at 350° for 15 minutes or until thoroughly heated. Yield: 8 servings (240 calories per serving).

PRO 25.6 / FAT 5.6 / CARB 20.6 / FIB 0.5 / CHOL 60 / SOD 436 / POT 366

 People who are active in sports are aware of the energy boosting benefits of eating high carbohydrate diets, but many of these active people may be ignoring the importance of including an adequate amount of protein in their diets as well.

The human body requires protein in order to maintain "lean body mass," such as muscle, organ tissue and bone. In order to keep functioning at peak performance levels, active people should eat about 0.7 grams of protein per pound of body weight compared to the 0.4 grams required by the average sedentary adult.

Consuming carbohydrate-rich foods for maximum energy output is fine, as long as it is not done at the expense of including protein in the diet to maintain the very muscles the carbohydrates are energizing.

CHICKEN LASAGNA ROLL-UPS

8 lasagna noodles (about 8 ounces)
Vegetable cooking spray
1 cup chopped onion
1 clove garlic, minced
1 (15-ounce) can no-added-salt tomato sauce
1 (6-ounce) can no-added-salt tomato paste
½ cup sliced fresh mushrooms
2 tablespoons chopped fresh parsley
2 tablespoons Burgundy or other dry red wine
1 teaspoon dried whole oregano
¼ teaspoon pepper
1 (12-ounce) carton low-fat cottage cheese
1 egg
½ cup (2 ounces) shredded mozzarella cheese
2 tablespoons grated Parmesan cheese
2 cups finely chopped, cooked chicken breast
   (skinned before cooking and cooked without salt)
2 tablespoons grated Parmesan cheese

Cook noodles according to package directions, omitting salt. Drain and set aside.

Coat a large skillet with cooking spray; place over medium heat until hot. Add onion and garlic; sauté until tender. Add next 7 ingredients, and bring to a boil. Cover; reduce heat, and simmer 30 minutes, stirring occasionally.

Combine cottage cheese, egg, mozzarella, and 2 tablespoons Parmesan cheese, stirring well. Chill thoroughly.

Spread 1 cup tomato sauce mixture in bottom of a 13- x 9- x 2-inch baking dish coated with cooking spray. Stir chicken into remaining tomato sauce mixture, and set aside.

Spread ¼ cup cheese mixture on each lasagna noodle. Spread 2 tablespoons chicken mixture over cheese; roll up jellyroll fashion, beginning at narrow end. Arrange lasagna rolls, seam side down, in prepared dish. Spoon remaining sauce over rolls; sprinkle with 2 tablespoons Parmesan cheese.

Cover and bake at 350° for 30 to 40 minutes. Yield: 8 servings (289 calories per serving).

PRO 25.2 / FAT 5.7 / CARB 33.7 / FIB 1.9 / CHOL 75 / SOD 308 / POT 686

CHICKEN LIVER STROGANOFF

Vegetable cooking spray
1 teaspoon vegetable oil
½ pound fresh mushrooms, sliced
1 medium onion, chopped
1 pound chicken livers
¼ cup dry vermouth
2 tablespoons tomato paste
¼ teaspoon salt
¼ teaspoon dried whole rosemary, crushed
¼ teaspoon dried whole thyme
⅛ teaspoon pepper
1 tablespoon margarine
1 tablespoon all-purpose flour
½ cup plain low-fat yogurt
Parsleyed Noodles

Coat a large skillet with cooking spray; add oil, and place over medium heat until hot. Add mushrooms and onion; sauté until tender. Add chicken livers; cook until browned, stirring occasionally. Add tomato paste and next 5 ingredients, stirring well. Cover; reduce heat, and simmer 10 minutes, stirring occasionally.

Melt margarine in a small heavy saucepan over low heat; add flour, stirring until smooth. Cook 1 minute, stirring constantly. Stir in yogurt; cook 1 minute or until thoroughly heated. (Do not boil.) Pour over liver mixture, stirring well. Serve hot over Parsleyed Noodles. Yield: 6 servings (161 calories per serving plus 110 calories per ½ cup cooked noodles).

Parsleyed Noodles:

1½ quarts water
½ teaspoon salt
½ (12-ounce) package medium egg noodles
2 tablespoons chopped fresh parsley

Combine water and salt in a small Dutch oven; bring to a boil. Add noodles, and boil 7 to 9 minutes, stirring occasionally; drain. Combine noodles and parsley; toss well. Yield: 6 servings.

PRO 19.7 / FAT 7.5 / CARB 30.9 / FIB 0.7 / CHOL 360 / SOD 397 / POT 500

CHICKEN LIVERS EN BROCHETTE

1 pound chicken livers
¼ cup white wine vinegar
1 tablespoon plus 1 teaspoon vegetable oil
1 teaspoon dried whole tarragon
¼ teaspoon salt
⅛ teaspoon pepper
12 pearl onions, peeled
12 cherry tomatoes
2 medium-size green peppers, seeded and cut into
    1-inch pieces

Place chicken livers in a 10- x 6- x 2-inch baking dish. Combine next 5 ingredients in a jar; cover tightly, and shake vigorously. Pour marinade over chicken livers; cover and chill at least 3 hours.

Cook onions in boiling water 8 to 10 minutes or just until tender; drain and set aside.

Drain livers, reserving marinade. Alternate livers, onions, tomatoes, and green peppers on 8 (10-inch) skewers; brush with marinade. Broil 6 to 8 inches from heating element 12 to 14 minutes, turning and brushing livers and vegetables often with marinade. Yield: 4 servings (190 calories per serving).

PRO 17.9 / FAT 8.6 / CARB 10.1 / FIB 1.2 / CHOL 429 / SOD 193 / POT 370

 Turkey, like all poultry, is generally low-fat and delicious. A three-ounce uncooked turkey breast has only 99 calories and 1.4 grams of fat, compared with a four-ounce uncooked regular hamburger, which has 245 calories and 18 grams of fat.

But don't just serve poultry instead of hamburger — serve it as hamburger. Ground turkey is now available in many supermarkets. If you can't find it in the frozen poultry section or right in the meat section, ask your butcher to grind it for you.

Made primarily from dark meat, ground turkey has 50% less fat than regular ground beef — and it's cheaper, too. Use it in your favorite burger, meat loaf, or casserole recipes. It's milder than ground beef, so you might want to spice it up a little, as we've done in the Spicy Turkey Patties recipe on page 157.

ORANGE-BAKED TURKEY

1 (4½-pound) turkey breast, skinned
2 cups water
1 cup unsweetened orange juice
2 teaspoons chicken-flavored bouillon granules
1 tablespoon cornstarch
3 tablespoons Cointreau or other orange-flavored
    liqueur
1 tablespoon grated orange rind
1½ cups unsweetened orange juice
¼ teaspoon pepper
Fresh parsley sprigs
Orange slices

Place turkey breast in a large roasting pan. Combine water, 1 cup orange juice, and bouillon granules, stirring until granules dissolve; pour over turkey. Insert meat thermometer into meaty portion of breast, if desired, making sure it does not touch bone. Cover and bake at 325° for 3 hours or until meat thermometer registers 185°, basting frequently.

Combine cornstarch, Cointreau, orange rind, 1½ cups orange juice, and pepper in a non-aluminum saucepan; stir until smooth. Cook over medium heat, stirring constantly, until thickened and bubbly.

Slice turkey; transfer to a large platter. Garnish with parsley and orange slices. Serve with 1 tablespoon orange sauce per serving. Yield: 12 servings (177 calories per serving).

PRO 28.4 / FAT 3.1 / CARB 5.2 / FIB 0.0 / CHOL 65 / SOD 61 / POT 350

TURKEY CUTLETS
WITH DIJON PECAN SAUCE

8 turkey breast cutlets (1 pound)
¼ cup all-purpose flour
⅛ teaspoon pepper
Vegetable cooking spray
1 tablespoon margarine
½ cup dry white wine
½ cup water
2 tablespoons Dijon mustard
2 teaspoons honey
½ teaspoon chicken-flavored bouillon granules
2 tablespoons chopped, toasted pecans
Fresh parsley sprigs

Place each turkey cutlet between 2 sheets of waxed paper; flatten to ¼-inch thickness, using a meat mallet or rolling pin. Combine flour and pepper; dredge cutlets in flour mixture.

Coat a large skillet with cooking spray; add margarine, and place over medium heat until margarine melts. Add cutlets, and cook 3 to 4 minutes on each side or until golden brown. Remove turkey, and drain on paper towels; transfer to a platter, and keep warm.

Wipe skillet dry with a paper towel. Combine wine, water, mustard, honey, and bouillon granules in skillet; cook, uncovered, 10 minutes or until liquid is reduced to ½ cup, stirring occasionally. Stir in pecans, and spoon evenly over cutlets. Garnish with parsley. Yield: 4 servings (246 calories per serving).

PRO 27.7 / FAT 8.9 / CARB 11.9 / FIB 0.3 / CHOL 61 / SOD 364 / POT 333

TURKEY STIR-FRY

1 pound turkey breast cutlets
¼ cup dry sherry
2 tablespoons reduced-sodium soy sauce
2 tablespoons water
1 teaspoon firmly packed brown sugar
Vegetable cooking spray
1 tablespoon vegetable oil
1 clove garlic, minced
1 cup broccoli flowerets
1 medium onion, thinly sliced
2 medium carrots, scraped and cut diagonally into
  ½-inch slices
1 cup sliced fresh mushrooms
1 medium-size sweet red pepper, seeded and cut
  into ¼-inch strips
2 teaspoons cornstarch
2 cups hot cooked brown rice, (cooked without salt
  or fat)

Cut turkey across the grain into 3- x ½-inch strips; place in a shallow container, and set aside. Combine sherry, soy sauce, water, and brown sugar; mix well. Pour over turkey, tossing to coat. Cover and refrigerate 30 minutes.

Coat a wok with cooking spray. Pour oil around top of wok; heat at medium-high (325°) for 2 minutes. Add garlic; stir-fry 1 minute. Drain turkey, reserving marinade. Add turkey strips to wok; stir-fry 2 minutes. Add broccoli, onion, and carrots; stir-fry 2 minutes. Add mushrooms and red pepper; stir-fry 2 minutes.

Add cornstarch to reserved marinade, stirring well. Pour over turkey mixture. Cook, stirring constantly, 2 minutes or until slightly thickened. Serve hot over brown rice. Yield: 4 servings (240 calories per serving plus 102 calories per ½ cup cooked rice).

PRO 30.9 / FAT 7.1 / CARB 33.4 / FIB 3.2 / CHOL 61 / SOD 365 / POT 633

SPICY TURKEY PATTIES

1 (1-pound) package raw ground turkey, thawed
¼ cup soft breadcrumbs
1 egg, beaten
1 tablespoon dried onion flakes
1 clove garlic, minced
1 tablespoon Worcestershire sauce
1 teaspoon prepared mustard
½ teaspoon chili powder
¼ teaspoon pepper
⅛ teaspoon hot sauce
Vegetable cooking spray
Pepper-Onion Sauce

Combine first 10 ingredients in a bowl; stir well. Shape mixture into 4 (¾-inch-thick) patties. Place patties on rack of a broiler pan coated with cooking spray; broil 5 inches from heating element 5 minutes on each side or until desired degree of doneness. Serve with 2 tablespoons sauce per serving. Yield: 4 servings (199 calories per serving).

Pepper-Onion Sauce:

Vegetable cooking spray
3 tablespoons finely chopped green pepper
3 tablespoons finely chopped onion
⅓ cup reduced-calorie catsup
½ teaspoon firmly packed brown sugar
¼ teaspoon prepared horseradish

Coat a small skillet with cooking spray; place over medium heat until hot. Add green pepper and onion, and sauté 3 minutes or until tender. Add remaining ingredients; cook, stirring constantly, until thoroughly heated. Serve warm or chilled. Yield: ½ cup.

PRO 27.3 / FAT 5.0 / CARB 8.8 / FIB 0.6 / CHOL 142 / SOD 194 / POT 603

CRISPY TURKEY BAKE

1 (10-ounce) package frozen English peas
2 cups cubed cooked turkey or chicken breast
   (skinned before cooking and cooked without salt)
½ cup (2 ounces) shredded sharp Cheddar cheese
½ cup chopped green onion
⅓ cup reduced-calorie mayonnaise
½ teaspoon Dijon mustard
⅛ teaspoon salt
⅛ teaspoon pepper
Vegetable cooking spray
1 medium tomato, cut into 6 slices
1 cup corn flakes cereal, crushed
2 teaspoons margarine, melted

Cook peas according to package directions, omitting salt and fat; drain. Combine peas, turkey, cheese, and onion in a medium bowl; set aside. Combine mayonnaise, mustard, salt, and pepper in a small bowl. Add to turkey mixture, tossing well.

Spoon into a 10- x 6- x 2-inch baking dish coated with cooking spray; arrange tomato slices on top. Combine crushed cornflakes and margarine; sprinkle over casserole. Bake at 350° for 20 minutes or until thoroughly heated. Yield: 6 servings (221 calories per serving).

PRO 19.7 / FAT 9.8 / CARB 13.2 / FIB 2.4 / CHOL 46 / SOD 367 / POT 331

ORIENTAL GRILLED CORNISH HENS

4 (1-pound, 6-ounce) Cornish hens
⅔ cup unsweetened pineapple juice
⅓ cup dry sherry
¼ cup reduced-sodium soy sauce
1 tablespoon sesame seeds
1 tablespoon honey
1 clove garlic, minced
⅛ teaspoon ground ginger or 1 teaspoon grated
   fresh gingerroot
Vegetable cooking spray

Remove giblets from hens; reserve for other uses. Rinse hens with cold water, and pat dry. Split each hen lengthwise, using an electric knife. Place hens, cavity side up, in a large shallow dish. Combine next 7 ingredients; pour over hens. Cover and marinate in refrigerator 8 hours or overnight.

Remove hens from marinade, reserving marinade. Coat grill with cooking spray. Grill hens 6 to 7 inches over medium coals 1 hour to 1 hour and 15 minutes or until done, turning hens and basting with marinade every 15 minutes. Yield: 8 servings (256 calories per serving).

PRO 33.1 / FAT 8.8 / CARB 6.4 / FIB 0.1 / CHOL 99 / SOD 388 / POT 315

CORNISH HENS WITH CRANBERRY-ORANGE SAUCE

4 (1-pound, 6-ounce) Cornish hens
¼ cup frozen orange juice concentrate, thawed and
   undiluted
¼ cup water
Cranberry-Orange Sauce

Remove giblets from hens; reserve for other uses. Rinse hens with cold water; pat dry. Split each hen lengthwise, using an electric knife. Place hens, cut side down, on a rack in a shallow roasting pan.

Combine orange juice concentrate and water in a small bowl. Baste hens with orange juice mixture. Bake at 350° for 1 hour or until done.

Transfer hens to a serving platter. To serve, spoon 2 tablespoons plus 2 teaspoons Cranberry-Orange Sauce over each hen half. Yield: 8 servings (261 calories per serving).

Cranberry-Orange Sauce:

1½ cups fresh cranberries, coarsely chopped
1 teaspoon grated orange rind
¾ cup unsweetened orange juice
2 tablespoons firmly packed brown sugar
2 teaspoons cornstarch

Combine all ingredients in a small saucepan; stir well. Bring to a boil. Reduce heat to medium, and cook 1 minute, stirring constantly, until thickened. Serve warm. Yield: 1⅓ cups.

PRO 32.5 / FAT 8.3 / CARB 12.5 / FIB 0.3 / CHOL 99 / SOD 97 / POT 399

Salads provide a wide variety of ingredients for the calorie conscious. Marinated Flank Steak Salad (page 170) can serve as a main dish. For side-dish salads, choose Congealed Apricot-Fruit Salad (page 160) or Fusilli Fruit Salad (page 162).

Salads & Salad Dressings

CONGEALED APRICOT-FRUIT SALAD

1 (12-ounce) can apricot nectar
1 envelope unflavored gelatin
1 (15¼-ounce) can unsweetened crushed
  pineapple, undrained
1 tablespoon lemon juice
1 (16-ounce) can unsweetened apricot halves,
  drained and chopped
1 medium banana, chopped
Vegetable cooking spray
Lettuce leaves
Mandarin orange slices (optional)

Combine apricot nectar and gelatin in a small saucepan; let stand 1 minute. Cook over medium heat 1 minute or until gelatin dissolves.

Drain pineapple, reserving ½ cup juice. Stir ½ cup pineapple juice and lemon juice into apricot mixture. Chill until consistency of unbeaten egg white.

Add pineapple, apricots, and banana to gelatin mixture, stirring gently. Spoon mixture into a 4-cup mold coated with cooking spray. Chill overnight or until firm. Turn salad out onto a lettuce-lined serving dish. Garnish with mandarin orange slices, if desired. Yield: 8 servings (84 calories per serving).

PRO 1.8 / FAT 0.4 / CARB 20.2 / FIB 1.4 / CHOL 0 / SOD 3 / POT 281

HONEYDEW-GRAPE SALAD WITH LIME DRESSING

2 cups honeydew balls
½ cup seedless green grapes, halved
½ cup seedless red grapes, halved
1 tablespoon vegetable oil
1 tablespoon white wine vinegar
⅛ teaspoon grated lime rind
1½ teaspoons lime juice
1½ teaspoons honey
Fresh mint leaves (optional)

Combine honeydew and grapes in a medium bowl. Combine oil, vinegar, lime rind, lime juice, and honey in a small bowl; stir with a wire whisk until blended. Pour over fruit; toss lightly. Chill 1 hour. Garnish with mint leaves, if desired. Yield: 6 servings (64 calories per serving).

PRO 0.6 / FAT 2.6 / CARB 10.7 / FIB 0.8 / CHOL 0 / SOD 8 / POT 195

STUFFED NECTARINES

½ (8-ounce) package Neufchâtel cheese, softened
1 teaspoon grated lemon rind
1 tablespoon plus 1 teaspoon lemon juice, divided
1 tablespoon sugar
2 tablespoons chopped walnuts
2 (6-ounce) nectarines, halved and pitted
Lettuce leaves

Combine cheese, lemon rind, 2 teaspoons lemon juice, and sugar in a bowl; beat until well blended. Fold in walnuts; set aside.

Sprinkle remaining lemon juice evenly over cut sides of nectarine halves. Place each on a lettuce-lined salad plate. Top each half with 1½ tablespoons cheese mixture. Chill thoroughly. Yield: 4 servings (145 calories per serving).

PRO 4.5 / FAT 9.2 / CARB 13.1 / FIB 0.5 / CHOL 22 / SOD 113 / POT 206

MINTED PEAR GREEN SALAD

2 cups torn spinach
2 cups torn Romaine lettuce
2 cups torn iceberg lettuce
2 medium pears, cored and cut into wedges
2 tablespoons lemon juice
Creamy Mint Dressing

Combine spinach, Romaine, and iceberg lettuce in a large bowl, and toss gently. Cover and chill. Divide salad greens among individual serving plates. Dip pear wedges in lemon juice, and arrange over salad greens. Serve with 1½ tablespoons Creamy Mint Dressing per serving. Yield: 8 servings (62 calories per serving).

Creamy Mint Dressing:

½ cup plain low-fat yogurt
¼ cup chopped fresh mint leaves
¼ cup reduced-calorie mayonnaise
1 teaspoon sugar
2 teaspoons white wine vinegar
2 teaspoons lemon juice
⅛ teaspoon white pepper

Combine all ingredients in a small bowl, and stir with a wire whisk until smooth. Cover and chill thoroughly. Yield: ¾ cup.

PRO 1.5 / FAT 2.5 / CARB 9.5 / FIB 1.4 / CHOL 3 / SOD 74 / POT 191

SPINACH-APPLE SALAD

1 medium-size Red Delicious apple, cored and
  thinly sliced
1½ teaspoons lemon juice
½ pound spinach, trimmed and torn
1 tablespoon plus 1½ teaspoons slivered almonds,
  toasted
2 tablespoons white wine vinegar
1½ teaspoons sugar
½ teaspoon dry mustard
1½ teaspoons reduced-sodium soy sauce
1½ teaspoons olive oil
½ teaspoon lemon juice
Dash of hot sauce
Dash of pepper

Combine apple slices and 1½ teaspoons
lemon juice; toss to coat. Add spinach and almonds; toss well. Combine remaining ingredients; mix well. Pour over spinach mixture; toss
lightly to coat. Cover; chill 1 hour. Yield: 4 servings (76 calories per serving).

PRO 2.0 / FAT 3.8 / CARB 10.0 / FIB 2.4 / CHOL 0 / SOD 105 / POT 288

ORANGE-GLAZED FRUIT SALAD

¾ teaspoon cornstarch
½ teaspoon grated orange rind
¼ cup plus 2 tablespoons unsweetened orange juice
1 tablespoon honey
1 medium orange, peeled, seeded, and sectioned
½ medium apple, cubed
½ medium banana, sliced
½ cup strawberries, halved
½ cup seedless green grapes, halved
1 (8-ounce) can unsweetened pineapple chunks,
  drained

Combine first 4 ingredients in a small non-aluminum saucepan. Bring to a boil. Cover; reduce
heat, and cook, stirring constantly, until mixture
thickens. Cool slightly; refrigerate 1 hour or until
thickened and thoroughly chilled.
Combine remaining ingredients in a large
serving bowl. Pour chilled dressing over fruit; toss
gently. Cover and chill until ready to serve.
Yield: 6 servings (82 calories per serving).

PRO 0.9 / FAT 0.4 / CARB 20.7 / FIB 1.8 / CHOL 0 / SOD 1 / POT 244

GINGERED CITRUS CONGEALED SALAD

1 envelope unflavored gelatin
2 cups unsweetened orange juice, divided
½ teaspoon ground ginger
2 medium oranges, peeled, seeded, and sectioned
1 medium grapefruit, peeled, seeded, and
  sectioned
¼ cup chopped celery
Vegetable cooking spray
Lettuce leaves (optional)

Sprinkle gelatin over ½ cup orange juice in a
medium bowl; let stand 1 minute. Bring remaining 1½ cups orange juice to a boil in a small
non-aluminum saucepan. Add to gelatin mixture; stir until gelatin dissolves. Stir in ginger, and
chill until consistency of unbeaten egg white.
Chop orange and grapefruit sections; drain
well. Stir oranges, grapefruit, and celery into
thickened gelatin.
Coat 6 (½-cup) molds with cooking spray;
pour gelatin mixture into molds. Chill overnight
or until firm. Unmold onto lettuce leaves, if desired. Yield: 6 servings (73 calories per serving).

PRO 2.3 / FAT 0.2 / CARB 16.8 / FIB 0.9 / CHOL 0 / SOD 7 / POT 299

FRUITY CABBAGE SALAD

4 cups shredded cabbage
1 (8-ounce) can unsweetened pineapple tidbits,
  drained
1 medium pear, cored and diced
1 medium-size Red Delicious apple, cored and
  diced
½ cup seedless green grapes, halved
1 (8-ounce) carton plain low-fat yogurt
2 teaspoons cider vinegar
1 teaspoon honey
½ teaspoon celery seeds
1 medium banana, sliced

Combine first 5 ingredients. Combine yogurt,
vinegar, honey, and celery seeds, stirring well;
pour over cabbage mixture, tossing to coat well.
Cover and chill 1 hour. Add banana just before
serving, and toss to coat. Yield: 12 servings (54
calories per ½-cup serving).

PRO 1.6 / FAT 0.6 / CARB 11.9 / FIB 1.3 / CHOL 1 / SOD 18 / POT 199

Marinated Green Bean Salad in the making. The result — a delicious salad with only 43 calories per serving.

FUSILLI FRUIT SALAD

1 cup fusilli pasta
1 (8-ounce) can unsweetened pineapple chunks, undrained
1 cup cantaloupe chunks
1 cup seedless white grapes, halved
1 (8-ounce) carton peach low-fat yogurt
1 cup strawberry halves
Lettuce leaves

Cook pasta according to package directions, omitting salt; drain and set aside.

Drain pineapple, reserving 2 tablespoons juice. Combine pasta, pineapple chunks, cantaloupe, and grapes in a medium bowl; set aside.

Combine yogurt and reserved 2 tablespoons pineapple juice in a small bowl; stir well. Spoon over pasta mixture, tossing lightly. Cover and refrigerate 2 hours.

Stir in strawberry halves, and serve on lettuce leaf-lined plates. Yield: 8 servings (109 calories per serving).

PRO 3.2 / FAT 0.8 / CARB 23.3 / FIB 1.5 / CHOL 1 / SOD 20 / POT 261

MARINATED GREEN BEAN SALAD

1 pound fresh green beans
1 (2-ounce) jar sliced pimiento, drained
1 medium tomato, chopped
½ cup chopped green pepper
½ cup reduced-calorie Italian salad dressing
¼ cup chopped fresh parsley
¼ teaspoon freshly ground pepper

Remove strings from green beans; wash thoroughly. Cut each bean lengthwise into 4 strips. Place in a steaming rack over boiling water. Cover and steam 5 minutes or until crisp-tender. Cool completely.

Combine beans, pimiento, tomato, and green pepper in a shallow container. Combine salad dressing, parsley, and pepper; stir well. Pour over bean mixture. Cover and refrigerate overnight. Yield: 6 servings (43 calories per serving).

PRO 1.9 / FAT 0.3 / CARB 9.7 / FIB 2.0 / CHOL 0 / SOD 190 / POT 264

CURRIED BEAN AND RICE SALAD

1 pound fresh green beans
1 cup water
1 teaspoon chicken-flavored bouillon granules
½ cup parboiled rice, uncooked
½ cup chopped onion
2 tablespoons slivered almonds, toasted
3 tablespoons white wine vinegar
1 tablespoon vegetable oil
1 teaspoon lemon juice
½ teaspoon curry powder
½ teaspoon prepared mustard
⅛ teaspoon pepper

Remove strings from beans; wash beans thoroughly, and cut into 1½-inch pieces. Place beans and water to cover in a medium saucepan. Bring to a boil. Cover; reduce heat, and simmer 10 minutes or until beans are crisp-tender; drain and cool.

Combine 1 cup water and bouillon granules in a small saucepan. Bring to a boil, and stir in rice. Cover; reduce heat, and simmer 20 minutes or until rice is tender. Cool.

Combine beans, rice, onion, and almonds in a medium bowl. Combine remaining ingredients in a jar. Cover tightly, and shake vigorously. Pour over bean mixture; toss gently. Cover and refrigerate overnight. Yield: 10 servings (74 calories per ½-cup serving).

PRO 1.9 / FAT 2.4 / CARB 11.8 / FIB 1.3 / CHOL 0 / SOD 45 / POT 134

CALICO RICE SALAD

1¾ cups water
⅛ teaspoon salt
½ cup brown rice, uncooked
¾ cup frozen English peas, thawed and drained
¾ cup frozen cut corn, thawed and drained
¼ cup reduced-calorie French salad dressing
⅓ cup diced sweet red pepper
¼ cup grated onion
¼ cup plus 2 tablespoons unsalted peanuts

Bring water and salt to a boil in a medium saucepan; add rice. Cover; reduce heat, and simmer 45 minutes or until rice is tender and water is absorbed. Transfer to a medium serving bowl, and set aside.

Cook peas and corn according to package directions, omitting salt and fat. Drain well. Combine rice, peas, corn, salad dressing, pepper, and onion, stirring well. Cover and refrigerate until thoroughly chilled. Top with peanuts just before serving. Yield: 6 servings (147 calories per serving).

PRO 5.4 / FAT 4.9 / CARB 22.0 / FIB 2.7 / CHOL 0 / SOD 178 / POT 199

DILLED BROCCOLI-CAULIFLOWER SALAD

2 cups fresh broccoli flowerets
2 cups fresh cauliflower flowerets
1 cup sliced fresh mushrooms
¼ cup chopped onion
2 tablespoons pine nuts, toasted
¼ cup low-fat cottage cheese
¼ cup reduced-calorie mayonnaise
1 teaspoon Worcestershire sauce
¼ teaspoon dried whole dillweed
⅛ teaspoon pepper
Boston lettuce leaves

Combine first 5 ingredients in a medium bowl; toss lightly. Place cottage cheese in container of an electric blender; process until smooth. Add mayonnaise, Worcestershire sauce, dillweed, and pepper; process until combined. Pour over broccoli mixture, tossing lightly. Cover and refrigerate at least 4 hours or overnight. Spoon mixture into a lettuce-lined bowl to serve. Yield: 8 servings (68 calories per serving).

PRO 3.1 / FAT 4.5 / CARB 5.2 / FIB 0.9 / CHOL 3 / SOD 102 / POT 273

 Running got you down? Skip around. By skipping you can avoid running's bone-jolting force, says former U.S. Olympic Sports Medicine Council chairman Dr. Irving Dardik.

When you jog, your body is pointed pretty much straight up, he explains. This means the pressure of landing on your feet goes right up your muscular-skeletal system.

But skip, and your body tilts forward coming down from the hop. So some of the pressure goes behind you, not into your knees and back.

For variety, jog a bit, and then skip for a few minutes. It may feel a little silly, but it's healthy!

Mexican Salad Bowl is a protein-rich fiesta of flavor!

CRISPY MARINATED CARROTS

1 pound carrots, scraped and sliced
½ medium onion, sliced and separated into rings
½ cup chopped green pepper
⅓ cup vinegar
¼ cup tomato juice
1 tablespoon sugar
1 tablespoon vegetable oil
1 teaspoon Worcestershire sauce
¼ teaspoon prepared mustard

Cook carrots in boiling water to cover 2 minutes or until crisp-tender; drain. Combine carrots, onion, and green pepper in a 10- x 6- x 2-inch baking dish; set aside.

Combine remaining ingredients in a small bowl; stir until well blended. Pour over vegetables; toss lightly. Cover and refrigerate 8 hours or overnight. Serve with a slotted spoon. Yield: 6 servings (71 calories per serving).

PRO 1.1 / FAT 2.5 / CARB 12.4 / FIB 1.4 / CHOL 0 / SOD 75 / POT 327

MEXICAN SALAD BOWL

1 (15-ounce) can kidney beans
4 ounces sharp Cheddar cheese, diced
1 (8¾-ounce) can whole kernel corn, drained
2 medium tomatoes, diced
½ cup chopped green pepper
4 green onions, thinly sliced
½ cup reduced-calorie French salad dressing
½ to ¾ teaspoon chili powder
1 medium head iceberg lettuce, shredded

Place kidney beans in a colander, and rinse under cold water 1 minute; set colander aside to let beans drain 1 minute.

Combine beans with next 5 ingredients in a large salad bowl. Combine salad dressing and chili powder; pour over bean mixture, tossing gently. Cover and refrigerate 1 hour. Add lettuce just before serving; toss lightly. Yield: 5 servings (205 calories per main-dish serving).

PRO 11.5 / FAT 8.6 / CARB 22.8 / FIB 7.3 / CHOL 24 / SOD 516 / POT 592

MARINATED BLACK-EYED PEA SALAD

1 (10-ounce) package frozen black-eyed peas
1 small head cauliflower (about ¾ pound)
½ cup chopped onion
¼ cup chopped green pepper
1 (2-ounce) jar sliced pimiento, drained
½ cup unsweetened apple juice
½ cup cider vinegar
½ teaspoon dried whole oregano
¼ teaspoon salt
¼ teaspoon pepper
⅛ teaspoon hot sauce
1 clove garlic, crushed

Cook peas according to package directions, omitting salt and fat; drain well. Set aside.

Break cauliflower into flowerets; place in a steaming rack over boiling water. Cover and steam 8 to 10 minutes or until crisp-tender.

Combine vegetables and pimiento. Combine remaining ingredients in a glass jar; cover tightly, and shake vigorously. Pour over vegetables. Cover and refrigerate 8 hours or overnight, stirring occasionally. Yield: 10 servings (61 calories per ½-cup serving).

PRO 3.4 / FAT 0.3 / CARB 12.2 / FIB 0.9 / CHOL 0 / SOD 68 / POT 304

HERB-GARLIC POTATO SALAD

1½ pounds red potatoes, cut into
    ¾-inch cubes
3 cups water
3 tablespoons plain low-fat yogurt
2 tablespoons sour cream
2 teaspoons Dijon mustard
1 clove garlic, minced
1 teaspoon dried whole basil
¼ teaspoon salt
¼ teaspoon dried whole thyme

Combine potatoes and water in a large saucepan; bring to a boil. Cover; reduce heat, and simmer 8 minutes or just until tender. Drain and transfer to a large bowl.

Combine yogurt, sour cream, mustard, garlic, basil, salt, and thyme in a small bowl; stir until well blended. Pour over potatoes, and toss gently until well coated. Serve warm or chilled. Yield: 8 servings (86 calories per serving).

PRO 2.0 / FAT 1.0 / CARB 17.8 / FIB 0.4 / CHOL 2 / SOD 95 / POT 303

SPECIAL ROMAINE SALAD

1 (14-ounce) can artichoke hearts, drained and
    quartered
1 (14-ounce) can hearts of palm, drained and
    sliced into ½-inch pieces
1 medium onion, thinly sliced and separated into
    rings
½ cup white wine vinegar
¼ cup water
1 tablespoon olive or vegetable oil
¼ teaspoon pepper
¼ teaspoon dried whole oregano
1 clove garlic, crushed
1 (10-ounce) head Romaine lettuce, torn
8 cherry tomatoes, halved
2 tablespoons grated Parmesan cheese

Combine artichokes, hearts of palm, and onion in a shallow baking dish. Combine vinegar and 5 ingredients in a glass jar; cover tightly, and shake vigorously. Pour over vegetable mixture, tossing well. Cover and refrigerate 8 hours or overnight, tossing occasionally.

Drain vegetable mixture, reserving marinade. Combine Romaine and marinated vegetables in a large salad bowl; toss gently. Arrange cherry tomatoes on top of salad, and sprinkle with Parmesan cheese. Serve with reserved marinade, if desired. Yield: 12 servings (53 calories per 1-cup serving).

PRO 1.9 / FAT 1.8 / CARB 9.5 / FIB 1.4 / CHOL 0 / SOD 75 / POT 237

ORIENTAL MARINATED VEGETABLES

2 cups fresh snow peas
1 (8-ounce) can sliced water chestnuts, drained
1 (8-ounce) can sliced bamboo shoots, drained
½ cup sliced fresh mushrooms
½ cup chopped green onion
¼ cup rice wine vinegar
2 tablespoons reduced-sodium soy sauce
1 teaspoon finely grated fresh gingerroot
1 tablespoon vegetable oil
2 teaspoons sesame oil
⅛ teaspoon garlic powder
⅛ teaspoon crushed red pepper

Trim ends from snow peas. Place snow peas in a steaming basket. Plunge basket into boiling water, and remove immediately. Drain well.

Combine snow peas, water chestnuts, bamboo shoots, mushrooms, and onion in a medium bowl; set aside. Combine vinegar, soy sauce, and gingerroot in a small bowl. Gradually add oil, beating constantly with a wire whisk. Add garlic powder and red pepper. Pour over vegetables; toss lightly. Chill 2 hours. Toss lightly before serving. Yield: 10 servings (51 calories per ½-cup serving).

PRO 1.4 / FAT 2.4 / CARB 6.4 / FIB 0.8 / CHOL 0 / SOD 120 / POT 227

GAZPACHO SALAD

2 medium tomatoes, chopped
1 medium cucumber, chopped
1 medium-size green pepper, seeded and chopped
1 stalk celery, finely chopped
¼ cup chopped onion
1 shallot, finely chopped
1 tablespoon chopped fresh parsley
1 tablespoon chopped ripe olives
Herbed Dressing
Lettuce leaves

Combine first 8 ingredients in a 13- x 9- x 2-inch baking dish. Pour Herbed Dressing over vegetables; toss gently. Chill at least 2 hours. Serve on lettuce leaves. Yield: 10 servings (50 calories per ½-cup serving).

Herbed Dressing:

3 tablespoons red wine vinegar
2 tablespoons lemon juice
2 tablespoons olive or vegetable oil
1 teaspoon Dijon mustard
½ teaspoon dried whole oregano
½ teaspoon dried whole basil
2 cloves garlic, minced
¼ teaspoon freshly ground pepper

Combine all ingredients in a glass jar; cover tightly, and shake vigorously. Yield: ½ cup.

PRO 1.1 / FAT 3.2 / CARB 5.2 / FIB 1.0 / CHOL 0 / SOD 32 / POT 227

For delectable salads, add one of these dressings: (clockwise from top) Spring Onion, Honey-Curry, Herbed Tomato, Tangy White Wine, and Creamy Pineapple (pages 171 and 172).

MINTED SUMMER VEGETABLE SALAD

1 medium zucchini squash, thinly sliced
1 medium-size yellow squash, thinly sliced
1 small cucumber, thinly sliced
1 medium tomato, coarsely chopped
¼ cup chopped onion
¼ cup chopped sweet red pepper
1 tablespoon finely chopped fresh mint
    leaves
2 tablespoons white wine vinegar
1 tablespoon lemon juice
1 tablespoon water
1½ teaspoons olive or vegetable oil
½ teaspoon sugar
⅛ teaspoon pepper

Combine zucchini squash, yellow squash, cucumber, chopped tomato, onion, and red pepper in a large bowl.

Combine remaining ingredients in a small bowl; stir until well blended. Pour mixture over vegetables, and toss lightly to coat well. Cover and chill at least 1 hour.

Toss vegetables again just before serving. Serve, using a slotted spoon. Yield: 8 servings (23 calories per serving).

PRO 0.7 / FAT 1.0 / CARB 3.4 / FIB 0.6 / CHOL 0 / SOD 3 / POT 149

VEGETABLE ASPIC

1 teaspoon unflavored gelatin
¾ cup unsweetened apple juice
⅓ cup cider vinegar
1 cup frozen English peas, thawed and
    drained
1 cup frozen French-style green beans,
    thawed and drained
1 (14-ounce) can artichoke hearts, drained and
    chopped
1 (2-ounce) jar diced pimiento, drained
2 tablespoons chopped ripe olives
1 tablespoon finely chopped onion
1½ teaspoons prepared horseradish
⅛ teaspoon pepper
Vegetable cooking spray
8 lettuce leaves

Combine gelatin and apple juice in a small saucepan; let stand 1 minute. Cook over medium heat 1 minute or until gelatin dissolves, stirring constantly. Remove from heat; stir in vinegar. Chill until mixture reaches consistency of unbeaten egg white.

Combine peas, green beans, artichoke hearts, pimiento, olives, onion, horseradish, and pepper in a large bowl; add gelatin mixture, stirring gently. Spoon mixture into 8 (½-cup) molds coated with cooking spray; cover and refrigerate overnight or until set.

Unmold onto individual lettuce-lined serving plates. Yield: 8 servings (56 calories per serving).

PRO 2.5 / FAT 0.6 / CARB 11.0 / FIB 0.9 / CHOL 0 / SOD 62 / POT 222

DILLED VEGETABLE MACARONI SALAD

½ (8-ounce) package elbow macaroni
½ cup shredded zucchini squash
¼ cup chopped celery
¼ cup shredded carrot
¼ cup chopped green pepper
2 medium-size green onions, sliced
2 medium radishes, thinly sliced
¼ cup reduced-calorie mayonnaise
2 tablespoons plain low-fat yogurt
1½ teaspoons vinegar
½ teaspoon lemon juice
¼ teaspoon dried whole dillweed or 1 teaspoon
    minced fresh dill
Fresh dill sprigs (optional)

Cook macaroni according to package directions, omitting salt. Drain macaroni well, and let cool completely.

Combine cooked macaroni, zucchini squash, celery, carrot, green pepper, onions, and radishes in a medium serving bowl; mix well. Combine mayonnaise, yogurt, vinegar, lemon juice, and ¼ teaspoon dillweed in a small bowl; stir until well blended. Pour dressing mixture over macaroni mixture, mixing well. Cover and chill at least 2 hours. Garnish with fresh dill sprigs just before serving, if desired. Yield: 8 servings (81 calories per serving).

PRO 2.3 / FAT 2.3 / CARB 12.8 / FIB 0.7 / CHOL 3 / SOD 64 / POT 102

CURRIED SHRIMP SALAD

1½ quarts water
2 pounds uncooked medium shrimp
1 (8-ounce) can sliced water chestnuts, drained
½ cup chopped celery
½ cup chopped green onion
¼ cup plain low-fat yogurt
¼ cup reduced-calorie mayonnaise
1 teaspoon curry powder
2 teaspoons reduced-sodium soy sauce
1 teaspoon lemon juice
¼ teaspoon pepper
Fresh celery leaves (optional)

Bring water to a boil; add shrimp, and reduce heat. Cook 3 minutes. Drain well, and rinse with cold water. Let shrimp cool; peel and devein.

Combine cooked shrimp, water chestnuts, celery, and onion in a large serving bowl; toss well. Combine remaining ingredients, except celery leaves, in a small bowl; mix well. Add to shrimp mixture, tossing lightly to coat. Cover and chill. Garnish with celery leaves, if desired. Yield: 6 servings (169 calories per main-dish serving).

PRO 21.8 / FAT 3.8 / CARB 10.2 / FIB 0.6 / CHOL 174 / SOD 317 / POT 468

CRABMEAT SALAD

½ pound fresh crabmeat, drained and flaked
1 tablespoon chopped green onion
1 tablespoon chopped fresh parsley
2 tablespoons plain low-fat yogurt
1 tablespoon reduced-calorie mayonnaise
1 teaspoon lemon juice
Dash of pepper
2 Bibb lettuce leaves
4 cherry tomatoes, halved

Combine crabmeat, onion, and parsley in a small bowl; stir well to combine. Combine yogurt, mayonnaise, lemon juice, and pepper in a small bowl, stirring until well blended. Pour over crabmeat mixture. Toss gently to mix well; cover and chill thoroughly. Spoon onto individual lettuce-lined serving plates, and surround with cherry tomato halves. Yield: 2 servings (144 calories per main-dish serving).

PRO 21.0 / FAT 4.5 / CARB 4.2 / FIB 0.5 / CHOL 117 / SOD 308 / POT 356

HOT SEAFOOD SALAD

1 quart water
¾ pound uncooked medium shrimp
¾ pound lump crabmeat, drained and flaked
3 medium stalks celery, thinly sliced
¼ cup chopped sweet red pepper
¼ cup reduced-calorie mayonnaise
2 tablespoons grated onion
1 tablespoon lemon juice
1 tablespoon Worcestershire sauce
2 teaspoons creole mustard
⅛ teaspoon red pepper
Vegetable cooking spray
2 tablespoons grated Parmesan cheese
Fresh parsley sprigs

Bring water to a boil; add shrimp, and reduce heat. Cook 3 minutes. Drain well; rinse with cold water. Let shrimp cool; peel and devein. Cut each shrimp in half.

Combine cooked shrimp and next 3 ingredients in a bowl; stir well. Combine mayonnaise, onion, lemon juice, Worcestershire sauce, mustard, and red pepper in a small bowl. Add to shrimp mixture; stir until well blended.

Spoon shrimp mixture into 6 baking shells or 6-ounce custard cups coated with cooking spray. Sprinkle 1 teaspoon Parmesan cheese over each. Bake at 350° for 15 minutes or until thoroughly heated. Garnish with parsley. Yield: 6 servings (137 calories per main-dish serving).

PRO 18.7 / FAT 4.8 / CARB 3.9 / FIB 0.3 / CHOL 125 / SOD 342 / POT 303

TUNA-RICE SALAD

2 (6½-ounce) cans water-packed tuna
1 cup water
½ teaspoon chicken-flavored bouillon granules
½ cup uncooked white parboiled rice
½ cup chopped celery
¼ cup chopped green onion
2 tablespoons thinly sliced ripe olives
2 tablespoons finely chopped dill pickle
1 (2-ounce) jar diced pimiento, drained
½ cup reduced-calorie mayonnaise
1 tablespoon Dijon mustard
8 lettuce leaves
2 medium tomatoes, each cut into 4 slices

Place tuna in a colander, and rinse under cold tap water 1 minute; set colander aside to let tuna drain 1 minute.

Combine 1 cup water and bouillon granules in a small saucepan; bring to a boil. Add rice. Cover; reduce heat, and simmer 20 minutes or until all liquid is absorbed. Chill.

Combine rice, tuna, celery, onion, olives, pickle, and pimiento in a large bowl. Combine mayonnaise and mustard in a small bowl; stir well. Add to tuna mixture, stirring well. Chill.

Place lettuce on plates. Place 1 slice tomato on each lettuce leaf. Spoon ½ cup tuna mixture on top. Yield: 8 servings (153 calories per main-dish serving).

PRO 12.6 / FAT 5.4 / CARB 13.5 / FIB 0.9 / CHOL 29 / SOD 284 / POT 286

 Go green! Salad greens, tangy and fresh, are a dieter's delight: A 1½-cup serving of romaine lettuce has only 12 calories — but lots of vitamins C and A, good amounts of potassium and even some B vitamins. There's a little iron and calcium, too, and practically no sodium. And the darker the green, the better source of vitamins it is.

CHICKEN-PASTA SALAD DELUXE

½ pound small bowtie pasta (2 cups)
1 pound boneless chicken breast halves, skinned
Vegetable cooking spray
1 teaspoon vegetable oil
¼ teaspoon paprika
1 cup water
¾ pound fresh broccoli, cut into 1-inch pieces
1 cup unsweetened orange juice
¼ cup plus 2 tablespoons cider vinegar
1 teaspoon ground ginger
½ teaspoon paprika
¼ teaspoon pepper
4 medium oranges, peeled, sectioned, and seeded
¼ cup sliced almonds, toasted

Cook pasta according to package directions, omitting salt. Drain and set aside in a large mixing bowl.

Trim excess fat from chicken, and cut chicken into 3- x ½-inch strips. Coat a large skillet with cooking spray; add oil. Place over medium heat until hot. Add chicken, and sauté 5 minutes or until chicken is tender. Stir in ¼ teaspoon paprika during last minute of cooking time. Add chicken to pasta, and set aside. Wipe skillet dry with a paper towel.

Add water to skillet; bring to a boil. Add broccoli. Cover; reduce heat, and simmer 3 minutes or until broccoli is crisp-tender. Drain well, and set aside to cool; chill.

Combine orange juice, vinegar, ginger, ½ teaspoon paprika, and pepper in a small bowl; stir until well blended. Pour over reserved pasta and chicken; add orange sections, and toss lightly to coat. Transfer to a 13- x 9- x 2-inch baking dish; cover and chill thoroughly.

Add broccoli and almonds just before serving, tossing well. Serve chilled. Yield: 8 servings (257 calories per main-dish serving).

PRO 19.2 / FAT 4.3 / CARB 36.5 / FIB 2.8 / CHOL 35 / SOD 44 / POT 532

TURKEY SALAD

½ cup low-fat cottage cheese
2 tablespoons tarragon wine vinegar
2 tablespoons skim milk
¼ teaspoon celery seeds
¼ teaspoon dry mustard
⅛ teaspoon dried whole thyme
3 cups diced cooked turkey breast
1½ cups thinly sliced celery
1½ cups diced apple
1 cup seedless green grapes
1 (8-ounce) can unsweetened pineapple tidbits, drained
Lettuce leaves
2 tablespoons slivered almonds, toasted

Combine first 6 ingredients in container of electric blender; process until smooth. Chill.

Combine turkey, celery, apple, grapes, and pineapple in a large bowl; add cottage cheese mixture, tossing gently. Arrange lettuce leaves in a large serving bowl; spoon salad into bowl. Sprinkle with almonds. Yield: 8 servings (148 calories per main-dish serving).

PRO 18.8 / FAT 3.5 / CARB 10.6 / FIB 1.4 / CHOL 38 / SOD 114 / POT 345

MARINATED FLANK STEAK SALAD

1 (1-pound) beef flank steak
Vegetable cooking spray
1 medium onion, thinly sliced
1 medium-size green pepper, seeded and cut into thin strips
1 cup sliced fresh mushrooms
1 (2-ounce) jar sliced pimiento, drained
Marinade (recipe follows)
Lettuce leaves
2 medium tomatoes, cut into wedges

Trim excess fat from steak; set steak aside. Coat a broiler rack with cooking spray. Place steak on rack. Broil 3 to 4 inches from heating element 5 to 7 minutes on each side or to desired degree of doneness. Cut steak diagonally across grain into thin slices; cut slices into 1½-inch pieces. Cool slightly.

Combine steak, onion, green pepper, mushrooms, pimiento, and marinade in a shallow container. Cover and refrigerate 8 hours or overnight. Spoon salad into a lettuce-lined serving bowl; garnish with tomato wedges. Yield: 6 servings (180 calories per main-dish serving).

Marinade:

½ cup red wine vinegar
2 tablespoons Dijon mustard
1 tablespoon olive or vegetable oil
1 tablespoon vegetable oil
1 tablespoon lemon juice
½ teaspoon dried whole basil
¼ teaspoon dried whole thyme
¼ teaspoon salt
¼ teaspoon pepper
1 clove garlic, minced

Combine all ingredients in a small bowl. Stir with a wire whisk until well blended. Yield: about 1 cup.

PRO 19.2 / FAT 8.2 / CARB 6.3 / FIB 0.9 / CHOL 37 / SOD 288 / POT 458

 Watch what you add to your salads. Cheese, bacon bits, and creamy dressings add fat and calories. A better bet: delicious low-calorie dressing. Add meat, seafood or beans and you'll have a whole meal — especially with a roll or slice of bread.

ZESTY BROCCOLI-HAM SALAD

1¼ pounds fresh broccoli
1½ cups cubed lean cooked ham
½ cup (2 ounces) shredded Swiss cheese
¼ cup chopped sweet red pepper
¼ cup chopped green onion
½ cup reduced-calorie Italian salad dressing
¼ cup cider vinegar
1 tablespoon Dijon mustard
½ teaspoon dried whole savory
⅛ teaspoon freshly ground pepper

Trim off large leaves of broccoli. Remove tough ends of lower stalks. Wash broccoli thoroughly; chop coarsely. Combine broccoli, ham, cheese, red pepper, and onion in a large serving bowl; toss gently.

Combine remaining ingredients in a small bowl; stir well. Pour over vegetable mixture; toss gently. Cover and refrigerate 8 hours or overnight. Yield: 6 servings (123 calories per main-dish serving).

PRO 12.4 / FAT 5.0 / CARB 8.2 / FIB 1.3 / CHOL 27 / SOD 721 / POT 390

FRESH BASIL DRESSING

¾ teaspoon unflavored gelatin
2 tablespoons cold water
½ cup boiling water
¼ cup red wine vinegar
2 tablespoons grated Parmesan cheese
2 tablespoons chopped fresh basil
1 tablespoon chopped fresh parsley
1 tablespoon lemon juice
1 clove garlic, crushed
⅛ teaspoon pepper

Soften gelatin in cold water; add ½ cup boiling water, stirring until gelatin dissolves. Set mixture aside.

Combine remaining ingredients in container of an electric blender; process until smooth. Add gelatin mixture, and process 30 seconds or until well combined. Cover and chill thoroughly. Stir well before serving. Yield: 1 cup (5 calories per tablespoon).

PRO 0.4 / FAT 0.2 / CARB 0.2 / FIB 0.0 / CHOL 0 / SOD 12 / POT 9

HONEY-CURRY DRESSING

½ cup water
2 tablespoons honey
2 teaspoons all-purpose flour
1 teaspoon curry powder
¼ teaspoon dry mustard
⅛ teaspoon salt
1 egg, beaten
2 tablespoons unsweetened orange juice
1 tablespoon vinegar

Combine first 6 ingredients in a non-aluminum saucepan. Add egg; stir well. Add orange juice and vinegar; stir until smooth. Cook over low heat, stirring constantly, until thickened. Cover and chill. Serve over fresh fruit. Yield: 1 cup (16 calories per tablespoon).

PRO 0.5 / FAT 0.4 / CARB 2.8 / FIB 0.0 / CHOL 17 / SOD 23 / POT 12

GINGERED PEACH DRESSING

1 (8-ounce) carton peach low-fat yogurt
1 tablespoon lemon juice
½ teaspoon grated fresh gingerroot

Combine all ingredients in a small bowl; stir with a wire whisk until well blended. Cover and chill thoroughly. Serve over fresh fruit. Yield: 1 cup (14 calories per tablespoon).

PRO 0.6 / FAT 0.2 / CARB 2.7 / FIB 0.0 / CHOL 1 / SOD 8 / POT 27

CREAMY PINEAPPLE DRESSING

¼ cup sugar
2 tablespoons all-purpose flour
1 cup unsweetened pineapple juice
¼ cup unsweetened orange juice
2 tablespoons lemon juice
1 egg, beaten
¼ teaspoon grated orange rind
½ cup low-fat cottage cheese

Combine sugar and flour in a small non-aluminum saucepan; mix well. Stir in fruit juice. Add egg, mixing until smooth. Cook over low heat, stirring constantly, until thickened. Remove from heat, and stir in orange rind. Chill thoroughly.
Place cottage cheese and ½ cup juice mixture in container of an electric blender; process until smooth. Fold cottage cheese mixture into remaining juice mixture. Serve over fresh fruit. Yield: 2 cups (19 calories per tablespoon).

PRO 0.8 / FAT 0.3 / CARB 3.5 / FIB 0.0 / CHOL 9 / SOD 17 / POT 22

RASPBERRY-ORANGE DRESSING

1 (8-ounce) carton raspberry low-fat yogurt
½ teaspoon grated orange rind
1 tablespoon unsweetened orange juice

Combine all ingredients in container of an electric blender; process until smooth. Cover and chill thoroughly. Serve over fresh fruit. Yield: 1 cup (14 calories per tablespoon).

PRO 0.6 / FAT 0.2 / CARB 2.8 / FIB 0.0 / CHOL 1 / SOD 8 / POT 27

LEMON-MUSTARD DRESSING

½ cup plain low-fat yogurt
½ cup commercial sour cream
2 tablespoons lemon juice
2 tablespoons white wine vinegar
1 tablespoon chopped fresh parsley
1 teaspoon sugar
1 teaspoon dry mustard

Combine all ingredients in a small bowl; stir with a wire whisk until well blended. Cover and chill thoroughly. Serve over salad greens. Yield: 1¼ cups (18 calories per tablespoon).

PRO 0.5 / FAT 1.3 / CARB 1.0 / FIB 0.0 / CHOL 3 / SOD 7 / POT 25

CREAMY PEPPER DRESSING

¾ cup plain low-fat yogurt
¼ cup reduced-calorie mayonnaise
1 tablespoon grated Parmesan cheese
1 tablespoon minced green onion
1½ teaspoons freshly ground pepper
1½ teaspoons cider vinegar
1 teaspoon lemon juice
½ teaspoon Worcestershire sauce

Combine all ingredients in a bowl. Stir with a wire whisk until smooth. Cover; chill thoroughly. Stir well before serving over salad greens. Yield: 1¼ cups (15 calories per tablespoon).

PRO 0.6 / FAT 1.0 / CARB 1.1 / FIB 0.0 / CHOL 2 / SOD 34 / POT 27

SPRING ONION SALAD DRESSING

1½ cups chopped green onion
½ cup finely chopped onion
1 cup low-fat cottage cheese
1 tablespoon lemon juice
½ teaspoon seasoned salt
⅛ teaspoon pepper

Combine all ingredients in container of an electric blender; process until smooth. Cover and chill thoroughly. Serve over salad greens. Yield: 1¾ cups (10 calories per tablespoon)

PRO 1.2 / FAT 0.2 / CARB 1.0 / FIB 0.2 / CHOL 1 / SOD 64 / POT 26

TARRAGON DRESSING

1 cup low-fat cottage cheese
¼ cup reduced-calorie mayonnaise
¼ cup tarragon vinegar
2 teaspoons sugar
½ teaspoon dried whole tarragon
½ teaspoon dry mustard
⅛ teaspoon salt
⅛ teaspoon pepper
1 tablespoon chopped fresh parsley

Combine first 8 ingredients in container of an electric blender; process until smooth. Stir in parsley. Cover and chill thoroughly. Serve over salad greens. Yield: 1½ cups (17 calories per tablespoon).

PRO 1.3 / FAT 0.9 / CARB 0.9 / FIB 0.0 / CHOL 2 / SOD 69 / POT 14

TANGY WHITE WINE DRESSING

1 cup water
½ cup white wine vinegar
2 tablespoons plus ¾ teaspoon powdered fruit
  pectin
2 tablespoons fresh lemon juice
1 green onion, chopped
1 clove garlic, crushed
1 teaspoon sugar
¼ teaspoon dried red pepper flakes, crushed
¼ teaspoon salt
¼ teaspoon white pepper

Combine all ingredients in container of an electric blender; process until smooth. Cover and chill. Stir well before serving over salad greens. Yield: 1¾ cups (5 calories per tablespoon).

PRO 0.0 / FAT 0.0 / CARB 1.2 / FIB 0.0 / CHOL 0 / SOD 22 / POT 5

HERBED TOMATO DRESSING

1 (14½-ounce) can no-salt-added tomatoes,
  undrained
1 (6-ounce) can vegetable cocktail juice
¼ cup red wine vinegar
2 tablespoons lemon juice
1 teaspoon dried whole oregano
½ teaspoon dried whole basil
½ teaspoon dried whole tarragon
½ teaspoon garlic powder
½ teaspoon onion powder
½ teaspoon pepper
2 tablespoons powdered fruit pectin
1 tablespoon chopped fresh parsley

Combine all ingredients in container of an electric blender; process until smooth. Cover and chill dressing several hours. Stir well before serving over salad greens. Yield: 3¼ cups (4 calories per tablespoon).

PRO 0.1 / FAT 0.0 / CARB 1.1 / FIB 0.1 / CHOL 0 / SOD 13 / POT 28

Selections to satisfy any snack or sandwich appetite: (clockwise) Tuna Stack (page 178), Bite-Size Burgers (page 176), and Open-Faced Fruit Sandwiches (page 174).

BREAKFAST SANDWICHES

¼ cup crunchy peanut butter
¼ cup wheat germ
2 tablespoons chopped dates
2 tablespoons skim milk
8 slices very thinly sliced whole wheat bread,
    toasted
1 medium banana

Combine crunchy peanut butter, wheat germ, chopped dates, and milk in a small bowl, mixing until well blended. Spread 2 tablespoons peanut butter mixture on 4 slices whole wheat toast. Peel and thinly slice banana. Arrange banana slices equally on top of peanut butter mixture. Top with remaining 4 toast slices, and serve. Yield: 4 servings (309 calories per serving).

PRO 13.4 / FAT 10.8 / CARB 46.2 / FIB 4.6 / CHOL 3 / SOD 379 / POT 521

OPEN-FACED FRUIT SANDWICHES

1 (8-ounce) can unsweetened crushed
    pineapple, drained
1 (8-ounce) package Neufchâtel
    cheese
⅓ cup grated carrot
⅓ cup grated apple
3 tablespoons finely chopped pecans,
    toasted
½ teaspoon vanilla extract
Curly leaf lettuce leaves (optional)
4 whole wheat English muffins,
    split
Red apple slices (optional)

Place pineapple on paper towels; drain well, pressing out excess juice.
Beat Neufchâtel cheese until fluffy; fold in well-drained pineapple, carrot, apple, pecans, and vanilla.
Place curly leaf lettuce leaves on English muffin halves, if desired. Spread fruit-cheese mixture evenly over lettuce leaves. Top with red apple slices, if desired. Yield: 8 servings (196 calories per serving).

PRO 5.9 / FAT 9.3 / CARB 22.8 / FIB 1.7 / CHOL 22 / SOD 283 / POT 172

VEGETARIAN CORNBREAD SQUARES

Vegetable cooking spray
1 teaspoon olive oil
½ cup chopped onion
½ cup coarsely chopped sweet red pepper
½ cup coarsely chopped green pepper
½ cup coarsely chopped sweet yellow pepper
½ teaspoon dried whole basil, crushed
½ teaspoon dried whole thyme, crushed
¼ teaspoon pepper
Cornbread (recipe follows)
1 cup (4 ounces) shredded extra-sharp Cheddar
    cheese

Coat a large skillet with cooking spray. Add oil, and place over medium heat until hot. Add onion, and sauté until tender. Stir in chopped pepper, basil, thyme, and pepper, and continue to cook over medium heat, stirring frequently, until vegetables are tender. Remove from heat, and set aside.
Remove hot cornbread from pan; slice in half horizontally. Place bottom half on a baking sheet; spoon sautéed mixture evenly over cut side of cornbread. Sprinkle with cheese, and broil 6 inches from heating element just until cheese melts. Cover with top half of cornbread.
Cut cornbread into 3-inch squares. Cut each cornbread square in half diagonally, if desired, and serve warm. Yield: 9 servings (244 calories per serving).

Cornbread:

2 cups yellow cornmeal
½ cup all-purpose flour
1 teaspoon baking soda
½ teaspoon salt
2 (8-ounce) cartons plain low-fat yogurt
2 eggs, beaten
Vegetable cooking spray

Combine first 4 ingredients in a medium bowl, stirring until well blended. Add yogurt and eggs; stir just until mixed.
Coat a 9-inch square baking pan with cooking spray; place pan in oven at 400° for 2 minutes. Remove from oven, and immediately pour batter into pan; bake at 400° for 20 minutes. Yield: 9 servings.

PRO 10.8 / FAT 7.3 / CARB 33.3 / FIB 3.5 / CHOL 77 / SOD 299 / POT 266

AVOCADO EGG SALAD SANDWICHES

4 hard-cooked eggs, chopped
1 medium tomato, seeded and chopped
¼ cup plus 2 tablespoons shredded Monterey
    Jack cheese
⅓ cup minced celery
⅛ teaspoon salt
⅛ teaspoon pepper
½ small ripe avocado
2 tablespoons reduced-calorie mayonnaise
1 tablespoon skim milk
2 teaspoons lemon juice
Dash of hot sauce
4 lettuce leaves
8 slices thinly sliced whole wheat bread

Combine first 6 ingredients in a medium bowl; mix well, and set aside.

Combine avocado, mayonnaise, milk, lemon juice, and hot sauce in container of an electric blender; process until smooth. Pour over egg mixture, mixing gently.

Place lettuce leaves on 4 slices of bread; top with egg mixture and remaining slices of bread. Cut sandwiches in half, if desired, and serve immediately. Yield: 4 servings (283 calories per serving).

PRO 14.3 / FAT 14.9 / CARB 25.4 / FIB 3.2 / CHOL 286 / SOD 496 / POT 435

CALIFORNIA SALAD PIZZAS

1 (8-ounce) can no-salt-added tomato
    sauce
½ teaspoon dried whole basil, crushed
½ teaspoon dried whole oregano, crushed
½ teaspoon dried whole marjoram,
    crushed
¼ teaspoon garlic powder
¾ cup low-fat cottage cheese
5 whole wheat English muffins, split
1 sweet red pepper, seeded and thinly
    sliced
¾ cup sliced fresh mushrooms
½ cup (2 ounces) shredded part-skim
    mozzarella cheese
1 cup shredded fresh spinach
1 medium tomato, diced

Combine first 5 ingredients in a small bowl; stir well, and set aside.

Process cottage cheese in container of an electric blender or food processor until pureed. Spread pureed cheese over each muffin half; top with tomato sauce mixture. Arrange pepper slices, mushrooms, and cheese on top of tomato sauce. Bake at 425° for 8 minutes or until cheese melts and pizzas are thoroughly heated. Place pizzas on individual serving plates. Top with shredded spinach and diced tomato. Serve warm. Yield: 10 servings (133 calories per serving).

PRO 7.1 / FAT 2.0 / CARB 21.7 / FIB 1.7 / CHOL 5 / SOD 272 / POT 290

INDIVIDUAL PIZZAS

1 (8-ounce) can no-salt-added tomato sauce
1 tablespoon Worcestershire sauce
½ teaspoon garlic powder
¼ teaspoon dried whole basil
¼ teaspoon dried whole oregano
¼ teaspoon dried whole marjoram
½ pound ground chuck
½ cup sliced fresh mushrooms
¼ cup chopped onion
¼ cup chopped green pepper
1 (5½-ounce) can refrigerated buttermilk biscuits
½ cup (2 ounces) shredded part-skim mozzarella
    cheese

Combine tomato sauce, Worcestershire sauce, garlic powder, basil, oregano, and marjoram in a small bowl; stir well. Set aside.

Combine ground chuck, mushrooms, onion, and green pepper in a large skillet; cook over medium heat 5 minutes or until meat is browned, stirring to crumble meat. Drain well in a colander; pat dry with paper towels.

Split each biscuit in half, and place on an ungreased baking sheet; press each into a 3-inch circle. Top each biscuit half with 1 tablespoon tomato sauce mixture; spoon 1 tablespoon meat mixture over each. Sprinkle with cheese. Bake at 425° for 10 minutes or until crusts are browned. Serve warm. Yield: 10 servings (105 calories per serving).

PRO 7.3 / FAT 4.9 / CARB 7.8 / FIB 0.3 / CHOL 20 / SOD 124 / POT 144

BARBECUE BEEF SANDWICHES

1 pound ground chuck
1 (8-ounce) can tomato sauce
¾ cup chopped onion
½ cup reduced-calorie catsup
2 tablespoons tomato juice
1 tablespoon lemon juice
1 tablespoon Worcestershire sauce
1½ teaspoons firmly packed brown sugar
¼ teaspoon pepper
3 hamburger buns, split and toasted
Fresh parsley sprigs

Cook ground chuck in a large skillet over medium heat until meat is browned, stirring to crumble meat. Drain meat well in a colander, and pat dry with a paper towel; wipe pan drippings from skillet with a paper towel.

Return meat to skillet, and stir in next 8 ingredients. Cover and cook over medium heat 10 minutes. Uncover and simmer 5 minutes or until thickened, stirring frequently.

To serve, spoon ⅓ cup meat mixture over each bun half. Garnish with parsley, and serve. Yield: 6 servings (228 calories per serving).

PRO 18.0 / FAT 8.3 / CARB 19.1 / FIB 0.7 / CHOL 60 / SOD 360 / POT 658

BITE-SIZE BURGERS

1 (8-ounce) package club rolls
1 pound ground chuck
1 tablespoon catsup
1 teaspoon Worcestershire sauce
½ teaspoon onion powder
⅛ teaspoon hot sauce
1 egg, beaten
Vegetable cooking spray
¼ cup Dijon mustard
¾ cup shredded iceberg lettuce
3 thin tomato slices, quartered

Separate rolls into twelve individual rolls; brown rolls according to package directions. Set aside, and keep warm.

Combine next 6 ingredients; mix well. Shape mixture into twelve 3-inch patties. Place on a broiler pan coated with cooking spray. Broil 5 inches from heating element 4 minutes on each side or until desired degree of doneness.

Spread each roll with 1 teaspoon mustard. Place a patty on each roll; top with lettuce and tomato, and serve. Yield: 12 servings (229 calories per serving).

PRO 12.7 / FAT 7.3 / CARB 26.8 / FIB 0.2 / CHOL 64 / SOD 494 / POT 240

ROAST BEEF SANDWICHES

¼ cup reduced-calorie Italian salad dressing
1 tablespoon water
1 teaspoon beef-flavored bouillon granules
1 medium onion, thinly sliced
1 medium-size green pepper, seeded and sliced
2 teaspoons cornstarch
½ cup water
2 teaspoons Worcestershire sauce
6 (½-inch-thick) slices Italian bread, toasted
¾ pound cooked roast beef (cooked without salt), thinly sliced
2 medium tomatoes, each cut into 6 slices
2 tablespoons grated Parmesan cheese

Combine first 3 ingredients in a large skillet; bring to a boil. Add onion and green pepper. Cover; reduce heat, and simmer 5 minutes or until onion is tender, stirring occasionally.

Combine cornstarch, ½ cup water, and Worcestershire sauce; add to onion mixture. Bring to a boil, and cook 1 minute, stirring frequently. Reduce heat, and cook until slightly thickened.

Place bread slices on an oven-proof serving platter; top each with equal amounts of meat. Spoon onion mixture over meat; place 2 tomato slices on each sandwich, and sprinkle 1 teaspoon Parmesan cheese over tomatoes.

Broil 6 inches from heating element until cheese is golden brown. Serve warm. Yield: 6 servings (258 calories per serving).

PRO 20.3 / FAT 8.7 / CARB 23.7 / FIB 0.8 / CHOL 53 / SOD 429 / POT 417

PARTY-SIZE HAM SANDWICH

¼ cup plus 2 tablespoons part-skim ricotta cheese
2 tablespoons reduced-calorie mayonnaise
1 tablespoon lemon juice
½ teaspoon dry mustard
¼ teaspoon garlic powder
Vegetable cooking spray
1 (1-pound) loaf frozen white bread dough, thawed
1 tablespoon margarine, melted
6 (1-ounce) slices lean cooked ham
2 medium tomatoes, thinly sliced
8 (⅔-ounce) slices Swiss cheese (at room temperature)
2 cucumbers, peeled and thiny sliced lengthwise
½ cup sliced green onion
4 ounces alfalfa sprouts, washed and drained

Combine first 5 ingredients in container of an electric blender; process until smooth. Set aside.

Coat a 15- x 10- x 1-inch jellyroll pan with cooking spray; set aside. Roll dough on a lightly floured surface in a 15- x 10-inch rectangle; transfer to pan. Pat to the edge of pan; brush entire surface with margarine. Let rise in a warm place (85°), free from drafts, 30 minutes or until doubled in bulk. Bake at 450° for 10 minutes or until golden brown. Remove from oven, and cool 3 minutes. (Crust may be left in pan to serve or may be carefully removed to a tray.) Spread crust with ricotta mixture.

Arrange remaining ingredients over ricotta mixture in order given. Cut into squares. Yield: 10 servings (234 calories per serving).

PRO 13.6 / FAT 9.4 / CARB 24.4 / FIB 2.1 / CHOL 27 / SOD 504 / POT 280

OPEN-FACED TURKEY ASPARAGUS SANDWICHES

24 thin spears fresh asparagus
Vegetable cooking spray
1 teaspoon margarine
4 (2-ounce) slices turkey breast, cooked
4 slices thinly sliced whole wheat bread, toasted
¼ cup reduced-calorie mayonnaise
1 tablespoon minced fresh parsley
1 tablespoon diced pimiento
1 teaspoon Dijon mustard
1 egg white

Place asparagus in a medium saucepan with a small amount of boiling water; cover and cook 6 minutes or until tender. Drain well.

Coat a large skillet with cooking spray; place over medium heat until margarine melts. Reduce heat to low, and add turkey; cook 3 to 4 minutes on each side or until turkey is done. Remove from heat, and drain on paper towels.

Place one turkey slice on each slice of toast; place on a broiler pan. Arrange 6 asparagus spears diagonally on each turkey slice; set aside.

Combine mayonnaise, parsley, pimiento, and mustard in a small bowl; stir well.

Beat egg white (at room temperature) in a small bowl until stiff peaks form. Fold mayonnaise mixture into beaten egg white. Spoon egg white mixture equally over each sandwich. Broil 3 inches from heating element 1 minute or until golden. Serve warm. Yield: 4 servings (219 calories per serving).

PRO 21.8 / FAT 7.8 / CARB 16.0 / FIB 1.8 / CHOL 45 / SOD 360 / POT 367

GRILLED CRAB TORTILLAS

¾ cup part-skim ricotta cheese
2 tablespoons finely chopped jalapeño pepper
2 tablespoons finely chopped fresh cilantro
2 tablespoons finely chopped green onion
1 tablespoon lime juice
¼ teaspoon salt
½ pound fresh crabmeat, drained and flaked
2 teaspoons margarine, softened
4 (8-inch) whole wheat flour tortillas
Vegetable cooking spray

Combine first 6 ingredients in a small bowl; mix well. Fold in crabmeat, and set aside.

Spread margarine equally on one side of each tortilla; set aside.

Place 1 tortilla, margarine side down, in a nonstick skillet coated with cooking spray. Spread ½ cup crab mixture over half of tortilla in skillet, leaving a ¼-inch margin on sides. Cook over medium heat 3 minutes or until underside of tortilla is golden brown. Fold in half. Transfer to a serving platter, and keep warm. Repeat with remaining ingredients. Serve hot. Yield: 4 servings (198 calories per serving).

PRO 17.6 / FAT 7.3 / CARB 16.1 / FIB 1.5 / CHOL 71 / SOD 522 / POT 261

OYSTER LOAVES

2 tablespoons plain low-fat yogurt
2 tablespoons sliced green onion
1 tablespoon chopped red or green pepper
1 tablespoon chopped celery
1 teaspoon reduced-calorie mayonnaise
1 teaspoon lemon juice
½ teaspoon chopped capers
⅛ teaspoon pepper
⅛ teaspoon hot sauce
2 (2½-ounce) hard dinner rolls
1 (12-ounce) container Standard oysters, drained
   and rinsed
⅓ cup cracker crumbs
Vegetable cooking spray
1 lemon, cut into wedges

Combine first 9 ingredients in a medium bowl, and set aside. Cut rolls in half, and scoop out centers, leaving ½-inch shells. (Reserve breadcrumbs for another use.) Place shells on a baking sheet, and bake at 300° for 10 minutes or until crisp. Set aside.

Dredge oysters in cracker crumbs. Coat a medium skillet with cooking spray, and place over medium-high heat until hot; add oysters, and cook 2 minutes on each side or until lightly browned.

Spread roll cavities with yogurt mixture. Divide oysters among rolls; serve with lemon. Yield: 4 servings (163 calories per serving).

PRO 9.2 / FAT 3.3 / CARB 23.4 / FIB 0.3 / CHOL 35 / SOD 442 / POT 154

SHRIMP BOATS

1 pound fresh medium shrimp, uncooked
3 tablespoons reduced-calorie mayonnaise
3 tablespoons plain low-fat yogurt
2 teaspoons lemon juice
¼ teaspoon salt
¾ teaspoon dry mustard
2 cloves garlic, minced
¼ cup finely chopped green onion
¼ cup finely chopped sweet red pepper
¼ cup finely chopped celery
8 whole wheat hot dog buns
2 tablespoons margarine, softened
8 lettuce leaves
Paprika

Bring 1½ quarts water to a boil in a small Dutch oven. Add shrimp, and cook 3 minutes. (Do not boil.) Drain and cool slightly. Peel and devein shrimp; coarsely chop, and set aside.

Combine mayonnaise, yogurt, lemon juice, salt, mustard, garlic, green onion, red pepper, and celery in a small bowl; mix until well blended. Fold in chopped shrimp. Cover and chill thoroughly.

Spread inside of buns evenly with margarine. Line each bun with a lettuce leaf, and fill each with ¼ cup shrimp mixture. Sprinkle with paprika, and serve immediately. Yield: 8 servings (199 calories per serving).

PRO 11.8 / FAT 7.6 / CARB 21.0 / FIB 1.5 / CHOL 79 / SOD 228 / POT 246

TUNA STACK

½ cup all-purpose flour
Dash of salt
¾ cup skim milk
1 egg, beaten
2 teaspoons margarine, melted
Tuna Salad
Apple Slaw
Vegetable cooking spray
Cucumber rose (optional)

Combine flour and salt in a small bowl; stir well. Gradually add milk, egg, and margarine, beating with a wire whisk until smooth. Cover and refrigerate batter at least 1 hour. (This allows flour particles to swell and soften so that crêpes are light in texture.)

Coat the bottom of a 10-inch nonstick crêpe pan or skillet with cooking spray; place pan over medium heat just until hot, not smoking. Pour 3 tablespoons batter into hot pan; quickly tilt pan in all directions so that batter covers pan in a thin film. Cook crêpe 2 minutes. Lift edge of crêpe to test for doneness. Crêpe is ready for flipping when it can be shaken loose from the pan. Flip crêpe, and cook 1 minute on other side. (This side is rarely more than spotty brown, and is the side on which the filling is placed.) Place crêpes on a towel to cool. Stack crêpes between layers of waxed paper to prevent sticking. Repeat procedure until all batter is used.

Place one crêpe on a serving platter; spread

⅓ cup Tuna Salad over crêpe. Top with another crêpe, and spread with ⅓ cup Apple Slaw. Repeat procedure, ending with a crêpe, until all crêpes, Tuna Salad, and Apple Slaw have been used. Cover and refrigerate overnight.

Garnish Tuna Stack with a cucumber rose, if desired. Cut into wedges to serve. Yield: 6 servings (183 calories per serving).

Tuna Salad:

1 (9¼-ounce) can water-packed white tuna, drained
¾ cup minced celery
¼ cup plus 2 tablespoons reduced-calorie salad dressing
¼ teaspoon onion powder
¼ teaspoon ground ginger
1¼ teaspoons lemon juice

Place tuna in a colander, and rinse under cold water 1 minute; set colander aside to let tuna drain 1 minute. Combine tuna and remaining ingredients in a small bowl; stir until well blended. Cover and chill thoroughly. Yield: about 1⅓ cups.

Apple Slaw:

¾ cup shredded cabbage
⅓ cup shredded apple
3 tablespoons plain low-fat yogurt
1 teaspoon sugar
1 teaspoon poppy seeds
2 teaspoons lemon juice

Combine all ingredients in a small bowl; stir until well blended. Cover and chill thoroughly. Yield: about 1 cup.

PRO 14.6 / FAT 7.1 / CARB 14.7 / FIB 0.7 / CHOL 75 / SOD 188 / POT 274

PARMESAN CHIPS

1 (16-ounce) package lasagna noodles
¼ cup vegetable oil
¼ cup water
Vegetable cooking spray
⅓ cup grated Parmesan cheese
2 teaspoons dried whole basil, crushed
2 teaspoons dried whole oregano, crushed
2 teaspoons dried parsley flakes, crushed
¾ teaspoon garlic powder

Cook noodles according to package directions, omitting salt. Drain well. Separate noodles carefully, and blot excess moisture with paper towels.

Combine oil and water in a small bowl; stir well, and brush both sides of lasagna noodles with oil mixture. Cut each noodle crosswise into 2-inch pieces, and arrange in a single layer on baking sheets coated with cooking spray. Set aside.

Combine Parmesan cheese, basil, oregano, parsley flakes, and garlic powder in a small bowl; stir well. Sprinkle a rounded ⅛ teaspoon herb mixture over each chip. Bake at 400° for 16 minutes or until crisp and golden. Cool and store in an airtight container until ready to serve. Yield: 12 dozen. Serving size: 1 chip (16 calories per serving).

PRO 0.5 / FAT 0.5 / CARB 2.4 / FIB 0.1 / CHOL 0 / SOD 4 / POT 8

*Tasty snacks to keep on hand:
(clockwise from top) Mexican
Nibbles (page 180), Popcorn and
Toasted Pumpkin Seed Snacks (page
180), and Parmesan Chips (at right).*

MEXICAN NIBBLES

1 egg white
2½ teaspoons chili powder
½ teaspoon ground cumin
¼ teaspoon garlic powder
3 cups bite-size crispy corn squares cereal
Vegetable cooking spray

Beat egg white (at room temperature) in a large bowl until foamy. Combine next 3 ingredients in a small bowl; stir well, and fold into egg white. Add cereal; stir gently to coat pieces evenly. Spread cereal mixture on a baking sheet coated with cooking spray. Bake at 325° for 15 minutes, stirring every 5 minutes. Let cereal mixture cool on baking sheet; store in an airtight container. Yield: 6 cups. Serving size: ½ cup (63 calories per serving).

PRO 1.7 / FAT 0.3 / CARB 13.2 / FIB 0.5 / CHOL 0 / SOD 155 / POT 43

POPCORN AND TOASTED PUMPKIN SEED SNACK

½ cup pumpkin seeds
1½ teaspoons reduced-sodium soy sauce
¼ cup unpopped popcorn
1 teaspoon vegetable oil

Toss pumpkin seeds with soy sauce in a 9-inch square baking pan; bake at 350° for 7 minutes or until seeds are brown and liquid is absorbed, stirring often. Set aside.

Combine popcorn and oil in a nonstick saucepan; cover and cook over medium-high heat 2 minutes or until popped, shaking pan after corn starts to pop. Toss with pumpkin seeds in a bowl. Yield: 4 cups. Serving size: ½ cup (76 calories per serving).

PRO 3.0 / FAT 4.9 / CARB 6.3 / FIB 1.2 / CHOL 0 / SOD 38 / POT 89

ORANGE-YOGURT CREAMSICLES

2½ cups plain low-fat yogurt
1 (12-ounce) can evaporated skim milk
1 (6-ounce) can frozen unsweetened orange juice
    concentrate, thawed and undiluted
16 (3-ounce) paper cups
16 wooden sticks

Combine first 3 ingredients in a large bowl; stir gently with a wire whisk to mix well. Pour evenly into 16 (3-ounce) paper cups. Cover tops with aluminum foil, and insert a stick through foil into each cup of yogurt mixture. Freeze until firm. Yield: 16 servings (56 calories per serving).

PRO 3.7 / FAT 0.6 / CARB 9.0 / FIB 0.0 / CHOL 3 / SOD 49 / POT 223

APRICOT ICICLES

2 (12-ounce) cans apricot nectar
1 cup skim milk
10 (3-ounce) paper cups
10 wooden sticks

Combine apricot nectar and milk; stir well. Pour evenly into 10 (3-ounce) paper cups. Cover tops with aluminum foil, and insert a stick through foil into center of each cup. Freeze until firm. Yield: 10 servings (47 calories per serving).

PRO 1.1 / FAT 0.1 / CARB 11.0 / FIB 0.2 / CHOL 0 / SOD 15 / POT 118

COTTAGE CHEESE BANANA SPLIT

⅔ cup low-fat cottage cheese
¼ cup plus 2 tablespoons vanilla low-fat yogurt
1 small banana, cut in half lengthwise
2 tablespoons unsweetened crushed pineapple,
    drained
4 small fresh strawberries, sliced
2 teaspoons wheat germ

Combine cottage cheese and yogurt; mix well. Spoon into 2 dessert bowls. Cut banana slices in half crosswise; arrange 2 banana slices on sides of each bowl. Top cottage cheese with equal amounts of pineapple and strawberries. Sprinkle each with 1 teaspoon wheat germ. Yield: 2 servings (164 calories per serving).

PRO 14.0 / FAT 2.8 / CARB 22.3 / FIB 1.4 / CHOL 9 / SOD 337 / POT 447

Light sauces to brighten tastes: (clockwise from top) Mixed Herb Vinegar, Apple-Pineapple Conserve, Salt-Free Seasoning Blend, Peach-Pear Chutney, Strawberry-Orange Spread, Hot Horseradish Mustard, and Mixed Squash Relish in center (pages 183 to 188).

Sauces & Condiments

APRICOT-ALMOND SAUCE

1 (16-ounce) can apricot halves in light syrup,
   undrained
¼ cup unsweetened pineapple juice
2 teaspoons sugar
¼ to ½ teaspoon almond extract
1 tablespoon cornstarch
2 tablespoons water

Place apricots with syrup in container of an
electric blender; process until smooth. Combine
pureed apricots, pineapple juice, sugar, and almond extract in a non-aluminum saucepan; stir
well. Combine cornstarch and water, stirring to
blend; stir into apricot mixture. Bring to a boil;
reduce heat, and cook, stirring constantly, until
thickened. Remove from heat; cool to room
temperature. Serve over ice milk or fresh fruit.
Yield: 1⅔ cups (15 calories per tablespoon).

PRO 0.1 / FAT 0.0 / CARB 3.7 / FIB 0.1 / CHOL 0 / SOD 0 / POT 44

 Fruit is naturally sweet. When making
syrups and sauces, use fresh fruit, frozen
unsweetened fruit, or canned fruit
packed in juice or a light syrup, rather than fruit
which has been sweetened and frozen or
canned in a heavy sugar syrup. You'll be reducing your intake of both sugar and calories.

BLUEBERRY SYRUP

¼ cup sugar
1 tablespoon plus 1½ teaspoons cornstarch
1¼ cups boiling water
1 (16-ounce) package frozen unsweetened
   blueberries, thawed and drained
1 tablespoon lemon juice

Combine sugar and cornstarch in a saucepan;
stir well. Stir in boiling water. Cook over medium
heat, stirring constantly, until mixture comes to a
full boil. Reduce heat; simmer 1 minute, stirring
constantly. Remove from heat; stir in blueberries
and lemon juice. Serve warm or chilled over
pancakes or pound cake. Yield: 2¼ cups (13
calories per tablespoon).

PRO 0.1 / FAT 0.1 / CARB 3.2 / FIB 0.4 / CHOL 0 / SOD 0 / POT 7

FRESH CITRUS SAUCE

2 tablespoons sugar
1 tablespoon cornstarch
½ to ¾ teaspoon grated orange rind
½ to ¾ teaspoon grated lemon rind
1 cup unsweetened orange juice
2 tablespoons lemon juice
1 tablespoon Grand Marnier or other
   orange-flavored liqueur

Combine sugar and cornstarch in a small non-
aluminum saucepan; stir until well blended. Stir
in remaining ingredients; bring to a boil. Reduce
heat, and cook, stirring constantly, until smooth
and thickened. Remove from heat; cover and
chill thoroughly. Serve over fresh fruit, ice milk,
or angel food cake. Yield: 1 cup (16 calories per
tablespoon).

Note: Fresh Citrus Sauce may be served warm
over pancakes, if desired.

PRO 0.1 / FAT 0.0 / CARB 3.9 / FIB 0.0 / CHOL 0 / SOD 0 / POT 32

MINTED PINEAPPLE-STRAWBERRY SAUCE

¼ cup water
2 tablespoons sugar
2 tablespoons chopped fresh mint
1 medium-size ripe pineapple
2 cups fresh strawberries, hulled and
   crushed
1 tablespoon lemon juice

Combine water, sugar, and mint in a medium
saucepan. Bring to a boil, stirring constantly; reduce heat to medium, and cook, stirring constantly, until sugar dissolves. Remove from heat,
and set aside.

Remove leaves and stem ends from pineapple. Peel pineapple, and trim out eyes; remove
core. Chop half of pineapple, and set aside; cut
remaining half into chunks. Place pineapple
chunks in bowl of a food processor. Add mint
mixture. Process until smooth.

Combine pineapple puree, chopped pineapple, and crushed strawberries in a saucepan.
Cook over low heat just until thoroughly heated,
stirring frequently. Transfer to a serving bowl,
and stir in lemon juice. Serve warm or chilled

over ice milk or angel food cake. Refrigerate any remaining sauce for later use. Yield: 4½ cups (5 calories per tablespoon).

PRO 0.1 / FAT 0.0 / CARB 1.3 / FIB 0.2 / CHOL 0 / SOD 0 / POT 13

HONEY-LEMON SAUCE

1 (8-ounce) carton plain low-fat yogurt
2 tablespoons honey
½ teaspoon grated lemon rind
2 tablespoons lemon juice

Combine all ingredients in a small bowl; stir with a wire whisk until blended. Chill thoroughly. Serve over fresh fruit. Yield: 1 cup (17 calories per tablespoon).

PRO 0.8 / FAT 0.2 / CARB 3.4 / FIB 0.0 / CHOL 1 / ·SOD 10 / POT 37

CREAMY CINNAMON SAUCE

1 (8-ounce) carton vanilla low-fat yogurt
½ cup low-fat cottage cheese
1 tablespoon firmly packed brown sugar
½ teaspoon ground cinnamon
½ teaspoon vanilla extract

Combine all ingredients in container of an electric blender; process until smooth, and chill thoroughly. Serve over fresh fruit or angel food cake. Store sauce in a covered container in refrigerator. Yield: 1½ cups (13 calories per tablespoon).

PRO 1.1 / FAT 0.2 / CARB 1.5 / FIB 0.0 / CHOL 1 / SOD 26 / POT 29

CHOCOLATE CUSTARD SAUCE

2 eggs
3 tablespoons sugar
1½ cups skim milk
3 tablespoons Dutch process cocoa
1 teaspoon vanilla extract

Beat eggs until frothy in a small bowl; add sugar, beating until thick and lemon colored. Set mixture aside.

Scald milk in top of a double boiler over simmering water; stir in cocoa. Gradually stir one-fourth of hot milk mixture into egg mixture; add to remaining milk mixture, stirring constantly. Cook over hot water, stirring constantly, 20 minutes or until mixture thickens and coats a metal spoon. Remove from heat, and stir in vanilla. Cover and chill thoroughly. Serve over fresh fruit or angel food cake. Yield: 1¾ cups (18 calories per tablespoon).

PRO 1.0 / FAT 0.6 / CARB 2.3 / FIB 0.0 / CHOL 20 / SOD 16 / POT 30

BLACKBERRY FREEZER SPREAD

3 cups fresh blackberries
1 (1¾-ounce) package powdered fruit pectin
¼ cup sugar
1 tablespoon unsweetened orange juice

Crush blackberries in a medium saucepan; stir in remaining ingredients. Bring to a boil; boil 1 minute, stirring constantly. Remove from heat; stir 3 minutes. Spoon into freezer containers, leaving ½-inch headspace. Cover at once with lids. Let stand at room temperature 24 hours; freeze.

Thaw to serve. Yield: 2¼ cups (16 calories per tablespoon).

PRO 0.1 / FAT 0.0 / CARB 4.1 / FIB 0.5 / CHOL 0 / SOD 0 / POT 24

STRAWBERRY-ORANGE SPREAD

1 teaspoon unflavored gelatin
¼ cup unsweetened orange juice
1 cup mashed, fresh strawberries
1 tablespoon sugar
1 teaspoon grated orange rind
¼ teaspoon ground coriander

Soften gelatin in orange juice in a small non-aluminum saucepan. Cook over low heat, stirring constantly, until gelatin dissolves and mixture comes to a boil. Remove from heat; stir in remaining ingredients. Cover and refrigerate until spread is firm. Spread will keep in refrigerator for up to 2 weeks. Yield: 1¼ cups (7 calories per tablespoon).

PRO 0.2 / FAT 0.0 / CARB 1.6 / FIB 0.1 / CHOL 0 / SOD 0 / POT 18

LIGHT BEER MARINADE

1 (12-ounce) can light beer
¼ cup reduced-calorie catsup
1 clove garlic, minced
1 teaspoon dry mustard
¼ teaspoon salt
¼ teaspoon pepper

Combine all ingredients in a medium bowl; stir well. Use to marinate flank steak or pork chops. Marinate meat in refrigerator several hours or overnight. Baste meat with remaining marinade during cooking. Yield: 1¾ cups (5 calories per tablespoon).

PRO 0.1 / FAT 0.0 / CARB 0.7 / FIB 0.0 / CHOL 0 / SOD 22 / POT 21

CURRY MARINADE

¾ cup Chablis or other dry white wine
¼ cup water
2 tablespoons reduced-sodium soy sauce
1 clove garlic, crushed
1½ teaspoons curry powder

Combine all ingredients in a glass jar; cover tightly, and shake vigorously. Use to marinate chicken, seafood, or pork chops before grilling. Pour over meat, and marinate in refrigerator several hours or overnight. Baste meat with remaining marinade during grilling. Yield: 1 cup (10 calories per tablespoon).

PRO 0.2 / FAT 0.0 / CARB 0.4 / FIB 0.0 / CHOL 0 / SOD 73 / POT 11

LEMON-TARRAGON MARINADE

½ cup lemon juice
1 tablespoon olive oil
1 teaspoon dried whole tarragon
1 teaspoon Dijon mustard
⅛ teaspoon pepper

Combine all ingredients in a glass jar; cover tightly, and shake vigorously. Use to marinate seafood before grilling. Marinate seafood in refrigerator several hours or overnight. Baste with remaining marinade during grilling. Yield: ⅔ cup (16 calories per tablespoon).

PRO 0.1 / FAT 1.4 / CARB 1.2 / FIB 0.0 / CHOL 0 / SOD 15 / POT 21

DILLED MUSTARD SAUCE

1 (8-ounce) carton plain low-fat yogurt
2 tablespoons Dijon mustard
1 teaspoon chopped fresh chives
1 teaspoon Worcestershire sauce
1 teaspoon lemon juice
½ teaspoon dried whole dillweed
Fresh dill sprig (optional)

Combine all ingredients, except dill sprig, in a small bowl; mix well. Cover and chill. Transfer to a serving container, and garnish with dill sprig, if desired. Serve chilled mustard sauce over chicken, fish, or vegetables. Yield: 1 cup (12 calories per tablespoon).

PRO 0.8 / FAT 0.3 / CARB 1.2 / FIB 0.0 / CHOL 1 / SOD 69 / POT 39

MAPLE APPLE SAUCE

¾ cup unsweetened apple juice
¼ cup water
2 tablespoons reduced-sugar maple-flavored syrup
½ teaspoon Dijon mustard
1 medium cooking apple, chopped
1 tablespoon cornstarch
1 tablespoon water
2 tablespoons cider vinegar

Combine first 4 ingredients in a small saucepan; add apple. Bring to a boil. Cover; reduce heat, and simmer 4 minutes. Dissolve cornstarch in 1 tablespoon water; add to apple juice mixture. Bring to a boil; cook 1 minute or until thickened, stirring constantly. Remove from heat; stir in vinegar. Transfer to a serving bowl. Serve warm with ham slices. Yield: 1⅔ cups (8 calories per tablespoon).

PRO 0.0 / FAT 0.0 / CARB 2.0 / FIB 0.1 / CHOL 0 / SOD 3 / POT 15

BRANDIED CRANBERRIES

¾ cup water
½ cup brandy
¼ cup honey
2 tablespoons lemon juice
¼ teaspoon ground cardamom
¼ teaspoon ground nutmeg
1 (12-ounce) package cranberries

Combine first 6 ingredients in a saucepan; stir well. Add cranberries. Bring to a boil; reduce heat, and simmer, uncovered, 10 minutes or until cranberries burst, stirring occasionally. Spoon into a bowl. Cover; chill 8 hours or overnight. Serve cold with turkey or ham. Yield: 3 cups (15 calories per tablespoon).

PRO 0.0 / FAT 0.0 / CARB 2.4 / FIB 0.1 / CHOL 0 / SOD 0 / POT 7

TANGY LEMON SAUCE

¾ cup water
1 teaspoon chicken-flavored bouillon granules
½ teaspoon sugar
½ teaspoon grated lemon rind
Dash of white pepper
2 teaspoons cornstarch
1 tablespoon water
¼ cup lemon juice
2 teaspoons chopped fresh parsley

Combine first 5 ingredients in a saucepan. Cook over low heat, stirring frequently, until bouillon and sugar dissolve.

Combine cornstarch and water, stirring to blend. Gradually add to hot mixture; bring to a boil. Reduce heat, and cook, stirring constantly, until mixture thickens. Remove from heat; stir in lemon juice and parsley. Serve warm over broccoli, asparagus, or fish. Yield: 1 cup (3 calories per tablespoon).

PRO 0.0 / FAT 0.0 / CARB 0.8 / FIB 0.0 / CHOL 0 / SOD 24 / POT 6

SWEET PEPPER SAUCE

3 medium-size sweet red peppers
1 medium-size green pepper, seeded and chopped
⅛ teaspoon salt
⅛ teaspoon ground red pepper

Place red peppers in a 9-inch square pan; bake at 400° for 30 minutes, turning every 10 minutes. Remove from oven; cool.

Cook green pepper, covered, in boiling water to cover 5 minutes; drain and set aside.

Peel red peppers over a medium bowl, collecting juice. Strain juice, and place in container of an electric blender. Add peeled red peppers, salt, and ⅛ teaspoon ground red pepper; process until smooth. Stir in reserved green pepper; transfer to a serving bowl. Cover and chill. Serve with poached white fish. Yield: 1⅔ cups (3 calories per tablespoon).

PRO 0.1 / FAT 0.1 / CARB 0.7 / FIB 0.2 / CHOL 0 / SOD 11 / POT 27

Sweet Pepper Sauce enhances the mild flavor of poached white fish.

MIXED SQUASH RELISH

1 cup finely chopped yellow squash
1 cup finely chopped zucchini squash
½ medium carrot, scraped and shredded
½ cup chopped onion
½ cup chopped green pepper
¼ cup plus 2 tablespoons white wine vinegar
2 tablespoons unsweetened apple juice
1½ teaspoons sugar
½ teaspoon dry mustard
¼ teaspoon minced fresh gingerroot
⅛ teaspoon salt
⅛ teaspoon pepper
1 (2-ounce) jar sliced pimiento, drained

Combine first 5 ingredients in a large saucepan. Combine vinegar, apple juice, sugar, dry mustard, gingerroot, salt, and pepper in a jar; cover tightly, and shake vigorously. Pour over vegetables; bring to a boil. Reduce heat, and simmer, uncovered, 5 minutes or until vegetables are crisp-tender. Transfer to a medium bowl; stir in pimiento. Cover and refrigerate at least 24 hours before serving. Serve with meats. Yield: 3 cups (4 calories per tablespoon).

PRO 0.1 / FAT 0.0 / CARB 0.7 / FIB 0.1 / CHOL 0 / SOD 7 / POT 24

SPAGHETTI SAUCE

Vegetable cooking spray
¾ cup chopped onion
¾ cup chopped green pepper
4 cloves garlic, minced
2 (14½-ounce) cans no-salt-added tomatoes, undrained
1 (6-ounce) can no-salt-added tomato paste
2 teaspoons dried whole oregano
1 teaspoon dried whole basil
½ teaspoon fennel seeds
¼ teaspoon dried whole thyme
¼ teaspoon red pepper flakes
1 bay leaf

Coat a Dutch oven with cooking spray; place over medium heat until hot. Add onion, green pepper, and garlic, and sauté 5 minutes or until tender. Add remaining ingredients, stirring well; bring to a boil. Cover; reduce heat, and simmer

1 hour, stirring occasionally. Remove and discard bay leaf. Serve sauce hot over cooked pasta or spaghetti squash strands. Yield: 1 quart (51 calories per ½-cup serving).

PRO 2.2 / FAT 0.4 / CARB 11.6 / FIB 1.4 / CHOL 0 / SOD 29 / POT 498

TOMATO PESTO

2 medium tomatoes, coarsely chopped
1 medium-size sweet red pepper, seeded and coarsely chopped
2 tablespoons minced fresh parsley
2 cloves garlic
¼ cup chopped fresh basil leaves
1 tablespoon plus 1½ teaspoons all-purpose flour
¼ teaspoon salt
⅛ teaspoon pepper
2 teaspoons grated Parmesan cheese

Combine first 5 ingredients in container of an electric blender, and process until thoroughly pureed. Add flour, salt, and pepper; process until combined. Transfer mixture to a saucepan, and bring to a boil. Simmer 15 minutes; add Parmesan cheese, stirring well. Serve over pasta or with steamed vegetables. Yield: 1½ cups (6 calories per tablespoon).

PRO 0.3 / FAT 0.1 / CARB 1.3 / FIB 0.2 / CHOL 0 / SOD 28 / POT 38

ZESTY SEAFOOD SAUCE

1 cup reduced-calorie mayonnaise
⅓ cup reduced-calorie catsup
¼ cup finely chopped green onion
2 tablespoons chopped fresh parsley
2 tablespoons prepared horseradish
1 tablespoon lemon juice
1 tablespoon chopped capers

Combine all ingredients in a medium bowl, mixing well. Cover and chill several hours. Serve chilled with seafood. Yield: 2 cups (22 calories per tablespoon).

PRO 0.1 / FAT 2.0 / CARB 0.9 / FIB 0.1 / CHOL 2 / SOD 113 / POT 29

SALT-FREE SEASONING BLEND

¼ cup plus 2 tablespoons onion powder
1 tablespoon garlic powder
3 tablespoons poultry seasoning
3 tablespoons paprika
2 tablespoons dry mustard
2 teaspoons ground oregano
2 teaspoons pepper
1 teaspoon chili powder

Mix all ingredients together, and store in an airtight container. Pour into a shaker to use with meat, poultry, or vegetables. Yield: 1 cup (7 calories per teaspoon).

PRO 0.3 / FAT 0.2 / CARB 1.3 / FIB 0.2 / CHOL 0 / SOD 1 / POT 26

MIXED HERB VINEGAR

3 sprigs fresh basil
3 sprigs fresh tarragon
6 sprigs fresh thyme
1 quart vinegar

Wash herbs; arrange in a sterilized wide-mouthed jar. Bruise leaves and stems, using a wooden spoon. Bring vinegar to a boil; pour over herbs in jar. Cover with a metal lid, and screw band tight. Let stand 10 days at room temperature; shake jar daily.

Strain vinegar through 4 layers of cheesecloth into a decorative bottle; discard herbs. Seal with a cork or other airtight lid. Use mixed herb vinegar in sauces and salad dressings. Yield: 1 quart (2 calories per tablespoon).

PRO 0.0 / FAT 0.0 / CARB 0.7 / FIB 0.0 / CHOL 0 / SOD 0 / POT 2

HOT SAUCE

2 teaspoons caraway seeds
3 tablespoons water
2 tablespoons vegetable oil
1 tablespoon red wine vinegar
1 clove garlic, minced
2 teaspoons ground cumin
½ to 1 teaspoon red pepper
¼ teaspoon salt

Place caraway seeds in container of an electric blender; process until finely ground. Add remaining ingredients, and process until smooth. Serve sparingly over cooked greens. Yield: ¼ cup plus 2 tablespoons (47 calories per tablespoon).

PRO 0.3 / FAT 4.8 / CARB 0.9 / FIB 0.2 / CHOL 0 / SOD 99 / POT 29

HOT HORSERADISH MUSTARD

⅔ cup dry mustard
¾ cup white wine vinegar
¼ cup water
2 tablespoons firmly packed brown sugar
½ teaspoon ground turmeric
¼ teaspoon salt
⅛ teaspoon onion powder
⅛ teaspoon red pepper
2 eggs, lightly beaten
1 tablespoon prepared horseradish

Combine first 8 ingredients in top of a double boiler; cover and let stand overnight.

Add eggs to mustard mixture, stirring well. Bring water in double boiler to a boil; reduce heat, and cook mustard mixture over simmering water, stirring constantly, 10 minutes or until thickened. Remove from heat, and stir in horseradish. Cool.

Place mixture in an airtight container; refrigerate 24 hours before serving. Serve with meats. Yield: 1⅓ cups (27 calories per tablespoon).

PRO 1.3 / FAT 1.5 / CARB 1.9 / FIB 0.1 / CHOL 26 / SOD 37 / POT 33

 Hot chili peppers aren't just an exciting substitute for salt. They're good for the heart and lungs. The peppers reduce the tendency of blood to clot, which is a risk factor for heart disease. Chili peppers also stimulate the mucus membranes and help prevent congestion in the lungs.

That's not all. The peppers, especially the red ones, are excellent sources of vitamins A and C. Of course, few of us would want to eat large quantities of jalapeño peppers. But that's okay: Sweet red bell peppers, while they don't have the heart and lung benefits of hot peppers, are also excellent sources of vitamins A and C.

APRICOT-PEACH CHUTNEY

1 cup peeled, sliced fresh apricots
½ cup peeled, sliced fresh peaches
1 tablespoon firmly packed brown sugar
3 tablespoons water
2 tablespoons white vinegar
1 tablespoon white raisins
1 tablespoon chopped onion
1 teaspoon mustard seeds
2 teaspoons lime juice
¼ teaspoon ground ginger

Combine all ingredients in a large non-aluminum saucepan. Bring to a boil. Cover; reduce heat, and simmer 30 minutes, stirring frequently. Cook, uncovered, 5 minutes or until mixture thickens, stirring frequently. Chill thoroughly before serving with pork. Yield: 1 cup (15 calories per tablespoon).

PRO 0.3 / FAT 0.1 / CARB 3.4 / FIB 0.3 / CHOL 0 / SOD 1 / POT 57

Whatever you call it — "snacking," "grazing," or just "eating on the run" — more and more of us are eating in bits and pieces. The more you snack, of course, the more important it is to eat healthy snacks. Many processed foods are full of saturated fat which should be avoided. It's not only bad for your heart, but for your mind, too. A recent study found that animals learned and remembered better on a diet that included polyunsaturated fats than one that was full of saturated fats.

PEACH-PEAR CHUTNEY

1½ cups peeled, diced pears
1½ cups peeled, sliced peaches
1 medium onion, chopped
⅔ cup cider vinegar
⅓ cup raisins
¼ cup firmly packed brown sugar
1 teaspoon mustard seeds
½ teaspoon ground ginger
¼ teaspoon ground cloves
⅛ teaspoon pepper
1 (3-inch) stick cinnamon

Combine all ingredients in a large non-aluminum saucepan; stir until well blended. Bring to a boil, stirring constantly. Cover; reduce heat, and simmer 1 hour, stirring frequently. Uncover and simmer an additional 5 minutes or until mixture thickens. Remove and discard cinnamon stick. Chill before serving with beef or pork. Yield: 2 cups (22 calories per tablespoon).

PRO 0.2 / FAT 0.1 / CARB 5.7 / FIB 0.6 / CHOL 0 / SOD 1 / POT 59

APPLE-PINEAPPLE CONSERVE

2 (20-ounce) jars unsweetened applesauce
1 (20-ounce) can unsweetened crushed pineapple, drained
1 (6-ounce) package dried apricots
½ cup golden raisins
2 tablespoons lemon juice
½ teaspoon ground cinnamon

Combine all ingredients in a large non-aluminum saucepan. Bring mixture to a boil. Reduce heat, and simmer, uncovered, 30 minutes, stirring frequently.

Spoon conserve into hot sterilized jars, leaving ¼-inch headspace; cover at once with metal lids, and screw bands tight. Process in boiling-water bath 15 minutes. Serve with meats or as a spread for toast. Yield: 6 half-pints (14 calories per tablespoon).

PRO 0.1 / FAT 0.0 / CARB 3.6 / FIB 0.2 / CHOL 0 / SOD 1 / POT 44

Color for the table and pleasure for the palate come naturally from these light side dishes: (clockwise from top) Fresh English Peas with Herbs (page 196), Tri-Colored Pepper Sauté (page 196), and Citrus Spiced Pears (page 200).

Side Dishes

ASPARAGUS WITH ORANGE SAUCE

1½ pounds fresh asparagus spears
½ cup reduced-calorie mayonnaise
3 tablespoons water
1 teaspoon grated orange rind
1 tablespoon unsweetened orange juice
Dash of hot sauce

Snap off tough ends of asparagus. Remove scales with a knife or vegetable peeler, if desired. Cook asparagus, covered, in a small amount of boiling water 6 minutes or until crisp-tender. Drain and place on a serving platter; set aside, and keep warm.

Combine mayonnaise, water, orange rind, juice, and hot sauce in a small non-aluminum saucepan; stir until well blended. Cook over low heat 3 minutes or until thoroughly heated, stirring constantly. Serve immediately over asparagus. Yield: 6 servings (79 calories per serving).

PRO 3.7 / FAT 5.6 / CARB 5.9 / FIB 1.1 / CHOL 7 / SOD 151 / POT 354

ASPARAGUS AND PEAS VINAIGRETTE

½ pound fresh asparagus spears, cleaned
1 cup fresh English peas
⅔ cup lemon juice
1 (2-ounce) jar diced pimiento, drained
½ teaspoon paprika
¼ teaspoon salt
¼ teaspoon pepper
1 hard-cooked egg, seived

Snap off tough ends of asparagus. Cook asparagus spears, covered, in a small amount of boiling water 6 minutes or until crisp-tender. Drain well; set aside, and keep warm.

Cook peas in boiling water to cover 20 minutes or just until tender. Drain; set aside, and keep warm.

Arrange asparagus in a ring on a large serving platter; spoon peas into center of ring. Combine lemon juice, pimiento, paprika, salt, and pepper in a small non-aluminum saucepan; cook over medium heat 2 minutes or until thoroughly heated. Spoon over asparagus and peas. Top with egg, and serve immediately. Yield: 4 servings (76 calories per serving).

PRO 5.5 / FAT 1.8 / CARB 11.8 / FIB 1.9 / CHOL 68 / SOD 169 / POT 355

GREEN BEANS WITH PEARL ONIONS AND TOMATOES

1 pound fresh green beans
18 pearl onions
1 cup water
1 teaspoon dried whole tarragon
1 medium tomato, coarsely chopped
1 tablespoon tarragon vinegar
¼ teaspoon freshly ground pepper

Remove strings from beans; wash and cut beans into 2-inch pieces. Place beans, onions, water, and tarragon in a large saucepan; bring to a boil. Cover; reduce heat, and simmer 18 minutes or until tender. Add tomato; cover and cook 2 minutes. Stir in vinegar and pepper; toss well. Yield: 6 servings (31 calories per serving).

PRO 1.6 / FAT 0.2 / CARB 7.3 / FIB 1.7 / CHOL 0 / SOD 8 / POT 230

 Not all calcium comes from milk and cheese. Dark green leafy vegetables, including turnip greens, collard greens, broccoli, kale, and mustard greens, are excellent sources of that important mineral. Other good sources are canned salmon or sardines (eaten with the bones), tofu, and beans.

CREOLE LIMA BEANS

Vegetable cooking spray
1 teaspoon margarine
½ cup chopped celery
½ cup chopped green pepper
½ cup chopped onion
1 (16-ounce) package frozen lima beans, thawed or 3 cups fresh lima beans
1 cup diced tomato
1 cup spicy-hot vegetable cocktail juice

Coat a large skillet with cooking spray; add margarine, and place over medium heat until margarine melts. Add celery, green pepper, and onion, and sauté until tender.

Stir in remaining ingredients; cover and bring to a boil. Reduce heat, and simmer 12 minutes or until beans are tender. Yield: 8 servings (90 calories per serving).

PRO 5.0 / FAT 0.7 / CARB 16.9 / FIB 1.6 / CHOL 0 / SOD 208 / POT 409

SEASONED WHITE BEANS

1 pound dried Great Northern beans
1 medium onion, chopped
1 medium carrot, scraped and
  chopped
1 (14½-ounce) can whole tomatoes, drained
  and chopped
2 teaspoons beef-flavored bouillon
  granules
¾ teaspoon fennel seeds
¼ teaspoon dried whole thyme
¾ cup Chablis or other dry white
  wine
3 tablespoons minced fresh parsley
¼ teaspoon red pepper

Sort and wash beans; place in a large Dutch oven. Cover with water 2 inches above beans; let soak overnight. Drain beans; add onion, carrot, tomatoes, bouillon granules, fennel seeds, thyme, and enough water to cover mixture. Bring to a boil. Cover; reduce heat, and simmer 2 hours or until beans are tender, stirring occasionally. Stir in wine, parsley, and red pepper. Simmer, uncovered, 30 minutes or until thickened, stirring occasionally. Yield: 16 servings (108 calories per ½-cup serving).

PRO 6.7 / FAT 0.6 / CARB 19.8 / FIB 7.2 / CHOL 0 / SOD 124 / POT 421

BEET PUREE

1½ pounds small beets, trimmed
1 teaspoon grated orange rind
⅔ cup unsweetened orange juice

Place beets in a medium non-aluminum saucepan with water to cover. Bring to a boil. Cover; reduce heat, and simmer 35 minutes. Drain and let cool. Rub off skins.
Position knife blade in food processor bowl. Add beets and remaining ingredients to processor bowl. Process 2 minutes or until smooth, scraping sides of bowl occasionally. Return mixture to saucepan; cook over low heat 5 minutes or until mixture is thoroughly heated, stirring occasionally. Yield: 6 servings (62 calories per serving).

PRO 1.9 / FAT 0.2 / CARB 14.4 / FIB 1.1 / CHOL 0 / SOD 82 / POT 420

BRAISED BELGIAN ENDIVE

2 heads Belgian endive (about ½ pound)
1 tablespoon diced celery
1 tablespoon chopped onion
1 tablespoon diced pimiento
¼ cup water
1 tablespoon lemon juice
¼ teaspoon chicken-flavored bouillon granules

Trim ends from endive, and remove any wilted or discolored outer leaves. Cut each endive in half lengthwise. Place in a medium skillet; sprinkle with celery, onion, and pimiento. Combine water, lemon juice, and bouillon granules, stirring well; pour over endive. Bring to a boil. Cover; reduce heat, and simmer 10 minutes or until tender. Yield: 2 servings (27 calories per serving).

PRO 1.6 / FAT 0.3 / CARB 5.5 / FIB 1.1 / CHOL 0 / SOD 78 / POT 405

BROCCOLI WITH GARLIC AND PARMESAN

1 cup water
2 cloves garlic, split
1 (1½-pound) bunch broccoli
⅛ teaspoon salt
1 tablespoon lemon juice
2 tablespoons grated Parmesan cheese

Combine water and garlic in a large saucepan; bring to a boil. Cover; reduce heat, and simmer 5 minutes.
Trim off large leaves and tough ends of lower stalks of broccoli. Wash broccoli thoroughly, and separate into spears. Add broccoli and salt to garlic mixture; cover and simmer 20 minutes or until tender. Drain well; transfer broccoli to a serving dish, and sprinkle with lemon juice and Parmesan cheese before serving. Yield: 6 servings (36 calories per serving).

PRO 3.6 / FAT 0.8 / CARB 5.6 / FIB 1.3 / CHOL 1 / SOD 106 / POT 316

LEMON-TARRAGON BRUSSELS SPROUTS

1 pound fresh brussels sprouts
½ teaspoon dried whole tarragon, crushed
¼ cup coarsely grated carrot
2 teaspoons grated lemon rind
2 tablespoons lemon juice

Combine brussels sprouts, tarragon, and water to cover in a saucepan; bring to a boil. Cover; reduce heat, and simmer 8 minutes. Add carrot, and cook 2 minutes or until crisp-tender. Drain.

Sprinkle lemon rind and juice over vegetables; toss lightly to coat well. Yield: 4 servings (37 calories per serving).

PRO 3.7 / FAT 0.2 / CARB 7.7 / FIB 2.6 / CHOL 0 / SOD 30 / POT 243

CONFETTI CABBAGE

1 cup thinly sliced cabbage
½ cup diced celery
½ cup chopped tomato
¼ cup finely chopped sweet red or green pepper
¼ cup diced onion
¼ cup water
1 tablespoon vinegar
¼ teaspoon salt
¼ teaspoon caraway seeds

Combine all ingredients in a large skillet. Cover and cook over low heat 6 minutes or until vegetables are crisp-tender, stirring occasionally. Yield: 4 servings (18 calories per serving).

PRO 0.7 / FAT 0.2 / CARB 4.0 / FIB 0.7 / CHOL 0 / SOD 165 / POT 169

CAULIFLOWER WITH GREEN CHILES

1 medium head cauliflower (about 1½ pounds)
Vegetable cooking spray
1 tablespoon margarine
½ cup chopped onion
2 hot green chile peppers, seeded and diced
2 tablespoons diced sweet red pepper
1 tablespoon plus 1½ teaspoons all-purpose flour
1 cup skim milk
½ teaspoon chicken-flavored bouillon granules
½ cup (2 ounces) shredded Monterey Jack cheese
¼ teaspoon paprika

Wash cauliflower, and break into flowerets. Cook, covered, in a small amount of boiling water 5 to 6 minutes or until crisp-tender. Transfer to a serving dish, and keep warm.

Coat a medium saucepan with cooking spray; add margarine, and place over medium heat until hot. Add onion, chile peppers, and red pepper; sauté until tender. Reduce heat to low, and add flour, stirring well. Cook 1 minute, stirring constantly. Gradually add milk and bouillon granules; cook over medium heat, stirring constantly, until mixture is thickened and bubbly. Stir in shredded cheese and paprika; remove mixture from heat, and stir with a wire whisk until well blended.

Pour sauce mixture evenly over warm cauliflower, and serve immediately. Yield: 8 servings (85 calories per serving).

PRO 5.0 / FAT 3.9 / CARB 8.9 / FIB 1.1 / CHOL 6 / SOD 111 / POT 444

When it comes to healthy eating, cabbages are truly kings. Nutritious, full of fiber and vitamin C, cabbages — in all varieties including green, red, savoy, bok choy, Chinese, and celery — may even help prevent cancer. In fact, the whole cabbage family, which includes cauliflower, broccoli, brussels sprouts, collard greens, and kohlrabi, is thought to have the same cancer-preventing value.

In a number of population studies, people who eat lots of cabbage-family vegetables have less risk of getting colon and rectal cancer than people who rarely eat them. Lab studies in animals find that certain chemicals in the vegetables actually inhibit tumors from developing.

That's why the National Cancer Institute recommends that we include cabbage-family vegetables in our diet. Of course, that's only part of a healthy lifestyle that minimizes the risk of cancer.

The NCI also recommends that Americans reduce intake of dietary fats and smoked or nitrate-cured meats, that we drink alcohol only in moderation and that we increase intake of complex carbohydrates and fiber, and fruit and vegetables high in vitamins C and A. Each of these actions will help reduce cancer risks, NCI scientists believe.

CARROTS AND PARSNIPS GLACÉ

½ pound carrots, scraped
½ pound parsnips, scraped
½ cup water
½ teaspoon chicken-flavored bouillon
 granules
1 tablespoon honey
Minced fresh parsley

Cut carrots and parsnips into julienne strips; set aside.

Bring water and bouillon granules to a boil in a medium saucepan. Add carrots; cook over medium heat 1 minute. Stir in parsnips, and cook an additional 6 minutes or until crisp-tender. Remove vegetables from saucepan, reserving ¼ cup broth in saucepan. Stir honey into saucepan, and cook until thoroughly heated. Add vegetables, and toss to coat well. Transfer to a serving dish, and sprinkle with parsley. Yield: 4 servings (84 calories per serving).

PRO 1.6 / FAT 0.5 / CARB 20.1 / FIB 3.4 / CHOL 0 / SOD 75 / POT 494

CARROT SOUFFLÉ

1 pound carrots, scraped and sliced
¼ cup skim milk
3 eggs
3 tablespoons all-purpose flour
1 teaspoon sugar
1 teaspoon baking powder
¼ teaspoon salt
⅛ teaspoon pepper
Vegetable cooking spray

Combine carrots and water to cover in a medium saucepan. Bring to a boil. Cover; reduce heat, and simmer 15 minutes or until carrots are tender. Remove from heat, and drain well.

Position knife blade in food processor bowl; add carrots and milk. Process until carrots are smooth. Drop next 6 ingredients through food chute with processor running. Process until light and fluffy.

Spoon carrot mixture into a 1-quart soufflé dish coated on bottom with with cooking spray. Bake at 350° for 40 to 45 minutes or until golden brown. Serve immediately. Yield: 6 servings (94 calories per serving).

PRO 4.7 / FAT 3.0 / CARB 12.6 / FIB 1.3 / CHOL 137 / SOD 214 / POT 299

MEXICAN CORN PUDDING

Vegetable cooking spray
1 medium onion, chopped
1 medium-size green pepper, seeded and
 chopped
1 (17-ounce) can whole kernel corn, drained
1 (10-ounce) can chopped tomatoes with green
 chiles, drained
¼ cup all-purpose flour
¼ teaspoon pepper
2 cups skim milk
1 egg, beaten
¼ cup (1 ounce) shredded extra-sharp Cheddar
 cheese

Coat a large skillet with cooking spray, and place over medium heat until hot. Add onion and green pepper. Sauté until tender. Remove from heat.

Position knife in food processor bowl; add corn, and pulse 10 to 12 times or until corn is coarsely chopped. Add corn and tomatoes with green chiles to mixture in skillet; add flour and pepper, stirring well. Gradually add milk, egg, and cheese, stirring until well blended.

Coat 8 (6-ounce) custard cups with cooking spray. Divide corn mixture evenly among them. Place 4 custard cups in a 9-inch square baking pan; fill pan with boiling water to a depth of 1 inch. Repeat with remaining custard cups.

Bake at 325° for 1 hour and 15 minutes or until knife inserted in center comes out clean. Remove cups from water; let stand 5 minutes. Serve hot. Yield: 8 servings (124 calories per serving).

PRO 6.1 / FAT 2.7 / CARB 20.7 / FIB 0.9 / CHOL 39 / SOD 121 / POT 322

CORN AND TOMATOES

6 ears fresh yellow corn
⅓ cup finely chopped onion
¼ cup finely chopped green pepper
1 tablespoon finely chopped green chiles
2 teaspoons margarine
¼ teaspoon white pepper
½ cup chopped tomato

Cut corn from cob, scraping cob to remove pulp. Combine corn, onion, green pepper, chiles, margarine, and white pepper in a medium saucepan. Cover and cook over medium heat 20 minutes, stirring frequently. Add tomatoes, and cook an additional 10 minutes or until corn is tender, stirring frequently. Yield: 4 servings (113 calories per serving).

PRO 3.6 / FAT 2.1 / CARB 23.8 / FIB 2.6 / CHOL 0 / SOD 35 / POT 236

EGGPLANT STACKS

Vegetable cooking spray
¼ pound sliced fresh mushrooms
⅛ teaspoon pepper
1 medium eggplant (about 1 pound)
Lemon juice (optional)
2 medium tomatoes
1 teaspoon garlic powder
1 teaspoon dried whole oregano, crushed
1 teaspoon dried whole basil, crushed
2 tablespoons vegetable oil
¼ cup plus 2 tablespoons (1½ ounces) shredded mozzarella cheese
Fresh parsley sprigs

Coat a small skillet with cooking spray; place over medium heat until hot. Add mushrooms, and sauté until tender. Sprinkle pepper over mushrooms. Set aside.

Cut eggplant into ½-inch-thick slices. Set 6 uniform slices aside. Reserve remaining slices for other uses; sprinkle with a small amount of lemon to prevent darkening, if desired. Cut tomatoes into ½-inch-thick slices. Set 6 uniform slices aside. Reserve remaining tomato slices for other uses.

Combine garlic powder, oregano, and basil; stir well, and set aside.

Coat rack of a broiler pan with cooking spray. Brush 6 eggplant slices on each side with vegetable oil; place eggplant slices on rack. Broil 5 inches from heating element 2 minutes or until lightly browned; turn and sprinkle eggplant slices evenly with reserved herb mixture. Broil an additional 2 minutes or until slices are lightly browned.

Top each eggplant slice with a tomato slice, 1 tablespoon sautéed mushrooms, and 1 tablespoon shredded mozzarella cheese. Broil 5 inches from heating element 1 minute or until cheese melts. Transfer to a serving platter, and garnish with parsley. Yield: 6 servings (100 calories per serving).

PRO 3.5 / FAT 6.9 / CARB 7.7 / FIB 1.5 / CHOL 7 / SOD 43 / POT 331

CAJUN-STYLE JICAMA

4 cups cubed, peeled jicama
1 medium-size green pepper, seeded and chopped
1 cup chopped onion
2 cloves garlic, crushed
1 cup water
½ teaspoon sugar
½ teaspoon salt
¼ teaspoon red pepper
3 medium tomatoes, peeled and chopped

Combine jicama, green pepper, onion, garlic, water, sugar, salt, and red pepper in a small Dutch oven; bring to a boil. Cover; reduce heat, and simmer 45 minutes or just until tender. Stir in chopped tomato; cover and simmer an additional 5 minutes. Yield: 10 servings (69 calories per ½-cup serving).

PRO 2.6 / FAT 0.5 / CARB 14.8 / FIB 1.6 / CHOL 0 / SOD 127 / POT 383

BAKED MUSHROOMS

1 pound medium-size fresh mushrooms
¼ cup Chablis or other dry white wine
¼ cup water
1 tablespoon finely chopped green onion
¾ teaspoon dried whole basil
¾ teaspoon dried whole marjoram
¼ teaspoon chicken-flavored bouillon granules
¼ teaspoon dried whole dillweed
¼ teaspoon freshly ground pepper
Fresh parsley sprigs (optional)

Clean mushrooms with damp paper towels; trim stems. Arrange in a 1½-quart baking dish. Combine remaining ingredients except parsley sprigs in a small bowl; pour over mushrooms. Cover and bake at 350° for 20 minutes or until tender. Garnish with fresh parsley sprigs, if desired. Yield: 6 servings (21 calories per serving).

PRO 1.6 / FAT 0.3 / CARB 4.1 / FIB 0.6 / CHOL 0 / SOD 20 / POT 289

OKRA STIR-FRY

Vegetable cooking spray
2 teaspoons vegetable oil
2 cups sliced fresh okra
½ cup chopped onion
1 medium-size sweet red pepper, seeded and diced
½ teaspoon dried whole basil
¼ teaspoon dried whole thyme
⅛ teaspoon pepper
1 medium tomato, chopped

Coat a large skillet with cooking spray; add oil, and place over medium-high heat until hot. Add sliced okra, onion, red pepper, basil, thyme, and pepper; stir-fry 6 minutes or just until tender. Add chopped tomato to mixture, and stir-fry an additional 2 minutes. Yield: 6 servings (41 calories per serving).

PRO 1.2 / FAT 1.7 / CARB 5.7 / FIB 0.9 / CHOL 0 / SOD 5 / POT 213

Eggplant Stacks are layers of hearty flavor topped with melted cheese and mushrooms.

FRESH ENGLISH PEAS WITH HERBS

2 cups shelled fresh English peas (about 2 pounds unshelled)
12 green onions, cut into 1-inch pieces
½ teaspoon sugar
1½ teaspoons dried whole basil, crushed
1½ teaspoons dried whole tarragon, crushed
1½ teaspoons minced fresh parsley
⅛ teaspoon pepper
1½ cups water

Combine all ingredients in a 2-quart saucepan; bring to a boil. Cover; reduce heat, and simmer 15 minutes or until peas are tender. Yield: 6 servings (50 calories per serving).

PRO 3.0 / FAT 0.3 / CARB 9.5 / FIB 2.4 / CHOL 0 / SOD 4 / POT 189

BLACK-EYED PEA JAMBALAYA

1¼ cups dried black-eyed peas, sorted and washed
5 cups water
1 cup chopped onion
½ cup chopped green onion
½ cup chopped green pepper
¼ cup chopped fresh parsley
1 clove garlic, pressed
1 (14½-ounce) can whole tomatoes, undrained and chopped
½ teaspoon red pepper
1½ teaspoons Worcestershire sauce
¼ teaspoon salt
⅛ teaspoon dried whole oregano
⅛ teaspoon dried whole thyme
1 bay leaf
¾ cup parboiled rice, uncooked
Additional chopped green onion (optional)

Place peas in a Dutch oven. Cover with water 2 inches above peas; let soak overnight. Pour water off peas. Add 5 cups water to peas; bring to a boil. Cover; reduce heat, and simmer 45 minutes. Add remaining ingredients except rice and additional green onion; cover and simmer 45 minutes. Add rice to pea mixture; stir well. Cover and simmer 20 minutes or until peas and rice are tender. Discard bay leaf. Garnish with additional green onion, if desired. Yield: 6 servings (154 calories per serving).

PRO 5.7 / FAT 0.7 / CARB 32.6 / FIB 6.2 / CHOL 0 / SOD 228 / POT 439

TRI-COLORED PEPPER SAUTE

Vegetable cooking spray
1 tablespoon water
2 teaspoons vegetable oil
2 green peppers, seeded and cut into strips
1 sweet red pepper, seeded and cut into strips
1 yellow pepper, seeded and cut into strips
1 clove garlic, crushed
¼ teaspoon salt
¼ teaspoon dried whole oregano
2 tablespoons vinegar

Coat a large skillet with cooking spray; add water and oil. Place over medium-high heat until hot. Add peppers, garlic, salt, and oregano; sauté 3 minutes, stirring constantly. Remove from heat, and stir in vinegar. Yield: 6 servings (41 calories per serving).

PRO 0.9 / FAT 2.0 / CARB 6.0 / FIB 1.2 / CHOL 0 / SOD 101 / POT 207

PEPPERED OVEN-FRIED POTATOES

1 tablespoon margarine, melted
1 tablespoon water
3 medium potatoes (¾ pound), peeled and cut into ½-inch strips
Vegetable cooking spray
1 tablespoon plus 1½ teaspoons chopped fresh cilantro
2 teaspoons minced onion
¼ teaspoon garlic powder
¼ teaspoon red pepper
⅛ teaspoon pepper

Combine margarine and water in a large bowl; stir until blended. Add potato strips, and toss lightly to coat well.

Arrange potato strips in a single layer on a baking sheet coated with cooking spray. Combine remaining ingredients, and sprinkle evenly over potatoes. Bake at 400° for 35 minutes or until crisp and golden brown. Remove to paper towels to drain, if necessary. Yield: 4 servings (77 calories per serving).

PRO 2.3 / FAT 3.0 / CARB 11.1 / FIB 1.6 / CHOL 0 / SOD 44 / POT 366

Pleated Potatoes provide an unusual look, and the richly-flavored skins eaten with the potatoes make them especially tasty.

PLEATED POTATOES

6 medium-size new potatoes (1 pound)
Vegetable cooking spray
2 tablespoons margarine, melted
2 tablespoons water
1 tablespoon chopped fresh chives
¼ teaspoon salt
¼ teaspoon chervil leaves
¼ teaspoon dried whole tarragon
⅛ teaspoon pepper

Cut potatoes crosswise into ¼-inch slices, taking care not to cut all the way through so that potato remains intact. Place cut side up in a shallow pan coated with cooking spray.

Combine remaining ingredients, stirring well. Brush potatoes with margarine mixture; bake at 400° for 1 hour or until tender and slices have fanned out. Baste occasionally with pan drippings. Yield: 6 servings (90 calories per serving).

PRO 1.7 / FAT 3.9 / CARB 12.6 / FIB 0.6 / CHOL 0 / SOD 150 / POT 390

POTATO-CHEESE PATTIES

3 medium potatoes, peeled and sliced (1½ pounds)
⅓ cup skim milk
½ cup (2 ounces) shredded extra-sharp Cheddar cheese
⅓ cup wheat bran flakes cereal, crushed
⅓ cup wheat germ
2 teaspoons dried parsley flakes
¾ teaspoon salt
¼ teaspoon garlic powder
¼ teaspoon onion powder

Combine potatoes and water to cover in a large saucepan; bring to a boil. Cover; reduce heat, and simmer 20 minutes or until tender. Drain; reserve potatoes in saucepan. Add milk, and beat at medium speed of an electric mixer until smooth; stir in cheese. Cover and chill mixture overnight.

Combine remaining ingredients in a small bowl, stirring well. Shape ⅓ cup potato mixture into a 3-inch pattie; coat with cereal mixture. Place on an ungreased baking sheet. Repeat procedure with remaining potato mixture and cereal mixture. Bake at 325° for 25 minutes. Yield: 11 servings (87 calories per serving).

PRO 4.1 / FAT 2.2 / CARB 14.0 / FIB 0.7 / CHOL 6 / SOD 211 / POT 391

TWICE-BAKED SWEET POTATOES

3 small sweet potatoes (1¼ pounds)
¼ cup plus 2 tablespoons plain low-fat yogurt
1 tablespoon plus 1½ teaspoons skim milk
⅛ teaspoon curry powder

Wrap sweet potatoes in aluminum foil; bake at 400° for 1 hour or until tender. Cool.

Cut potatoes in half lengthwise; carefully scoop out pulp, leaving a ⅛-inch-thick shell. Combine potato pulp, yogurt, milk, and curry powder in a medium bowl; beat until fluffy. Stuff potato shells with potato mixture; place on a baking sheet. Bake at 350° for 20 minutes or until thoroughly heated. Yield: 6 servings (110 calories per serving).

PRO 2.4 / FAT 0.5 / CARB 24.2 / FIB 2.0 / CHOL 1 / SOD 24 / POT 233

SWEET POTATO PUFFS

4 medium-size sweet potatoes (1½ pounds)
1 tablespoon margarine, softened
½ teaspoon sugar
¼ teaspoon ground cinnamon
Dash of ground nutmeg
2 cups cornflakes, finely crushed
¼ teaspoon ground cinnamon
Vegetable cooking spray

Place potatoes on center rack in oven. Bake at 400° for 1 hour or until potatoes yield to pressure. Let cool to touch. Peel and discard skin. Place potato pulp in a medium bowl; mash until smooth. Add margarine, sugar, ¼ teaspoon ground cinnamon, and nutmeg, stirring until well blended. Cover and refrigerate overnight.

Combine cornflakes and ¼ teaspoon ground cinnamon. Shape potato mixture into 2-inch balls; roll in crumb mixture. Place on a baking sheet coated with cooking spray. Bake at 350° for 25 minutes or until crisp. Serve hot. Yield: 10 servings (100 calories per serving).

Note: To freeze, place balls on a baking sheet, and freeze until firm. Transfer balls to a heavy-duty zip top plastic bag or an airtight container. Seal and freeze for up to 1 month. Bake frozen balls at 350° for 35 minutes or until crisp.

PRO 1.5 / FAT 1.4 / CARB 20.7 / FIB 0.7 / CHOL 0 / SOD 79 / POT 130

STEAMED SPINACH WITH RED RADISHES

1½ pounds fresh spinach
1 (6-ounce) package radishes, cleaned and thinly sliced
¼ cup water
2 tablespoons lemon juice
¼ teaspoon salt
⅛ teaspoon pepper

Rinse spinach under cold running water; pat dry. Place spinach, radishes, and ¼ cup water in a large Dutch oven; cover and cook over medium heat 10 minutes. Drain well; transfer spinach mixture to a serving bowl.

Combine lemon juice, salt, and pepper; pour over spinach, and toss well. Yield: 6 servings (31 calories per serving).

PRO 3.4 / FAT 0.5 / CARB 5.4 / FIB 3.8 / CHOL 0 / SOD 194 / POT 700

STUFFED YELLOW SQUASH

3 medium-size yellow squash
Vegetable cooking spray
1 tablespoon plus 1½ teaspoons minced onion
1 teaspoon chopped fresh parsley
1 tablespoon fine, dry breadcrumbs
1 hard-cooked egg, finely chopped
1 tablespoon diced pimiento
⅛ teaspoon salt
⅛ teaspoon pepper
1 tablespoon grated Parmesan cheese

Place whole squash in a medium saucepan with boiling water to cover. Cook 8 minutes or until tender but firm. Drain squash well, and let cool to touch.

Cut squash in half lengthwise; remove and reserve pulp, leaving a firm shell. Set aside. Chop pulp, and set aside.

Coat a small skillet with cooking spray; place over medium-high heat until hot. Add onion and parsley to skillet, and sauté until onion is tender. Stir in squash pulp, breadcrumbs, egg, pimiento, salt, and pepper. Spoon mixture into squash shells; sprinkle each with ½ teaspoon Parmesan cheese. Place in a baking dish coated with cooking spray. Bake, uncovered, at 350° for 20 minutes or until thoroughly heated. Yield: 6 servings (34 calories per serving).

PRO 2.2 / FAT 1.4 / CARB 3.7 / FIB 0.6 / CHOL 46 / SOD 86 / POT 131

SAUTÉED SQUASH

Vegetable cooking spray
3 tablespoons Chablis or other dry white wine
1 small white onion, thinly sliced and quartered
2 medium zucchini squash, thinly sliced
2 medium-size yellow squash, thinly sliced
½ teaspoon chicken-flavored bouillon granules

Coat a large skillet with cooking spray; add wine. Place over medium heat until hot; add onion, and sauté 1 minute. Add zucchini, yellow squash, and bouillon granules; sauté 3 minutes or until crisp-tender. Yield: 6 servings (17 calories per serving).

PRO 1.0 / FAT 0.2 / CARB 3.8 / FIB 0.6 / CHOL 0 / SOD 35 / POT 193

HERBED SPAGHETTI SQUASH TOSS

1 medium spaghetti squash (3 pounds)
1 (2-ounce) jar diced pimiento, drained
3 tablespoons chopped fresh parsley
2 tablespoons water
1 tablespoon margarine, melted
½ teaspoon dried whole oregano
½ teaspoon dried whole basil
¼ teaspoon garlic powder
¼ teaspoon white pepper

Wash squash; cut in half lengthwise, discarding seeds. Place squash halves, cut side down, in a large Dutch oven; add a small amount of water. (Water should be about 2 inches deep.) Bring to a boil. Cover; reduce heat, and simmer 25 minutes or until tender. Drain. Remove spaghetti-like strands from squash, using a fork.

Combine 3 cups squash and remaining ingredients in a large skillet; toss gently. Reserve remaining squash for other uses. Cook over low heat 5 minutes or until thoroughly heated. Yield: 6 servings (86 calories per serving).

PRO 1.7 / FAT 2.6 / CARB 15.4 / FIB 3.3 / CHOL 0 / SOD 66 / POT 294

ITALIAN HERB TOMATOES

2 tablespoons fine, dry breadcrumbs
1 tablespoon grated Parmesan cheese
¾ teaspoon dried whole basil
¾ teaspoon chopped fresh parsley
¼ teaspoon dried whole oregano
Dash of garlic powder
Dash of pepper
4 medium tomatoes
2 teaspoons margarine, melted
Fresh parsley sprigs (optional)

Combine first 7 ingredients in a small bowl; stir well, and set aside.

Cut tomatoes in half crosswise; place on a broiler pan cut side up. Brush tomato halves with margarine; sprinkle with breadcrumb mixture. Bake at 350° for 15 minutes; broil 4 inches from heating element until golden brown. Transfer to a serving plate, and garnish with fresh parsley sprigs, if desired. Yield: 8 servings (31 calories per serving).

PRO 1.1 / FAT 1.4 / CARB 4.4 / FIB 0.6 / CHOL 1 / SOD 41 / POT 154

RELISH-TOPPED TURNIP GREENS

1 medium-size green pepper, seeded and chopped
½ cup chopped onion
1 clove garlic, minced
2 tablespoons mild picante sauce
1 medium tomato, chopped
3 pounds fresh turnip greens, cleaned
½ cup water
½ teaspoon salt
1 teaspoon lemon juice

Combine green pepper, onion, garlic, and picante sauce in a small saucepan; stir well. Bring to a boil. Cover; reduce heat, and simmer 2 minutes, stirring frequently. Add tomato, and cook an additional 2 minutes. Remove from heat; cover and refrigerate at least 1 hour.

Wash turnip greens; combine with water and salt in a large Dutch oven. Bring to a boil. Cover; reduce heat, and simmer 1½ hours or until greens are tender, stirring occasionally. Drain well, and toss with lemon juice. Transfer to a serving dish, and serve immediately with 2 tablespoons relish per serving. Yield: 8 servings (51 calories per serving).

PRO 2.6 / FAT 0.6 / CARB 10.9 / FIB 1.6 / CHOL 0 / SOD 233 / POT 517

HERBED VEGETABLE SAUTÉ

½ pound fresh green beans
1 cup sliced carrots
½ cup chopped onion
2 tablespoons chopped fresh parsley
½ teaspoon salt-free 14 herb-and-spice blend
½ teaspoon dried whole thyme
½ teaspoon dried whole basil
¾ cup water
½ cup sliced fresh mushrooms
1 medium tomato, cut into 12 wedges

Remove strings from beans; wash and cut beans into 1½-inch pieces. Combine beans and next 7 ingredients in a large skillet; bring to a boil. Cover; reduce heat, and simmer 15 minutes. Add mushrooms; simmer 5 minutes. Stir in tomato; cook, stirring frequently, 3 minutes or until hot. Serve with a slotted spoon. Yield: 6 servings (32 calories per serving).

PRO 1.4 / FAT 0.2 / CARB 7.2 / FIB 1.5 / CHOL 0 / SOD 12 / POT 247

WALDORF BAKE

⅓ cup reduced-calorie mayonnaise
½ cup unsweetened apple juice
1 cup diced celery
¼ cup raisins
2 tablespoons chopped walnuts
2 medium apples

Combine mayonnaise and apple juice in a medium bowl, stirring until mixture is smooth.

Stir in diced celery, raisins, and walnuts. Core apples; dice and immediately fold into mayonnaise mixture, stirring well. Transfer mixture to a 1-quart casserole; cover and bake at 350° for 20 minutes or until mixture is thoroughly heated. Serve immediately. Yield: 6 servings (108 calories per serving).

PRO 1.1 / FAT 5.3 / CARB 15.7 / FIB 1.7 / CHOL 4 / SOD 119 / POT 196

APPLE-PEAR PUREE

1½ pounds Granny Smith apples, peeled and coarsely chopped
1 pound pears, peeled and coarsely chopped
1 quart water
1 tablespoon sugar
2 tablespoons unsweetened orange juice
½ teaspoon vanilla extract
¼ teaspoon ground nutmeg
⅛ teaspoon ground cloves

Combine apples, pears, and water in a medium saucepan. Bring to a boil. Cover; reduce heat, and simmer 20 minutes or until tender, stirring occasionally. Drain.

Combine apple mixture and remaining ingredients in a bowl. Mash until mixture resembles chunky applesauce. Serve hot or cold. Yield: 6 servings (109 calories per serving).

PRO 0.8 / FAT 0.6 / CARB 27.8 / FIB 4.1 / CHOL 0 / SOD 3 / POT 215

DIJON PEARS

3 ripe pears
1 tablespoon honey
1 tablespoon unsalted margarine, softened
1 teaspoon Dijon mustard
¼ cup water

Cut pears in half lengthwise, and remove cores; place pears, cut side up, in a 10- x 6- x

2-inch baking dish. Combine honey, margarine, and mustard in a small bowl, stirring until smooth; brush over pears. Pour water into dish. Cover and bake at 350° for 40 minutes or until pears are tender. Serve warm. Yield: 6 servings (76 calories per serving).

PRO 0.3 / FAT 2.3 / CARB 15.2 / FIB 2.0 / CHOL 0 / SOD 25 / POT 105

CITRUS SPICED PEARS

2 (3-inch) sticks cinnamon
8 whole cloves
1 (29-ounce) can pear halves in their own juice, undrained
1 orange, thinly sliced
1 lemon, thinly sliced
Additional orange or lemon slices (optional)
10 (3-inch) strips lemon or orange rind (optional)

Place cinnamon and cloves on a cheesecloth square. Bring edges of cheesecloth together at top, and tie securely. Combine spice bag, pears,

1 orange, and 1 lemon in a medium-size non-aluminum saucepan; bring to a boil. Cover; reduce heat, and simmer 15 minutes. Remove from heat, and cool. Transfer to a serving dish; cover and chill 8 hours or overnight.

Discard spice bag, orange, and lemon. Serve chilled on a bed of orange or lemon slices, if desired. To garnish, tie strips of lemon or orange rind into knots, and arrange on pears, if desired. Yield: 6 servings (69 calories per serving).

PRO 0.5 / FAT 0.1 / CARB 17.7 / FIB 1.3 / CHOL 0 / SOD 5 / POT 132

Introduce your family to a new vegetable by serving Baked Plantains. Like the banana, the plantain is a rich source of potassium.

BAKED PLANTAINS

3 medium plantains, peeled and cut into ½-inch
  slices
Vegetable cooking spray
1 tablespoon sherry
¼ teaspoon curry powder
¼ teaspoon ground cinnamon
2 teaspoons unsalted margarine, softened

Arrange sliced plantains in a 10- x 6- x 2-inch baking dish coated with cooking spray. Sprinkle with sherry, curry powder, and cinnamon. Dot with margarine. Cover and bake at 375° for 15 minutes. Uncover and bake an additional 5 minutes. Serve hot. Yield: 8 servings (113 calories per serving).

PRO 1.0 / FAT 1.3 / CARB 26.8 / FIB 0.4 / CHOL 0 / SOD 5 / POT 331

 It's true that getting too much sun can be unhealthy, prematurely aging the skin and increasing the risk of skin cancers. Protection against overexposure can be achieved by using sunscreens and sun blocks.

However, scientists are finding that almost everyone needs a certain amount of sunlight each day to remain healthy both physically and mentally. Just 20 to 30 minutes of sunlight a day can affect the way we look and feel. Research is indicating that the older we get, the more exposure to sunlight we need. When our skin is exposed to the sun, it starts providing vitamin D, a nutrient that helps our bodies absorb calcium for stronger bones and teeth. As we age, our skin becomes less efficient at turning sunlight into vitamin D thus decreasing our ability to absorb calcium.

Sunlight may also affect our mental health. SAD, or Seasonal Affective Disorder, is a common form of depression that affects people during the winter months. New research indicates that daily exposure to sunlight, especially in the morning, often helps SAD people feel better. One possible reason is that exposure to sunlight sparks those hormonal changes that are related to waking up, hence improving mood.

So take some 20-minute walks in the sun this week. You'll be getting some exercise, strengthening your bones, and maybe even lifting your spirits enough to make it a healthy habit.

SPICED PINEAPPLE STICKS

1 medium-size fresh pineapple
1½ teaspoons whole cloves
1 teaspoon whole allspice
1 (3-inch) stick cinnamon
1 medium orange, sliced
1 cup unsweetened orange juice
2 tablespoons sugar
2 tablespoons vinegar

Peel and trim eyes from pineapple; remove core. Cut pineapple lengthwise into 16 sticks. Set aside.

Place cloves, allspice, cinnamon stick, and orange on a cheesecloth square. Bring edges together at top, and tie securely to form a bag. Combine spice bag, orange juice, sugar, and vinegar in a non-aluminum Dutch oven; bring to a boil. Add pineapple. Reduce heat; simmer, uncovered, stirring occasionally, 35 minutes or until pineapple is transparent. Discard spice bag. Transfer pineapple and cooking liquid to a large bowl. Cover and chill 8 hours or overnight. Drain pineapple, and serve cold. Yield: 8 servings (77 calories per serving).

PRO 0.6 / FAT 0.5 / CARB 19.4 / FIB 1.6 / CHOL 0 / SOD 1 / POT 175

WARM FRUIT COMPOTE WITH MUSTARD

1 (8-ounce) can unsweetened pineapple chunks, undrained
1 medium banana, sliced
1 (16-ounce) can peach slices in light syrup, drained
1 (16-ounce) can pear slices in light syrup, drained
3 tablespoons firmly packed brown sugar
1 tablespoon prepared mustard

Drain pineapple, reserving juice. Toss banana in pineapple juice; drain, reserving juice. Combine pineapple, banana, peaches, and pears in a 1-quart baking dish.

Combine reserved pineapple juice, brown sugar, and mustard in a small bowl; pour over fruit. Bake, uncovered, at 325° for 20 minutes or until thoroughly heated. Yield: 8 servings (82 calories per serving).

PRO 0.8 / FAT 0.4 / CARB 20.7 / FIB 2.1 / CHOL 0 / SOD 28 / POT 231

MAPLE FRUIT SKEWERS

1 (16-ounce) can apricot halves in light syrup, drained
1 (8-ounce) can unsweetened pineapple chunks, drained
16 seedless red grapes
2 tablespoons reduced-calorie maple syrup, divided

Thread fruit alternately onto 8 wooden skewers. Place on a jellyroll pan. Brush with 1 tablespoon syrup. Bake at 350° for 5 minutes; turn and baste with remaining syrup. Bake an additional 5 minutes. Serve hot. Yield: 8 servings (40 calories per serving).

PRO 0.4 / FAT 0.2 / CARB 10.3 / FIB 0.6 / CHOL 0 / SOD 2 / POT 123

SPICED RHUBARB

1 pound rhubarb, trimmed and cut into ½-inch-thick slices
1 cup water
3 tablespoons firmly packed brown sugar
1 tablespoon margarine
1 teaspoon ground cinnamon

Combine rhubarb and water in a medium saucepan; bring to a boil. Cover; reduce heat, and cook 5 minutes or until tender. Drain; add remaining ingredients, and toss well. Yield: 4 servings (83 calories per serving).

PRO 0.8 / FAT 3.1 / CARB 14.3 / FIB 0.7 / CHOL 0 / SOD 42 / POT 284

Paella Stew (page 210), with its combination of shrimp, chicken, and vegetables, will satisfy the appetite at only 128 calories per serving.

Soups & Stews

ICED APPLE SOUP

2 red cooking apples, peeled, cored, and quartered
2 medium Granny Smith apples, quartered, cored, and peeled
2 cups unsweetened apple juice
2 tablespoons lemon juice
1 tablespoon lime juice
2 (3-inch) sticks cinnamon
1 teaspoon vanilla extract
2 cups unsweetened pineapple juice
2 cups skim milk
2 tablespoons apple brandy
¼ cup plus 3 tablespoons shredded red cooking apple

Combine first 6 ingredients in a large saucepan; bring to a boil. Cover; reduce heat, and simmer 20 minutes or until apples are very soft, stirring occasionally. Remove from heat, and stir in vanilla. Cool; cover and refrigerate overnight.

Discard cinnamon stick; place apple mixture in container of an electric blender. Process until smooth. Add pineapple juice and milk; process until blended. Stir in apple brandy. Cover and chill thoroughly. Pour into individual bowls; top each serving with 1 tablespoon shredded cooking apple. Serve immediately. Yield: 7 cups (192 calories per 1-cup serving).

PRO 3.0 / FAT 0.8 / CARB 43.2 / FIB 3.5 / CHOL 1 / SOD 40 / POT 477

CHILLED HONEYDEW SOUP WITH MINT

2 tablespoons lime juice
1 tablespoon fresh mint leaves
1 medium honeydew melon, halved and seeded
1 cup unsweetened orange juice
¼ cup Sauterne or other sweet white wine
Fresh mint sprigs (optional)

Combine lime juice and fresh mint leaves in a small bowl. Bruise leaves with a wooden spoon; let stand 15 minutes. Remove mint leaves, and discard. Set lime juice aside.

Scoop out honeydew balls from one half of melon with a small melon baller; set aside. Peel remaining half; cut pulp into cubes. Combine honeydew cubes, orange juice, Sauterne, and reserved lime juice in container of an electric blender; process until smooth.

Combine pureed mixture and honeydew balls in a large bowl; cover and chill thoroughly. Stir well before serving in chilled bowls. Garnish with fresh mint sprigs, if desired. Yield: 6 cups (141 calories per 1-cup serving).

PRO 3.0 / FAT 1.1 / CARB 31.5 / FIB 2.0 / CHOL 0 / SOD 42 / POT 946

CREAMY PAPAYA SOUP

4 cups cubed, peeled papaya
3 cups unsweetened orange juice
1 cup vanilla low-fat yogurt
½ cup lime juice
½ cup honey
Lime twists (optional)

Combine all ingredients except lime twists in container of an electric blender; process until smooth. Pour into a bowl; cover and chill thoroughly. Stir before serving. Pour into individual bowls; garnish with lime twists, if desired. Yield: 7 cups (185 calories per 1-cup serving).

PRO 3.0 / FAT 0.6 / CARB 45.3 / FIB 0.7 / CHOL 2 / SOD 26 / POT 509

Two soups: Chilled Honeydew and Creamy Papaya.

CARROT SOUP

1 teaspoon vegetable oil
Vegetable cooking spray
½ medium onion, chopped
1 large clove garlic, minced
6 medium carrots, scraped and sliced
⅛ teaspoon pepper
1 tablespoon all-purpose flour
4 cups water
2 teaspoons chicken-flavored bouillon granules
Fresh dill sprigs (optional)

Pour vegetable oil into a large skillet coated with cooking spray; place over medium heat until hot. Add onion and garlic, and sauté until tender. Add sliced carrots and pepper. Cover and cook over low heat 15 minutes or until carrots are tender.

Stir in flour; cook 1 minute. Add water and bouillon granules; bring to a boil. Reduce heat, and simmer, uncovered, 5 to 10 minutes, stirring occasionally. Cool. Transfer mixture in batches to a blender or food processor. Process until smooth. Chill thoroughly before serving. Garnish with fresh dill sprigs, if desired. Yield: 4 cups (80 calories per 1-cup serving).

Note: Soup may be served hot.

PRO 1.9 / FAT 1.7 / CARB 15.5 / FIB 2.0 / CHOL 0 / SOD 231 / POT 418

CHILLED SUN-DRIED TOMATO BISQUE

2 cups water
2 ounces unsalted, sliced sun-dried tomatoes (dry-packed)
2 cups tomato juice, divided
½ medium onion, chopped
1 small clove garlic, minced
1 teaspoon sugar
1 teaspoon dried whole dillweed
¼ teaspoon pepper
½ cup skim milk

Bring 2 cups water to a boil in a small saucepan; add sun-dried tomatoes. Cover; reduce heat, and simmer 4 minutes. Drain. Cover tomatoes with cool water, and soak for 5 minutes; drain thoroughly.

Place tomatoes, 1 cup tomato juice, onion, garlic, sugar, dillweed, and pepper in container of an electric blender; process until smooth. Add remaining 1 cup tomato juice and milk; process until blended. Chill thoroughly. Yield: 3 cups (121 calories per 1-cup serving).

PRO 6.0 / FAT 0.9 / CARB 26.9 / FIB 3.5 / CHOL 1 / SOD 636 / POT 1382

ARTICHOKE BISQUE

1 (14-ounce) can artichoke hearts, drained and divided
2 tablespoons margarine
2 tablespoons all-purpose flour
⅛ teaspoon ground nutmeg
Dash of white pepper
2 cups skim milk
1 cup water
1 teaspoon chicken-flavored bouillon granules
1 teaspoon lemon juice
4 twists fresh lemon

Coarsely chop 2 artichoke hearts; set aside. Place remaining artichoke hearts in container of food processor; process until pureed. Set aside.

Melt margarine in a medium saucepan over low heat; add flour, nutmeg, and pepper. Cook over medium heat 1 minute, stirring constantly. Gradually add milk, water, bouillon granules, and lemon juice, stirring constantly. Add reserved chopped artichokes and pureed artichokes, stirring well. Cook over medium heat, stirring constantly, 10 minutes or until thickened and bubbly. Ladle into soup bowls; garnish each serving with a lemon twist. Yield: 4 cups (140 calories per 1-cup serving).

PRO 6.2 / FAT 6.3 / CARB 16.0 / FIB 0.7 / CHOL 2 / SOD 271 / POT 381

CUBAN BLACK BEAN SOUP

1 (16-ounce) package dried black beans
9 cups water
2 cloves garlic, halved and crushed
1 teaspoon salt
2 tablespoons lemon juice
3 cloves garlic
1½ teaspoons ground cumin
½ teaspoon dried whole oregano
2 to 4 drops hot sauce
1 medium onion, finely chopped
1½ cups finely chopped green pepper
Marinated Rice

Sort and wash beans; place in a large Dutch oven. Cover with water 2 inches above beans; let soak overnight. Drain beans, and return to Dutch oven. Add 9 cups water, 2 cloves garlic, and salt; bring to a boil. Cover partially; reduce heat to medium-low, and cook 2 hours or until beans are tender, stirring occasionally.

Combine lemon juice, 3 cloves garlic, cumin, oregano, and hot sauce in a pestal; crush well. Add lemon juice mixture, onion, and green pepper to beans. Bring to a boil; reduce heat and simmer, partially covered, 30 to 45 minutes, stirring occasionally. Ladle into soup bowls; garnish each with 2 tablespoons Marinated Rice. Yield: 8 cups (236 calories per 1-cup serving).

Marinated Rice:

⅔ cup cooked brown rice (cooked without salt or fat)
⅓ cup finely chopped tomato
1 green onion, chopped
2 teaspoons lemon juice
1 teaspoon olive oil

Combine all ingredients in a bowl; mix well. Cover; chill at least 3 hours. Yield: 1 cup.

PRO 13.8 / FAT 1.8 / CARB 43.0 / FIB 15.2 / CHOL 0 / SOD 311 / POT 727

EGG DROP SOUP

1 quart water
2 teaspoons chicken-flavored bouillon granules
2 teaspoons reduced-sodium soy sauce
1 green onion, chopped
2 eggs, beaten

Combine first 4 ingredients in a large saucepan; bring to a boil. Slowly pour eggs into boiling broth. Serve immediately. Yield: 4 cups (45 calories per 1-cup serving).

PRO 3.5 / FAT 3.0 / CARB 1.0 / FIB 0.1 / CHOL 137 / SOD 322 / POT 46

MUSHROOM CONSOMMÉ

3 cups water
½ cup chopped green onion
¼ cup chopped celery
1½ teaspoons chicken-flavored bouillon granules
½ teaspoon dried whole marjoram, crushed
½ teaspoon dried whole rosemary, crushed
Dash of pepper
2½ cups sliced fresh mushrooms

Combine first 7 ingredients in a large saucepan; bring to a boil. Cover; reduce heat, and simmer 15 minutes or until vegetables are tender. Stir in mushrooms, and continue to cook until mushrooms are thoroughly heated. Serve hot. Yield: 6 cups (13 calories per 1-cup serving).

PRO 0.8 / FAT 0.3 / CARB 2.4 / FIB 0.5 / CHOL 0 / SOD 101 / POT 146

 Soup is a dieter's friend, and now new research finds that low-calorie soup is just as hunger-soothing as high-calorie soup.
At Johns Hopkins University, researchers fed two groups of volunteers tomato soup, telling each to eat as much as they wanted. One group ate high-calorie soup, the other, low-calorie soup.
Each group felt full after eating about the same amount with the high-calorie eaters consuming 146 calories and the low-calorie eaters only 17.

FETTUCCINE RIBBON SOUP

1 medium carrot, peeled and cut into
   julienne strips
1 medium-size sweet red or green pepper, seeded
   and cut into very thin slices
2 quarts water
1½ teaspoons chicken-flavored bouillon
   granules
½ teaspoon dried whole basil
½ teaspoon dried whole oregano
1 cup packed fresh spinach, thinly sliced
¼ pound fresh mushrooms, thinly sliced
2 ounces whole wheat fettuccine, broken
2 tablespoons plus 2 teaspoons grated Parmesan
   cheese

Combine first 6 ingredients in a Dutch oven.
Bring to a boil. Cover; reduce heat, and simmer
5 minutes or just until vegetables are tender.
Add spinach, mushrooms, and fettuccine; simmer 5 to 6 minutes or until fettuccine is tender
but slightly firm. Ladle into serving bowls, and
sprinkle each with 1 teaspoon cheese. Yield: 8
cups (44 calories per 1-cup serving).

PRO 2.2 / FAT 1.1 / CARB 7.2 / FIB 0.9 / CHOL 1 / SOD 111 / POT 173

TORTILLA SOUP

Vegetable cooking spray
½ cup chopped onion
1 (4-ounce) can chopped green chiles,
   undrained
2 cloves garlic, crushed
3¾ cups water
1½ cups tomato juice
1 medium tomato, peeled and chopped
1 teaspoon beef-flavored bouillon
   granules
1 teaspoon ground cumin
1 teaspoon chili powder
1 teaspoon Worcestershire sauce
¼ teaspoon pepper
2 to 4 drops hot sauce
3 (6-inch) corn tortillas, cut into ½-inch strips
½ cup (2 ounces) shredded Monterey Jack
   cheese
Fresh cilantro sprigs

Coat a small Dutch oven with cooking spray;
place over medium heat until hot. Add onion,
chiles, and garlic, and cook until onion is tender,
stirring frequently. Add water, tomato juice, tomato, bouillon granules, cumin, chili powder,
Worcestershire sauce, pepper, and hot sauce; stir
well. Bring to a boil. Cover; reduce heat, and
simmer 1 hour. Add tortillas; cover and simmer
10 minutes.

Ladle hot soup into serving bowls. Sprinkle 1
tablespoon cheese over each, and garnish with
a cilantro sprig. Yield: 8 cups (89 calories per
1-cup serving).

PRO 3.6 / FAT 2.9 / CARB 13.0 / FIB 0.7 / CHOL 6 / SOD 299 / POT 265

VEGETARIAN CHILI

Vegetable cooking spray
1 teaspoon olive or vegetable oil
1½ cups chopped onion
1½ cups chopped green pepper
1 cup chopped celery
2 (16-ounce) cans pinto beans,
   undrained
2 (14½-ounce) cans no-salt-added
   tomatoes, undrained
1 (6-ounce) can tomato paste
1 cup water
1 cup chopped fresh mushrooms
1 jalapeño pepper, seeded and chopped
1 tablespoon chili powder
1½ teaspoons ground cumin
1 teaspoon dried whole oregano, crushed
½ teaspoon pepper
1 (20-ounce) package tofu, drained and
   cut into small cubes

Coat a Dutch oven with cooking spray; add
oil, and place over medium heat until hot. Add
onion, green pepper, and celery; sauté 5 minutes or until onion is tender.

Add remaining ingredients except tofu to
Dutch oven; bring to a boil. Cover; reduce heat,
and simmer 30 minutes. Add tofu; stir gently.
Cover and simmer an additional 10 minutes or
until tofu is thoroughly heated. Yield: 12 cups
(146 calories per 1-cup serving).

PRO 8.7 / FAT 3.4 / CARB 22.6 / FIB 9.2 / CHOL 0 / SOD 316 / POT 644

VEGETABLE GUMBO

3 cups sliced fresh okra
1 (16-ounce) can whole tomatoes, undrained
1½ cups water
1 medium-size green pepper, seeded and chopped
1 cup fresh or frozen lima beans
1 cup fresh corn cut from cob
½ cup chopped onion
1 teaspoon vegetable-flavored bouillon granules
1 teaspoon chopped fresh parsley
¼ teaspoon garlic powder

Combine all ingredients in a small Dutch oven; bring to a boil. Cover; reduce heat, and simmer 45 minutes or until vegetables are tender, stirring occasionally. Yield: 6 cups (95 calories per 1-cup serving).

PRO 4.6 / FAT 0.7 / CARB 19.8 / FIB 6.7 / CHOL 0 / SOD 204 / POT 537

HAMBURGER SOUP

Vegetable cooking spray
¾ pound ground chuck
1 medium onion, chopped
1 quart water
1 (16-ounce) can stewed tomatoes, undrained
1 teaspoon beef-flavored bouillon granules
1 teaspoon Worcestershire sauce
½ to ¾ teaspoon pepper
1 (10-ounce) package frozen mixed vegetables
½ cup medium egg noodles, uncooked
½ teaspoon dried whole thyme
Croutons (recipe follows)

Coat a small Dutch oven with cooking spray, and place over medium heat until hot. Add ground chuck and chopped onion; cook until meat is browned, stirring to crumble. Drain meat mixture in a colander; pat dry with paper towels to remove excess fat. Wipe Dutch oven clean with paper towels.

Return meat mixture to Dutch oven; add water, tomatoes, bouillon granules, Worcestershire sauce, and pepper. Bring to a boil. Cover; reduce heat, and simmer 30 minutes. Add vegetables, noodles, and thyme. Bring to a boil; reduce heat and simmer, uncovered, 20 minutes, stirring occasionally. Ladle into serving bowls. Serve warm with 4 croutons per serving. Yield: 6 cups (197 calories per 1-cup serving).

Croutons:

1 hamburger bun, split
2 teaspoons margarine, softened
½ teaspoon dried whole dillweed.

Spread each cut side of hamburger bun with 1 teaspoon margarine. Sprinkle with dillweed; cut each bun half into 12 cubes. Bake at 250° for 20 minutes or until crisp. Yield: 2 dozen.

PRO 15.0 / FAT 7.3 / CARB 17.7 / FIB 1.1 / CHOL 43 / SOD 355 / POT 517

ORIENTAL PORK-VEGETABLE SOUP

2¾ cups water
1 tablespoon vinegar
1 tablespoon reduced-sodium soy sauce
1 teaspoon beef-flavored bouillon granules
1 cup chopped fresh broccoli
1 cup fresh snow peas
3 tablespoons sliced green onion
½ cup chopped, cooked lean pork

Combine first 4 ingredients in a saucepan; bring to a boil. Add remaining ingredients; reduce heat. Simmer, uncovered, 5 minutes or until vegetables are crisp-tender. Serve hot. Yield: 4 cups (65 calories per 1-cup serving).

PRO 7.4 / FAT 2.1 / CARB 4.3 / FIB 0.9 / CHOL 17 / SOD 282 / POT 214

CHICKEN MINISTRONE

1 quart water
2 teaspoons chicken-flavored bouillon granules
½ teaspoon dried whole basil
½ teaspoon dried whole oregano
1 (10-ounce) package frozen mixed vegetables
3 ounces spaghetti, broken
1 pound fresh mushrooms, sliced
2 cups cubed, cooked chicken breast
2 medium zucchini squash, sliced
1 (16-ounce) can tomatoes, undrained and chopped

Combine first 6 ingredients in a Dutch oven. Bring to a boil. Cover; reduce heat, and simmer 5 minutes. Add mushrooms, chicken, zucchini squash, and tomatoes. Cover; reduce heat, and simmer 5 minutes or until tender. Yield: 9 cups (136 calories per 1-cup serving).

PRO 13.7 / FAT 1.8 / CARB 16.8 / FIB 1.6 / CHOL 26 / SOD 310 / POT 530

TURKEY BARLEY SOUP

1 pound cubed, cooked turkey breast
2 cups sliced fresh mushrooms
1 cup sliced carrots
1 cup sliced celery
¾ cup diced parsnips
¾ cup chopped onion
½ cup barley, uncooked
¼ cup chopped fresh parsley
1½ quarts water
½ teaspoon salt
½ teaspoon pepper
½ teaspoon dried whole thyme
½ cup frozen English peas

Combine all ingredients except peas in a large Dutch oven; bring to a boil. Cover; reduce heat, and simmer 30 minutes. Add peas, and simmer an additional 5 minutes. Yield: 9 cups (151 calories per 1-cup serving).

PRO 17.4 / FAT 2.0 / CARB 15.8 / FIB 2.2 / CHOL 35 / SOD 194 / POT 432

SOUTHWESTERN BEEF STEW

1½ pounds lean round steak (about ½-inch thick)
1 cup water
1 cup cubed potatoes
1 cup sliced carrots
¾ cup light beer
¼ cup chopped sweet red pepper
¼ cup chopped fresh cilantro or 1 tablespoon dried whole coriander
1 (16-ounce) can whole tomatoes, undrained and chopped
1 medium onion, chopped
1 clove garlic, minced
1 jalapeño pepper, seeded and chopped
2 teaspoons dried whole oregano
1½ teaspoons chili powder
1 teaspoon beef-flavored bouillon granules
2 tablespoons all-purpose flour
2 tablespoons water

Trim excess fat from steak; cut meat into 1-inch pieces. Combine all ingredients except flour and 2 tablespoons water in a large Dutch oven; bring to a boil. Cover; reduce heat, and simmer 1 hour to 1 hour and 15 minutes or until meat is tender, stirring occasionally.

Combine flour and 2 tablespoons water, stirring to form a smooth paste. Gradually add to meat mixture; cook over medium heat until thickened and bubbly. Yield: 6 cups (294 calories per 1-cup serving).

PRO 38.6 / FAT 6.6 / CARB 18.1 / FIB 1.9 / CHOL 74 / SOD 521 / POT 945

 Bring out the iron in your vegetables. Eat them with vitamin C, and a little meat, fish, or chicken. Many vegetables, such as beans, broccoli, and leafy greens, are good sources of iron. But vegetable iron is not absorbed as easily as is the iron in meat. Vitamin C, found in tomatoes, red peppers, even potatoes, helps us absorb that iron.

CHICKEN VEGETABLE STEW

4 chicken breast halves (about 2 pounds), skinned
1½ quarts water
1 small onion, chopped
1 teaspoon salt-free 14 herb-and-spice blend
¾ teaspoon salt
½ teaspoon poultry seasoning
¼ teaspoon pepper
¼ teaspoon rubbed sage
2 cups cut fresh green beans
3 medium carrots, scraped and sliced
½ pound fresh mushrooms, sliced
2 tablespoons all-purpose flour
2 tablespoons water

Trim excess fat from chicken; combine chicken and next 7 ingredients in a large Dutch oven. Bring to a boil. Cover; reduce heat, and simmer 30 minutes or until chicken is tender. Remove chicken from broth; skim off any layer of fat from broth. Set broth aside. Bone chicken, and cut meat into bite-size pieces.

Combine chicken, broth, green beans, carrots, and mushrooms in Dutch oven. Bring to a boil. Cover; reduce heat, and simmer 30 minutes or until vegetables are tender. Combine flour and 2 tablespoons water, blending until smooth. Stir into stew. Cook over medium heat until thickened and bubbly. Yield: 8 cups (131 calories per 1-cup serving).

PRO 18.6 / FAT 2.2 / CARB 9.3 / FIB 1.6 / CHOL 46 / SOD 273 / POT 431

LOUISIANA CRAB GUMBO

Vegetable cooking spray
1 stalk celery, chopped
1 clove garlic, minced
1 medium onion, chopped
½ green pepper, seeded and chopped
3 (14½-ounce) cans stewed tomatoes, undrained
3 cups sliced fresh okra
2 cups tomato juice
1 bay leaf
1 small red pepper pod, seeded
1 tablespoon salt-free creole seasoning
¼ teaspoon pepper
1 pound fresh lump crabmeat, drained and flaked
5 cups hot cooked parboiled rice (cooked without salt or fat)

Coat a large Dutch oven with cooking spray; place over medium heat until hot. Add celery, garlic, onion, and green pepper. Sauté 5 minutes or until tender. Stir in next 7 ingredients; bring to a boil. Cover; reduce heat, and simmer 1 hour, stirring occasionally. Stir in crabmeat; cook 2 minutes over low heat or until heated. Discard bay leaf and pepper pod. Ladle gumbo over ½-cup portions of rice. Serve warm. Yield: 10 cups (198 calories per 1-cup serving).

PRO 12.6 / FAT 1.4 / CARB 34.2 / FIB 2.0 / CHOL 45 / SOD 513 / POT 801

CIOPPINO

1 medium-size green pepper, seeded and diced
1 small onion, diced
1 clove garlic, minced
1 (16-ounce) can no-salt-added whole tomatoes, undrained and chopped
1 (8-ounce) can no-salt-added whole tomatoes, undrained and chopped
½ cup clam juice
2 tablespoons minced fresh parsley
2 tablespoons dry sherry
¼ teaspoon pepper
⅛ teaspoon rubbed sage
9 littleneck clams, cleaned
½ pound fresh cod fillets, cut into 1-inch pieces
½ pound scallops, cut in half

Combine first 6 ingredients in a large saucepan. Bring to a boil. Cover; reduce heat, and simmer 10 minutes or until onion and pepper are tender. Stir in remaining ingredients; bring to a boil. Cover; reduce heat, and simmer 8 minutes or until fish flakes easily when tested with a fork, clams are open, and scallops are opaque. Serve hot. Yield: 6 cups (150 calories per 1-cup serving).

PRO 20.4 / FAT 0.8 / CARB 10.8 / FIB 0.6 / CHOL 80 / SOD 409 / POT 671

PAELLA STEW

3½ cups water
2 teaspoons chicken-flavored bouillon granules
1 (8-ounce) can tomatoes, undrained
1 cup chopped celery
½ cup chopped onion
1 clove garlic, minced
¼ teaspoon dried whole oregano
¼ teaspoon ground saffron
1 pound fresh medium shrimp, peeled and deveined
1 (14-ounce) can artichoke hearts, drained and quartered
1 cup frozen English peas, thawed
1 cup hot cooked parboiled rice (cooked without salt or fat)
¾ cup cubed, cooked chicken (cooked without salt)

Combine first 8 ingredients; bring to a boil. Cover; reduce heat, and simmer 30 minutes or until onion is tender. Add remaining ingredients; bring to a boil. Cover; reduce heat, and simmer 5 minutes or until shrimp are done. Yield: 8 cups (128 calories per 1-cup serving).

PRO 14.7 / FAT 1.1 / CARB 15.1 / FIB 1.7 / CHOL 75 / SOD 407 / POT 394

The best dessert is one that's guilt-free; experience pleasure without penitence when you serve a fruit-based dish such as Rum Compote in Tortilla Shells (page 212).

Desserts

PEACH MERINGUES WITH FRESH STRAWBERRY SAUCE

6 egg whites
½ teaspoon cream of tartar
1 teaspoon vanilla extract
1 cup superfine sugar
5 cups thinly sliced fresh peaches
Fresh Strawberry Sauce

Beat egg whites (at room temperature) in a large bowl at high speed of an electric mixer until foamy. Sprinkle cream of tartar and vanilla extract over beaten egg whites; continue beating until soft peaks form. Gradually add sugar, 1 tablespoon at a time, beating until stiff peaks form and sugar dissolves. (Do not underbeat mixture.)

Spoon meringue mixture into 10 equal portions on baking sheets covered with parchment or unglazed brown paper. (Do not use recycled paper.) Using the back of a spoon, shape meringues into circles 4 inches in diameter; shape each circle into a shell. (Sides of shells should be about 1½ inches high.) Bake at 200° for 1 hour. Turn oven off, and leave meringues in oven overnight. (Do not open door.) Carefully remove baked meringue shells from paper. Fill each meringue shell with ½ cup sliced fresh peaches. Spoon 2 tablespoons Fresh Strawberry Sauce over each serving. Yield: 10 servings (143 calories per serving).

Fresh Strawberry Sauce:

3 cups fresh strawberries, washed, hulled, and halved
2 tablespoons orange juice concentrate, thawed and undiluted
1 tablespoon sugar
1 teaspoon grated orange rind
½ teaspoon grated lemon rind

Place all ingredients in container of an electric blender. Process until smooth, scraping sides of container as necessary. Pour mixture into a small bowl; cover and chill thoroughly. Yield: 1⅓ cups.

Note: Use meringues immediately or store in airtight containers.

PRO 2.8 / FAT 0.2 / CARB 33.8 / FIB 2.6 / CHOL 0 / SOD 42 / POT 280

FRESH RASPBERRIES IN PEACH SAUCE

2 medium peaches, peeled and pitted
2 teaspoons lemon juice
2 teaspoons sugar
2 cups fresh raspberries, chilled
Fresh mint leaves (optional)

Place peaches, lemon juice, and sugar in container of an electric blender; process until smooth. Chill thoroughly.

To serve, spoon ½ cup raspberries into each of 4 individual stemmed glasses; top with peach puree. Garnish with fresh mint, if desired. Yield: 4 servings (55 calories per serving).

PRO 0.8 / FAT 0.4 / CARB 13.6 / FIB 3.9 / CHOL 0 / SOD 0 / POT 185

RUM COMPOTE IN TORTILLA SHELLS

1 cup sliced, peeled fresh peaches
1 cup sliced plums
1 cup honeydew melon chunks
1 cup fresh pineapple chunks
1 tablespoon sugar
2 tablespoons rum
½ teaspoon grated lemon rind
1 tablespoon lemon juice
6 (6-inch) flour tortillas
2 tablespoons sugar
½ teaspoon ground cinnamon
2 tablespoons margarine, melted and divided

Combine first 8 ingredients in a medium bowl; toss lightly. Cover and refrigerate 2 hours.

Stack tortillas, and wrap in aluminum foil; bake at 350° for 7 minutes to soften. Set aside, and keep warm.

Combine 2 tablespoons sugar and cinnamon, stirring well. Brush one side of each tortilla with ½ teaspoon melted margarine; sprinkle with ½ teaspoon sugar-cinnamon mixture. Turn tortillas over, and repeat procedure on other side. Place tortillas in each of six 10-ounce custard cups; gently place a 6-ounce custard cup in center of each tortilla, shaping tortilla into a bowl. Bake at 475° for 5 minutes; remove tortillas from custard cups, and place on cookie sheet. Bake an additional 5 minutes or until lightly browned and crisp. Remove tortillas to wire racks, and cool completely.

Place tortilla shells on individual serving plates. Drain fruit, discarding liquid. Spoon fruit into shells; serve immediately. Yield: 6 servings (232 calories per serving).

PRO 3.1 / FAT 5.8 / CARB 41.8 / FIB 2.5 / CHOL 0 / SOD 51 / POT 241

 Fruit has what we need. In addition to vitamin C, apples, bananas, kiwifruit and many other fruits are rich sources of fiber, potassium and natural sugar.

Studies show that we eat less than half the fiber we need to maintain the smooth functioning of our digestive systems. By eating more fruit and therefore, taking in more fiber, we can help protect ourselves against digestive problems.

We need the potassium in fruit, too. Many scientists believe that getting enough potassium is as important in preventing high blood pressure as is avoiding too much sodium.

Fruit is also full of natural sugar, which is absorbed more slowly into the bloodstream than refined sugar. Consequently, a piece of fruit offers more sustained energy than a candy bar.

MOCHA YOGURT PARFAIT

1 envelope unflavored gelatin
1/3 cup cold water
3 tablespoons Dutch process or unsweetened cocoa
2 (8-ounce) cartons coffee low-fat yogurt
2 egg whites
1/3 cup sugar
Chocolate Crunch

Soften gelatin in cold water in top of a double boiler; cook over boiling water until gelatin dissolves, stirring constantly. Stir in cocoa, and cook until cocoa dissolves. Remove from heat, and cool to room temperature. Fold in yogurt. Chill until mixture reaches consistency of unbeaten egg white.

Beat egg whites (at room temperature) in a large bowl until soft peaks form. Gradually add sugar, 1 tablespoon at a time, beating until stiff peaks form. Fold yogurt mixture into egg whites.

Spoon alternate layers of yogurt mixture and Chocolate Crunch into 8 individual parfait glasses. Chill 3 to 4 hours. Yield: 8 servings (157 calories per serving).

Chocolate Crunch:

1/4 cup plus 2 tablespoons all-purpose flour
1/4 cup regular oats, uncooked
1 tablespoon plus 1 1/2 teaspoons sugar
1 tablespoon Dutch process or unsweetened cocoa
3 tablespoons unsalted margarine, melted
1 tablespoon water

Combine first 4 ingredients. Sprinkle margarine and water over dry ingredients; mix well. Spread in a 9-inch square baking pan. Bake at 450° for 8 to 10 minutes or until crunchy; stir once. Cool completely. Yield: 3/4 cup.

PRO 6.1 / FAT 6.0 / CARB 21.0 / FIB 0.7 / CHOL 3 / SOD 73 / POT 178

PEAR CREAM TART

1 cup gingersnap crumbs
2 tablespoons margarine, melted
Vegeable cooking spray
1/2 (8-ounce) package Neufchâtel cheese, softened
1 tablespoon sugar
1/4 teaspoon grated lemon rind
1/4 cup plus 1 tablespoon lemon juice, divided
1/2 cup unsweetened orange juice
2 teaspoons cornstarch
3 medium pears, peeled, cored, and thinly sliced

Combine gingersnap crumbs and margarine in a small bowl; mix well. Press mixture evenly on bottom of a 12-inch pizza pan coated with cooking spray. Bake at 375° for 5 minutes. Remove tart shell from oven, and cool completely.

Combine cheese, sugar, lemon rind, and 1 tablespoon lemon juice in a small bowl; beat until well blended. Spread mixture evenly over cooled crust. Set aside.

Combine orange juice, 2 tablespoons lemon juice, and cornstarch in a non-aluminum saucepan; beat with a wire whisk until well bended. Bring to a boil. Cover; reduce heat, and cook until mixture thickens, stirring frequently wth wire whisk. Remove glaze from heat; cool.

Dip pear slices in remaining 2 tablespoons lemon juice; drain well. Arrange pear slices over tart. Drizzle glaze over pears. Cover; chill tart thoroughly. Cut into wedges to serve. Yield: 10 servings (131 calories per serving).

PRO 2.2 / FAT 6.8 / CARB 16.3 / FIB 0.9 / CHOL 12 / SOD 88 / POT 163

NECTARINE CREAM PIE

¼ cup sugar
2 tablespoons cornstarch
1½ cups skim milk
2 egg yolks, beaten
½ teaspoon vanilla extract
¼ teaspoon almond extract
½ cup peach low-fat yogurt
3 fresh nectarines, peeled and thinly sliced
Spiced Crumb Crust
2 tablespoons flaked coconut, toasted

Combine sugar and cornstarch in a medium saucepan; stir well. Gradually add milk, stirring until smooth. Cook over medium heat, stirring constantly, until thickened.

Gradually stir one-fourth of hot mixture into egg yolks; add to remaining hot mixture, stirring constantly. Cook, stirring constantly, 1 minute or until mixture thickens. Remove from heat, and stir in flavorings. Cool 15 minutes. Stir in yogurt.

Arrange nectarine slices in Spiced Crumb Crust; pour filling over fruit. Sprinkle with coconut. Chill thoroughly. Yield: 8 servings (192 calories per serving).

Spiced Crumb Crust:

1½ cups crushed corn flakes
2 tablespoons sugar
½ teaspoon ground cinnamon
¼ teaspoon ground nutmeg
¼ cup unsalted margarine, melted
Vegetable cooking spray

Combine first 4 ingredients in a medium bowl; add margarine, and mix well. Press mixture into bottom and up sides of a 9-inch pieplate coated with cooking spray. Bake at 350° for 15 minutes. Cool. Yield: one 9-inch piecrust.

PRO 3.7 / FAT 8.2 / CARB 26.9 / FIB 0.4 / CHOL 70 / SOD 91 / POT 230

 Trying to cut the cream in your coffee? Start with light cream. If that tastes okay, experiment with a light cream/ whole milk combo. Soon, you might even find that whole milk, or better yet, low-fat milk, suits your purpose. Limit your use of nondairy creamers, though. Most are made with oils that are even more saturated than heavy cream.

PUMPKIN-BANANA PIE

3 medium bananas, quartered
1 cup canned pumpkin
1 cup evaporated skim milk
3 eggs, beaten
¼ cup firmly packed brown sugar
1 tablespoon all-purpose flour
1 teaspoon ground cinnamon
½ teaspoon ground nutmeg
Gingersnap Crust

Place bananas in container of an electric blender or food processor; process until smooth. Add pumpkin, milk, eggs, sugar, flour, cinnamon, and nutmeg; process 30 seconds or until smooth. Pour mixture into Gingersnap Crust. Bake at 350° for 45 minutes or until a knife inserted in center comes out clean. Serve at room temperature or chilled. Yield: 8 servings (219 calories per serving).

Gingersnap Crust:

1 cup gingersnap crumbs
2 tablespoons margarine, melted
Vegetable cooking spray

Combine crumbs and margarine in a small bowl; stir well. Press mixture into a 9-inch pieplate coated with cooking spray. Yield: one (9-inch) piecrust.

PRO 6.5 / FAT 7.5 / CARB 33.1 / FIB 1.2 / CHOL 109 / SOD 119 / POT 486

MANGO-LIME ICE

2 medium mangos, peeled and cubed
¼ cup sugar
1 teaspoon grated lime rind
2 tablespoons lime juice
3 cups unsweetened orange juice
¾ cup water
Lime twists (optional)

Combine mangos, sugar, lime rind, and lime juice in container of an electric blender or food processor; process until smooth. Combine pureed mixture, orange juice, and water in a large bowl; stir well.

Pour mixture into freezer can of a hand

turned or electric freezer. Freeze according to manufacturer's instructions. Scoop ice into serving bowls; garnish with lime twists, if desired, and serve immediately. Yield: 6 cups (63 calories per ½-cup serving).

PRO 0.6 / FAT 0.1 / CARB 15.7 / FIB 0.3 / CHOL 0 / SOD 1 / POT 162

BANANA-STRAWBERRY SHERBET

3 medium-size ripe bananas, quartered
1½ cups low-fat buttermilk
¼ cup sugar
2 tablespoons lemon juice
1 teaspoon vanilla extract
2 cups fresh strawberries, hulled and mashed
1 egg white, stiffly beaten

Combine bananas, buttermilk, sugar, lemon juice, and vanilla in container of an electric blender or food processor; process until smooth. Pour mixture into a 9-inch square baking pan; freeze until mixtures becomes slushy.

Scoop mixture into container of an electric blender or food processor; process until smooth. Fold in strawberries and egg white; return mixture to baking pan. Freeze until firm. Scoop mixture into individual serving dishes. Yield: 5 cups (82 calories per ½-cup serving).

PRO 2.1 / FAT 0.6 / CARB 18.1 / FIB 1.1 / CHOL 1 / SOD 44 / POT 254

PINEAPPLE-MINT SHERBET

½ cup sugar
½ teaspoon unflavored gelatin
2 cups skim milk
2 (15¼-ounce) cans unsweetened crushed pineapple, drained
2 tablespoons lemon juice
1 tablespoon plus 1½ teaspoons green crème de menthe
1 egg white
Fresh mint sprigs (optional)
Pineapple chunks (optional)

Combine sugar and gelatin in a small saucepan; gradually add milk, stirring well. Cook over

low heat, stirring constantly, until sugar and gelatin dissolve. Remove from heat, and cool. Stir in crushed pineapple, lemon juice, and crème de menthe.

Beat egg white (at room temperature) in a small bowl until stiff peaks form. Fold into pineapple mixture. Spoon mixture into an 8-inch square baking pan; cover and freeze 4 hours or until slushy, stirring at 1 hour intervals. Spoon mixture into container of an electric blender or food processor; process until smooth. Cover and freeze 8 hours or overnight. Process mixture again in electric blender just prior to serving. Scoop into individual dessert bowls; garnish with fresh mint sprigs and pineapple chunks, if desired. Yield: 4½ cups (104 calories per ½-cup serving).

PRO 2.6 / FAT 0.4 / CARB 22.6 / FIB 1.0 / CHOL 1 / SOD 35 / POT 171

For light and cool endings, serve (clockwise):
Pineapple-Mint Sherbet, Banana-Strawberry Sherbet,
and Mango-Lime Ice.

AMARETTO JAVA SUNDAES

2 cups vanilla ice milk
4 teaspoons finely ground amaretto-flavored coffee, divided
4 tablespoons Amaretto or other almond-flavored liqueur, divided

Scoop ice milk into 4 individual parfait glasses. Sprinkle each with 1 teaspoon coffee; spoon 1 tablespoon Amaretto over each. Serve immediately. Yield: 4 servings (140 calories per serving).

PRO 2.6 / FAT 2.8 / CARB 18.9 / FIB 0.0 / CHOL 9 / SOD 52 / POT 159

KAHLÚA CRÈME CUSTARDS

¼ cup ground chocolate-flavored coffee beans
2 cups skim milk, scalded
3 eggs
3 tablespoons firmly packed brown sugar
2 teaspoons Kahlúa or other coffee-flavored liqueur
Vegetable cooking spray
2 tablespoons Kahlúa or other coffee-flavored liqueur, divided

Place a coffee filter in a large strainer; place strainer over a medium bowl. Spoon ground coffee into filter. Pour hot milk over coffee; set aside until all of the milk has dripped through.

Combine eggs, brown sugar, and 2 teaspoons Kahlúa in a medium bowl; beat at high speed of an electric mixer until well blended. Gradually add reserved milk mixture, beating constantly. Spoon mixture into six (6-ounce) custard cups coated with cooking spray.

Place custard cups in a 13- x 9- x 2-inch baking dish; pour hot water into baking dish to a depth of 1 inch. Bake at 325° for 40 minutes or until a knife inserted halfway between center and edge of custard comes out clean. Remove cups from water; cool to room temperature. Chill thoroughly. Turn custard out onto individual serving plates; spoon 1 teaspoon Kahlúa over each. Serve immediately. Yield: 6 servings (116 calories per serving).

PRO 5.9 / FAT 2.9 / CARB 12.9 / FIB 0.0 / CHOL 139 / SOD 79 / POT 245

Raspberry Pudding, baked in individual custard cups.

PEANUT-BANANA PUDDING

2 egg yolks, beaten
⅓ cup sugar
3 tablespoons cornstarch
2 cups skim milk
2 tablespoons creamy peanut butter
1 teaspoon vanilla extract
2 medium bananas, thinly sliced

Combine egg yolks, sugar, cornstarch, and milk in a medium saucepan. Cook over medium heat, stirring constantly, until mixture boils. Cook an additional 1 minute, stirring constantly. Remove saucepan from heat; add peanut butter and vanilla. Stir well; cover and chill thoroughly.

Layer half of bananas in 6 individual dessert dishes. Spoon half of pudding over bananas in each dish. Repeat layers, ending with pudding. Chill thoroughly. Yield: 6 servings (178 calories per serving).

PRO 5.7 / FAT 5.0 / CARB 28.9 / FIB 0.7 / CHOL 92 / SOD 72 / POT 335

RASPBERRY PUDDING

2 eggs, separated
¼ cup sugar
1 tablespoon plus 1½ teaspoons cornstarch
¼ cup skim milk
1¾ cups skim milk, scalded
½ teaspoon vanilla extract
1 cup fresh raspberries
⅛ teaspoon cream of tartar
2 tablespoons sugar

Combine egg yolks, ¼ cup sugar, cornstarch, and ¼ cup milk in top of a double boiler, stirring to blend. Slowly add 1¾ cups hot milk, stirring constantly. Place over boiling water, and cook, stirring frequently, 10 minutes or until thickened. Remove from heat; stir in vanilla. Cool slightly.

Divide raspberries evenly into 6 (6-ounce) custard cups. Pour pudding over raspberries.

Beat egg whites (at room temperature) and cream of tartar until foamy. Gradually add 2 tablespoons sugar, 1 tablespoon at a time, beating until stiff peaks form. Spoon or pipe meringue onto pudding, covering entire surface and sealing edges. Bake at 425° for 3 to 4 minutes or until golden brown. Serve immediately. Yield: 6 servings (122 calories per serving).

PRO 5.0 / FAT 2.1 / CARB 20.9 / FIB 1.0 / CHOL 93 / SOD 70 / POT 191

SWEET POTATO PUDDING

2 eggs, beaten
1 cup mashed cooked sweet potatoes
¼ cup firmly packed brown sugar
½ teaspoon ground cinnamon
½ teaspoon grated orange rind
1 (12-ounce) can evaporated skim milk
Vegetable cooking spray

Combine first 5 ingredients; beat well. Stir in milk. Pour into a 1-quart casserole coated with cooking spray. Place in a 13- x 9- x 2-inch baking dish; pour boiling water into dish to a depth of 1 inch. Bake at 325° for 1 hour or until a knife inserted comes out clean. Serve warm. Yield: 6 servings (154 calories per serving).

PRO 7.4 / FAT 2.1 / CARB 26.5 / FIB 0.4 / CHOL 94 / SOD 102 / POT 337

WHOLE WHEAT BREAD PUDDING

3 slices whole wheat bread, cubed
¼ cup raisins
2 eggs, beaten
2 cups skim milk
2 tablespoons sugar
1 teaspoon ground cinnamon
1 teaspoon vanilla extract

Combine bread and raisins in a 1-quart casserole. Combine remaining ingredients, stirring well; pour over bread mixture. Stir well.

Place casserole in a 13- x 9- x 2-inch baking pan; pour warm water into baking pan to a depth of 1 inch. Bake at 350° for 45 minutes or until a knife inserted in center comes out clean. Spoon into dessert bowls, and serve warm. Yield: 4 servings (183 calories per serving).

PRO 9.5 / FAT 3.6 / CARB 29.3 / FIB 1.7 / CHOL 140 / SOD 200 / POT 359

HOT APRICOT WHIP

1 (6-ounce) package dried apricots
1½ cups water
¼ teaspoon ground cinnamon
4 egg whites
¼ teaspoon cream of tartar
¼ cup sugar
Vegetable cooking spray

Combine apricots and water in a saucepan. Bring to a boil. Cover; reduce heat, and simmer 15 minutes or until tender. Place undrained apricots and cinnamon in container of an electric blender or food proessor; process until smooth. Spoon into a bowl; cover and chill.

Beat egg whites (at room temperature) and cream of tartar until stiff but not dry. Add sugar, 1 tablespoon at a time, beating until stiff peaks form. Fold one-third of egg white mixture into apricot puree. Fold in remaining egg whites.

Spoon mixture into a 1½-quart soufflé dish coated on bottom with cooking spray. Place dish in a 13- x 9- x 2-inch baking pan; pour hot water into baking pan to a depth of 1 inch. Bake at 350° for 35 minutes or until puffed and firm. Spoon into individual dessert bowls, and serve. Yield: 8 servings (83 calories per serving).

PRO 2.5 / FAT 0.1 / CARB 19.6 / FIB 0.6 / CHOL 0 / SOD 34 / POT 319

GINGER SOUFFLÉ

2 tablespoons margarine
3 tablespoons all-purpose flour
¾ cup skim milk
3 egg yolks
⅓ cup firmly packed brown sugar
1 teaspoon grated lemon rind
1 teaspoon ground ginger
1 teaspoon vanilla extract
¼ teaspoon ground cinnamon
⅛ teaspoon ground cloves
4 egg whites
Vegetable cooking spray

Melt margarine in a small saucepan over low heat; add flour, stirring until smooth. Cook 1 minute, stirring constantly (mixture will be dry). Gradually add milk. Cook over medium heat, stirring constantly with a wire whisk, until mixture is thickened and bubbly. Remove mixture from heat.

Beat egg yolks and sugar in a small bowl until thick and lemon colored. Gradually stir one-fourth of hot mixture into yolks; add yolk mixture to remaining hot mixture, stirring constantly. Pour mixture into a large bowl; stir in next 5 ingredients. Cool.

Beat egg whites (at room temperature) in a medium bowl until stiff, but not dry; gently fold into yolk mixture. Spoon into a 1½-quart soufflé dish coated on bottom with cooking spray. Place dish in an 8-inch square baking pan; pour hot water into baking pan to a depth of 1 inch. Bake at 350° for 50 minutes or until puffed and golden. Spoon into individual dessert bowls; serve immediately. Yield: 6 servings (152 calories per serving).

PRO 5.2 / FAT 6.8 / CARB 17.5 / FIB 0.2 / CHOL 137 / SOD 104 / POT 141

Comparative Nutritional Analysis of Frozen Dairy Products (½-cup serving)			
TYPE	CALORIES	FAT	CALCIUM
Super Premium Ice Cream	175	12 g	75 mg
Premium Ice Cream	134	7 g	88 mg
Ice Milk	92	3 g	88 mg
Frozen Low-Fat Yogurt	110	1 g	100 mg

SPICY APPLESAUCE CAKE SQUARES

½ cup sugar
¼ cup vegetable oil
1 egg
1 cup all-purpose flour
½ cup whole wheat flour
1 teaspoon baking soda
1 teaspoon ground cinnamon
¼ teaspoon ground ginger
¼ teaspoon ground allspice
⅛ teaspoon ground cloves
⅛ teaspoon salt
1 cup unsweetened applesauce
1 teaspoon vanilla extract
Vegetable cooking spray

Combine sugar, oil, and egg in a medium bowl; beat at medium speed of an electric mixer until well blended. Combine flour, soda, cinnamon, ginger, allspice, cloves, and salt in a small bowl; add to sugar mixture, beating well. Stir in applesauce and vanilla.

Spoon batter into an 8-inch square baking pan coated with cooking spray. Bake at 350° for 25 minutes or until a wooden pick inserted in center comes out clean. Cool completely, and cut into squares. Yield: 9 servings (197 calories per serving).

PRO 3.2 / FAT 7.0 / CARB 31.0 / FIB 1.2 / CHOL 30 / SOD 80 / POT 70

ORANGE CARROT CAKE

1 cup all-purpose flour
1 teaspoon baking powder
1 teaspoon ground allspice
½ teaspoon ground cinnamon
¼ teaspoon baking soda
⅛ teaspoon salt
2 eggs, lightly beaten
½ cup sugar
⅓ cup vegetable oil
⅓ cup frozen unsweetened orange juice concentrate, thawed and undiluted
1 cup grated carrots
Vegetable cooking spray
1½ teaspoons sifted powdered sugar

Combine flour, baking powder, allspice, cinnamon, soda, and salt in a medium bowl; set mixture aside.

Combine eggs, ½ cup sugar, oil, and orange juice concentrate in a large bowl; beat well. Add flour mixture and carrots, stirring well.

Spoon batter into an 8-inch square baking pan coated with cooking spray. Bake at 350° for 30 minutes or until a wooden pick inserted in center comes out clean. Cool cake completely in pan. Sprinkle with powdered sugar, and cut into squares to serve. Yield: 9 servings (212 calories per serving).

PRO 3.4 / FAT 9.5 / CARB 28.8 / FIB 0.7 / CHOL 61 / SOD 96 / POT 141

SPICY ZUCCHINI BARS

1 cup all-purpose flour
1 cup whole wheat flour
1 teaspoon baking powder
1 teaspoon baking soda
2 teaspoons ground cinnamon
½ teaspoon ground cloves
¼ teaspoon salt
2 eggs
½ cup vegetable oil
½ cup firmly packed brown sugar
1 (8-ounce) carton plain low-fat
  yogurt
1 teaspoon vanilla extract
1½ cups shredded zucchini squash
Vegetable cooking spray
2 tablespoons sifted powdered
  sugar

Combine flour, baking powder, soda, cinnamon, cloves, and salt in a medium bowl; set mixture aside.

Combine eggs, oil, sugar, yogurt, and vanilla in a large bowl; beat well. Stir in zucchini; add flour mixture, and stir just until moistened. Pour batter into a 13- x 9- x 2-inch baking dish coated wih cooking spray. Bake at 350° for 30 minutes or until a wooden pick inserted in center comes out clean. Cool completely in pan. Sprinkle with powdered sugar, and cut into bars. Yield: 36 bars (75 calories each).

PRO 1.4 / FAT 3.2 / CARB 8.5 / FIB 0.4 / CHOL 14 / SOD 40 / POT 52

CHOCOLATE ORANGE CREPÊS

1½ cups part-skim ricotta cheese
¼ cup semisweet chocolate mini-morsels
3 tablespoons sugar
1 tablespoon Cointreau or other orange-flavored
  liqueur
1 teaspoon grated orange rind
½ teaspoon vanilla extract
Chocolate Crêpes
1 orange, thinly sliced

Combine first 6 ingredients in a medium bowl, stirring well. Spoon 2 tablespoons mixture in center of each crepe; roll up, and place, seam side down, on individual dessert plates. Garnish with orange slices. Yield: 8 servings (160 calories per serving).

Chocolate Crêpes:

1 egg
⅓ cup all-purpose flour
½ cup skim milk
1 tablespoon unsweetened cocoa
1 teaspoon vegetable oil
¼ teaspoon vanilla extract
Dash of salt
Vegetable cooking spray

Combine all ingredients except cooking spray in container of an electric blender; process 30 seconds. Scrape sides of blender with rubber spatula; process 30 seconds. Refrigerate batter 1 hour. (This allows flour particles to swell and soften so crepes are light in texture.)

Coat the bottom of a 6-inch crêpe pan with cooking spray; place pan over medium heat until just hot, not smoking. Pour 2 tablespoons batter onto pan. Quickly tilt pan in all directions so batter covers bottom of pan. Cook crêpe 1 minute. Lift edge of crêpe to test for doneness. Crêpe is ready for flipping when it can be shaken loose from pan. Flip crêpe, and cook 30 seconds. (This side is rarely more than spotty brown, and is the side on which the filling is placed.) Place on paper towels to cool. Stack crêpes between layers of waxed paper to prevent sticking. Repeat procedure until all batter is used, stirring batter occasionally. Yield: 8 (6-inch) crêpes (44 calories each).

PRO 7.6 / FAT 7.0 / CARB 16.3 / FIB 0.3 / CHOL 49 / SOD 93 / POT 129

CHOCOLATE PEANUT CUPCAKES

2 ounces Neufchâtel cheese, softened
3 tablespoons crunchy peanut butter
3 tablespoons honey
1 tablespoon skim milk
⅓ cup shortening
½ cup firmly packed brown sugar
1 egg
1 cup all-purpose flour
3 tablespoons Dutch process or unsweetened
  cocoa
1 teaspoon baking soda
⅛ teaspoon salt
½ cup skim milk
1 teaspoon vanilla extract

Combine Neufchâtel cheese, peanut butter, honey, and 1 tablespoon skim milk in a small bowl, stirring well; set mixture aside.

Cream shortening in a medium bowl; gradually add brown sugar, beating well. Add egg, beating well. Combine flour, cocoa, soda, and salt in a small bowl; add to creamed mixture alternately with ½ cup skim milk, beginning and ending with flour mixture. Mix well after each addition. Stir in vanilla.

Spoon 1 tablespoon batter into each of 12 paper-lined muffin cups. Spoon 2 teaspoons peanut butter mixture into each cup. Fill each two-thirds full with remaining batter. Bake at 375° for 20 minutes. Remove from pans, and cool completely on wire racks. Yield: 1 dozen (186 calories each).

PRO 3.9 / FAT 8.7 / CARB 24.0 / FIB 0.5 / CHOL 27 / SOD 116 / POT 114

Especially for chocolate lovers: Chocolate-Filled Almond Cake garnished with chopped almonds.

CHOCOLATE-FILLED ALMOND CAKE

Vegetable cooking spray
3 eggs, separated
½ cup sugar
½ teaspoon vanilla extract
½ teaspoon almond extract
⅛ teaspoon salt
½ cup sifted cake flour
Chocolate Almond Filling
2 tablespoons finely chopped almonds, toasted

Coat an 8- x 2½-inch round cakepan with cooking spray; line with waxed paper, and coat waxed paper with cooking spray. Set aside.

Beat egg yolks 5 minutes or until thick and lemon colored. Gradually add sugar, beating well. Beat in flavorings and salt. Slowly stir in flour, blending well; set mixture aside.

Beat egg whites (at room temperature) until stiff peaks form. Stir one third of beaten egg whites into yolk mixture. Carefully fold remaining egg whites into yolk mixture.

Spoon batter into prepared pan, and bake at 325° for 25 minutes or until cake springs back when lightly touched. Cool in pan 10 minutes. Carefully remove cake from pan to wire rack, and peel off paper. Cool completely.

Slice cake layer in half horizontally, using a

long serrated knife. Spread two-thirds of Chocolate Almond Filling between layers and on top and sides of cake. Spoon remaining filling into pastry bag fitted with a star tip. Pipe filling on top and around bottom edges. Sprinkle chopped almonds on top of cake. Chill thoroughly. Yield: 10 servings (178 calories per serving).

Chocolate Almond Filling:

1 (1.25-ounce) envelope whipped topping mix
⅓ cup Dutch process or unsweetened cocoa
¼ cup sifted powdered sugar
⅓ cup skim milk, chilled
6 ounces Neufchâtel cheese, softened and cut into cubes
½ teaspoon almond extract

Combine whipped topping mix, cocoa, and sugar in a deep narrow-bottomed bowl; add milk. Beat at high speed of an electric mixer 4 minutes or until light and fluffy. Add Neufchâtel cheese, beating until well blended. Stir in almond extract. Yield: about 2 cups.

PRO 5.1 / FAT 8.4 / CARB 21.6 / FIB 0.3 / CHOL 95 / SOD 159 / POT 88

MANDARIN ANGEL CAKE

¼ cup sugar
2 teaspoons cornstarch
½ cup unsweetened orange juice
¼ cup unsweetened apricot nectar
2 (10¼-ounce) cans unsweetened mandarin oranges, drained
Angel Cake
1 cup frozen whipped topping, thawed

Combine sugar and cornstarch in a saucepan. Add orange juice and apricot nectar, stirring until smooth. Cook over medium heat, stirring constantly, 5 minutes or until thickened. Remove from heat; stir in oranges, reserving ¼ cup oranges for garnish. Chill thoroughly.

Slice Angel Cake in half horizontally, using a long serrated knife. Place one layer on a cake plate; spoon chilled orange mixture over layer. Top with second cake layer. Spread whipped topping over top of cake; garnish with reserved orange sections. Chill thoroughly. Yield: 8 servings (151 calories per serving).

Angel Cake:

6 egg whites
½ teaspoon cream of tartar
⅛ teaspoon salt
¼ cup plus 2 tablespoons sugar
½ cup sifted cake flour
½ teaspoon vanilla extract
¼ teaspoon orange extract

Beat egg whites (at room temperature) until foamy. Add cream of tartar and salt; beat until soft peaks form. Gradually add sugar, 2 tablespoons at a time, beating until stiff peaks form.

Sprinkle flour over egg white mixture; fold in carefully. Gently fold in flavorings. Pour batter into an ungreased 9-inch round cakepan. Bake at 325° for 30 minutes or until a wooden pick inserted in center comes out clean. Cool in pan 40 minutes. Remove cake from pan, and cool completely. Yield: one 9-inch cake layer.

PRO 3.1 / FAT 2.4 / CARB 30.5 / FIB 0.1 / CHOL 0 / SOD 93 / POT 158

 Does that midafternoon slump have you craving a candy bar or some other sweet? Take a hike — instead.

In studies at California State University in Long Beach, California, volunteers rolled dice at appointed times. Depending on the number that came up, they would either walk around the block or eat a candy bar.

The outdoor walk boosted energy for two hours and lowered tension, the walking volunteers reported. The candy bar, on the other hand, boosted energy only briefly for the candy eaters, and, after 30 minutes, their tension levels went up.

A gentle walk after dinner but before dessert might be a good idea too — for your whole family. It's not just the fresh air and the chance to get your blood circulating after sitting down that's beneficial. It's also time for your meal to settle. When you eat, your stomach sends signals to your brain that you're getting full. But it takes about 20 minutes or so after eating for those "satiety" signals to fully register.

So if you take a walking break before dessert, you'll likely be a little less hungry when you sit down again. And a nice light dessert will seem just fine.

NUTMEG CAKE
WITH WARM PEACH SAUCE

6 eggs, separated
¼ cup water
1 teaspoon vanilla extract
¾ cup sugar
⅛ teaspoon salt
1¼ cups sifted all-purpose flour
1 teaspoon ground nutmeg
½ teaspoon baking powder
½ cup sugar
1 teaspoon cream of tartar
Warm Peach Sauce

Beat egg yolks at high speed of an electric mixer 6 minutes or until thick and lemon colored. Combine water and vanilla; add to egg yolks. Beat at low speed of an electric mixer until thoroughly blended. Beat at medium speed 4 minutes or until mixture thickens. Gradually beat in ¾ cup sugar and salt; continue beating 5 to 6 minutes or until smooth.

Combine flour, nutmeg, and baking powder. Sprinkle one-fourth of flour mixture over yolk mixture, and carefully fold in. Repeat procedure with remaining flour mixture; set aside.

Beat egg whites (at room temperature) until foamy; add cream of tartar, and continue beating until soft peaks form. Gradually add ½ cup sugar, 2 tablespoons at a time, beating until stiff peaks form. Gently fold 1 cup beaten egg whites into yolk mixture. Gently fold yolk mixture into remaining egg whites.

Pour batter into an ungreased 10-inch tube pan, spreading evenly with a spatula. Bake at 350° for 45 minutes or until cake springs back when touched. Remove from oven; invert pan. Cool 40 minutes; remove cake from pan to wire rack to cool completely. Serve with 2 tablespoons Warm Peach Sauce per serving. Yield: 16 servings (155 calories per serving).

Warm Peach Sauce:

1 (16-ounce) can unsweetened sliced peaches, undrained
2 tablespoons sugar
1½ teaspoons cornstarch
1½ teaspoons lemon juice
2 teaspoons margarine, melted
¼ cup evaporated skim milk

Drain peaches, reserving juice. Place peaches in container of an electic blender; process until smooth. Set aside.

Combine sugar and cornstarch in a small heavy saucepan. Add peach juice, lemon juice, and margarine, stirring well. Bring to a boil; reduce heat to low, and simmer 10 minutes, stirring frequently. Remove from heat; stir in milk and pureed peaches. Serve warm. Yield: 2 cups.

PRO 3.7 / FAT 2.7 / CARB 29.4 / FIB 0.4 / CHOL 103 / SOD 78 / POT 92

CHOCOLATE-RASPBERRY CAKE ROLL

Vegetable cooking spray
¾ cup sifted cake flour
¼ cup Dutch process or unsweetened cocoa
⅛ teaspoon salt
5 eggs, separated
½ cup sugar
2 tablespoons sifted powdered sugar
Creamy Raspberry Filling

Coat a 15- x 10- x 1-inch jellyroll pan with cooking spray, and line with waxed paper. Coat waxed paper with cooking spray; set aside.

Sift together flour, cocoa, and salt; set aside. Beat egg yolks at high speed of an electric mixer 5 minutes or until thick and lemon colored. Gradually add ½ cup sugar, beating well. Gradually fold in flour mixture, ¼ cup at a time.

Beat egg whites (at room temperature) until stiff, but not dry. Fold one-third of egg whites into chocolate mixture. Gently fold chocolate mixture into remaining egg whites. Spread batter evenly in pan. Bake at 350° for 15 minutes or until surface springs back when touched.

Sift powdered sugar in a 15- x 10-inch rectangle on a linen towel. When cake is done, immediately loosen from sides of pan, and turn out onto powdered sugar; peel off waxed paper. Starting at narrow end, roll up cake and towel together, jellyroll fashion; let cool on a wire rack, seam side down.

Unroll cake, and remove towel. Spread cake with Creamy Raspberry Filling, reserving 2 tablespoons; reroll. Place on a serving plate, seam side down; dollop with 2 tablespoons reserved Creamy Raspberry Filling. Chill at least 1 hour. Cut into 1-inch slices to serve. Yield: 10 servings (177 calories per serving).

Creamy Raspberry Filling:

1 (10-ounce) package frozen raspberries in light syrup, thawed and undrained
1 tablespoon cornstarch
1 tablespoon Cointreau or other orange-flavored liqueur
1 (1.25-ounce) envelope whipped topping mix
½ cup skim milk, chilled

Drain raspberries, reserving juice. Combine juice and cornstarch in a small saucepan; cook over medium heat, stirring constantly, until mixture comes to a boil. Cook 1 minute or until thickened, stirring constantly. Remove from heat, and stir in liqueur. Cool slightly, and stir in raspberries. Chill.

Combine whipped topping mix and chilled skim milk in a deep, narrow-bottomed bowl. Beat at high speed of an electric mixer 4 minutes or until topping is light and fluffy. Fold chilled raspberry mixture into whipped topping mixture. Yield: about 2¾ cups.

PRO 4.8 / FAT 4.6 / CARB 29.3 / FIB 0.9 / CHOL 137 / SOD 92 / POT 106

APPLE PIE

1 (6-ounce) can frozen unsweetened apple juice concentrate, thawed and undiluted
2 tablespoons cornstarch
1 tablespoon margarine
1 teaspoon ground cinnamon
1 teaspoon vanilla extract
6 medium cooking apples, peeled, cored, and sliced
Vegetable cooking spray
Pastry (recipe follows)

Combine apple juice concentrate and cornstarch in a medium saucepan, stirring well. Cook over medium heat until thickened and bubbly. Stir in margarine, cinnamon, and vanilla. Add apples; toss well to coat. Pour into a 9-inch pieplate coated with cooking spray.

Roll pastry to ⅛-inch thickness on a lightly floured surface; cut into rounds with a 1½-inch cookie cutter. Arrange pastry rounds over apples. Bake at 425° for 30 minutes or until lightly browned. Serve warm. Yield: 8 servings (167 calories per serving).

Pastry:

½ cup all-purpose flour
⅛ teaspoon salt
⅛ teaspoon ground nutmeg
2 tablespoons shortening
1 to 1½ tablespoons cold water

Combine flour, salt, and nutmeg; cut in shortening with a pastry blender until mixture resembles coarse meal. Sprinkle cold water evenly over surface; stir with a fork until all dry ingredients are moistened. Shape into a ball. Yield: pastry for one 9-inch pie.

PRO 1.2 / FAT 4.6 / CARB 31.7 / FIB 2.5 / CHOL 0 / SOD 60 / POT 214

PEACH COBBLER

4 cups peeled and sliced very ripe peaches
3 tablespoons sugar
1 tablespoon quick-cooking tapioca, uncooked
1 tablespoon lemon juice
½ teaspoon ground cinnamon
⅛ teaspoon ground cloves
1 cup all-purpose flour
1 tablespoon sugar
1 teaspoon baking powder
3 tablespoons cold margarine, cut into bits
4 to 5 tablespoons skim milk
2 teaspoons superfine sugar

Combine first 6 ingredients in a 9-inch pieplate; toss well. Let stand 15 minutes.

Combine flour, 1 tablespoon sugar, and baking powder in a medium bowl; cut in margarine with a pastry blender until mixture resembles coarse meal. Stir in milk wih a fork to form dough into a ball. Roll dough into a 10-inch circle on a lightly floured surface; place over filling in pieplate. Crimp edges of dough decoratively; chill 30 minutes. Cut slits in top to allow steam to escape; sprinkle with superfine sugar. Bake at 375° for 30 minutes or until crust is golden and filling is bubbly. Yield: 8 servings (169 calories per serving).

PRO 2.6 / FAT 4.6 / CARB 30.3 / FIB 2.5 / CHOL 0 / SOD 96 / POT 206

PLUM COBBLER

3 tablespoons sugar
2 tablespoons cornstarch
1 cup unsweetened white grape juice
1½ pounds ripe plums, pitted and thinly sliced
½ teaspoon almond extract
½ cup all-purpose flour
2 tablespoons firmly packed brown sugar
¼ teaspoon ground cinnamon
3 tablespoons margarine

Combine sugar and cornstarch in a medium saucepan; stir in grape juice, mixing well. Cook over medium heat, stirring constantly, until clear and thickened. Remove from heat, and stir in plums and almond extract. Spoon plum mixture into a 10- x 6- x 2-inch baking dish.

Combine flour, brown sugar, and cinnamon in a small bowl. Cut in margarine with a pastry blender until mixture resembles coarse meal; sprinkle over plum mixture.

Bake at 350° for 45 minutes or until browned and bubbly. Serve warm. Yield: 8 servings (182 calories per serving).

PRO 1.3 / FAT 4.4 / CARB 36.0 / FIB 3.6 / CHOL 0 / SOD 57 / POT 287

BLUEBERRY CRISP

2 (16-ounce) packages frozen unsweetened blueberries, thawed and drained
3 tablespoons all-purpose flour
2 tablespoons sugar
2 teaspoons lemon juice
Vegetable cooking spray
½ cup quick-cooking oats, uncooked
⅓ cup all-purpose flour
⅓ cup firmly packed brown sugar
1 teaspoon ground cinnamon
3 tablespoons margarine

Dredge blueberries in 3 tablespoons flour in a medium bowl; stir in sugar and lemon juice. Spoon mixture into an 8-inch square baking dish coated with cooking spray.

Combine oats, ⅓ cup flour, brown sugar, and cinnamon in a small bowl. Cut in margarine with a pastry blender until mixture resembles coarse meal. Sprinkle topping over blueberry mixture. Bake at 350° for 30 minutes or until lightly browned. Serve warm. Yield: 8 servings (225 calories per serving).

PRO 3.1 / FAT 6.0 / CARB 41.8 / FIB 5.9 / CHOL 0 / SOD 57 / POT 151

Any of these cookies will make a healthy lunchbox treat: (clockwise from top) Chocolate Coffee Drops, Almond Meringue Cookies, Peanut Butter Fingers, and Crunchy Cereal Cookies (page 225).

ALMOND MERINGUE COOKIES

2 egg whites
⅓ cup sugar
⅓ cup finely chopped toasted almonds
½ teaspoon almond extract

Beat egg whites (at room temperature) in a medium bowl until soft peaks form. Gradually add sugar, 1 tablespoon at a time, beating until stiff peaks form. Fold in almonds and almond extract.

Drop meringue by heaping teaspoonfuls 1 inch apart onto waxed paper-lined cookie sheets. Bake at 300° for 35 minutes. Cool slightly on cookie sheets; gently remove from waxed paper, and cool completely on wire racks. Yield: 3½ dozen (11 calories each).

PRO 0.3 / FAT 0.4 / CARB 1.7 / FIB 0.0 / CHOL 0 / SOD 2 / POT 8

CRUNCHY CEREAL COOKIES

1 cup all-purpose flour
1 teaspoon ground cinnamon
¾ teaspoon baking soda
½ teaspoon baking powder
⅛ teaspoon salt
⅓ cup margarine, softened
½ cup firmly packed brown sugar
1 egg
1 teaspoon vanilla extract
1 cup quick-cooking oats, uncooked
1 cup corn flakes cereal
2 tablespoons wheat germ
Vegetable cooking spray

Combine flour, cinnamon, soda, baking powder, and salt. Set aside.

Cream margarine in a medium bowl; gradually add sugar, beating well. Add egg and vanilla; beat well. Stir in flour mixture, mixing well. Stir in oats, corn flakes, and wheat germ.

Drop dough by rounded teaspoonfuls 2 inches apart onto cookie sheets coated with cooking spray. Bake at 325° for 10 to 12 minutes. Cool slightly on cookie sheets. Remove cookies to wire racks to cool completely. Yield: 3½ dozen (53 calories each).

PRO 1.2 / FAT 1.9 / CARB 8.1 / FIB 0.7 / CHOL 6 / SOD 41 / POT 30

CHOCOLATE COFFEE DROPS

⅓ cup margarine
⅓ cup sugar
1 egg
3 tablespoons Kahlua or other coffee-flavored liqueur
1 tablespoon skim milk
1½ cups all-purpose flour
2 tablespoons Dutch process or unsweetened cocoa
½ teaspoon baking soda
Vegetable cooking spray

Cream margarine in a medium bowl; gradually add sugar, beating well. Add egg, Kahlua, and milk; beat well.

Combine flour, cocoa, and soda; gradually add to creamed mixture, stirring just until blended. Drop dough by rounded teaspoonfuls 2 inches apart onto cookie sheets coated with cooking spray. Bake at 375° for 8 to 10 minutes. Remove from cookie sheets, and cool on wire racks. Yield: 3 dozen (50 calories each).

PRO 0.8 / FAT 2.0 / CARB 6.7 / FIB 0.2 / CHOL 8 / SOD 30 / POT 10

PEANUT BUTTER FINGERS

¼ cup plus 2 tablespoons margarine, softened
¼ cup plus 2 tablespoons creamy peanut butter
½ cup firmly packed brown sugar
2 cups all-purpose flour
½ teaspoon ground cinnamon
1 egg
2 tablespoons skim milk
½ teaspoon vanilla extract

Cream margarine and peanut butter in a medium bowl. Add sugar, beating well.

Combine flour and cinnamon; add to creamed mixture, mixing until well blended. Add remaining ingredients, and beat well.

Press dough from a cookie press into 2-inch strips onto ungreased cookie sheets, following manufacturer's instructions. Bake at 400° for 6 minutes or until edges are lightly browned. Remove from cookie sheets, and cool completely on wire racks. Yield: 9 dozen (24 calories each).

Note: Cookies may be sealed in an airtight container and frozen for later use.

PRO 0.6 / FAT 1.2 / CARB 3.0 / FIB 0.1 / CHOL 2 / SOD 13 / POT 13

Marketplace

The growing trend toward eating light and staying fit is reflected in the many changes showing up in the marketplace. New and lighter foods are appearing on supermarket shelves. Standard foods that we've been buying for years are arriving in newly designed packages that include more specific nutritional labeling.

Sports and athletic equipment is changing too. For instance, the running shoe now comes in as varied an assortment of styles and podiatric features as do the runners. This year, with soft and low-impact aerobics being recommended by exercise physiologists, the walking shoe is beginning to replace the running shoe in popularity.

On these pages, we've included a few tips to help you make choices from the many available options in the marketplace. Use this information as you begin your quest for a healthier life-style.

Legumes Are In

When you think about foods that are rich in protein, chances are red meat, chicken, fish, dairy products, and eggs come to mind. Unfortunately, these animal sources of protein also tend to be high in saturated fat. A healthier alternative may be to choose foods from the other basic source of protein — vegetable protein. The richest source of vegetable protein is legumes represented by dried peas and beans and peanuts. Low in fat, readily available, and less expensive, legumes are also able to provide high-quality protein.

In order for our bodies to efficiently utilize protein, it must be complete. The protein must contain nine essential amino acids. Unlike animal proteins, legumes do not contain all nine amino acids. However, when combined with complementary foods such as rice, wheat, corn, barley, oats, nuts, and seeds which supply the amino acids they are lacking, they become complete proteins.

Pictured here are a variety of the legumes available in your supermarket. By combining legumes and a complementary food there is no end to the number of interesting dishes you can prepare.

Legumes come in many different sizes and colors; (starting at back row, reading left to right) red kidney beans, green flageoles, lentils, soy beans, black beans, navy beans, large lima beans, garbanzo beans, October cranberries, green split peas, black-eyed peas, and yellow split peas.

New Labeling For Meats

Red meat can be a healthy part of our diet as long as it is low-fat or lean. New regulations by the United States Department of Agriculture (USDA), proposed to go into effect by March 1987, strictly define what "lean" means for beef, pork, lamb, and poultry.

To be "lean," meat or poultry must be no more than 10% fat by weight. "Extra lean" must be no more than 5% fat by weight. Remember, however, that a food that's 10% fat by weight probably gets more than 10% of its calories from fat.

The USDA is also defining the term "leaner" this year. For a meat or poultry product to be labeled "leaner," it must have 25% less fat than USDA standards. Such foods must also carry labels that compare the food's fat to the standard. For example, "leaner ground beef," must also carry a phrase that states, "This product contains 20% fat, which is 33% less fat than is in most ground beef."

There is a change that appears likely to occur in 1987. The meat industry is petitioning the USDA to change the name of Good beef to Select. Presently beef is graded Prime, Choice, Good, or Standard.

The higher grades — Prime and Choice have more fat than Good or Standard grades of meat. Because many consumers want lean red meat, they are discovering Good grades, which are sometimes a little tougher but are high quality and much lower in fat. But because "Good" doesn't sound appealing, the grade name is being changed to "Select." Look for it in your market soon; it is as nutritious, calorie for calorie, as Prime or Choice, and lower in fat.

Sometime late in 1987, another voluntary label may start appearing on beef and other red meats. It's an NEF label. NEF stands for Nutritional Effects Foundation, a nonprofit group composed of physicians, nutritionists, and livestock experts. They are planning to label cuts of red meat that are low enough in fat to qualify for the American Heart Association's general recommendations (less than 30% of calories from fat), and also those cuts that are low enough to be part of the AHA's therapeutic diets (20% of calories from fat). NEF labels will also guarantee that the meat is free of drugs and antibiotics.

Walking In Comfort

Although walking is perhaps the least expensive sport, it does require an investment in good shoes. Fortunately, shoe manufacturers are helping America lace up and walk. Ask at your local sporting goods or athletic shoe store for new shoes designed especially for walking.

Walking exerts less force on your feet than running so that you need less cushioning in your shoes. However, walking requires that your feet bend more; for that reason, your shoes should allow for more flexibility. A good walking shoe requires less shock absorption in the heel but a more flexible, curved sole designed for the natural rocking motion of stepping forward.

Look for thin, flexible cushioning and flat, low profile soles. Heel counters should be reinforced.

And the uppers should be made of materials that will allow the foot to breath. In fitting, make sure you have enough room for your toes to spread naturally as you walk.

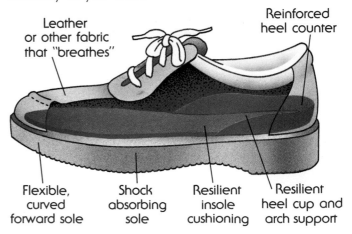

Leather or other fabric that "breathes"

Reinforced heel counter

Flexible, curved forward sole

Shock absorbing sole

Resilient insole cushioning

Resilient heel cup and arch support

Calorie/Nutrient Chart

FOOD	APPROXIMATE MEASURE	FOOD ENERGY (CALORIES)	PROTEIN (GRAMS)	FAT (GRAMS)	CARBOHYDRATES (GRAMS)	SODIUM (MILLIGRAMS)	CALCIUM (MILLIGRAMS)
Alfalfa sprouts	½ cup	5	0.7	0.1	0.6	1	5
Apple							
Fresh, with skin	1 medium	77	0.2	0.4	20.0	0	9
Juice, unsweetened	1 cup	117	0.1	0.2	29.0	7	17
Applesauce, unsweetened	½ cup	52	0.2	0.1	13.8	2	4
Apricot							
Fresh	3 medium	53	1.3	0.4	12.3	1	16
Canned, in light syrup	½ cup	75	0.7	0.1	19.0	1	12
Dried, uncooked	3 medium	50	0.8	0.1	13.0	2	9
Artichokes, fresh, cooked	1 medium	53	2.6	0.2	12.4	79	47
Asparagus							
Fresh, cooked	4 medium spears	15	1.5	0.2	2.6	2	14
Canned, regular pack	½ cup	22	2.2	0.4	3.5	474	22
Avocado	1 medium	322	3.9	30.6	14.8	20	22
Bacon, fried and drained							
Cured, sliced	1 medium slice	43	2.3	3.7	0.0	120	1
Canadian-style	1 (⅔-ounce) slice	35	4.6	1.6	0.2	292	2
Bamboo shoots, raw	1 cup	41	3.8	0.5	7.5	6	20
Banana							
Whole	1 medium	109	1.2	0.5	27.6	1	7
Mashed	1 cup	202	2.2	1.0	51.6	2	13
Beans							
Garbanzo, cooked	½ cup	169	10.0	1.1	30.5	13	75
Great Northern, canned	½ cup	96	6.5	0.4	16.4	465	55
Green, fresh, cooked	½ cup	22	1.2	0.2	4.9	2	29
Green, canned, regular pack	½ cup	18	1.0	0.1	4.2	442	29
Kidney, red, dark, canned	½ cup	114	7.8	0.4	19.9	418	35
Lima, canned, regular pack	½ cup	88	5.0	0.4	16.5	490	32
Lima, immature seeds, cooked	½ cup	105	5.8	0.3	20.1	14	27
Lima, mature seeds, cooked	½ cup	131	7.7	0.6	24.3	2	28
Yellow or wax, fresh, cooked	½ cup	22	1.2	0.2	4.9	2	29
Yellow or wax, canned, regular pack	½ cup	23	1.2	0.2	4.9	353	41
Bean sprouts, mung, raw	1 cup	31	3.1	0.2	6.2	6	14
Beef, trimmed of excess fat							
Chuck roast (arm and round bone cuts), braised and drained	3 ounces	152	25.9	6.0	0	45	12
Flank steak, braised and drained	3 ounces	162	25.9	6.2	0	45	12
Round steak, broiled	3 ounces	161	26.6	5.2	0	65	11
Rump roast, roasted	3 ounces	162	24.7	7.9	0	61	10
Sirloin, broiled	3 ounces	178	27.4	6.5	0	67	11
Beef, corned, boneless, canned	3 ounces	157	22.4	6.8	0.0	1480	18
Beef, dried, chipped, uncooked	1 ounce	58	9.7	1.8	0.0	1219	6
Beef, ground, lean, broiled	3 ounces	243	20.6	17.2	0.0	40	9
Beet greens, cooked	½ cup	13	1.2	0.1	2.3	55	72
Beets							
Fresh, diced, cooked	½ cup	26	0.9	0.4	5.7	42	9
Canned, regular pack	½ cup	38	1.0	0.1	9.2	264	12

Tr = Trace amount of nutrient   Dash (-) indicates insufficient data available

FOOD	APPROXIMATE MEASURE	FOOD ENERGY (CALORIES)	PROTEIN (GRAMS)	FAT (GRAMS)	CARBOHYDRATES (GRAMS)	SODIUM (MILLIGRAMS)	CALCIUM (MILLIGRAMS)
Beverages, alcoholic							
Beer	1 ounce	9	0.1	0.0	0.6	3	3
Beer, light	1 ounce	8	0.1	0.0	1.1	2	1
Champagne	1 ounce	22	0.1	0.0	0.4	1	1
Cognac brandy	1 ounce	72	-	-	-	-	-
Créme de menthe liqueur	1 ounce	99	-	-	8.9	-	-
Curaçao liqueur	1 ounce	92	0.0	0.1	8.3	-	-
Gin, rum, vodka, whiskey (90 proof)	1 ounce	78	0.0	0.0	0.0	0	0
Sherry, dry	1 ounce	34	0.1	0.0	0.4	3	2
Sherry, sweet	1 ounce	40	0.1	0.0	2.0	4	2
Vermouth, dry	1 ounce	35	0.0	0.0	1.6	5	2
Vermouth, sweet	1 ounce	45	0.0	0.0	4.7	8	2
Wine, dessert	1 ounce	41	0.0	0.0	2.2	1	2
Wine, dessert, after cooking	1 ounce	9	0.0	0.0	2.2	1	2
Wine, table	1 ounce	25	0.0	0.0	1.2	1	3
Wine, table, after cooking	1 ounce	5	0.0	0.0	1.2	1	3
Beverages, nonalcoholic							
Carbonated, artificially sweetened dietary drinks	1 ounce	-	0	0	-	-	-
Carbonated, cola type, sweetened	1 ounce	14	0.0	0.0	3.6	0	0
Carbonated, ginger ale	1 ounce	10	0.0	0.0	2.8	2	-
Carbonated, unsweetened (club soda)	1 ounce	0	0.0	0.0	0.0	0	0
Biscuit, homemade	1 biscuit	127	2.3	6.4	14.9	224	65
Blackberries, fresh	½ cup	37	0.5	0.3	9.2	0	23
Blueberries, fresh	½ cup	41	0.5	0.3	10.2	4	4
Bouillon, dry							
Beef-flavored cubes	1 cube	3	0.1	0.0	0.2	400	-
Beef-flavored granules	1 teaspoon	5	0.0	0.5	0.0	461	-
Chicken-flavored cubes	1 cube	7	0.2	0.1	0.5	800	-
Chicken-flavored granules	1 teaspoon	5	0.2	0.5	0.2	381	-
Bran							
Oat	½ cup	168	8.4	4.2	23.8	4	28
Wheat, raw	½ cup	59	4.0	1.3	7.5	3	36
Bread, cut into approximately 1-ounce slices							
French or Vienna	1 slice	72	2.3	0.5	13.9	145	11
Italian	1 slice	83	2.7	0.2	16.9	175	5
Pumpernickel	1 slice	76	2.8	0.4	16.4	176	26
Raisin	1 slice	65	1.6	0.7	13.4	91	18
Rye	1 slice	61	2.3	0.3	13.0	139	19
White	1 slice	67	2.2	0.8	12.6	127	17
Whole wheat	1 slice	61	2.6	0.8	11.9	132	25
Breadcrumbs, dry	1 cup	392	12.6	4.5	73.4	736	122
Broccoli, fresh, cooked, chopped	½ cup	26	2.8	0.1	4.9	22	47
Brussels sprouts, fresh, cooked	½ cup	30	2.0	0.4	6.8	16	28
Bulgur, dry	1 cup	602	18.9	2.5	128.5	7	49
Butter							
Regular type	1 tablespoon	102	0.1	11.5	0.0	117	3
Unsalted	1 tablespoon	102	0.1	11.5	0.0	2	3
Whipped type	1 tablespoon	68	0.1	7.7	0.0	78	2
Cabbage, common varieties							
Raw, shredded	1 cup	17	0.8	0.1	3.7	13	33
Cooked	½ cup	16	0.7	0.2	3.6	14	25
Bok choy	1 cup	9	1.0	0.1	1.5	45	73
Cake							
Angel food, unfrosted	1 (2-ounce) slice	166	3.3	0.1	38.1	56	4
Chocolate, (2 layers) with chocolate frosting, cut into 12 slices	1 slice	365	4.5	16.2	55.2	233	20

FOOD	APPROXIMATE MEASURE	FOOD ENERGY (CALORIES)	PROTEIN (GRAMS)	FAT (GRAMS)	CARBOHYDRATES (GRAMS)	SODIUM (MILLIGRAMS)	CALCIUM (MILLIGRAMS)
Cake (continued)							
Pound, without frosting	1 (1-ounce) slice	113	1.8	6.3	12.3	92	13
Sponge, without frosting, homemade	1 slice	122	1.8	5.1	17.5	55	32
Candy							
Chocolate, milk	1 ounce	156	2.1	9.1	16.1	26	54
Fudge, chocolate	1 ounce	113	0.8	3.4	21.3	54	22
Gum drops	1 ounce	98	0.0	0.2	24.8	10	2
Hard	1 ounce	109	0.0	0.0	27.5	9	6
Marshmallows, regular-size	1 marshmallow	26	0.2	0.0	6.4	3	1
Cantaloupe, diced	1 cup	56	1.4	0.4	13.4	14	18
Carrot							
Raw	1 medium	30	0.7	0.1	7.1	24	19
Fresh, sliced, cooked	½ cup	35	0.8	0.1	8.1	51	24
Canned, regular pack	½ cup	24	0.7	0.1	5.7	298	22
Catsup							
No salt added	1 tablespoon	15	0.0	0.0	4.0	6	-
Regular type	1 tablespoon	18	0.3	0.1	4.3	178	4
Cauliflower							
Raw, sliced	1 cup	20	1.7	0.2	4.2	13	25
Fresh, sliced, cooked	½ cup	15	1.2	0.1	2.8	4	17
Celery, raw, diced	½ cup	10	0.4	0.1	2.2	53	23
Cereal							
Bran, whole	½ cup	106	6.1	0.7	31.6	480	34
Bran flakes	1 cup	127	4.9	0.7	30.5	363	19
Corn flakes	1 cup	88	1.8	0.1	19.5	281	1
Granola	½ cup	251	5.7	9.8	37.7	116	36
Shredded wheat, large biscuit	1 biscuit	83	2.5	0.3	18.8	0	10
Wheat, puffed	1 cup	56	3.2	0.3	11.1	4	65
Chard, Swiss, cooked	½ cup	16	1.5	0.2	2.8	75	64
Cheese, natural							
Blue or Roquefort	1 ounce	100	6.0	8.1	0.7	395	150
Brie	1 ounce	95	5.9	7.8	0.1	178	52
Camembert	1 ounce	85	5.6	6.9	0.1	239	110
Cheddar	1 ounce	114	7.0	9.4	0.3	176	204
Cottage (4% milk-fat)	½ cup	108	13.1	4.7	2.8	425	63
Cottage, low-fat (2% milk-fat)	½ cup	102	15.5	2.2	4.1	459	77
Cream	1 ounce	99	2.1	9.9	0.8	84	23
Farmers, dry curd, no salt added	1 ounce	24	4.9	0.1	0.5	4	9
Gruyère	1 ounce	117	8.4	9.2	0.1	95	287
Monterey Jack	1 ounce	106	6.9	8.6	0.2	152	211
Mozzarella, part skim	1 ounce	72	6.9	4.5	0.8	132	183
Muenster	1 ounce	104	6.6	8.5	0.3	178	203
Neufchâtel	1 ounce	74	2.8	6.6	0.8	113	21
Parmesan, grated	1 tablespoon	23	2.1	1.5	0.2	93	69
Ricotta, part skim	½ cup	170	14.0	9.7	6.3	154	335
Romano	1 ounce	110	9.0	7.6	1.0	340	302
Swiss	1 ounce	107	8.1	7.8	1.0	74	272
Cheese, American, Lite-Line	1 ounce	50	6.9	2.0	1.0	407	198
Cheese, process American	1 ounce	106	6.3	8.9	0.5	405	175
Cherries, pitted							
Fresh, sour	½ cup	39	0.8	0.2	9.4	2	12
Fresh, sweet	½ cup	41	0.6	0.1	9.9	1	16
Sweet, canned, in light syrup	½ cup	100	1.1	0.3	25.2	1	19
Candied	½ cup	264	0.4	0.2	67.5	2	17
Chicken, skinned and roasted							
Breast meat	3 ounces	140	26.4	3.0	0.0	63	13
Dark meat	3 ounces	174	23.3	8.3	0.0	79	13
Chili, canned, with beans	1 cup	357	17.8	17.8	33.1	1288	64

Tr = Trace amount of nutrient   Dash (-) indicates insufficient data available

FOOD	APPROXIMATE MEASURE	FOOD ENERGY (CALORIES)	PROTEIN (GRAMS)	FAT (GRAMS)	CARBOHYDRATES (GRAMS)	SODIUM (MILLIGRAMS)	CALCIUM (MILLIGRAMS)
Chocolate							
Semisweet	1 ounce	144	1.2	10.1	16.2	1	9
Sweer	1 ounce	150	1.2	9.9	16.4	9	27
Unsweetened	1 ounce	141	3.1	14.7	8.5	1	23
Chocolate syrup	1 tablespoon	49	0.6	0.2	11.0	13	3
Clams							
Raw, hard or round, meat only	5 large	80	11.1	0.8	5.9	205	69
Raw, soft, meat only	5 large	102	17.5	2.2	1.5	45	86
Canned, drained	½ cup	78	12.6	2.0	1.4	96	44
Cocoa							
Dutch process	1 tablespoon	16	0.9	1.3	2.4	39	7
Regular type	1 tablespoon	24	1.6	0.7	2.6	0	8
Coconut, fresh, grated	1 cup	526	5.5	51.4	18.8	30	21
Coffee, prepared as beverage	1 cup	2	0.0	0.0	0.0	2	5
Collards, fresh, cooked	½ cup	12	0.9	0.1	2.2	16	66
Cookies							
Chocolate chip, homemade	1 cookie	69	0.9	4.6	6.8	30	7
Oatmeal, plain	1 cookie	57	0.9	2.7	7.2	46	13
Vanilla sandwich type	1 cookie	55	0.5	7.0	2.5	-	0
Vanilla wafers	1 cookie	19	0.2	0.9	2.5	16	2
Corn							
Fresh, kernels, cooked	½ cup	89	2.6	1.0	20.6	14	2
Canned, cream-style, regular pack	½ cup	103	2.5	0.8	25.0	295	4
Cornmeal							
Enriched, dry	1 cup	453	10.9	1.7	95.2	1	8
Self-rising, dry	1 cup	465	11.4	4.3	95.8	1849	402
Cornstarch	1 tablespoon	29	0.0	0.0	7.0	0	0
Crab							
Fresh, steamed	3 ounces	79	14.6	1.5	0.4	179	37
Canned, drained, flaked	½ cup	98	18.1	1.9	0.5	220	45
Crackers							
Animal	1 cracker	12	0.1	0.4	1.9	13	0
Butter, round	1 cracker	15	0.2	0.7	2.0	37	-
Graham, rectangular	1 rectangle	54	1.1	1.3	10.3	94	6
Saltines	1 cracker	13	0.3	0.3	2.0	43	5
Cranberries, fresh, whole	½ cup	23	0.2	0.1	6.0	0	3
Cranberry sauce, sweetened, canned	¼ cup	105	0.1	0.1	26.9	20	3
Cream							
Half-and-half	1 cup	315	7.2	27.8	10.4	99	254
Sour	1 tablespoon	31	0.5	3.0	0.6	8	17
Whipping, unwhipped	1 cup	821	4.8	88.1	6.6	90	155
Cucumber, raw							
Whole, unpeeled	1 medium	39	1.6	0.4	8.7	6	42
Sliced, unpeeled	1 cup	14	0.6	0.1	3.1	2	15
Currants	1 tablespoon	25	0.3	0.2	6.1	3	8
Dates, pitted	5 medium	102	0.7	0.2	27.4	1	12
Doughnuts							
Cake type	1 doughnut	156	1.8	7.4	20.6	200	16
Plain	1 doughnut	186	3.0	10.0	21.0	181	20
Egg							
Substitute	¼ cup	30	6.0	0.0	1.0	90	20
Whole	1 large	79	6.2	5.6	0.6	69	28
White	1 white	16	3.2	0.0	0.4	49	4
Yolk	1 yolk	63	2.8	5.6	0.0	8	26
Eggplant, cooked without salt	½ cup	13	0.4	0.1	3.2	1	3

FOOD	APPROXIMATE MEASURE	FOOD ENERGY (CALORIES)	PROTEIN (GRAMS)	FAT (GRAMS)	CARBOHYDRATES (GRAMS)	SODIUM (MILLIGRAMS)	CALCIUM (MILLIGRAMS)
Extracts							
Almond	1 teaspoon	10	-	-	-	-	-
Coconut	1 teaspoon	6	-	-	-	-	-
Vanilla	1 teaspoon	12	-	-	-	-	-
Fig, raw	1 medium	11	0.1	0.0	3.0	0	5
Fish, raw							
Bass, striped	4 ounces	119	21.3	3.1	0.0	77	23
Cod	4 ounces	88	20.0	0.8	0.0	79	11
Catfish, freshwater	4 ounces	117	20.0	3.4	0.0	68	26
Flounder	4 ounces	90	18.9	0.9	0.0	88	14
Haddock	4 ounces	90	20.6	0.7	0.0	69	26
Halibut	4 ounces	110	22.3	1.5	0.0	61	15
Mackerel	4 ounces	217	21.5	13.7	0.0	84	6
Perch, white	4 ounces	134	21.8	4.5	0.0	57	57
Salmon, pink	4 ounces	135	22.7	4.2	0.0	73	144
Salmon, pink, canned	1 (7¾-ounce) can	310	45.0	13.0	0.0	850	431
Snapper, red and gray	4 ounces	105	22.3	0.9	0.0	18	243
Sole	4 ounces	90	18.9	0.9	0.0	88	14
Trout	4 ounces	191	20.6	11.3	0.0	92	29
Tuna, solid white, canned in oil	1 (7-ounce) can	571	48.1	40.7	0.0	830	12
Tuna, solid white, canned in water	1 (6½-ounce) can	235	51.6	1.5	0.0	620	30
Flour							
All-purpose, sifted	1 cup	419	12.1	1.1	87.4	2	18
Rye, sifted	1 cup	314	8.2	0.9	68.6	1	19
Unbleached	1 cup	401	12.0	1.0	86.3	5	0
Whole wheat	1 cup	400	16.0	2.4	85.2	4	49
Frankfurter, all meat, raw	1 frankfurter	130	5.8	11.2	1.1	484	3
Fruit cocktail							
Canned, in light syrup	½ cup	71	0.5	0.1	18.5	8	8
Canned, in water	½ cup	39	0.5	0.1	10.4	5	6
Garlic	1 clove	4	0.2	0.0	1.0	1	5
Gelatin							
Unflavored, dry	1 envelope	25	6.2	0.0	0.0	8	-
Flavored, prepared with water	½ cup	80	2.0	-	18.9	90	-
Grapefruit							
Fresh	½ grapefruit	43	0.9	0.1	10.7	0	14
Juice, unsweetened	1 cup	94	1.2	0.2	22.1	2	17
Grapes							
Green, seedless	1 cup	114	1.1	0.9	28.4	3	18
Juice, unsweetened	1 cup	172	1.0	0.0	42.5	9	25
Grits, cooked without salt	½ cup	73	1.6	0.2	15.7	0	0
Honey	1 tablespoon	64	0.1	0.0	17.5	1	1
Honeydew, diced	1 cup	56	1.4	0.5	12.9	20	24
Horseradish, prepared	1 tablespoon	6	0.2	0.0	1.4	14	9
Ice cream, vanilla, 10% fat	½ cup	134	2.3	7.2	15.9	58	88
Ice milk, vanilla	½ cup	92	2.6	2.8	14.5	52	88
Jams and Jellies	1 tablespoon	51	0.0	0.0	13.2	3	4

Tr = Trace amount of nutrient   Dash (-) indicates insufficient data available

FOOD	APPROXIMATE MEASURE	FOOD ENERGY (CALORIES)	PROTEIN (GRAMS)	FAT (GRAMS)	CARBOHYDRATES (GRAMS)	SODIUM (MILLIGRAMS)	CALCIUM (MILLIGRAMS)
Kale, cooked	½ cup	21	1.1	0.3	3.7	15	47
Kiwifruit	1 medium	46	0.7	0.3	11.2	4	19
Lamb, trimmed of excess fat							
Leg, roasted	3 ounces	156	24.4	6.0	0	60	11
Loin chop, broiled and drained	2.3 ounces	120	18.3	4.9	0	45	8
Lard	1 tablespoon	116	0.0	12.8	0.0	0	0
Leeks, leaf portion, raw	½ cup	32	0.8	0.2	7.3	10	31
Lemon							
Fresh	1 medium	16	0.6	0.2	5.2	1	15
Juice	1 tablespoon	4	0.1	0.0	1.3	0	1
Lemonade, frozen, sweetened, diluted	1 cup	109	0.2	0.0	28.0	0	2
Lentils, cooked	½ cup	106	7.8	0.0	19.2	13	25
Lettuce							
Boston or Bibb, chopped	1 cup	7	0.7	0.1	1.3	3	-
Chicory	1 cup	18	1.1	0.3	3.3	8	77
Endive or Escarole	1 cup	8	0.6	0.1	1.7	11	26
Iceberg, chopped	1 cup	7	0.5	0.1	1.1	5	10
Romaine, chopped	1 cup	9	0.9	0.1	1.3	4	20
Lime	1 medium	19	0.4	0.1	6.8	1	21
Liver							
Beef, fried	3 ounces	195	22.3	9.0	4.5	156	9
Chicken, simmered	3 ounces	140	22.5	3.7	2.6	52	9
Lobster, cooked, meat only	3 ounces	81	15.9	1.3	0.3	179	55
Luncheon meats							
Bologna, all meat	1 ounce	90	3.3	8.0	0.8	289	3
Salami	1 ounce	74	3.9	6.3	0.6	283	-
Lychees, raw	1 each	18	0.2	0.1	4.6	1	2
Macaroni, cooked tender without salt	½ cup	78	2.4	0.3	16.1	Tr	6
Mango, raw, diced	½ cup	54	0.4	0.2	14.0	2	8
Margarine							
Regular type	1 tablespoon	101	0.1	11.4	0.1	133	4
Unsalted	1 tablespoon	101	0.1	11.3	0.1	0	2
Mayonnaise							
Reduced-calorie	1 tablespoon	40	0.1	4.0	1.0	111	0
Regular type	1 tablespoon	99	0.2	11.0	0.3	82	2
Milk							
Buttermilk	1 cup	98	7.8	2.1	11.7	257	284
Skim	1 cup	86	8.3	0.4	11.9	127	301
Low-fat (2% fat)	1 cup	122	8.1	4.7	11.7	122	298
Whole (3.5% fat)	1 cup	159	8.5	8.5	12.0	122	288
Evaporated	1 cup	338	17.1	19.0	25.3	267	658
Evaporated skim	1 cup	200	19.3	0.5	29.1	294	742
Sweetened condensed	1 cup	982	24.2	26.3	166.5	389	869
Instant nonfat dry	1 cup powder	434	43.4	0.9	62.4	642	1508
Molasses, cane, light	1 tablespoon	52	0.0	0.0	13.3	3	34
Mushrooms, fresh	1 cup	17	1.4	0.3	3.3	3	3
Mustard, prepared	1 teaspoon	4	0.2	0.2	0.3	65	4
Mustard greens, cooked	½ cup	10	1.6	0.1	1.4	11	52
Nectarine, fresh	1 medium	67	1.3	0.6	16.1	0	7
Noodles, chow mein	½ cup	110	2.9	5.3	13.0	225	7
Oatmeal, cooked without salt	1 cup	145	5.8	2.3	25.3	1	19

FOOD	APPROXIMATE MEASURE	FOOD ENERGY (CALORIES)	PROTEIN (GRAMS)	FAT (GRAMS)	CARBOHYDRATES (GRAMS)	SODIUM (MILLIGRAMS)	CALCIUM (MILLIGRAMS)
Oil, vegetable	1 tablespoon	121	0.0	13.6	0.0	0	0
Okra							
Cooked	½ cup	26	1.5	0.1	5.8	4	50
Raw	½ cup	19	1.0	0.0	3.8	4	40
Olives							
Green	½ cup	78	0.9	8.5	0.8	1620	41
Ripe	½ cup	124	0.8	13.6	2.2	506	72
Onions							
Mature, raw, chopped	½ cup	29	1.0	0.2	6.2	2	21
Mature, cooked	½ cup	15	0.4	0.1	3.3	4	14
Green, chopped	1 tablespoon	2	0.1	0.0	0.5	0	3
Orange							
Fresh	1 medium	64	1.3	0.3	15.9	1	54
Juice, unsweetened	1 cup	112	1.5	0.2	26.4	2	22
Oysters, raw, meat only	1 cup	158	19.9	4.1	8.2	175	226
Papaya, fresh, cubed	½ cup	27	0.4	0.1	6.9	2	17
Parsley, fresh, chopped	1 tablespoon	1	0.1	0.0	0.3	1	5
Parsnip, diced, cooked	½ cup	51	1.2	0.4	11.5	6	35
Pasta, egg type, cooked without salt	½ cup	100	3.2	1.2	18.6	2	8
Peach							
Fresh	1 medium	47	0.8	0.1	12.0	1	11
Canned, unsweetened	½ cup	29	0.5	0.1	7.4	4	2
Canned, in light syrup	½ cup	74	0.5	0.1	19.3	3	5
Dried	3 each	244	3.7	0.8	62.4	8	28
Peanuts, roasted, unsalted	1 tablespoon	53	2.4	4.5	1.7	1	8
Peanut butter	1 tablespoon	95	4.6	8.3	2.6	79	5
Pear							
Fresh	1 medium	96	0.6	0.7	24.6	0	18
Canned, unsweetened	½ cup	35	0.2	0.0	9.5	2	5
Canned, in light syrup	½ cup	70	0.2	0.2	17.9	1	6
Dried	3 each	267	1.9	0.6	70.9	6	35
Peas							
Black-eyed, fresh cooked	½ cup	90	6.7	0.7	15.0	3	23
Black-eyed, canned, regular pack	½ cup	89	6.4	0.4	15.7	301	23
English, fresh, cooked	½ cup	67	4.3	0.2	12.5	2	22
English, canned, regular pack	½ cup	61	3.7	0.3	11.1	340	22
Split, dry	½ cup	115	8.0	0.3	20.7	13	11
Pecans, chopped	1 tablespoon	50	0.6	5.0	1.4	0	3
Peppers							
Chili, hot	1 medium	18	0.9	0.1	4.3	3	8
Green, sweet, raw	1 medium	23	0.7	0.5	4.8	3	5
Jalapeño	1 medium	6	0.2	0.0	1.6	3	2
Red, sweet, raw	1 medium	23	0.8	0.4	4.8	3	5
Pickle							
Dill, whole	1 medium	7	0.4	0.1	1.4	914	17
Dill, sliced	¼ cup	4	0.2	0.1	0.9	553	10
Sweet, whole	1 large	50	0.2	0.1	12.4	242	4
Sweet, chopped	¼ cup	57	0.2	0.2	14.1	276	5
Pie, baked, 9-inch diameter, cut into 8 slices							
Apple, with top crust	1 slice	401	3.5	20.5	52.8	397	14
Chocolate meringue	1 slice	302	4.7	10.0	49.6	269	93
Pecan	1 slice	510	5.1	22.9	71.4	510	15
Pumpkin custard	1 slice	324	6.5	11.3	48.6	518	102
Pimiento	1 (4-ounce) jar	31	0.9	0.6	6.6	28	8
Pineapple							
Fresh, diced	½ cup	38	0.3	0.3	9.6	1	5

Tr = Trace amount of nutrient   Dash (-) indicates insufficient data available

FOOD	APPROXIMATE MEASURE	FOOD ENERGY (CALORIES)	PROTEIN (GRAMS)	FAT (GRAMS)	CARBOHYDRATES (GRAMS)	SODIUM (MILLIGRAMS)	CALCIUM (MILLIGRAMS)
Pineapple *(continued)*							
Canned, in juice	½ cup	81	0.6	0.1	21.0	1	22
Canned, in light syrup	½ cup	82	0.4	0.1	21.3	1	15
Juice, unsweetened	1 cup	137	1.0	0.2	33.7	2	37
Plum, fresh	1 each	35	0.5	0.4	8.3	0	3
Popcorn							
Unpopped	1 cup	742	24.2	9.4	147.6	6	20
Popped, plain without fat or salt	1 cup	23	0.8	0.3	4.6	0	1
Pork, trimmed of excess fat							
Ham, fresh, baked	3 ounces	187	25.2	8.5	0	55	11
Loin chop, broiled and drained	2 ounces	146	17.1	8.6	0	42	7
Picnic, cured, baked	3 ounces	179	24.1	8.4	0	863	11
Spareribs, braised	3 ounces	330	17.7	33	0	31	8
Potato							
Whole, with skin, baked	1 medium	218	4.4	0.2	50.4	16	20
Diced, boiled	½ cup	67	1.3	0.1	15.6	4	6
Potato chips	10 chips	105	1.3	7.1	10.4	94	5
Pretzels, thin sticks	10 pretzels	106	2.1	0.0	23.3	772	9
Prunes							
Dried, pitted	5 medium	127	1.1	1.4	30.9	23	21
Juice	1 cup	182	1.6	0.0	44.7	10	31
Pumpkin							
Fresh, cubed	½ cup	15	0.6	0.1	3.8	1	12
Canned, mashed	½ cup	42	1.3	0.3	9.9	6	32
Radishes, raw, sliced	½ cup	10	0.3	0.3	2.1	14	12
Raisins, seedless	1 tablespoon	27	0.3	0.0	7.2	1	5
Raspberries, fresh							
Black	½ cup	33	0.6	0.4	7.7	0	15
Red	½ cup	30	0.6	0.3	7.1	0	14
Rhubarb							
Cooked, added sugar	½ cup	190	0.7	0.1	48.6	3	105
Raw, diced	½ cup	13	0.5	0.1	2.8	2	52
Rice							
Brown, cooked without salt	½ cup	102	2.0	0.6	21.9	2	9
White, cooked without salt	½ cup	118	2.2	0.1	25.9	1	8
White, parboiled, cooked without salt	½ cup	93	1.7	0.1	20.3	2	17
Roll							
Bun, frankfurter or hamburger	1 bun	136	3.2	3.4	22.4	112	19
Hard	1 (1-ounce) roll	88	2.8	0.9	16.9	177	13
Plain, brown-and-serve	1 (1-ounce) roll	85	2.2	1.9	14.3	145	13
Rutabaga, cubed, cooked	½ cup	30	0.7	0.1	6.9	3	50
Salad dressing, commercial							
Blue cheese	1 tablespoon	84	0.4	9.2	0.3	216	3
French	1 tablespoon	96	0.3	9.4	2.9	205	6
Italian	1 tablespoon	84	0.1	9.1	0.6	172	1
Russian	1 tablespoon	76	0.2	7.8	1.6	133	3
Thousand Island	1 tablespoon	59	0.1	5.6	2.4	109	2
Mayonnaise-type	1 tablespoon	21	0.2	2.0	0.8	18	3
Salt	1 teaspoon	0	0.0	0.0	0.0	2343	15
Sauerkraut	½ cup	22	1.1	0.2	5.0	780	35
Sausage, pork, cooked							
Link (4 inches long)	1 (1-ounce) link	48	2.6	4.1	0.1	168	4
Patty (3⅞ inches in diameter)	1 (2-ounce) patty	100	5.3	8.4	0.3	349	9
Scallops, steamed	3 ounces	95	20.0	1.2	-	228	98

FOOD	APPROXIMATE MEASURE	FOOD ENERGY (CALORIES)	PROTEIN (GRAMS)	FAT (GRAMS)	CARBOHYDRATES (GRAMS)	SODIUM (MILLIGRAMS)	CALCIUM (MILLIGRAMS)
Sesame seeds	1 tablespoon	52	1.6	4.5	2.1	1	88
Shallot, bulbs, raw, chopped	½ cup	58	2.0	0.1	13.4	10	30
Sherbet, orange	½ cup	135	1.1	1.9	29.3	44	52
Shortening	1 tablespoon	121	0.0	13.6	0.0	0	0
Shrimp							
Fresh, raw, peeled	½ pound	206	41.0	1.8	3.4	318	143
Canned, drained	½ cup	74	15.5	0.7	0.4	90	74
Soups, condensed, prepared with equal amount of water							
Beef broth or bouillon	1 cup	16	2.7	.5	.1	782	15
Chicken, cream of	1 cup	116	3.4	7.3	9.2	986	34
Chicken noodle	1 cup	75	4.0	2.5	9.4	1107	17
Mushroom, cream of	1 cup	129	2.3	8.9	9.3	1031	46
Tomato	1 cup	86	2.1	2.0	16.6	872	13
Vegetable	1 cup	81	3.0	1.9	13.1	810	18
Soy sauce							
Reduced-sodium	1 tablespoon	14	1.2	0.0	1.6	582	0
Regular type	1 tablespoon	12	1.6	0.0	1.5	1030	3
Soybeans, dry, cooked	½ cup	117	9.9	5.0	9.7	2	66
Spaghetti, cooked without salt	½ cup	78	2.4	0.3	16.1	Tr	6
Spinach							
Raw, chopped	1 cup	12	1.6	0.2	2.0	44	55
Fresh, cooked	½ cup	21	2.7	0.2	3.4	63	122
Canned, regular pack	½ cup	22	2.3	0.5	3.5	397	99
Squash							
Acorn, cooked	½ cup	57	1.1	0.1	14.9	4	45
Butternut, cooked	½ cup	41	0.8	0.1	10.7	4	42
Spaghetti, cooked	½ cup	22	0.5	0.2	5.0	14	16
Yellow, sliced, cooked	½ cup	18	0.8	0.3	3.9	1	24
Winter, cooked, mashed	½ cup	40	0.9	0.6	9.0	1	14
Zucchini, sliced, cooked	½ cup	14	0.6	0.0	3.5	3	12
Strawberries, fresh, whole	1 cup	55	0.9	0.7	12.4	1	31
Sugar							
Brown, packed	1 tablespoon	51	0.0	0.0	13.3	4	12
Granulated	1 tablespoon	48	0.0	0.0	12.4	0	0
Powdered	1 tablespoon	29	0.0	0.0	7.5	0	0
Sunflower kernels, unsalted	¼ cup	205	8.2	17.8	6.8	1	42
Sweet potato							
Whole, baked	1 potato	115	1.9	0.1	27.2	11	31
Boiled, without skin, mashed	½ cup	172	2.7	0.5	39.8	21	34
Syrup, maple	1 tablespoon	50	0.0	0.0	12.8	2	20
Tangerine, fresh	1 medium	38	0.5	0.1	9.6	1	12
Tapioca, dry	1 tablespoon	32	0.1	0.0	7.8	0	1
Tofu	4 ounces	82	8.8	4.6	2.7	8	145
Tomato							
Juice	1 cup	41	1.8	0.1	10.3	881	22
Fresh, raw	1 medium	27	1.2	0.3	6.1	11	10
Fresh, cooked	½ cup	30	1.3	0.3	6.8	13	10
Canned, peeled, regular pack	½ cup	25	1.2	0.2	5.1	155	38
Paste, regular pack	1 (6-ounce) can	143	6.4	1.5	32.0	111	60
Puree, regular pack	1 (29-ounce) can	321	13.6	0.8	82.3	3280	123
Turkey, ground, raw	3 ounces	101	18.5	2.4	0.0	60	12
Turkey, roasted							
Breast meat, without skin	3 ounces	134	25.3	2.7	0.0	54	16
Dark meat, without skin	3 ounces	159	24.3	6.1	0.0	67	27

Tr = Trace amount of nutrient   Dash (-) indicates insufficient data available

FOOD	APPROXIMATE MEASURE	FOOD ENERGY (CALORIES)	PROTEIN (GRAMS)	FAT (GRAMS)	CARBOHYDRATES (GRAMS)	SODIUM (MILLIGRAMS)	CALCIUM (MILLIGRAMS)
Turnip, cubed, cooked	½ cup	14	0.5	0.1	3.8	39	17
Turnip greens							
Fresh, cooked	½ cup	14	0.8	0.2	3.1	21	99
Canned, regular pack	½ cup	16	1.6	0.4	2.8	324	138
Veal, trimmed of excess fat							
Loin cut, broiled	3 ounces	199	22.4	11.4	0	55	9
Round, broiled	3 ounces	184	23.0	9.4	0	56	9
Vegetable juice cocktail	1 cup	46	1.5	0.2	11.0	883	27
Vinegar							
Distilled	1 tablespoon	2	0.0	0.0	0.8	0	0
Red wine	1 tablespoon	2	Tr	Tr	Tr	1	-
White wine	1 tablespoon	2	Tr	Tr	Tr	2	-
Water chestnuts							
Chinese	4 each	38	0.5	0.0	8.6	5	4
Canned, sliced	¼ cup	17	0.3	0.0	4.4	3	1
Watercress, leaves with stems, raw, chopped	1 cup	4	0.7	0.0	0.4	14	41
Watermelon, fresh, diced	1 cup	51	1.0	0.7	11.5	3	13
Yeast, dry	1 (¼-ounce) package	20	2.6	0.1	2.8	4	3
Yogurt, plain							
Fruit varieties, low-fat	1 cup	225	9.0	2.6	42.3	120	313
Plain, low-fat	1 cup	143	11.9	3.5	16.0	159	415
Plain, made from whole milk	1 cup	138	7.9	7.4	10.6	104	275

Sources of Data:

Adams, Catherine F. *NUTRITIVE VALUE OF AMERICAN FOODS*. Washington: U. S. Government Printing Office, 1975.

Computrition, Inc., Chatsworth, California. Primarily comprised of *The Composition of Foods; Raw, Processed, Prepared*. Agriculture Handbooks - 8 series. United States Department of Agriculture, Human Nutrition Information Service, 1976-1986.

Index

Subject Index

Favorite Light Recipes

*Record your favorite light recipes
below for quick and handy reference*

Recipe	Source/Page	Calories

Recipe	Source/Page	Calories